MW00654820

CODE 1244

KAHUNA BOOKS
© 2019 Ric Conrad

First Edition, October 2019

Manufactured in the United States of America
Edited by Sheri Conrad
Cover design by Mark Myers and Sheri Conrad
Book design, art direction, typography, and layout by Mark Myers and Sheri Conrad

Frontispiece: Ralph Summers in the parking lot of Wy'East Day Lodge, May 14, 1986. Historic Images ORA86720.

Library of Congress Cataloguing-in-Publication Data

Library of Congress Control Number: 2019903356

Conrad, Richard J, 1967-
CODE 1244: The 1986 Mount Hood Tragedy/Ric Conrad.

Includes bibliographical references.

ISBN: 978-0-9887339-5-4 (Hardcover)

    1. Mountaineering—United States—History.
    2. Mountaineering—Oregon (State)—Hood, Mount—Description

I. Title: CODE 1244: The 1986 Mount Hood Tragedy.

Published by Kahuna Books
Beaverton, Oregon
www.kahunabooks.com

TABLE OF
CONTENTS

THURSDAY, MAY 15, 1986

ACKNOWLEDGMENTS

I am greatly indebted to the following members of Portland Mountain Rescue for their recollections of their SAR efforts on Mount Hood during the tragedy: Mike Craig, Ed Hall, Rocky Henderson, Jerry Janeck, Mark Kelsey, Ky Krank, Hal Lillywhite, Cheryl Maslen, Dave McClure, Sue Shultz, Tom Stringfield, and Barry Wright.

I thank the members of Corvallis Mountain Rescue Unit, who were kind enough to share their memories and observations: Bob Freund, Gene Griswold, Jody Leach, Bill O'Brien, and Scott Olson. Their contributions are paramount to an understanding of what took place on the mountain during Thursday's portion of the SAR operation.

I also thank the employees of RLK & Company for sharing their recollections of the tragedy: Linny Adamson, Curator; Bill Brett, retired Mountain Maintenance Manager; and Jon Tullis, Director of Public Affairs.

Other members of the SAR community, who took their time and shared their memories of the operation, include: Charlie Ek and Ken McFadden of the 304th ARRS; Deputy Mike Hattan of the Clackamas County Sheriff's Department; Mike Moffitt of Hillsboro Helicopters; Greg Prothman and Pete Bustanoby of Seattle Mountain Rescue; Kathleen Sheridan of the Mt. Hood Nordic Ski Patrol.

Individuals from the Oregon Episcopal School community who agreed to interviews include Courtney Fuller, Mick Garrett, Mar Goman, Jeff Hicks, Amy Horwell, Frank McGinness, Don Penater, Sandy Radtke, Lorca Smetana, John Whitson, and Diana Yates. Their willingness to share speaks volumes about their desire to perpetuate the memories of their friends and loved ones. I thank them for trusting me with the responsibility of portraying this story as accurately as possible.

Mo Copeland, the headmaster of Oregon Episcopal School, met with us on October 19, 2015. We appreciate her candor concerning the tragedy and recognize that it continues to affect the OES student body. We kept Ms. Copeland on our email distribution list to keep the school informed of the book's progress.

We reached out to several people with an invitation to interview but did not receive a response. I respect these individual's right to privacy and their decision to keep their memories private: Molly and Sue Schula, Ralph Summers, and Dee Zduniak via the U.S. Postal Service; David Armstrong, Dr. Brinton Clark, Connie Haeder, Brian Litzenberger, David Mullen, Giles Thompson, and Hilary Spray via social media; Chuck Reynolds, Dave Rich, Marc Sellers, Jon Swails, and John Young via email. Scott Russell and Dave Kennell declined interviews. Ed Krebs passed away during the production of this book.

I'm grateful to those individuals who were kind enough to read the manuscript and provide back cover endorsements: Dave McClure and Barry Wright, who co-led operations for Portland Mountain Rescue; Tom Stringfield, a member of Team 10; and Ed Hall, an honorary member of the Crag Rats. I appreciate the time and energy they spent to help me with this project.

Special thanks are extended to Marsha Jared, RN, BSN, who reviewed the notes taken by Base Operations' personnel during the evacuation procedures. Through her work, we have a better understanding of what medics were requesting, when, and for what reasons.

I'd like to thank photographer Alecia Sensor for taking the images used for the dust jacket. Thanks to my stepson, Jackson Long, for serving as the model for the SAR worker on the front cover. By using clothing and equipment, loaned to us by Dave McClure—used during the actual rescue—Sensor and Long managed to capture the sense of isolation and confusion that permeates this tragic story.

I thank Mark Myers, who created the dust jacket, and laid out the book in Adobe InDesign.

Six photos in this book have been altered. Five of these images are used to separate the story into daily sections: a portrait of Fr. Tom Goman. The original reflection has been altered; a portrait of Lorca Smetana; a portrait of Ralph Summers; a picture of Mike Moffitt in his helicopter. The aircraft's identification number has been removed; a portrait of Major Kenneth McFadden. These images were sent through a handful of filters and enhancement software to emerge as unique works of art.

The sixth picture to have been altered concerns members of Teams 3 and 4 preparing to board a snowcat. Barry Wright snapped two photos from the same standing position. Mark Myers created a composite image for the photo insert, incorporating the best portions of each of these two pictures.

I need to take this opportunity to thank those individuals and companies that generously allowed me to publish photographs from their collections: Mike Craig, Mar Goman, Mark Kelsey, Cheryl Maslen, Dave McClure, Frank McGinness, Mike Moffitt, Sandy Radtke, Lorca Smetana, Barry Wright, the Historic Images Outlet, and the Associated Press. Of the twenty-seven photographs that appear in the book, twenty-one of them are being published here for the first time.

I want to thank my wife for editing the manuscript and working with Mark Myers. This project began as an effort to understand the complexities of one of the nation's largest mountain SAR operations but—through Sheri—it became more personal. Her kindness and understanding helped those most closely affected by the tragedy to believe in this project and share their stories.

–Ric Conrad

June 16, 2019

DEDICATION

This book is respectfully dedicated to the Search and Rescue (SAR) organizations who volunteered their time and services during the 1986 Mount Hood Tragedy.

304th AEROSPACE RESCUE AND RECOVERY SQUADRON (AIR FORCE)

FLIGHT CREWS

Lt. Colonel David Mullen, Pilot
Major Charles Jones, Pilot
Major David Schildmeyer, Pilot
Major Fred Stovel, Pilot
Major Jack Kaseburg, Pilot
Major John Baczuk, Pilot

Major Kenneth McFadden, Pilot
Captain William Moore, Squadron
Spokesman
Sergeant Cliff Peckens, Flight Engineer
Sergeant Ron Carpenter, Flight Engineer
Sergeant Wes Lohman, Flight Engineer

PARARESCUE

Master Sergeant Charlie Ek
Master Sergeant Jan Nesbit
Master Sergeant Rick Harder
Sergeant David Bourland
Sergeant Jeffrey Youngbluth
Sergeant John Harkness
Sergeant John Olson

Sergeant Jon Swails
Sergeant Mark Ross
Sergeant Mark Schneider
Technical Sergeant Joel Kasprzak
Airman David Armstrong
Airman Gary Dugan

ALPINE AMBULANCE
Phil Moyer

ALPINEES
Gerald Donahue
Jim Holloway
Scott Walker

AMERICAN RED CROSS

CLACKAMAS COUNTY SHERIFF'S OFFICE (CCSO)

Sheriff Bill Brooks
Chief Deputy W. Ris Bradshaw
Captain J.T. Grolbert
Lt. Don Vicars
Lt. Gene Hanners
Lt. Sherwood Stillman
Deputy Dave Kennell

Deputy Ed Krebs
Deputy Lou Serafin
Deputy Mike Hattan
Deputy Russ Williams
Deputy Carl Witt
ME Doug Pratt
EM coordinator Casey Marley

COLUMBUS SEARCH DOGS

Doug Martinson and "Ranger"

CORVALLIS MOUNTAIN RESCUE UNIT (CMRU)

John Blaisdell	Wayne Lederer
Hollis Ferguson	Dale Nelson
Bob Freund	Bill O'Brien
Gene Griswold	Scott Olson
Frank Howard	Jim Ruef
Jody Leach	Sterling Thomas

GERMAN SHEPHERD SEARCH DOGS (GSSD)

Bruce Cheshire and "Polly"	Dick Reininger and "Rascal"
Christy Pierce and "Mica"	

HILLSBORO HELICOPTERS, INC.

Mike Moffitt

HOODLAND FIRE DISTRICT NO. 74

Neale Brown	David Summer
Richard Curtis	Lane Wintermute

HOOD RIVER CRAG RATS

John Arens	Ken Hukari
Dick Arnold	Kent Lambert
Cam Axford	Craig McCurdy
Bill Bryan	Don Pattison
Bruce Hukari	Tom Wells

LIFE FLIGHT

Barbara Dobbert	Susan Galeski
Sarah Evenson	Michele Kelly
JoAnne Fairchild	Mark Kohnstadt
Michael Fletcher	Susan Waters

MT. HOOD MEADOWS

Brandy Johnson	Warren Johnson
Martin Johnson	

MT. HOOD NORDIC SKI PATROL

Scott Clark	Ray Patrick
Don Cossel	Paul Rishel
Eric Hagstrum	Kent Romney
Mark Parker	Kathleen Sheridan
Francis Patrick	

MT. HOOD SKI PATROL

Craig Petrie	Lew Russell
Keith Petrie	Scott Russell
Pete Rue	

MT. HOOD SNOWMOBILE CLUB

Ken Gilbertson	Clinton Peterson

OUTWARD BOUND

Ralph Summers	Dee Zduniak
Brad Wade	

PORTLAND MOUNTAIN RESCUE (PMR)

Dennis Alexander	Hal Lillywhite
David Allen	Cheryl Maslen
Steve Belding	Dave McClure
Mike Blailock	Larry McDaniels
Jim Boucher	Dave McNeil
Bob Caldwell	Matt Nauman
Sandy Childs	Harry Oakes, Jr.
Mike Craig	Allen O'Bannon
Jim Dixon	Mark Powers
Chet Edwards	Al Radys
Richard Ernst	Dave Rich
Ted Forgeron	Gary Salberg
Harvey Frisco	John Schneider
Steve Glenn	Mike Seeley
Ed Hall	Marc Sellers
Carl Harbour	Sue Shultz
Jeff Hartley	Bill Stevenson
Michael Hauty	Tom Stringfield
Les Hedquist	Terry Swicegood
Rocky Henderson	Gary Uhland
Jerry Janeck	Barry Wright
Mark Kelsey	Jim Wright
Ky Krank	

SEATTLE MOUNTAIN RESCUE (SMR)

Gordon Adams
Jim Baker
Brian Beaman
Ed Boulton
Pete Bustanoby
Jim Cleary
Pete Frickland
Diane Hoff

Russ Kroeker
Chris Madden
Allen McGuire
Steve Plate
Greg Prothman
Bob Ricker
George Sainsbury
Paul Williams

TIMBERLINE LODGE

Linny Adamson
Bill Brett
Bill Conerly
Tom Jackson
Richard L. Kohnstamm

John O'Neill
Judy O'Regan
Jon Tullis
John Young

UNITED STATES FOREST SERVICE

Bruce Haynes
Richard Hoffmann
Hal Reese

SUNDAY

May 11, 1986

CHAPTER 1
MOTHER'S DAY

Frank McGinness opened the freezer door and pulled out a box of frozen waffles.

There were several such boxes inside, but not much else. Grabbing the butter from the refrigerator, he caught a glimpse of the feast he would be cooking later tonight for his two sons: a small rack of ribs, a jar of applesauce, and a jar of sauerkraut–young Patrick's favorite meal.

Legally separated, and navigating the challenging rapids of divorce proceedings, Frank had been feeding his boys on a steady diet of Eggo waffles and spaghetti.

Patrick was recovering from a cold. Still feeling under the weather, he was busy struggling with a colossal pile of the family laundry. A member of the stage crew for the school play, he had returned home from a cast party after midnight. Pat was giving Frank a lively report of the highlights of the play and the party, the highlights that a fifteen-year-old boy would share with his dad.[1]

Upbeat, positive, and prone to laughter, Pat was attending the prestigious Oregon Episcopal School (OES) on a full scholarship.[2] The private college preparatory school, in the Raleigh Hills district of Portland, saw many of their graduates move on to nationally ranked universities.

Pat's little brother, Chris, was drying the dishes and complaining at the apparent lack of equality in household chore assignments. Chris wanted to know why his big brother got to do the laundry while he slaved away in the kitchen.

"It's because of who you are in the pecking order," Frank chuckled, playfully ribbing his youngest son. "Now, shut up and dry."[3]

Frank glanced at his oldest, concerned that Pat was still fighting off the cold. "Look, you're lying low today," he said. "Just do the laundry and go back to bed."

O'LEARY RESIDENCE
PORTLAND

Only sixteen, Erin O'Leary had landed a lead role in the school's production of *You Can't Take It with You*. She'd celebrated immediately after the show with the rest of the cast and crew. Erin was running for class president in the school election, which was only days away.[4] Her opponent was her good friend, Rich, who had taken her to the prom a year earlier.[5]

Following her rapidly approaching ascent of Mount Hood, the sophomore would be traveling to Washington, D.C., to participate in a nationwide debating contest.[6]

Erin had come to OES during her eighth-grade year, having spent the previous two years in Ireland. On her first day of school, she found herself walking across campus with a small group of bubbly girls, including Sandy Douthit. As it often does in Oregon, the rain started falling.

"I'll have to get my bumbershoot out!" Erin exclaimed.[7] The group of teens exploded in laughter at this strange remark.

"Here in Oregon," Sandy whispered, coming to Erin's rescue, "we just call it an *umbrella*."

Erin and Sandy were soon great friends.

Erin's dad was worried about the weather forecast.[8] A frontal system from the Gulf of Alaska had moved into the region, causing rainfall throughout the day. The snow level in the Cascade Mountains was expected to drop to 4,000'.[9]

Mr. O'Leary phoned Father Tom Goman, the teacher who would be leading the school-sponsored attempt on Mount Hood. O'Leary expressed his concerns about the forecast. Goman assured him, if the team encountered any trouble, they'd simply make a token hike in order to fulfill the requirements of the school's wilderness Basecamp program.[10]

Knowing he would be climbing an ice-clad mountain during the night, Erik crawled into bed to try to catch some sleep. The outgoing sophomore had a trademark grin and was considered by his peers to be the class clown. He thoroughly enjoyed entertaining his friends, conjuring up a wide variety of impersonations at a moment's notice. He could instantly become a sizzling piece of bacon, or King Kong, hard at work washing dishes.[11] In the middle of one memorable school assembly, Erik stood up and pretended to be a lawn sprinkler. The act came complete with an uncanny sound effect that turned heads.[12]

"I got some fossil flowers today from the Petrified Florist!" he would joke. Or, "Did you hear about the baker with Extra Sensory Perception? He was éclair-voyant!"[13] In a letter to a friend, Erik had written, "How does a Polish priest bless people? Like *this*. Ha-ha! Oh, you can't see me right now. Well, ask me to show you the punchline when you come here." He was always kidding around.[14]

Erik was active on campus. He ran track, he was a National Merit Scholar, and he played bass in the jazz band.[15] He enjoyed theater, appearing in the school's latest production.[16]

The first of the Sandvik family to try mountain climbing, he was anxious—yet excited—about the journey ahead.[17]

"Dad!" Pat called down the hallway. "I can't find one of my polypropylene socks."[18]

"What?" Frank yelled back, knowing his son would need proper protection on a snow-covered volcano.

"It's okay, Dad," Pat noted. "I know how broke we are. I can go up without it."

"You are *not* going up without socks," his father replied with conviction. Frank telephoned the local REI clothing and equipment store, learning they would close in twenty minutes.

Frank and his boys piled into the family car, arriving at their destination with only five minutes to spare. Replacement socks were purchased for

$5.00, and Frank breathed a sigh of relief.

"Dad, thank you," Pat said, brandishing a heart-melting smile.[19] He gave his dad a big hug. "I love you."

"Well, thanks," Frank laughed, somewhat surprised by the unexpected display of emotion. "I really appreciate that. It's just a pair of socks."

The trio drove home to cook Pat's favorite dinner.

HAEDER RESIDENCE
PORTLAND

The Haeder Family was all chipping in to assist sixteen-year-old Rich.[20] The girls helped their big brother fill his backpack with trail mix, chocolate bars, fruit, sodas, and four ham and cheese sandwiches. Rich folded his parka and set it on the table next to his pack. No one in the family had experience scaling peaks, so they relied heavily on a list of equipment suggestions that Ralph Summers—a consultant—had provided.[21]

Mr. Haeder entered the room, brandishing his son's hiking boots. The proud father had spent the previous evening ensuring that the protective footwear would be water-proof, applying layer after layer of wax.[22]

Aware of the forecasted storm front, young Rich called Father Goman, asking if the field trip had been canceled. Hanging up the phone, he informed his mother that the attempt was still on, but they were only expected to hike part-way up the mountain. They'd turn around and return to the Lodge by 2:00 p.m. Mrs. Haeder was put at ease. It appeared as if the students would simply play around in the snow.[23]

~8:30 P.M.
GOMAN-YATES RESIDENCE
PORTLAND

Tom and Mar Goman had married eighteen years earlier.[24] About seven years later, the Gomans were joined by Diana Yates. Together, they'd formed the Community of St. Michael and All Angels. The trio were the only permanent members of the community, though others would stay in their home if needed.[25]

An Episcopal priest, Tom completed a Ph.D. from the School of Theology at Claremont while he was teaching at OES. Some of the students acknowledged that accomplishment by addressing him as Father Doctor Tom, which they soon shortened to "FurDur Tom," or simply "Furdur." The *father* half of his impressive titles always preceded the *doctor* half. Most students, however, continued to call him Father Tom.[26]

Goman, forty-one, had been working at OES for seven years.[27] On campus, the popular teacher taught calculus, chemistry, ethics & religion, and was the advisor for the chess team. He was known to be selfless in nearly every aspect of his life. Whether it was his time, attention, money, clothing, food, books, or climbing equipment, he shared generously and without the need for reciprocity.[28]

Returning home from her niece's wedding, Diana was relieved to have arrived in time to see Tom before he departed for the climb. She grew troubled when Mar told her that Tom hadn't gotten much sleep during the day.[29]

Shouldering his bulging backpack, Tom took a big swig of milk straight from the jug. Mar leaned in to kiss him goodbye but stopped suddenly.

"You have milk in your mustache," she chuckled.[30] Her husband laughed and waved off the observation, kissing his wife affectionately. Adjusting his thick, prescription glasses, Tom said his goodbyes to the two women and departed.[31]

~9:30 P.M.
JACKSON HOUSE
OREGON EPISCOPAL SCHOOL

Marion Horwell and her twelve-year-old daughter, Amy, lived in a split-level apartment within the school's dormitory complex. The living room and kitchen were on the upper floor, and two bedrooms were on the lower level.

Marion had been appointed the dean of students for the upper school. As such, the forty-one-year-old was responsible for the kids who lived on campus.[32] The students in the dorms found her to be firm, yet fair.[33]

As Amy was preparing for bed, her mother walked in to ask if she was ready. Grabbing what she needed, the girl walked with her mom to an unfamiliar dorm room.

Amy was welcomed by one of the senior girls who supervised her whenever Marion needed a sitter.[34] The room had two beds, and Amy crawled into the available one. The light was turned off.

Marion tucked her daughter in tight, kissing her goodnight. Then, she walked towards the exit and turned around.

Amy could see her mother, framed in the doorway and silhouetted by the illuminated hallway behind her.

"Goodbye," Marion whispered. "I'll see you tomorrow, around dinnertime."[35]

Amy rolled over to get some sleep; it was a school night after all. Marion turned and walked down to the school's bus stop, a few hundred yards away.

~9:40 P.M.
BELL TOWER
OREGON EPISCOPAL SCHOOL

Parking in the school lot, it appeared that the McGinness men were the first to arrive. Team members had been told to rendezvous at the school around 10:00 p.m., so Pat was a bit early.

Frank helped his son extract his pack and equipment from the back seat of the family car. He turned to give Pat one of his trademark bear hugs.

"Pasta tomorrow night?" Frank suggested.[36]

"Yeah," the boy grinned. "Pasta tomorrow night."

Frank released his hold on Pat and watched his son walk away, toward the Bell Tower.

Driving away, Frank suddenly felt strange. He felt pain in his stomach. It increased as he sped along the freeway and over the Fremont Bridge, heading for home. Soon, he was practically doubled over in pain.

~9:50 P.M.
BOATSMAN RESIDENCE
PORTLAND

Her spirits were high as Courtney climbed into the back seat of her mom's car. Her older brother had been on one of the school's climbing parties during his sophomore year. At sixteen, Courtney was more than ready to follow in her brother's boot prints.[37]

Mrs. Boatsman wasn't concerned about her daughter's participation in the field trip as she backed out of the family driveway. Fr. Goman was known as a safety-conscious mountaineer and had led climbs for years.[38]

Courtney looked out at the dark streets, looking forward to the ascent. This was one more athletic challenge to overcome. She had always respected her brother and knew his experience on the mountain had been very educational for him. She expected a similar experience, a great outdoor adventure, mid-way through her high school years.[39]

It was Mother's Day, and eleven sophomores were arriving, one-by-one, in the parking lot. It was time for the school's annual rite of passage.

Rich Haeder Jr. wandered through the minefield of backpacks and climbing equipment, scattered about the sidewalk.[40] Like Pat, Rich was attending school on a full-ride scholarship, even though his dad was a successful attorney. Academically advanced, and skilled in the field of mathematics, Rich enjoyed serving as a tutor for other students. Recently, his interests had expanded into the world of government and politics. He had been vice president of the middle school student body, he currently served as class treasurer for the high school, and he was now running for class president.[41]

Rich was a devout Latter-day Saint, but attending an Episcopal school was not considered new or peculiar.[42] Although students were required to attend chapel once a week, the institute was open to people of various denominations. Most of the teens had already taken the required World Religions course, where instructors taught everyone to respect others, regardless of race or creed.[43]

Courtney, with her close-cropped, dark curls, arrived. She checked in with the two juniors and two seniors who were performing pack-checks on her classmates.[44] The school had held an equipment and supply check a few days earlier, a second would occur before students were permitted to board the bus, and a third and final screening was scheduled to occur up on the mountain.[45]

Mr. Sandvik had woken his son thirty minutes earlier and had made him some eggs.

Erik was on the phone with his mother, who lived in California. She was thrilled to hear her son wish her a happy Mother's Day and to learn that he was excited about the rugged adventure he was embarking upon.[46]

Kristin, a year older than her brother, had volunteered to drive Erik to the school. Mr. Sandvik appeared somewhat nervous as his kids climbed into the family car, asking Erik to be extra careful and to stay warm. The youth tried to reassure his dad, telling him not to worry.

Kristin drove her brother to the school. As he was walking toward the bus, his big sister called out to him.

"Don't die," she teased.[47]

"Don't worry," Erik laughed.

Tasha Amy was quietly observing the activity around the school bus.[48] She was considered shy by most of her peers.[49] For the past five years, she'd studied the violin. Tasha's proficiency with the instrument, coupled with a growing list of friends on campus, appeared to be boosting her self-confidence. Now sixteen, she was an honor student and an active member in the theater program.[50] Her burgeoning self-confidence had made an appearance during history class as well. Tasha climbed atop a table and started tap dancing. Her soft-shoe routine terminated, quite abruptly, when she ran out of table and found herself sprawled on the floor, nursing a sprained ankle.[51]

Brinton Clark, sixteen, was smart and athletic, but somewhat shy.[52] A straight-A student, she was well-rounded and outgoing within her group of friends.[53] She was excited at the prospect of ascending the slopes of Mount Hood.[54]

John Whitson did not share Brinton's current optimism. He had attended a non-school-sponsored cast party and, after drinking and getting high, found himself recovering from a brutal hangover. When asked what he had been up to on Sunday, he merely confessed, "sucking on ice chips."[55] Husky, outgoing—almost gregarious—he was looking forward to the climb, just without the same level of enthusiasm as some of his fellow students.

Although an extrovert, John was not especially close to his classmates. This, his sophomore year, was his first at OES. His dad had earned a coveted position in Saudi Arabia and John, now sixteen, was deemed too old to stay with him overseas. As his father's employer was willing to pay for private education, the youth found himself enrolled at OES.

He lived off-campus with his mother, so she had driven him to the school. Running his hands through his mop of unkempt hair, John boarded the bus and navigated down the narrow aisle of bench seats. Taking up a position near the rear of the vehicle, he was hoping to catch some sleep during the journey to the mountain.[56]

Only sixteen, Giles Thompson was one of the strongest kids on campus. One night in the boy's dorms, the students undertook an arm-wrestling contest. Giles, a sophomore, bested the strongest among them—decisively.[57] He was confident, athletic, and kind to his fellow students.[58] He liked listening to older bands such as "The Grateful Dead" and "Crosby, Stills, and Nash."[59]

Giles had no climbing experience, but his older brother had successfully participated in a school-sponsored ascent of Mount Hood. Like Courtney, Giles was dutifully following in an elder sibling's footsteps.[60]

Another car pulled into the parking lot. It was the Sprays—Hilary and her mom, Sharon. They were running late. Because her daughter had diabetes, Sharon had agreed to accompany the students on the field trip. She had climbed Mount Hood once before and was concerned by the heavy packs several of the kids were loading onto the bus.[61] Due to their tardiness, the contents of the Sprays' packs were not inspected.[62]

Hilary was an artistic sophomore that many considered to be a free spirit. She was close friends with Erin O'Leary.[63]

Quick-witted and sarcastic, Alison Litzenberger was known to be extremely bright.[64] She sang in the school choir, babysat neighborhood children, took advanced classes in school, and enjoyed horseback riding.[65] Her parents had been divorced for a year, and the fifteen-year-old was living with her mother.

During their freshman year, Alison had dated Erik Sandvik. Though the romantic aspect of their relationship had ended, their friendship remained. Their mutual sense of humor bonded them like kindred spirits.[66]

Alison was looking forward to the climb, but she wished her best friend, Sandy Douthit, had been able to come with her. The two should be sharing laughs as they sat near the front of the bus.

CHAPTER 2
FATHER TOM'S POSSE

The school bus pulled onto Scholls Ferry Road, beginning the seventy-mile journey to Timberline Lodge.[1] Winding through the city streets, it was heading for Highway 26. The bus would stay on this thoroughfare until the town of Government Camp, only six miles before their final destination.

"Hey, guys!" Rich suddenly exclaimed. "See that field over there? That's where my dad and I fly our model airplanes."[2]

Courtney smiled. As a student at OES since the fifth grade, she knew every student on board, at least to some degree. Feeling that the school encouraged a climate of confidence, she was ready for the climb.[1]

Once the city lights of Portland were left behind, the boisterous teenagers simmered down. The vehicle's large headlights pierced the darkness along the quiet, forest-lined highway, tracing the old vestiges of an offshoot of the Oregon Trail.

In the back of the bus, John was eavesdropping on a nearby conversation. The topic was Fr. Goman. There was a rumor that the priest had once met God on a mountain. The students were speculating as to the story's authenticity.

"Do you think that's true?" one of them asked.[2] John chuckled to himself, thinking the anecdote amusing. Then, he thought, *I wish I could sleep on a bus.*

With thick glasses and a beard, people often mistook Father Tom for a mild-mannered librarian, but he was invariably the most powerful member in any climbing party. He always seemed willing, and able, to ascend to the next prominent landmark.[3]

Goman had been climbing mountains since the age of thirteen. In the decades that followed, he'd tackled most of the major Cascade peaks in

Oregon and Washington. There were also rock climbing adventures in the Pacific Northwest and the San Gabriel Mountains of California.[4] He joined the American Alpine Club and had been to the summit of Mount Hood on at least a dozen occasions.[5]

There were undoubtedly other topics to discuss during the journey: who was taking whom to Friday night's prom, the pending ascent, the success of the school's play, upcoming graduation ceremonies for the seniors, and potential college preferences.

Because of school activities the previous evening, some of the students were suffering from a lack of sleep. Molly, Erin, Rich, Erik, John, and Susan had all performed in the school's production of the 1936 Broadway comedy, "You Can't Take It with You." As part of the stage crew, Giles and Pat had helped build the sets. There had been two performances on Saturday night. Following the final curtain call, there had been a cast party at a private residence. Some of the students didn't get home until midnight or later.[6]

Four students on board were members of the Advanced Climbing Team (ACT). These upperclassmen were: Molly, Susan, Mick, and Lorca. The ACT members would watch over and inspire the sophomores during the ascent. If a younger student desired to turn around and descend, an ACT member would serve as their escort.

Molly Schula, seventeen, lived in Beaverton.[7] She was a senior, and this was her second year as an ACT member, having made successful ascents of Hood since her sophomore climb. Her mother was not surprised when, a year earlier, Molly had enrolled in a three-week wilderness education course with Pacific Outward Bound School.[8]

On a previous ascent of the mountain, Molly had experienced a severe chill. Her mother made sure that Molly brought her new balaclava to keep her face and neck warm on this climb.

"It's cloudy," Mrs. Schula had said to her daughter, as Molly departed home to rendezvous at the school bus.[9]

"Well," Molly had replied, "that might be better because sometimes the clouds make it warmer."

The other senior ACT member was Susan McClave. She was active in the school's theater program, both on stage and in production. An all-league soccer player, the seventeen-year-old was captain of the varsity team. She was a natural leader. Academically, she had won the Oregon State Physical Science competition as an underclassman. Susan was designated a William

Carlton Scholar at Carlton College, where she would begin classes in the fall.[10]

Susan was a friend Lorca could trust with her secrets.[11]

Lorca Fitschen, one of the juniors, had a rather lively and animated personality. At sixteen, she possessed a phenomenal vocabulary.[12] She grew up knowing mountains and the men and women who scaled their slopes. Her father, Joe Fitschen, was a highly-respected rock climber, author, and poet. He was a member of the climbing party that made the second ascent of The Nose on El Capitan. The rugged mountaineer had raised his daughter to respect the outdoors and to expect the unexpected.

Since Lorca lived in the dorms, she was familiar with Marion, Giles, and Mick. She knew Alison but was closer friends with her older brother.[13]

Lorca had made two attempts to summit Mount Hood on school-sponsored teams. Father Tom had led both of those climbs. The first was during her sophomore year in the Basecamp program. Her second was an attempt in April, only a few weeks earlier. Father Tom had taken his ACT members up the South Side Route, to gain experience on the mountain. On each of these attempts, their teacher had turned the team around and retreated when faced with inclement weather.[14]

Lorca respected Father Tom, appreciating his sense of humor and considering him a mentor. He had made her laugh in geometry class, explaining his interesting intellectual conflicts to the students.

"You think you have problems," he had remarked, "I'm a physicist and a priest—at the same time!"[15]

Lorca knew the difference between old-school mountain climbers—cautious, methodical, and safety-conscious—and a new breed of tourist climbers. Having been raised beside campfires that warmed climbing luminaries such as Chuck Pratt, Royal Robbins, and Tom Frost, Lorca admired Father Tom for his climbing style and ethics. She had never detected an ego emanating from the man during their mountaineering adventures or their rock climbing scrambles. To her, he seemed to be the epitome of the classic alpinist, a man with quiet confidence.[16]

For one subdued young man aboard the bus, the drive up to the mountain felt more like a commute to a day's work. Mick Garrett, the second ACT member from the junior class, had successfully ascended the mountain a year earlier, as a sophomore. Like Lorca, there wasn't the nervousness or excitement of one making the journey for the first time. *I'm here to help*, he thought to himself, not feeling particularly social.

Mick had three brothers; eight to eleven years older than him. By the time Mick was old enough to explore the outdoors, his brothers were hanging out with friends and beginning lives of their own. Growing up in a little town in Washington State, he had spent a considerable amount of time exploring the Wenatchee National Forest. He had a virtual Huckleberry Finn existence until he was thirteen.[17]

His father had been working at the Grand Coulee Dam when an offer to work overseas in Saudi Arabia suddenly arose. Mick had moved with his parents to a satellite village, next to King Khalid International Airport. Here, Mr. Garrett became superintendent of power and electricity for the airport that served the nation's capital city—Riyadh—home to over a million inhabitants.

Like John, when Mick reached a certain age, the Saudi government wanted him to attend boarding school. Mick's grandparents lived in Oregon. The thought of returning to the forest trails of the Pacific Northwest, coupled with the knowledge that he would have family nearby, pointed Mick firmly in the direction of the Beaver State.

Arriving on campus, his sophomore year, Mick learned about the institution's "Basecamp program." There were lessons designed to separate the individual from his or her surroundings—family, friends, and the physical environment of the suburbs. Satisfactory participation in the program was a prerequisite for graduation.[18]

During the first two years of the program, the concept of teamwork was encouraged. As freshmen, students attended a four-day camping excursion in early September, before the official start of classes.[19] Each May, sophomores were to make an attempt on Mount Hood's popular South Side Route. Summiting was not a requirement. If they hiked only 500 feet up the mountain slopes, the obligation would be considered fulfilled.[20] Students, not wishing to participate in the climb, had the option of performing community service.[21]

The final two years of the program stressed the importance of volunteering and serving others. The juniors worked on a variety of outdoor projects for the Forest Service. Seniors splintered into various smaller groups, studying wilderness first aid techniques, compass navigation, backpacking, and rappelling. These skills were used during a five-day adventure in the Ochoco National Forest.[22]

The Basecamp program was extremely popular, and the sophomore ascent of the mountain was a highlight of the curriculum. This was the thirty-sixth team to make an attempt in fourteen years.[23]

At fall orientation, during his sophomore year, Mick was thinking, *what if no one else has the strength to press on near the summit, and I alone want to make it to the top?*

In May of that school year, Mick discovered that he didn't have to worry about that scenario. It had been a bright sunny day when, under cobalt blue skies, his sophomore team stood on the summit of Mount Hood. Mount Jefferson stood due south. The view took his breath away.

A cloud cap descended upon Mount Hood, just as Mick's rope team began their descent. If they were starting to tumble, students had been instructed to yell out, "Falling!" As the group was descending the upper section of the mountain, Mick suddenly dropped his ice axe. He watched, helplessly, as it fell from his hand.

He yelled out something that started with an "F"—but it wasn't "falling."[24]

Mick crouched down, stretched his arm out, and narrowly recovered the axe before it slid down the mountain and into a crevasse. He turned to see his companions in the self-arrest position, the adzes of their axes buried in the snow.

An Outward Bound employee, who had accompanied the team, did not appear amused. Perhaps it was Mick's reckless maneuver and how it had potentially endangered his classmates. Maybe it was merely because the youth had called out the wrong "F" word. Mick didn't ask.

OES had two or three groups making an attempt on Hood's South Side Route on an annual basis. During Mick's sophomore year, all three teams had been led by Father Tom with the assistance of a technical consultant, hired from Outward Bound. This year, there were four groups scheduled to climb.[25]

Each year, students were required to perform sixty hours of community service. If a junior or senior participated as an ACT member, this service requirement was fulfilled. Accompanying underclassmen on conditioning hikes in the Columbia Gorge, attending training sessions at Mt. Hood Ski Bowl, and the climbs in the spring, was considered equivalent to sixty hours of work.[26]

Father Tom had sole decision-making authority on ACT member selection. Interested students had to write a one-page essay on why they should be selected for one of the coveted positions.[27] This year, Goman had received two dozen essays.

Mick was thrilled when he learned that he had been chosen. His excitement was not generated by the thought of a return journey to the summit, but by the hiking opportunities the position promised.[28] He was already an outdoorsman at heart, and here was a chance to enjoy the forest, while simultaneously accruing community service credit.

Eight students had been selected this year. The seniors were Susan McClave, Michael Rubovitz, Joel Schalit, Eric Utz, and team leader Molly Schula. The three juniors included Justin Akkerman, Lorca Fitschen, and Mick Garrett.[29] Of these eight upperclassmen, half of the group would be assisting Father Tom on the first of the four planned ascents.

The ACT members were instructed on how to work individually and in a group setting. They were receiving ongoing lessons on navigation and wilderness survival. They were to share their respect and appreciation of the outdoors with the underclassmen. They were student mentors.[30]

There was a natural sense of accomplishment and a sense of exclusiveness amid their ranks. The ACT members enjoyed their hiking and camping experiences, apart from the rest of their schoolmates. On one occasion, the ACT members went to the Oregon Coast to practice rock climbing along the rugged shoreline. During the winter holiday, they practiced rappelling. The group had recently completed an Outward Bound rope course, conducted in a grove of trees.[31]

During Mick's junior year, Father Tom became his academic advisor, his geometry teacher, and his chess club advisor. Now, they had the ACT connection as well.

The priest was a definite mentor to Mick. They played chess, discussed matters of science and philosophy, and shared hiking adventures. Mick felt honored to have been entrusted with responsibility by someone he admired and tried to emulate. He thoroughly enjoyed being a member of Father Tom's Posse."[32]

John, near the back of the bus, did not share Mick's optimistic assessment of the popular teacher. Goman was not one of John's instructors, but he was undoubtedly a well-known figure on campus. The sophomore found the man's beard and Dutch Boy haircut somewhat off-putting. John didn't care for the commonly-used nickname of Furdur Tom. All year, John had considered the title, and his hair, somewhat weird and unsettling.[33]

As the bus continued to wind its way up the dark mountain highway, Goman stood and reminded everyone that, should they encounter any trouble on the mountain, they would simply turn back.[34]

Ric Conrad

Ralph Summers had been hired as the technical consultant for all four of the OES outings on the mountain. After accepting the position, he discovered that he had a scheduling conflict with the May 23rd climb. He contacted Dee Zduniak, a fellow employee of Outward Bound, and asked if the thirty-year-old would be the consultant for that particular climb. She would receive seventy-five dollars for her services. Summers wanted her to accompany the team, for free, on tonight's attempt. This would familiarize her with Fr. Goman, the route, and how to interact with the teacher and his students.[35]

Zduniak had driven to the Lodge from her home in the little town of Mount Hood, northeast of the mountain. The woman was several hours early for the scheduled climb and had been milling about the main lounge for some time.

She had climbed the mountain five times, but this would be her first ascent of the South Side Route. She was looking forward to adding this achievement to her professional resume.

Jon Tullis, the manager on duty, had noticed Zduniak was wearing climbing clothing. A mountaineer himself, he approached her. She seemed pleasant, and they fell into conversation.[36] Tullis could feel a change in the weather. Knowing there was an unfavorable forecast, he questioned her about the approaching front.

Zduniak said she had been monitoring the forecast and thought the students were likely to experience the power of nature on this climb.[37] She acknowledged that the team would likely turn around, short of their goal. Outward Bound was known for teaching respect for the outdoors, so this made some sense to Tullis.

Zduniak explained that she was waiting to meet up with Summers, to discuss final departure plans.

Tullis invited her to remain in the Lodge and wished her well.[38]

Judy O'Regan, a bartender in the Ram's Head Bar, bumped into Zduniak. They were acquainted. When Zduniak began speaking of the pending trip, O'Regan was surprised.

"You guys are going out tonight?"[39]

"We'll just climb a few pitches," Zduniak replied, "and then turn back."

MONDAY

May 12, 1986

Ric Conrad

CHAPTER 3
A WEATHER EYE

In the town of Government Camp, at the base of Mount Hood, four inches of fresh snow had fallen on the existing snowpack.[1] The school bus stopped here, about six miles before the final destination. The temperature was brisk, so those who weren't already properly dressed opted to prepare for the pending ascent.[2]

Fr. Goman was a bit of an old school mountaineer. He still wore clothing that had proven their worth to him over the decades; a cotton base layer, a pair of wool knickers, a wool shirt, and his rainbow-striped suspenders. He wore under socks, covered by wool socks, and leather climbing boots. Gloves, purchased from an Army surplus store, a down parka, and a knitted wool cap completed his signature attire.[3]

His prized possession was a one-of-a-kind "nose cozy" his crafty and creative wife had fashioned from an old sock. She had cut off the end of the hosiery and attached elastic onto it so that it would keep Tom's nose warm. Diana and Mar always teased that it made him look like an elephant, with a tiny trunk. Even so, the cozy had served its purpose on several climbs.[4]

Courtney had prepared much like the majority of students. She had Thinsulate base layers, wool socks, Gore-Tex gloves, and layered clothing to keep her comfortable. Her jacket, ski pants, gloves, and hiking boots were all waterproof. She had a wool hat that fit snuggly. In her backpack was a two-day supply of food and water, extra clothing, and her crampons.[5]

John put on long underwear, wool pants, and a parka—items that kept him warm and dry during the ski season. After lacing his leather hiking boots, he reached for his nylon rucksack, purchased on a family vacation in Switzerland. It had a shock absorber that permitted the pack to bounce off his lower back. He had selected all of his clothing and equipment himself, as his parents had taken a hands-off approach concerning the high-altitude adventure.[6]

Instead of a thermal top, Mick had opted for a thin wool sweater and a down-filled jacket. After exchanging his jeans for water-resistant ski pants, he put on wool socks, a wool cap, and his hiking boots.

Stuffing thick, winter gloves into his coat pockets, he turned to inspect the contents of his backpack. Being a vegetarian, Mick had brought various types of trail-mix and granola bars. He had several quarts of water, as he recalled getting quite thirsty on his previous climb.[7]

Absent from their ranks was a girl named Sandy Douthit. She was not only Erin's bumbershoot-companion, but she was also Alison's best friend. Sandy had attended OES during seventh and eighth grade. Her parents, feeling the girl was too young to live in the dorms, had taken her with them when the family had moved to Sacramento.

Returning to Oregon, to visit Alison during the winter break of their freshman year, Sandy had met the handsome new student, Patrick McGinness. Instant attraction turned into a long-distance romance.

By their sophomore year, Sandy convinced her parents to let her return to OES. Marion Horwell was now supervising Sandy and the other girls who resided in the dorms.

Sandy was initially slated to be with her friends on this climb. Earlier in the week, however, her father had convinced her to withdraw from the trip. He believed she was overwhelmed by school assignments, tests, and activities.

Sandy shifted her attention to helping her boyfriend prepare for the adventure. Pat didn't own base layers, so Sandy made it her mission to find him some. A friend was glad to loan Patrick long johns but wanted to ensure they were promptly returned for his own upcoming attempt on the mountain.

Tucking a note into the long johns, Sandy had hidden the care package on one of the shelves in the school's Bell Tower. Pat had picked these up, just before equipment inspections in the parking lot. Now, in Government Camp, he found his girlfriend's note:

Please wear these.
I love you.[8]

Smiling, he gratefully donned the borrowed garments.[9]

Pat had chosen his meals, snacks, and water. The athlete was very health-conscious, often teasing his dad about the quality and quantity of

Ric Conrad

food he consumed. In regards to clothing and equipment for his son, Frank had overseen everything, except for the long johns. Within the confines of Pat's pack, there was a 35mm camera with a new roll of film, ready to capture what promised to be the thrill of a lifetime.[10]

Erin, like John, had been skiing on the mountain before and knew the importance of layering.[11] Mr. Sandvik had taken his son, Erik, to an outdoor store, where they rented a backpack and a pair of climbing boots. The young man's supplies included fruit, water, and Snickers candy bars.[12]

Dressed for the elements, the group climbed back aboard the bus for the final six-mile journey up Timberline Highway. During this short drive, Giles and Brinton made a quiet pact. They would look after each other on the mountain.[13]

2:00 A.M.
PARKING LOT
WY'EAST DAY LODGE

The technical consultant, hired by the school, had been told that the busload of teenagers should be arriving around 2:00 a.m. That consultant, thirty-year-old, Ralph Summers, was living in a small community on the southwestern side of the mountain.[14] A ski instructor at Mt. Hood Meadows resort, Summers also worked for the Pacific Crest Outward Bound School in Portland.[15]

He had arrived quite early so, finding no activity in Timberline Lodge, the man chose to catch some sleep inside his rig. He listened to a marine weather radio. A storm front was predicted by late afternoon.[16] Continuing to wait for the bus, he fell back asleep.

The school had hired Summers to assist Goman in a snow school field exercise and as the consultant on all four of the school-sponsored climbs. Summers had been told that the teacher wanted him to provide advice on solving technical climbing problems and the use of first aid. In dealing with the individual students, however, Goman believed he had the requisite history in directing the Basecamp program. Authorizing students to turn around and retreat would be at his discretion.[17]

The sound of the school bus woke Summers around 2:30 a.m.[18] The driver pulled up close to Wy'East Day Lodge.[19]

Exiting the bus, John found himself feeling excited about the pending ascent. *Maybe, I'll make it the whole way, in spite of the way I feel.* He resolved to climb at a moderate pace, to see for himself how far he could ascend this volcanic peak. Facing the southern slopes of Oregon's highest mountain, the sophomore was struck by how quiet and beautiful everything looked.[20]

Courtney stepped off the bus, up for the challenge and wanting the entire team to summit. She followed some of the others into the Climber's Cave, at the eastern edge of the Lodge. There was a note on the wall, indicating a forecast of snow flurries, but she didn't notice anything of significance. Walking back outside, Courtney saw bright stars overhead.[21]

Goman called the students together to introduce the two consultants from Outward Bound. The majority of teens had already met Ralph Summers from their snow school day at Mt. Hood Ski Bowl. Summers was pleased to see that everyone was appropriately dressed for the journey ahead.[22]

As a senior ACT member, Molly was busy making trips, in and out of the bus, during these formal pleasantries. She was bringing coils of rope and mountain climbing hardware out of the vehicle, stationing them in various caches.[23]

Before departing the school, students had been provided multiple items to carry in their backpacks: a Prusik sling, two metal carabineers, a pre-fabricated climbing harness, or polypropylene webbing that could be used to fashion a makeshift harness. They were each given a boxed breakfast and lunch. Now, in the parking lot, each of the climbers was issued an ice axe and a climbing helmet.[24]

Goman believed in proper planning. Lorca had once asked him how he would prepare the night before a math test.

"With a bath and a glass of wine," Father Tom replied, with a twinkle in his eye. "Because, I would have been ready, long before the night before the exam."[25]

The ACT members divided the sophomores into groups of three. In addition to the individual gear they had already been assigned, group equipment now needed to be distributed. One coiled climbing rope was handed to each team with instructions that the burden of carrying this additional weight would need to be passed from member to member as the hours unfolded.[26] There were two first aid kits, essentially military-style field kits attached to a wide belt, which would be passed from one ACT member to another as climbing positions rotated.[27] There was a large backpack, which held additional climbing hardware. This pack, weighing considerably more than the daypacks students were carrying, would also be the responsibility of ACT members. Susan volunteered to be the first to shoulder this burden.[28]

After the equipment distribution, Goman asked to speak privately with Summers and Zduniak. There were scattered high clouds, but stars were out, and the mountain slopes looked inviting. Summers mentioned the weather forecast he had heard over the radio, acknowledging that there was a storm front predicted for the afternoon. They'd need to keep an eye on the weather.[29]

After this brief meeting, Goman motioned for Mick to accompany him to the Climber's Cave.

The teenagers were excited to try on the new gear, posing with their ice axes and packs. Rich placed a coiled climbing rope around his shoulders and then donned his white helmet. He was beaming with pride when Pat suddenly snapped a portrait of him—capturing the first image of the long-anticipated adventure. The camera flash lit up the immediate vicinity, catching everyone by surprise.[30]

~2:45 A.M.
CLIMBER'S CAVE
WY'EAST DAY LODGE

Mick watched as Father Tom filled out the requisite climbing permit. This was a Forest Service document that requested: all party members by name; what equipment they possessed; their destination and route; estimated time of return; and an emergency contact.[31] Climb leaders fill this document out and place it in a register box, indicating that they are out climbing. When the party returns, the document is to be removed, signed, and placed into another box.[32]

"There's a storm coming in," Father Tom informed Mick. "We're probably going to have to call this one early."[33]

CHAPTER 4
THAT NAGGING
FEELING

As most of the climbers took their first steps toward the summit, wind speeds were mild, around seventeen mph.[1]

Molly took the lead, post-holing up to her calves in the snow.[2] Her headlamp illuminated the terrain directly in front of her, while the students she was leading used flashlights. Father Tom had instructed her to maintain a steady pace, keeping the Magic Mile chair lift towers far off to her left, as a guide.[3]

Pat was right behind Molly, eager to reach the summit. Stepping into the boot prints Molly was making proved to be less taxing than breaking virgin terrain in the snow as individuals. Susan, the other senior ACT member, brought up the rear.[4]

Goman, Summers, Zduniak, and Mick remained behind at the Climber's Cave, completing the registration documentation.[5]

Molly noticed that the younger students needed a break, only fifteen minutes into the journey. They peeled off their backpacks and complained about the pace she was setting. Molly told them to remove one layer of their outer clothing if they felt too warm. Shining the light from her headlamp onto the students' faces, to gauge their conditions, Molly noticed that Sharon Spray and her daughter were breathing hard. This break lasted about ten minutes, allowing the party's leadership to catch up.

Molly called for the ascent to be resumed, promising to modify her pace.[6] With all twenty climbers together on the mountain for the first time, they continued climbing.

Nearly 10,000 climbers plod up the slopes of Mount Hood annually.[7]

It's the second-most climbed peak in the world, just behind Mount Fuji in Japan.[8] Both mountains intrigue their various pilgrims, and both jut high enough into the sky for altitude sickness and inclement weather to become a problem. Hood symbolizes rugged adventure and seems to beckon thrill-seekers.

Most make their attempt during the late spring or early summer. During this brief window, the majority of the winter storms have subsided. The risk of avalanche is reduced, while the mid to late summer thaw has yet to release the mountain's icy grip on volcanic boulders inside the upper crater walls. Experienced mountaineers know to begin climbing around midnight. The colder temperatures make for better snow conditions throughout the ascent.[9]

The students, hiking in silence, trudged up the mountain along the eastern edge of Palmer Snowfield. Courtney marveled at the view. The sophomore couldn't believe how clear and gorgeous the stars appeared, now that they were far from the lights of Portland. She was warm, even with the cold breeze. It felt like the team had the mountain to themselves. Courtney had never experienced such splendid isolation before.[10] John was overwhelmed by the tranquility of his surroundings, the stars, and the unique crunching sounds made as their boots compressed the snow.[11] Mick knew that this calf-deep snow would hinder progress, and the team's overall pace would suffer as a result.[12]

Molly asked if the bulk of the party could turn off their flashlights, as they produced a glare on the surface of the snow.[13]

Summers traveled up and down the line of climbers as the distance between each began to expand. He checked on their conditions and boosted the morale of a handful who needed encouragement. The vibrant lights of Timberline Lodge continued to recede into the distance.[14]

When Summers caught up with Molly, he asked her how she was faring. Her legs were feeling the effects of post-holing in the snow. They spied a pristine piste, made by a snow groomer. Recognizing that the terrain there would be firmer, Molly urged the team to follow her lead.[15]

Reaching firmer footing, they were able to pick up the pace. Summers suggested that Molly take a break and allow one of the boys to take a turn as the designated pathfinder.[16]

Patrick, Giles, and Rich seemed to be filled with energy and offered to lead the charge.[17] Pat ran track at school. He was lean, athletic, and was known for his favorite catchphrase, "Okay...let's go!"[18]

When Pat started dating Sandy, they attended a social function at a church one evening. The couple took a stroll together out in the snow. Caught up in each other's company, they placed quite a bit of distance between themselves and the church. When Pat realized it was only a few minutes before the time his father had agreed to pick them up, he grasped Sandy's hand, and they began running back to the party.

Unlike her new boyfriend, Sandy was not on the track team and was quickly winded. In the dark, she missed seeing a speed bump and found herself flat in the snow. Embarrassed, she searched for something funny to say while Pat helped her up and dusted her off. Learning that she was okay, Pat knew just the right words.

"Okay," he called out, grasping her hand again. "Let's go!"[19]

The young man was goal-oriented.

Pat took the lead position on the mountain now, followed closely by Giles and Rich. Molly and Summers stood still for a few moments while these three eager youths gained some ground. The consultant then made a rapid descent to the back of the line, checking on the students he passed. Molly occupied a new position, directly in front of Goman and Zduniak.[20]

Around 3:15 a.m., Hilary began to feel sick.[21] Her mother asked her a few questions and then stated the obvious.

"Hilary," she noted. "This climb is not worth your life."[22] Hilary had diabetes.

Concerned, Sharon spoke with Goman and informed him that she would accompany her daughter back to the Lodge. Although it was only thirty minutes into the ascent, Hilary would be credited with making an attempt, fulfilling the requirement of the school's Basecamp program.[23]

Zduniak spied the Sprays turning around. She suddenly recognized that she had no idea how the climbing party was organized. Who could authorize individuals or portions of the party to peel off and retreat in the darkness?[24]

The climbing party was down to eighteen.

Susan, who had occupied the rear position, handed the first aid belt over to Mick. Susan, Summers, Zduniak, and Goman began to pick up their pace so they could evaluate other members of the team as they passed them. Mick found himself as the last man in the lineup. Directly in front of him was John, and ahead of John was Marion Horwell.[25]

Zduniak positioned herself next to Goman and started asking questions concerning the Basecamp program.[26] She had a general understanding of what was required of her on the mountain, but she pressed him for specifics concerning her role. She asked if she had any decision-making authority. Goman told her that he would take into consideration any advice she or Summers might care to provide, but that he was ultimately responsible for making the decisions.[27]

The team found themselves climbing in pairs, ascending in a line. Courtney noticed that people weren't passing each other as much as she had predicted. The climbers pretty much stayed in formation, with Summers and two of the ACT members ascending and descending along the line to check on the condition of the sophomores.[28] Courtney could tell that the team was proceeding only as fast as its slowest members.[29]

The team took another short break, merely enough time to catch one's breath and speak briefly with a companion. Summers urged everyone to remain hydrated and to eat a snack.[30]

5:00 A.M.
SILCOX HUT
PALMER SNOWFIELD

During the summer of 1939, a stone and timber structure was constructed at 6,950', roughly a mile uphill from Timberline Lodge.[31] The structure had been virtually abandoned since 1962, and time and vandalism were taking their toll on the cabin.[32]

The Magic Mile chairlift whisks skiers from Timberline Lodge up to 7,000', only two hundred yards west of Silcox Hut. Passengers disembark here and walk to yet another structure, to board a secondary chairlift—Palmer. Skiers can use the Palmer lift to be delivered up to an upper shack at 8,540'.

As students approached Silcox Hut, they used the building as a wind block for their third break. Looking at his watch, Father Tom remarked that they were already an hour behind schedule.[33]

A year earlier, Mick and his friends had walked right past the derelict cabin in the dark. Now, the stars were rapidly disappearing as sunrise was approaching.[34]

Mick did the math. The overall elevation gain of the ascent would be 5,245 feet. The climbing party had taken two hours to gain their first 1,000 feet in elevation. The terrain ahead, especially above 9,500', would be steeper and more challenging. If they intended to reach the summit, Goman's party would need to devote more hours to climbing than originally planned.

During this break, students found themselves in somewhat of a quandary. Some had been sweating and felt quite warm. They started removing their coats and stashing them in their packs.[35] Standing still, even in the lee of the cabin, the students grew cold rather quickly. The weather remained stable.[36]

Along the eastern side of the shack, someone discovered the door to the hut was missing, so the students stepped inside to get out of the cold.[37] Summers, again, encouraged everyone to hydrate. He wanted them to consume the contents of their water bottles and fill them with snow.[38] When the party emerged back out into the elements, ten or fifteen minutes later, they were surprised at how light the sky had become.

"Oh, my God," Giles remarked to Mick, seeing that dawn was fast approaching. "It's going to be really hot."[39] Giles wanted to remove extra layers of clothing, knowing he'd have hours of exercise ahead of him. The trouble was, the party was already departing.

Pat and Susan took the lead, taking turns breaking trail.[40] Molly found herself near the back of the pack, tired from her previous role as the trailblazer.[41]

Mick approached Father Tom, relaying Giles' request to stay behind for a quick change.

"We can easily catch up," Mick assured his mentor.[42] Summers and Zduniak were just outside of the structure, so adult supervision was, therefore, already on the scene.[43]

After receiving authorization to stay longer, Giles and Mick returned to the interior of the cabin. Giles was very excited about the ascent, and Mick found his friend's enthusiasm to be contagious.[44]

5:41 A.M.
PALMER SNOWFIELD

Sunglasses and goggles were fished out of pockets and packs. Patrick snapped another photo just as dawn spilled its golden rays onto the pristine slopes of Palmer Snowfield.[45] The team paused to watch the apex of the shimmering gold disk rise in the east. Moments later, Pat pointed his camera south, capturing Mount Jefferson as its peak glowed, bathed in the early morning sunlight. Slipping his sunglasses on, Pat looked up towards the summit of Mount Hood. Amber rays illuminated the many crags and cornices of the mountain's crater region.[46] The sophomores received their first glimpse of the technical challenges that awaited them.

As the team hiked parallel to the Palmer chairlift, Summers noticed that Rich and Marion were both breathing hard. The consultant paid close attention to Marion, asking her how she was feeling. She said that her chest hurt, it was hard to breathe, and she was a bit dizzy. Summers advised her to take slower, deeper breaths.[47] Goman joined Marion, to keep an eye on her.

Zduniak noticed that the wind had picked up, yet the climbers continued to peel off layer after layer of clothing.[48]

Students who hadn't already donned sunglasses were instructed to wear whatever eye protection they had brought with them. Zduniak sported amber ski goggles.[49] Molly had an identical pair.[50]

A sizeable gap began to develop between the party members. The climbers appeared to be divided, with those faring better than others pulling ahead of the rest of the team. Marion continued to complain of dizziness, and several students slowed down to assist her.[51]

They were all climbing a mountain—everyone was struggling, to a certain extent. Courtney had witnessed Marion making repeated inquiries as to the physical condition of others, during the initial ascent and at Silcox Hut. Courtney thought that the dean was faring quite well for a typical, middle-aged person ascending a mountain.[52] Goman decided to stay by Marion's side.

Courtney was accustomed to achieving her goals, and she wanted to climb the mountain.[53] It was very unlike her to contemplate quitting any athletic endeavor. Still, she began experiencing a bizarre, nagging feeling that she should retreat. An inner voice began speaking to her as she continued to climb. It was troubling. *Go down.*[54]

~8:20 A.M.
PALMER SNOWFIELD

Telling herself that she was just feeling lazy, Courtney had ignored the urge to quit, but now her back pain was undeniable. She had been preparing for a national track and field competition. Weeks of practice with the discus and javelin, compounded by the strenuous ascent in the cold, had taken its toll. She knew she could push through, but would it affect her performance at the competition?[55]

Looking up, she saw Lorca sitting in the snow. Lorca was privately suffering from wave after wave of painful cramps, the kind that only girls could understand. She was considering whether she should continue with the ascent or not.[56]

Marion Horwell, having her own difficulties, was standing beside the youth, concerned about her condition.

"I don't feel well," Lorca confided to her dorm mother.[57]

"Just rest a few minutes and see how you feel," Horwell said encouragingly.

Zduniak arrived and probed the teen for more information. Lorca, slightly embarrassed about the cause of her discomfort, merely replied that she felt pain below her rib cage.[58]

Goman, noticing the gathering, descended to investigate as John and Mick arrived from below.

Lorca wanted to continue climbing, but Father Tom wanted her to descend to safety.

"Aren't you going to need me?" the junior ACT member asked.[59]

"We're probably going to turn around anyway," he reassured her. "Don't worry about not making the summit." He then turned and called out to the others. "Is anyone considering going back?"[60] Goman didn't want Lorca descending alone.

"I could take her down," Mick offered. The teacher brushed aside this suggestion. Goman didn't want to lose two ACT members at once.[61]

Courtney, torn between the desire to continue, and that voice inside her head that kept telling her to descend, said she might head down soon, but not immediately.[62]

"It's okay," said the teacher. "If you want to come up with the next group, we'll get you in."[63] This assurance helped Courtney decide to descend.

Father Tom directed her to make her way down to the resort while also keeping an eye on her partner. If Lorca still wasn't feeling well upon their return to lower elevations, Courtney was to telephone a doctor.[64] Goman mentioned that the party's return to the Lodge should be expected no later than 6:00 that evening.[65]

Courtney turned and began descending with Lorca, leaving the remaining students in good spirits—exuberant even. They seemed confident in their training.[66]

The climbing party was down to sixteen.

Since the Sprays' departure, over five hours earlier, Mick had been keeping his eye on John and Marion from the back of the line. John appeared to have a touch of altitude sickness. The exertion was taking its toll on Marion.[67]

Goman descended to speak with John privately.

Mick was unable to overhear their conversation. When he found an opportunity, he asked the sophomore what had been discussed. John confessed that he'd expressed the hope of turning around, but Goman wanted him to continue climbing.[68]

~9:05 A.M.
TIMBERLINE LODGE

As Courtney and Lorca arrived back at the Lodge, they turned around to face the mountain. They could see their classmates, continuing with the ascent. The site was disheartening for Courtney. She wished she was back with the team, already second-guessing her decision to descend.

Why did I do that?[69]

~9:15 A.M.
PALMER SNOWFIELD

Just shy of the upper shack of Palmer chairlift, Summers noticed the summit was visited by broken clouds. Wind speeds had increased, and the temperature began to dip. Zipping up his parka, the consultant saw that clouds were also building in the valleys below. He called for the team to take another break.[70]

Here, at 8,500', John plopped down in the snow, exhausted and complaining about the way he felt. Most of the kids used the break to start putting warmer protection on. Pat trotted off to the east, fishing in his pocket for his camera. He snapped another photo, this time with his friends bundled up, faces covered to protect them from the dropping temperatures.[71]

Some of the students discussed the possibility of turning back. Giles was hoping for someone to announce a retreat but didn't mention this to many of his fellow students.[72] He figured they should already be enjoying the summit slopes but, they were only halfway to their destination.[73] Most surprisingly, Marion still hadn't requested to turn around, even when Summers formally asked if anyone wished to descend.[74]

John couldn't continue with the ascent. Mick had been climbing directly behind the husky sophomore for the last 2,500 feet in elevation gain and could confirm the teen's condition.[75] Quietly, John told Mick that he wanted to head back down.

Mick wasn't wearing a balaclava and didn't have any protection for his face, which had been cold for hours. He felt no burning ambition to reach the summit, as he'd been there a year earlier, and he was scheduled to accompany two more of the school-sponsored climbs in the weeks ahead. Treading the summit slopes on this particular day was not a pressing concern. He'd make it some other day. He felt ready to descend.[76]

Looking around, he observed that the team had separated into splinter groups. Summers and Zduniak were standing together, speaking quietly. Seated in one group were Giles, Rich, Erik, and Alison. A few yards away were Erin, Pat, and Tasha.[77]

John had been extremely impressed with Tasha's performance during the ascent. Legally blind in one eye, the girl was performing well and appeared to be going strong.[78]

Goman gathered his three remaining ACT members together. Mick informed Father Tom that John was ready to head back down the mountain and volunteered to be his escort. Surprised, Goman wanted to speak privately with the sophomore.

John saw the man approaching and braced himself, determined to leave. When it appeared that the student could not be swayed to continue the ascent, the teacher seemed to grow incredulous.

"What?" Goman remarked. "You're going to give up on what could possibly be the greatest moment of your life?"[79]

John thought the man's words were ridiculous, as the sophomore was only sixteen years old. Surely, he would have adventures in his future that could rival, or even surpass, mountain climbing. Besides, Hood wasn't going anywhere. John knew he could make another attempt for the summit one day. Goman rubbed him the wrong way.

Marion approached the pair and collapsed in the snow to rest. She was red in the face and seemed to have lost her motivation. John watched as the teacher, seemingly unsympathetic, shot her a look.

"What's the matter, Marion?" Goman chided. "Can't take it anymore?"[80] Horwell offered no reply. She continued to breathe and take stock of her surroundings.

As Goman walked away, John shook his head in disbelief. Taunting Horwell seemed unwarranted. John had been raised in the public-school system and had felt betrayed by several teachers during his formative years.

He had hoped things would change as he aged, yet Goman's interactions left him with the impression that educators at private institutions were no better.[81]

Molly was also tired and offered to be John's escort down the mountain. Mick was surprised by this, as nearly everyone understood how much energy and drive Molly was known to possess. When Mick mentioned that his face was cold, Molly offered him the balaclava she was wearing. Envisioning what fluids could be inside the face mask, after seven hours of climbing, Mick declined the offer as politely as he could.[82]

Susan was still filled with energy and encouraged Mick to continue.[83] Molly joined her, both assuming it was Mick's first ascent of the mountain.

"I've been to the top before," he countered. "So, I could go back down at this point, and that would be alright with me."[84]

Mick had made his request, and Molly had made hers. It was now up to Goman to consider the issue and decide. While the teacher conversed with Molly and Susan, Mick noticed that Marion was sitting in the snow, all alone. Curious, he walked up to her and asked how she was faring. Marion said that she felt she was doing okay, but she was tired.[85]

Mick walked over and sat down next to Rich and Giles. Rich was handing out cans of Coke, saving one for himself.[86]

"So, what's going on?" some students inquired of Mick.

"I think I'm still going up at this point," he replied, believing Father Tom would defer to Molly. She looked tired, whereas Mick still had something in reserve.

Goman asked Marion if she wished to descend. After some encouragement, she declined to turn around. Goman turned to Molly and asked about her condition. Molly acknowledged that she was fine, but whenever Horwell desired to retreat, she'd be happy to escort her down the mountain.[87]

Mick rose as Goman approached him.

"Marion wants to go on," the teacher informed him, only inches away from Mick's face.[88] This announcement was unexpected as Mick was sure that Marion would have wanted to turn around. "Molly will go on as far as Marion wants to go," Goman continued.

"All right," Mick replied, glancing over at Horwell. He believed the dean should turn around but didn't press the issue. Before departing, Mick had one last thing to say to his mentor.

"You know...you have icicles in your beard?"

Father Tom chuckled and waved off the observation as inconsequential. He hugged the teen.

The students, observing this scene of departure, said their goodbyes to Mick and John. Giles expressed empathy to his fellow dorm-mate, Mick.

"Too bad you have to go back," he noted.

Rich was also clearly disappointed. "I wish you were continuing on," he said to Mick.

John looked up at the remaining 2,700 feet of elevation gain that stretched towards the summit. He had been looking forward to the climb for weeks and was disappointed that he was cold enough to turn around.[89]

The climbing party was down to fourteen.

~10:45 A.M.
FRANK MCGINNESS WOOD FINISHING
PORTLAND

Frank was experiencing flu-like symptoms, and his voice had been raspy throughout the morning. He suffered periodic stomach cramps, which had started as soon as he had dropped Pat off at the school last night. Frank had just finished a phone interview with *Design West* magazine, concerning his wood-finishing work for Atwater's Restaurant in Portland. With his head in his hands, feeling miserable, he wondered if Pat had shaken off the last of his virus, up on the mountain.[90]

~10:55 A.M.
BASE OF TRIANGLE MORAINE

After passing the upper shack for the Palmer chairlift, Goman and Susan took turns, not only breaking trail but carrying the pack that held the team's equipment.[91] Goman also began placing trail wands about every 200 feet along the ascent line, marking their path so they could return the way they had come.[92]

Susan and Giles were the first to arrive at an area known as Triangle Moraine, between 9,300' and 9,600'. Marion told Molly that she was feeling dizzy again. Someone had an antacid and, believing it would help alleviate the dean's dizziness, gave it to her.[93]

Molly, Erin, and Alison excused themselves to walk behind a snow hummock, out of site, to answer the call of nature. Alison, complaining of nausea, hunched over and started retching. Goman overheard the noise and, when the girls returned to the group, asked about her condition.[94]

The team brought out their boxed meals and delicacies from home. Tasha had peanuts and commented that she had rinsed the salt from them. Susan shared Wheat Thins with Molly and others nearby. Erin consumed a sandwich while Rich enjoyed a candy bar. Goman declined to eat. Alison, not feeling like eating, mentioned that she had consumed a rather large breakfast. Erik took some good-natured ribbing over a bowl of Cheerios he had consumed the night before the climb. Summers snacked on a mixture of raisins, nuts, seeds, and dried fruits.[95] He noticed that students who were consuming snacks, did so with their gloves off. The majority seemed warm from their physical exertions. Molly asked Marion how she was feeling, after having taken the antacid. Horwell indicated she wanted to go just a little farther.[96]

Susan and Goman had been taking turns carrying the heavy backpack. She said she felt great. Although Molly was an ACT member and, as such, should have been sharing that burden, she knew Susan and Goman were not handing the pack to her because she was visibly tired.[97]

As he had done earlier, Pat stepped away to snap a group photo. Members of the team, seeing that their picture was about to be taken, waved and flashed the "peace" sign, mugging for the camera.[98]

~11:30 A.M.
UPPER TRIANGLE MORAINE

Near the top of Triangle Moraine, Zduniak started having difficulty with her eyesight and immediately recognized what was wrong.[99] On an ascent of Mount Adams, she had experienced the pain and cloudy vision associated with snow blindness, causing her to remain in a high camp an extra day before making her descent. Here, on Mount Hood, her symptoms had returned.[100]

"How are your eyes doing?" she asked Molly since the two were wearing identical ski goggles.[101]

Molly said the glare off the ice was not hurting too much. She was still wearing her balaclava and, with her goggles in place, her entire face stayed protected from the mountain winds.

A gray wash came over Zduniak's vision, and she could no longer see shadows. There didn't appear to be any difference between light or dark objects. She removed her goggles to see if her sunglasses would be better.[102] If her snow blindness continued to worsen, she would not be able to assist the group.

Zduniak approached Summers and Goman, to inform them of her condition. She asked them whether they had a "summit or bust" attitude and was pleased when both replied that they would turn around should the need arise.[103]

Summers handed his colleague his crampons and even considered giving her the team's lone shovel. They discussed the topic, but they decided that Summers should retain the tool.[104] If Zduniak did not feel comfortable driving home, she could wait for Summers, and he would drive her home.[105] With a last goodbye, Dee began a solitary retreat down the mountain.[106]

The climbing party was down to thirteen.

As Zduniak departed, she noticed that clouds were lowering over the summit region. A cloud cap descended quickly, and soon she couldn't see down the mountain. The upper shack of Palmer chairlift was no longer visible. Using the trail wands as guides, she eventually emerged below the cloud cover.

Reaching the ski slope area, she encountered two maintenance specialists who were working near a snowcat. She was secretly hoping the men would offer her a ride down the slopes, but she didn't want to vocalize such a request. She did mention the pain in her eyes to explain why she'd turned around, but the workmen merely exchanged pleasantries and went about their duties.[107]

The two repairmen periodically caught glimpses of the climbing party, through breaks in the clouds. Soon, those figures disappeared from view.[108]

CHAPTER 5
THE DEVIL'S KITCHEN

Just downhill from the repairmen, Dee Zduniak decided to eat her lunch. She removed her gloves and sat down. She was facing south with a clear view of Timberline Lodge and Wy'East Day Lodge below her. Zduniak glanced over her left shoulder to view the upper slopes of the mountain. Unable to see the climbing party, she wondered whether it was due to cloud cover, natural terrain features, or just because her vision remained gray.[1]

~12:00 P.M.
PARKING LOT
WY'EAST DAY LODGE

Only a few hundred yards from the parking lot, Mick and John had nearly finished their descent. Mick's journey down the mountain a year earlier had been fun, filled with jog-trotting and sitting glissades. This year, it seemed like it was taking them forever to reach their destination.

John felt sure that Mick was angry with him, for costing him a bid for the summit.[2]

"John," Mick announced when he spied the school bus so tantalizing close in the lot. "I'll meet you down there."[3]

When Mick arrived back in the parking lot, he encountered Courtney. Once John arrived on the scene, she escorted them both into the resort.[4]

~12:15 P.M.
TIMBERLINE LODGE

The Sprays had rented a chalet room in the historic inn.[5] It had European-style bunk beds and plaid carpeting. There was no television, and bathrooms were down the hall. Hilary and her mom had left the mountain already, but Lorca was resting in the room. She was curled up in a ball, still feeling poorly.[6] John was thrilled to have a place to relax and unwind. Courtney and Mick, feeling energetic, opted to explore the Lodge.[7]

~12:30 P.M.
PARKING LOT
WY'EAST DAY LODGE

Zduniak had made a hasty descent to Timberline Lodge. There was no need for her to sign the check-in sheet for the Forest Service, as Fr. Goman had not even listed her name as being among the party members. Her snow blindness had decreased enough that she felt comfortable driving the fifty-mile journey to her home.[8]

~1:00 P.M.
DEVIL'S KITCHEN
CRATER REGION

Goman and his remaining twelve climbers were still moving slowly as they entered the crater region of the volcano. In an area east of Crater Rock, Susan assumed the lead position. Goman continued placing trail wands in the snow every 200 feet or so.

Summers noticed the weather was beginning to change.[9] Clouds were increasing, and they were lower now. Much lower. He kept an eye on Marion's progress. As her pace continued to slow, Summers advised the dean not to push herself.[10]

Giles noticed that Goman continued spending a considerable amount of time with Marion. When Giles was taking a break, and Marion caught up to him, he overheard the teacher telling her that climbing was good for her and she should continue to press on with the ascent.[11]

"How much farther?" some of the students inquired.[12] The snow remained soft and deep, which was extremely difficult on their knees and hamstrings. Looking up, team members could see that the summit region was now completely shrouded in cloud cover.

Rich was complaining to Molly. He just wanted to be back at the Lodge. Molly chalked this up to normal sophomore behavior. She had seen it during previous ascents. It was only natural to want to be back in the comforts of the inn, next to a roaring fireplace.[13]

Molly was thinking about the upcoming ascent of the Hogsback, a natural feature within the crater. The services of the remaining two ACT members would be needed above the Hogsback, so Molly told Rich that he should hold on a little longer.[14]

Team members began to smell sulfur.[15] It was pungent, like a truckload of rotten eggs. Volcanic fumaroles dotted the crater floor and the base of the steep eastern wall, known as Steel Cliff. These volcanic shafts run deep into the heart of the mountain, and the steam melts the snow surrounding each vent. Only four feet below the surface, temperature readings in these shafts range between 106° and 120° Fahrenheit.[16] This noxious, steaming brew gave rise to the region's name—Devil's Kitchen.

Summers took over the lead position and soon stopped to permit the party members to congregate around him. Visibility was growing poor, and Molly noticed that no one was talking. Everyone huddled together, trying to keep warm.

The consultant knew they should be near the Hogsback but could not see it due to the cloud cap that had descended upon them. The summit only appeared periodically, through breaks in the clouds. He felt as if the ceiling had dropped. Summers instructed the students to remain where they were, so he could go ahead and investigate. The group watched as the man ascended a steep slope and vanished into the clouds.[17]

Winds were consistently strong and, though it wasn't snowing, Molly could feel the moisture in the air. Visibility was fifty feet at best.[18]

Summers' emerged, back from the clouds. When he reached the students, he informed them that they still had two switchbacks to navigate before reaching the base of the Hogsback. The party resumed climbing.

Strong winter winds whip through the crater region. Due to the topography of the high-altitude basin, these winds cause the snow to pile, forming a unique feature. Here, at 10,400', the Hogsback is a snow ridge, running from Crater Rock up to two natural gaps in the crater's rock wall, known as the Pearly Gates.

The climbers slowly wound their way up the final two switchbacks, bringing them to the base of this lengthy, narrow ridge.

~2:00 P.M.
LOWER HOGSBACK
COALMAN GLACIER

As they crested the snow ridge, the climbers were exposed to the harsh winds. These conditions only taxed the climbers further, and they opted for another break. Summers told everyone to eat and drink, even suggesting that they stuff snacks into their jacket pockets.[19]

Summers pulled Goman aside and asked about abandoning the bid for the summit. The team was due back in the parking lot within four hours. The consultant emphasized Marion's poor condition. Still, Goman opted to continue climbing.[20] Summers deferred to his leadership and decision, with the understanding that the party would only progress a short distance.[21]

Pat sat in the snow and dropped his head into his hands. He was sick and didn't want to continue. Goman and Summers told him that, if he remained where he was, he'd only get colder. Erin volunteered to walk beside him.[22]

For the final push for the summit, Goman and Summers opted not to rope-up because the snow was soft. If anyone stumbled, they'd simply land in a cushion of snow. The risk of an uncontrolled slide appeared minimal.[23] Students were already wearing helmets and brandishing ice axes. They brought out extra equipment for the final assault—snow pickets, flukes, and two coils of rope.[24]

Leaving their backpacks in the snow, the party proceeded forward along the Hogsback, shielding their faces from the wind. Summers assumed the lead position. Susan was directly behind him, followed by Erik, Tasha, Giles, Alison, and Brinton. Erin followed, escorting Pat at a slower pace. Behind this pair was Molly, Rich, Marion, and Goman.[25] Snow began to fall.

Molly couldn't see the summit. Like frustrated children in the back seat of a car, the climbers were asking her how far it was to the top.

"I wish you guys could see it," Susan called out in response. "It's so close!"[26]

It can take mountaineers six or seven hours to ascend from Timberline Lodge to the summit.[27] Goman's party had been trudging uphill for over eleven hours but still hadn't reached the Pearly Gates.

Rich continued complaining to Molly. He didn't appear to be focused, and he seemed to be on the verge of tears. Molly tried to ignore what she interpreted as whining, but the boy specifically called out to her as he plopped down in the snow. She turned around and returned to him, directing him to get on his feet. Rich was complaining about the temperature and the difficulty he was having in locating the steps that the team was making in the snow.

"Okay, Rich," said Molly. "I'm gonna walk right ahead of you, and when I move my foot, you put yours there."[28] She was somewhat short with him. The pair began to execute this plan, but they fell behind the group.

Molly told Rich the story of her first ascent of Hood, which seemed to calm him down.

"Thanks, Molly," said Rich.

Molly apologized for losing her patience, and both of their spirits appeared to rally.[29] Up ahead, the bulk of the climbing party slowed to the point where they both could catch up.

The party paused near an exposed rock. Erin glanced at her watch and informed her teammates how long they had been climbing. This announcement caused some controversy as some of the students refused to believe her.[30]

~3:15 P.M.
UPPER HOGSBACK
COALMAN GLACIER

Since leaving their backpacks on the lower reaches of the Hogsback, the party had climbed for roughly an hour and fifteen minutes. During that time, they had only gained a few hundred feet in elevation.

Summers called for the team to rest while he evaluated their situation. He knew a significant obstacle was somewhere nearby, an expansive bergschrund, or crevasse. Depending on how much snow was nestled inside this large crevasse, one could cross it on a snow bridge or choose to go around it on the western side. Past the crevasse were the Pearly Gates, two snow chutes between crumbling towers of rock. Passing successfully through one of these chutes brings climbers to an open, easy ascent to the summit. During clear visibility, Summers would have been able to see the crevasse and the Pearly Gates, but too much snow was falling. The consultant directed the team to remain where they were while he scouted the terrain ahead.[31]

Summers began ascending into the blowing snow. He traveled only thirty or forty feet when he turned around, unable to see the students behind him. Even without definable landmarks, he knew he was still below the bergschrund.[32]

Back at the huddled group, Rich told Father Tom how great Molly was for assisting him up the mountain. Teasingly, Molly agreed with him, causing the two students to smile at one another.[33]

As quickly as Summers had disappeared, he returned, trotting down the Hogsback, buffeted by high winds.

"Tom!" he called. "You better come up here with me."[34] Goman maneuvered around the students and made his way to his consultant. "I think we should get out of here," Summers stated emphatically.[35] Goman agreed, and the call for retreat was officially made.[36]

The team was somewhere around 10,700'. Above them, out of reach and hidden by the shroud of the developing storm, was the summit.[37]

Frank McGinness had come home from work early, still sick. When his youngest son, Chris, arrived home from elementary school, the boy found his father asleep.

"Dad," the seven-year-old inquired in a loud voice. "Are you alright?"[38]

"No, Chris," Frank winced. "I'm really sick, but I'll get up and cook you something."

"No, dad. You stay in bed. I'll cook you some chicken soup."

Frank slowly rose. His thoughts wandered to Pat. Looking at the clock, he reasoned that the climbing team must be back down to the parking lot by now. What adventures had they had? What stories would they be able to tell?

Adding their names to the summit register would be a goal the students would not achieve. The call for retreat had been made, and team members shifted positions. They readied themselves for the descent.[39]

As climbers turned to face downhill, Summers directed Goman to the front of the group. The consultant wanted to ensure that the teacher followed the tracks the team had made during their ascent. It was the easiest way to ensure they were returning along their original course considering the lack of visibility.[40]

Summers gave a brief review of the plunge step they had all practiced during their snow day weeks earlier.[41] It was at this point, after the party had been ascending for over twelve hours, that the consultant assumed more of the leadership duties of the climbing party.[42] This transition was not discussed with Goman, and there seemed to be no debate. It was just a fact that everyone assembled seemed to accept. Summers would bring up the rear, so he could personally handle anyone that fell too far behind.

As Molly and Rich found themselves in the front of the party for the retreat, Molly asked the priest what was going on.

"It's time to turn around," Father Tom replied.[43]

Molly was having difficulty seeing, so she raised her overmit and started wiping her goggles. They were icing over.[44]

The weather had deteriorated considerably, and a long descent lay ahead of them. Gusts of wind exceeded forty mph, and visibility was less than fifty feet.[45]

The consultant soon found himself escorting Tasha.[46] The duo fell so far behind that they lost sight of their companions. Summers did his best to motivate and inspire the girl. These overtures appeared to work. Their pace increased, and they eventually caught up to the party.

People began passing one another. Marion and Tasha continually needed assistance. Pat repeatedly wanted to sit down in the snow to rest. Molly, among others, successfully urged him to forgo a break, at least until they reached their backpacks.[47]

Summers called out for the party members to walk slightly to the left, as they were nearing a drop-off. Giles suddenly slipped on a patch of ice and began sliding. He used his ice axe in the self-arrest technique, saving himself from sliding into a large volcanic fumarole.[48]

"Molly!" Summers called out over the din of the wind, "To the left!"[49] The consultant gave this warning as the girl came precariously close to the edge of the drop-off.

When the team had descended a few hundred vertical feet and found themselves back at their packs, they stopped. Goman trotted over to Summers and asked him if he would lead the way; Goman could tend to Tasha and serve as her escort.[50] Summers agreed.

Passing a handful of students, Summers noticed one seemed off balance. Giles and Susan were on each side of this faltering climber, assisting him to the best of their ability.

It was Patrick McGinness.[51]

Pat suddenly fell over, bringing down the other two climbers in the process. The youth rose and continued to press on, but something was clearly wrong.

"Pat is real cold," Susan informed Summers.[52]

Pat was hunched over, clearly exhausted. The boy's speech was slurred and incoherent. Likewise, his physical coordination was impaired. He was disoriented. Pat made motions with his hands, indicating that he wanted to sit down. He mumbled something about wanting to sleep. Summers looked around. The winds were increasing, and visibility had dropped to only twenty or thirty feet.[53]

Pat, who had been sick recently, was showing signs of hypothermia, and Summers knew the teen needed immediate assistance. He advised Goman that they'd have to assist Pat before continuing with the descent.[54]

Efforts to help Pat began in earnest. All the team's coiled climbing ropes were tossed onto the snow, to act as a barrier from the cold.[55] Summers spread out his waterproof nylon tarp over the ropes. The students held it in place on the ground. The consultant's red sleeping bag was unrolled atop the tarp, and Pat was helped into the bag.[56] The boy still had his boots on.[57] Volunteering to share her body heat, Susan removed her jacket, hat, and gloves, and climbed into the bag with Patrick. The ends of the tarp were wrapped around the two teens. Everyone else huddled over and around the bundled pair, sharing their collective body heat and providing protection from the wind.[58] Summers retrieved a first aid kit, found a hypothermic thermometer, and handed it to Susan. Repositioning herself, Susan carefully inserted the device into Pat's mouth.[59]

While this rewarming process was underway, Summers broke out his climber's stove, and Giles heated some water. Susan mentioned that she had some lemon drops somewhere in her bag. They added two lemon drops to a cup of hot water.[60] Summers handed the cup to Giles to hold, briefly, while he read the thermometer. Pat's temperature was only 96° F.[61]

Molly was holding the sleeping bag's flaps, periodically checking on Susan and Pat. Now, she reached down and lifted Pat's head so he could take a few sips from the cup. Pat said he didn't want more but, with further coaxing, managed to consume almost two cups of the hot lemon water.[62]

Throughout this process, Susan kept offering Pat words of encouragement. She made inquiries that necessitated a verbal response from the boy. She rubbed his hands and asked whether he felt any throbbing in them. Pat stated that it was painful.

"That's good," Susan replied, "you're getting a little feeling back."[63]

Pat's condition didn't seem to improve much over the next forty-five minutes. His fellow students—who had ceased their descent to help him—were now shivering. Anxious glances were exchanged between students and faculty.

The teens began stomping their feet to keep warm.
    It was time to move.

CHAPTER 6
ALABASTER SKIES

Due to the steep terrain, it would be nearly impossible to carry Pat down the mountain. Summers hoped that the boy had recovered enough to escape the storm under his own steam. He reasoned that once the teen got moving, he'd warm up and show signs of improvement.[1]

Fr. Goman stated that the team needed to move fast.[2]

With this strategy in place, Susan was helped out of the sleeping bag. She threw on her jacket while others extracted Pat from the bag. The sleeping bag and tarp were rolled up and stashed in Summers' backpack.[3]

Summers removed his own parka and put it on Pat. The teen needed assistance with the zipper as well as the hood, but he seemed coherent and understood that his friends were helping him. Giles donned Summers' backpack, which had a set of skis lashed to the back.[4] Brinton carried her own pack and offered to carry Giles' as well. She accomplished this by carrying one on her chest and one on her back.[5] Summers told the students that Goman would be the last man in line, ensuring that no one was left behind. The group was to stay close to one another and to yell out, if need be, to achieve that objective.

"Tom!" Summers called out. "You guys stay here, collect the gear. I'm going to start down with Pat. He needs to start moving."[6]

The party continued their descent. Pat was unable to walk unassisted. As the group surged forward, Summers and Susan positioned themselves with Pat between them.[7] Even with these stabilizing forces, the boy lurched sideways or pitched forward at awkward moments. The task was made all the more difficult because of the snow that had fallen during the last hour. The party's tracks were growing challenging to spot with the recent accumulation.

Team members were post-holing, and the snow was blowing all around them.[8] The temperature was around 20° Fahrenheit.[9] When wind gusts reached sixty mph, the wind chill factor plummeted to -50° F.[10] Through these conditions, the party continued their descent.

The blowing snow began swirling around the students. Landscape features disappeared. Downhill and uphill seemed indistinguishable. The skies became as white as the snow underneath. Students could only see a few feet, and it was like living inside a ping-pong ball.[11]

Molly, the designated pathfinder, was concerned. Summers and Susan, escorting Pat, had managed to pull ahead and were now invisible because of the blizzard. Molly couldn't detect the presence of any distinguishable path.[12] *Where have our original prints gone?*

As Molly no longer knew where to go, she employed the telephone game. She turned to the person behind her and shouted a message—a plea for directions from Father Tom. This crude form of communication worked, and word was successfully transmitted up the line to Goman. While Molly waited for the response, she removed her ski goggles in the hopes that she would be able to see better. The snow was blowing too hard, and she was forced to replace her eye protection.[13]

When Molly finally received the return message from Goman, via the grapevine, she wasn't reassured. The teacher had advised her to keep to the left and look for the trail wands he had placed hours earlier. Molly was feeling very uncomfortable in the lead position when she heard the teacher yelling out to her.

"Can you see Ralph?" he shouted, as he approached.[14] Molly turned and began yelling out to the consultant who was somewhere below, cloaked by a wall of blinding snow.

Pat suddenly pitched forward and slid, his weight and momentum caught Susan and Summers off guard. All three began to slide, taking them twenty or thirty feet down a steep slope. By blind luck, they managed to stop their forward movement. Summers rose but discovered the two students were in a bad predicament. Pat had stopped right above Susan, on a steep area, and it looked like the two could begin sliding again at any moment. Summers stomped his feet, using his boots to create a little platform which Susan could stand on. She used her position, her weight, and her arms to hold Pat in place.[15] *Now what?*

Summers needed to fetch an ice axe. He carefully began climbing. Once the terrain became more level, Molly suddenly appeared before him.

"There you are!" he called out to her.[16]

Summers took an axe from one of the students and descended back to Pat's position. Handing the tool to the boy, Summers positioned himself below the youth. As Pat began ascending, employing the axe, the consultant used his shoulder to brace the teen's rear end, in case Pat slipped again.[17] Susan was told to remain where she was; Summers would return for her.

The consultant escorted Pat back up to the team. He then used his boots to level out a spot for his client to stand on and lean against a friend. Retrieving the ice axe, Summers yelled through the noise of the wind.

"Hold him...Don't let him sit down!"[18]

Summers descended once more. He returned to Susan's side, handed her the axe, and escorted her back up to the group in the same manner he had with Pat.

The consultant noticed that most of the group was doing well, physically, but they were beginning to show signs of fear. They were quiet, crowded close together, and appeared to realize they were involved in a very serious situation.[19]

Summers wrapped one of Pat's arms around his own shoulders. He held the boy's hand, asking him to squeeze it periodically. Summers continually asked questions, forcing Pat to converse, to remain coherent, and above all—to keep moving.[20]

~4:40 P.M.
DEVIL'S KITCHEN
CRATER REGION

Even though the team remained shrouded in the whiteout, they could tell by the topography that they were off the steep switchbacks below the Hogsback. They were somewhere in the lower reaches of the Devil's Kitchen. Goman produced his compass and called out to those in his vicinity.

"Go left! To the left!"[21]

Molly was tired. She had to force herself to concentrate and keep her vision on the climber directly in front of her. The high winds repeatedly forced her off balance and sent her to her knees. Not wanting to lose sight of the student in front of her, she quickly rose after each fall.[22]

Nearby, Brinton was also struggling. She was wearing her pack on her back and Giles' pack on her chest. It was proving very difficult for her to maintain her balance.

"Can anyone take one of Brinton's packs?" Erin yelled to those nearby.[23] There was no reply.

After descending more than a thousand feet since their highest point, and by following a generally southerly bearing, Giles suddenly came upon a trail wand in the snow.[24] It was one of the markers Goman had placed during the team's ascent.

There were no visible landmarks. Summers' energy was focused on escorting Pat down the seemingly endless slopes.

Goman suddenly handed his compass to Summers. Puzzled, the consultant received it while still hanging on to Pat. Summers noticed that the teacher had set a bearing of 160°.

"Let's pass it to someone closer to the front!" Summers suggested.[25]

Since Giles was wearing a bright yellow raincoat and matching ski pants, he took the lead. He would be easier to spot in the foul weather than his companions.[26]

Summers handed Susan the compass and told her she'd be the navigator, directly behind Giles. She was one of only two ACT members left on the team. As Summers still held Pat to his side, he reminded Susan how to take a bearing and directed the party to move forward.[27]

Giles was still carrying the consultant's backpack with a pair of skis strapped on the back. Whenever strong gusts of wind struck, the skis acted like sails, propelling Giles forward or backward.[28]

He came upon a second trail wand, off to his left.[29] It appeared as if the team remained on course.

Molly was not so sure about this. When the climbing party suddenly leveled out in an area where volcanic rock was visible, she felt the team was off track. She recalled a rather steep section of snow that the group had traversed during their ascent. To her knowledge, the team had not encountered this section of terrain during their retreat.[30]

"Stay left! Stay left!" Susan called out to Giles.[31] Goman also called out for the team to keep to the left.[32]

Giles turned to the left at each request.[33] Winds were blowing forty mph, with sudden gusts up to fifty. The snow was coming down almost sideways. Visibility extended only twenty feet.[34]

~5:00 P.M.
GUEST ROOM
TIMBERLINE LODGE

There was a knock on the door. Mick, Courtney, Lorca, and John, awakened to learn that the cleaning crew had arrived. The teenagers knew it was time to return to the school bus.[35]

Courtney and Mick had spent hours exploring every nook and cranny of the inn. Mick was confident that they had walked down corridors where only employees were allowed. They had examined the Blue Ox Bar, the Cascade Dining Room, intricately carved newel posts, hand-hewn wooden furniture, rare paintings, and intricate ironwork.

Around 3:00 p.m., Courtney had glanced out a window. She'd noticed that clouds were moving in really fast.[36]

Eventually, the two explorers had returned to the room and caught some sleep near their companions. Now, rustled from their slumber, the group of four made their way downstairs, through the lobby, and out the structure's front doors.[37]

"Whoa!" Mick exclaimed when they emerged into the elements. "Where did this storm come from?"[38] Visibility was limited to twenty yards, the winds were howling, and snow was falling. He couldn't believe his eyes. Only then did Mick recall that a storm front had been predicted to move in during the afternoon hours.

~5:05 P.M.
DINING HALL
OREGON EPISCOPAL SCHOOL

Amy Horwell was walking into the dining hall on campus, a pair of ice skates slung over one shoulder. After school, she had gone to the local skating rink.

She was excited about the evening ahead. On her twelfth birthday, only six weeks earlier, Amy's mother had purchased tickets to watch the 68th annual Memorial Cup competition, hosted by the Portland Winter Hawks.[39] As an ardent fan of hockey, Amy had received tickets to all of the games at the Memorial Coliseum in Portland. She had already attended the game that pitted the Winter Hawks against the Guelph Platers.[40] Tonight, after dinner, she'd see the Hull Olympiques take on the Platers.[41] She'd be escorted to these games by a family friend, Jeff Hicks.[42] Together, they looked forward to cheering on the chaotic knots of men on the ice.[43]

As Amy entered the hall, someone stopped her, saying that the climbing team was overdue and would be returning home later tonight.

~6:45 P.M.
MOUNT HOOD WILDERNESS

Molly was staggering, trying in vain to maintain her balance in these high winds. The terrain here did not seem familiar. Pausing to catch her breath, she saw a gathering ahead of her.[44] She could see Father Tom among them.

Suddenly, Goman pitched forward into the snow. Unable to rise under his own power, he was assisted back onto his feet by Brinton.[45] The teacher was bearing two backpacks and two coils of rope.

Summers noticed a crack in the snow just ahead. Only an inch wide, its length extended beyond view. Unable to tell whether it was a mere crack, or a hidden crevasse, he yelled for Giles and Susan to stop. The consultant asked two nearby students to tend to Pat while he went ahead to investigate.[46]

Employing his ice axe, Summers probed the areas on opposing sides of the crack. Both sides seemed firm.

The balance of the party had caught up, and everyone huddled together for warmth. Summers returned and informed them that they had encountered either a pressure ridge or a possible crevasse. The students were directed to follow precisely in his footsteps as they proceeded over and beyond this potential trap.[47]

Giles found it strange to see snow blowing horizontally. He felt as if all hell was breaking loose.[48] One of his steps took him too close to the crack, sinking his leg into deep snow.[49] Giles managed to extricate himself, but Summers was displeased, reminding his clients to follow "precisely" in his own footsteps.[50]

Visibility dropped to around ten feet, and the wind speeds increased. Topography features seemed almost impossible to identify ahead of time. Summers was forced to probe the snow ahead with his axe, his boots, and his best judgment.[51] The group successfully followed the consultant over the hidden obstacle.

Minutes later, Summers' foot found the edge of an unseen, sudden dropoff. It was everything he could do to maintain his balance and not fall over the lip of this mysterious ledge. Summers directed the students to head in an easterly direction—far to their left—to avoid the hazard.[52]

The team hadn't proceeded very far when the consultant encountered a large crevasse, roughly thirty feet deep and five feet across at its widest point.[53]

It was evident that the team was no longer on the relatively smooth Palmer Snowfield. In the whiteout, it was unclear where they were. *We're lost.*

Summers gave the order for the party to back away and regroup.[54] He guessed that they were somewhere in Zigzag Canyon.[55] The climbers closed ranks, facing one another in a huddle.

"I guess we should try to take them down," Summers remarked to the teacher.[56]

"Yeah," Goman agreed, "unless we should dig in?"

"What time is it?" the consultant asked.

"Seven o'clock," Goman said, looking at his watch.

Night was approaching. Unsure how long the storm would last, Summers felt compelled to get the students out of the wind.[57]

"Yeah," he replied. "We should dig."

CHAPTER 7
PUZZLE BOX

Fr. Goman retrieved the tarp and laid it out on a relatively level patch of snow. The sleeping bag was unrolled and placed atop the tarp. Pat was assisted into the bag again.[1] The backpacks were placed around him to act as a windshield. The kids sat huddled together near one edge of the tarp for warmth. Someone discovered a secondary tarp and pulled it over the group. Heavy snowfall continued to rage, quickly covering the equipment cache with a layer of snow.[2]

Molly shivered as she watched Summers digging out a snow cave. Her boots were sticking out of the makeshift tent. Part of the tarp kept flapping in the wind, hitting her in the face.[3]

"I'm cold," Tasha said, adding that her feet were freezing."[4]

"Keep wiggling your toes inside your boots," Erik offered.

Brinton managed to change one sock, remarking during the process that she could no longer feel her feet.[5]

The students heard a voice in the distance, calling out to Father Tom. It was Marion. The teens were shocked to realize that Marion had not been with them under the tarp. The kids started yelling out, leading her to them. She appeared, out of the storm, and joined the huddle.[6]

Occasionally, students would assist Summers, using whatever tools they had at their disposal: mittens, hats, and ice axes. Erin and Alison, hoping that manual labor would warm them up a bit, volunteered to assist for a while.[7]

Goman trudged over to the huddled group and leaned down.

"Does anyone have a flashlight?"[8]

Molly looked at the man. She heard his words, but she couldn't figure out why it was taking her so long to mentally process his request. *I know what a flashlight is, and I can understand why he wants one; do I have one? Why is this taking so long?* Molly felt like it was taking twenty minutes for the group to procure the requested tool. She knew it wasn't taking that long, but she felt as if it was. Finally, someone handed a flashlight to Goman. He hiked over to the burgeoning cave to deliver it to Summers.[9]

Frank received a telephone call from the wife of the OES headmaster. Frank had met her a few times and recognized her voice.

"They're running a little late," she stated. "They've run into a little bit of snow. If they get back today, it could be as late as eleven o'clock. Do you still want to come and pick Pat up? Or, do you want us to have him stay here at the school and have him sleep over?"[10]

"Let him just stay there," Frank conceded.

As he hung up the telephone, memories of Frank's former military days suddenly flooded back to him. He had a nagging feeling that he wasn't getting the whole story.

He looked out his living room window and was immediately witness to impressive flashes of lightning, followed by the rumble of distant thunder. *If it's this bad here, what's it like on the mountain?* Concerned, he picked up the phone and dialed a friend.

Dave Buck was a recreational mountaineer, who had climbed Mount Hood multiple times. After bringing Buck up to speed on his son's field trip, and the call he had just received, Frank asked if his buddy had any thoughts.

"Well...what the hell are they doing climbing on Mount Hood?" Buck asked in dismay.[11] "I just got a weather forecast from flight service. The weather isn't going to clear for another forty-eight hours. It's just totally socked in. The area is caught in a massive storm." Buck was training for his instrument flight rules rating and had hoped to get some air time. Flight service personnel had simply laughed at his request.

"How are the kids equipped?" Buck asked.

"Dave," Frank replied, "I have no idea."

"Well, if they have a snow shovel, they can dig in," Buck explained how a snow cave could be made. "If they have the right equipment, they should be in pretty good shape."

This telephone call, intended to soothe his own fears, had the opposite effect on Frank. He believed conditions on the mountain were worse than the school had relayed.

Holding the flashlight in one hand, or in his mouth, Summers continued to carve away at the interior walls and ceiling, throwing the snow debris into the cave's entrance. When he got winded, he handed the shovel out to Goman. The teacher removed the loose snow from the tunnel, handed the tool back to the consultant, and the time-consuming chore repeated.[12]

~8:25 P.M.
SALMON RIVER PARKING LOT
WY'EAST DAY LODGE

Mick looked out the window of the school bus. It was technically sunset.[13] There had been no fleeting amber colors of dusk, nor had a lavender horizon given way to a canopy of stars. Where was the famed alpenglow associated with high-altitude peaks? All he could see was a lingering charcoal veil, punctuated with blowing snow. A blizzard had engulfed the mountain.

Mick, Courtney, John, and Lorca had been sitting in the bus for a few, uneventful hours.[14] They were concerned about the tardy climbing team.

Lorca sat on the floor, leaning against the driver's seat. She remembered a recent day in Goman's math class.

"Okay," the teacher announced to his students. "If you get this one right, then we're all going out for ice cream."[15] Someone got the correct answer, and the whole class piled into cars, setting out on a quest for Haagen-Dazs.

Initially, John hadn't even recognized that Goman's party was behind schedule. The bus driver was thoroughly entertaining him. The man had driven some of the students to and from school for years. He would occasionally roll out a red carpet, down the step treads of the bus, for big occasions such as birthdays. The driver regaled this group with tales of past trips and some of the best gossip John had ever heard.[16]

Courtney and Lorca had been told to expect the team's return no later than six o'clock. When that milestone passed, and there had been no sign of the party, those on the bus thought the party was overdue. There was no cause for concern. When 7:00 p.m. had arrived, eyebrows were raised, but there didn't appear to be any cause for alarm. The storm would, understandably, delay any team descending the mountain. The bus driver, stretched out on one of the bench seats, agreed.

"Let's wait just a little longer," he sighed.[17]

Mick glanced out the window again, expecting his mentor's silhouette to materialize out of the haze of the storm, leading his team to safety.[18]

The finished snow cave was roughly six by eight feet. It was about four feet at the peak of its domed ceiling.[19] Smaller than a four-person tent, it would have been ideal for a few grown men, but not three adults and ten teenagers. Summers knew it would be extremely cramped quarters, but he believed each minute out of the elements was crucial to their survival.[20]

"Get all your extra, warm clothing out of your packs!" he called out to the huddled group under the tarp. "Someone bring the space blanket!"[21]

Molly had a silver emergency blanket. Resembling tin foil, it could be used to construct an emergency shelter in the forest. Tonight, it would be a barrier from the icy floor of the snow cave. Summers led Molly over to the shelter's entrance. Goman was there to meet her.

Bending down, Molly crawled through the tunnel and into the cave. She unfolded the blanket and laid it out flat on the compacted snow.[22] It didn't cover the entire floor.

Summers began escorting the students, one or two at a time, over to the cave's entrance.[23] Each person crawled through the short tunnel that led into the snow cocoon.

Next, Summers turned his attention to Pat. Snow was accumulating on the tarp and had to be cleared away as it was beginning to bury the youth.

"Scoot out from under there!" Summers shouted to Pat. "I need to help you to the cave."[24]

As Pat began squirming out of the sleeping bag and from under the tarp, Summers started to look for his own backpack in the pile of equipment. Not seeing it, he pulled his head out from under the tarp. As the storm howled, Summers realized he was alone. The sleeping bag was empty.

Patrick was gone.[25]

The climbing party was almost three hours overdue, and the mountain was enveloped in a blizzard.[26] Mick and his companions were now convinced that something was terribly wrong.

Courtney wondered if the storm was just a ring of chaos around the lower elevations of the peak, and—higher up—their friends might be descending amid better weather.[27]

They formulated a plan. Courtney and the driver would depart the bus together and make their way to Timberline Lodge. There, they'd alert authorities.

During the journey through the windswept parking lot, Courtney recalled that some official paperwork had been left in the Climber's Cave of Wy'East Day Lodge. She told the bus driver to continue to Timberline Lodge, and she would be there shortly.

Courtney trotted into the Climber's Cave and was soon inspecting the Forest Service documentation Father Tom had submitted. An emergency contact was listed, should anything go wrong. Courtney copied his phone number on a scrap of paper and then hiked up the road that led to the inn.

~8:47 P.M.
SNOW CAVE

Pat had wiggled his way out from under the tarp and vanished into the darkness. As the storm howled, the consultant spied Goman, emerging from the snow cave.

"Is Pat in there?" Summers yelled.[28]

"No!" Goman replied.

Summers lifted the tarp for a second time, using his flashlight to scan underneath. The boy was gone. Summers made his way to the edge of the platform they had created and peered over the edge.

"Patrick!" he called out, using his flashlight to search for the student. He continued shouting the youth's name.

"I'm climbing up toward you," Pat cried out from somewhere in the darkness. Summers continued to shine the light over the lip of the platform. Finally, an apparition began to take shape amid the blowing snow. Patrick McGinness, the teen who had needed assistance at 10,000' in the crater, was now fighting for his life. Hand over hand, the goal-oriented youth slowly ascended towards safety.

Summers dug an ice axe into the snow at the edge of the platform and shouted for the boy to grab the shaft and use it to pull himself up. Pat raised himself close enough for Summers to grab hold of him and pull him over the snow berm. They laid there together for a minute, catching their breath. Extremely relieved, Summers rose and escorted the teen to the tunnel and into the welcoming arms of his friends.[29]

It was cramped inside. Giles was pressed up against the back wall. Brinton was pressed against one of his shoulders. Another student was butted up against Giles' hip while, yet another teen was on top of his legs.[30] Pat, near the tunnel, was shivering, so his fellow students surrounded him to the best of their ability, lending their collective body heat.[31]

Outside, Summers was heading back to the equipment cache where the party's backpacks were covered by a tarp. He wanted to retrieve some of the equipment. At least two feet of snow now covered the area. Grasping the edges of the tarp, he tried desperately to lift it. It was too heavy.[32] The climber's stove, which could be used to melt snow for drinking water, would remain outside the cave—useless inside his buried pack.

Staring at the equipment cache, Summers thought about their predicament. He then realized that something was wrong with his own body. His limbs didn't seem to want to obey his mental commands as fast as usual. One thought kept repeating in his mind.

You need to get inside.[33]

~8:50 P.M.
REYNOLDS RESIDENCE
PORTLAND

Charles Reynolds, one of the Basecamp leaders, set his telephone down. He had just taken a call from the bus driver up on Mount Hood. *Goman's party was hours overdue.* Reynolds, who was slated to lead a party of students up the mountain in the weeks ahead, called the school, relaying that the team was overdue. He also phoned the Sheriff's department.[34]

8:57 P.M.
CLACKAMAS COUNTY SHERIFF'S OFFICE
OREGON CITY

Working under Sheriff Bill Brooks, Lieutenant Gene Hanners oversaw search and rescue (SAR) operations in Clackamas County. The greater portion of the southern side of Mount Hood falls under their jurisdiction. Having received the call from Charles Reynolds, Lt. Hanners was already writing in his log book; nine high school-aged children failed to return after climbing Mount Hood.[35]

Having six trained SAR coordinators at his disposal, Lt. Hanners allocated two for the task at hand. The first, Deputy David Kennel, was in the town of Sandy, only thirty-four miles from Timberline Lodge.[36] The second, Deputy Ed Krebs, was contacted at his residence.[37]

~9:00 P.M.
SNOW CAVE

As Summers wiggled his way into the snow cave, Erin urged the others to make room for him. There wasn't any extra space, and the consultant found himself lying atop the others.[38] Through chattering teeth, Summers asked for assistance in rewarming.[39]

Bodies intertwined with bodies, locked in various positions, like pieces of a Chinese puzzle box. Molly found herself at the bottom of this pile. Wriggling free, she moved to a spot on top of Marion and Susan.[40] Marion expressed to Molly her concern for her daughter, Amy. The concerned mother was hoping someone would take care of her.[41]

Movement was extremely restricted. It became obvious that two or three people would need to stay outside to provide room within the shelter. Three of the kids crawled out through the tunnel. About every twenty minutes or so, students and faculty rotated positions to promote decent blood circulation.[42] The students did their best to keep the air hole in the ceiling free of accumulating snow. Improper ventilation was a concern.

Pat was actually faring better than some of his companions. He had spent over an hour recuperating inside the sleeping bag during the construction of the cave. Even after his frightening slide near the equipment cache, he appeared warmer than those with their backs pressed against the icy walls.[43]

Molly was alarmed at Father Tom's condition when he crawled inside the cave. His cap was missing, and he was shivering so violently, he was unable to speak. Molly threw the down-filled bag over him, noticing that the interior was wet, and his clothing was soaked. Someone handed Tom a set of dry gloves, but he was unable to put them on himself. Molly and Marion rendered assistance. A replacement stocking cap was placed on Father Tom's head.[44]

They waited for his shivering to slacken, to the point where he could communicate.

"I'm...I'm warmer now," Tom said.[45] Molly didn't believe him.

Tasha was shivering too, so the priest surrendered the sleeping bag in deference to the girl.[46]

~9:05 P.M.
PENATER RESIDENCE
PACIFIC CITY

Don Penater, forty-three, had been attending real estate classes in Salem. The twice-daily commute of ninety minutes was wearing him down, and he was happy to remove his shoes and relax in the comfort of his own home.

Don's mother lived just down the street, in a house Don had built. She'd called to inform him that someone from OES had phoned her. Don's sister—

Marion Horwell—and the climbing team were overdue. Don did his best to alleviate his mom's fears and then wrapped the conversation up.

"Well," he remarked to her. "We'll give it a day and see what's what."[47]

~9:20 P.M.
SNOW CAVE

When it came time for Giles to come back in, after his rotation out in the elements, he removed his bright yellow jacket and placed it over the entrance to the tunnel. It would help to keep the wind and snow out, and it should be easily spotted from the outside.

Molly's head was awkwardly jammed between Marion and Susan. She could see that Father Tom was lying partially over Marion. Reaching out to hold his hand for a minute, Molly asked him if he could speak.

"Yeah," he replied through chattering teeth.[48]

It was time for Molly to take a turn outside. She spied Giles and Brinton huddled together. Everyone was quiet.[49] Molly slowly made her way to the cave entrance, passed through the tunnel, and emerged outside.

She entered the teeth of the storm and couldn't believe how rapidly it stole her body heat. With arms crossed, head bent, and stomping her feet, she took her turn outside. She thought of home and her mother. Then, she forgot why she had emerged from the cave in the first place. It took a few minutes for reality to sink back in.[50]

9:30 P.M.
GOMAN-YATES RESIDENCE
PORTLAND

Mar Goman pulled into her driveway. She had just taught a class at the Episcopal Parish of St. John the Evangelist Church and expected her husband to be home. As soon as Mar realized Tom wasn't inside, she telephoned the school's Basecamp coordinator, Sam Dibbins, to determine if the team had returned.

"Oh," Dibbins remarked. "They're overdue, but they'll be down. No problem. Everything will be fine."[51]

Mar discussed the report with Diana. The women agreed that when the climbing party returned from the storm, they'd be wet, cold, and in need of warmth and nourishment.

The two women went to a large trunk they kept in the basement. From its contents, they gathered parkas, down booties, hats, gloves, and sweaters. After grabbing a few blankets as well, they loaded everything into Diana's gray Subaru. They started the station wagon and began their drive towards the mountain.[52]

~9:30 P.M.
FRONT DESK
TIMBERLINE LODGE

Courtney walked up to the front desk. She explained to the manager on duty, Jon Tullis, that she was one of the students who had turned around. She and a handful of others were now cold, hungry, confused, and hunkered down in a school bus in the parking lot.[53] Tullis went to retrieve some blankets.

It was going to be a long night.

CHAPTER 8
GRAPEVINE

Dressed in their official tan and brown uniforms, the two deputies from the Clackamas County Sheriff's Department (CCSO) walked into the ski patrol office, located in the town of Government Camp.[1] Thirty-eight-year-old, Deputy Ed Krebs, sporting a dark brown mustache, announced that he and Deputy David Kennel were responding to a call concerning missing climbers.[2]

Deputy Kennel used the office phone to call Chuck Reynolds, who had reported the missing group, to see if there were any more facts to glean concerning Fr. Goman's party.

Reynolds told the deputy that there were about eight sophomores: three or four boys and four to five girls. There were three adults and one senior student—two of which had experience climbing the mountain. The teens were well-equipped, had some snow training, and were wearing wool and rain gear. The party had departed Timberline Lodge around 2:30 a.m. and planned on making an attempt of the traditional South Side Route.

Kennel scribbled notes in his log and thanked Reynolds for his time.[3]

Lorca, Mick, and John spied figures approaching the bus. Courtney had returned, accompanied by Jon Tullis, laden with blankets from the resort.

As Tullis boarded the bus and started passing out blankets to the chilled students, he asked them how they were doing. Their responses were similar to Courtney's previous report: they were cold, hungry, and wondering what they should do now that Father Tom's team was missing. They asked if they could go inside.

"Of course you can come into the Lodge," Tullis replied.[4]

For Mick and his friends, there was a momentary pause, as the reality of the seriousness began to sink in. Then, as one, the group started gathering their belongings and stuffing loose articles into their backpacks.[5]

~9:58 P.M.
MCGINNESS RESIDENCE
PORTLAND

Frank McGinness was surprised that the phone was ringing this late at night.

"Look," began a woman, who was calling from the school. "The latest update is that, unfortunately, we consider them lost on the mountain. The weather is really bad. We have notified the Clackamas County Sheriff's Department."[6]

Frank was unable to set the receiver down, even after the woman had ended the conversation.

What does this mean?

~10:05 P.M.
INFIRMARY
OREGON EPISCOPAL SCHOOL

Hearing that the school had received authorization for Patrick to spend the night on campus, once the group returned from their climb, Sandy walked into the school's infirmary. The word on campus was that the climbers were overdue, but there was no cause for alarm.

The sickbay had two small beds. Sandy hoped she could occupy one of the beds, and when Goman's team returned to the campus, Pat could sleep in the second bed.

"Can I wait here for Pat?" she asked the nurse on duty.[7]

"Sure," the woman replied with a smile.

Sandy had been scheduled to have a third-year French exam, a physics exam, the attempt on the mountain, and the school play, which her friends were featured in, all within one week. The school prom was just days away as well. When her father learned of this hectic schedule, he said his daughter had too much on her plate and would need to give something up. Sandy and Pat had discussed her options.

"The mountain will always be there," Pat had stressed. "I want to go to prom with you."[8] Flattered, Sandy had met with an academic advisor and officially withdrew from the pending climb. The counselor was not pleased by this choice, but Sandy informed him of her family's wishes, Pat's thoughts, and her own decision.

Tullis escorted the four students to a European-style Chalet room and requested food be delivered. Rustically designed, the paneled walls were dotted with textiles and paintings. There was a small table surrounded by chairs, wooden coat hooks to hang their damp coats, and a small window in which to permit natural light to illuminate the interior.

After Tullis departed, each of the students seemed alone with their thoughts. Lorca opted to lie down. She was still suffering periodic cramps.[9] John was faring better but didn't consider himself operating at peak performance.[10] Mick felt fine, physically, but was greatly troubled with what their new accommodations meant. He should have been returned to his dorm room over two hours ago. Still, he was grateful to have a roof over his head.[11]

Jon Tullis had authorized the complimentary accommodations for Mick and his fellow students. He made sure food was delivered to their room, all while fielding a sudden flurry of incoming telephone calls.[12] Courtney had made a call home. Her mom had then contacted some of the other parents, which resulted in incoming calls at the switchboard.

Tullis informed callers that the climbing party was overdue, that he had provided accommodations for the children who had turned around, and that he would personally contact worried relatives as soon as he learned any updates regarding the situation.

Tullis spoke with the resort's general manager, John O'Neill, informing him of what was unfolding up on the mountain. O'Neill approved the complimentary room and food and asked Tullis to start keeping a log of developments, as well as all incoming and outgoing calls.[13]

As he had seen scores of storms strike the mountain over the years, Tullis contacted the Clackamas County Sheriff's Department.[14] Officers there informed him that they were aware of the situation and that the matter was already under investigation.

Deputies Krebs and Kennel had driven the six miles from Government Camp to Wy'East Day Lodge.[15] They were still investigating the report of a missing climbing team, determining what SAR assets would be needed, and needed to make their recommendations to their superior.[16]

Krebs, a former Navy diver and sonar technician during the Vietnam War, had experience in marine patrols, narcotics, and had driven patrol cars in three different counties.[17] Lt. Hanners trusted Krebs' judgment and would be relying heavily upon the man's assessment of the situation.

Noting that the school bus was still in the Salmon River parking lot, Krebs and Kennel walked into the Climber's Cave and pulled the Forest Service documentation Goman had filled out twenty hours earlier. This "Climbing and Backcountry Travel Register" was a two-sided document that listed party members and their equipment.

According to the form, the missing climbers had a whistle, extra food and clothing, sunglasses, flashlights, a compass, a knife, waterproof matches, one sleeping bag, a first aid kit, a stove, several ropes, ice axes, and—next to the line concerning crampons—Goman had scrawled, "some."[18] Those items listed as lacking from their packs were: altimeter, ensolite pads, candles, snowshoes, flares, fuel, tent, and a fire starter.

The teacher's entries on the form outlined his intentions. The planned destination was the summit, and next to the question regarding planned campsites, Goman had written, "None."[19]

The deputies split their responsibilities. One checked the weather forecast while the other determined snowcat assets on hand. They then walked across the street to Timberline, to interview the manager on duty.[20]

Jeff Hicks, thirty, and Amy Horwell were returning to campus after attending an exciting hockey game. Wayne Gretzky had been in Section 15, watching the competition. Amy had been thrilled to be so near the twenty-five-year-old hockey phenom.[21]

Jeff escorted the girl into her apartment, and both were surprised her mother wasn't there to greet them. Instead, Amy's babysitter was there with an update on the school's climbing party. There had been another delay. Some-thing to do with the weather. Amy heard the words, but she was too young to comprehend the potential implications of what a delay might entail.

"You go to bed, now," said the sitter. "By the time you wake up, I'm sure they'll be home."[22]

Jeff walked to his apartment in Rodney House. *An unplanned, overnight stay on the mountain?* During the previous three years, he had been on four school-sponsored ascents of Mount Hood. On each occasion, he had been properly outfitted for an overnight bivouac. Marion had borrowed Jeff's knee-length wool socks and his wool ski pants. Giles was wearing Jeff's non-breath-able, yellow rubber pants and matching raincoat. *What was everyone else wearing?*

During the weekdays, Jeff taught second grade at a local elementary school. At night, he was a resident advisor at OES, receiving $500 a month plus room and board on campus for his services. For six years, he was a father-figure to the nearly forty students who lived in the dorms. Jeff monitored the Dining Hall during dinner, helped the kids transition to Study Hall, Sunday through Thursday evenings, and performed room checks. He would stick his head into room after room, ensuring students were at least pretending to study.

Entering his apartment, he couldn't shake the feeling that something was wrong. He didn't share the babysitter's optimistic appraisal of the situation. Picking up his phone, he dialed a messaging service. He requested a substitute teacher for his class at Beaver Acres Elementary School for the following day. He had the feeling he'd need to be available on campus in the morning.[23]

~11:40 P.M.
FRONT DESK
TIMBERLINE LODGE

The night auditor, Tom Jackson, arrived to reconcile the books. He would staff the front desk and provide all-around coverage for the hotel throughout the night.[24]

Tullis briefed Jackson on the students housed in the chalet room and the concerns about the overdue climbing party. Deputies Krebs and Kennel were in the Lodge and would remain at the resort, to use the house phone to make their reports to their superior.[25]

The weather conditions were appalling and were forecasted to grow even worse.

Reminding Jackson that several of the staff members would be attending a promotional outing in the morning, Tullis excused himself, stating he had some paperwork to do before heading home.[26]

Molly worried that she would never get home to see her mother.[27] She noticed there wasn't any particular order or fixed positions for people within the cave. Significant position changes occurred as needed. If someone complained that their legs felt crushed, the teens would work together to reposition themselves and accommodate the needs of others. Blood circulation was a continual topic of conversation.[28]

In addition to the poor ventilation and crowded conditions inside the shelter, the body heat of the climbers was melting the snow underneath them. In an ever-growing pool of icy water, the group passed the time—hour after agonizing hour.[29] Sleep was nearly impossible. They tried to keep their spirits up by conversing with one another.[30]

Brinton was scared. She'd heard crying. She'd seen students panic and bolt for the cave's entrance, only to emerge into the storm.[31]

The occupants of the cave heard Father Tom, outside, screaming at the top of his lungs.[32]

TUESDAY

May 13, 1986

CHAPTER 9
THE CALL OUT

The numeric pager, tucked underneath Dave McClure and Cheryl Maslen's bed, woke the couple.[1] Rising and retrieving the device, McClure walked into another room and called the number listed on the pager. A deputy from CCSO answered, informing him that something was going on up on the mountain. Portland Mountain Rescue (PMR) could be receiving an official request for their help at any minute. McClure, a member of PMR for five years, thanked the deputy for the heads-up and hung up the phone.

Scratching his silver, close-cropped beard, he walked back into the bedroom and informed his wife that PMR was on standby. Maslen, a thirty-one-year-old graduate student at Oregon Health & Science University and a member of PMR, began assembling their gear while her husband phoned a friend.[2]

Barry Wright had climbed Mount Hood twenty-four times, by most of the standard routes. He had broken his shoulder only four years earlier, involuntarily riding an avalanche partway down Reid Glacier. The thirty-eight-year-old understood, all too well, the importance of mountain rescue.[3] Married, with two young daughters, Wright was troubled when he received the call from McClure. He put on his glasses and sighed deeply. He knew a storm had descended on the mountain, and he shook his head in disbelief.[4]

Why would anyone be up on the mountain when there was an unfavorable forecast?

After placing Barry Wright on official standby, McClure called Deputy Kennell on a hunch, guessing that Kennell would be one of the preliminary investigators the sheriff would dispatch to the scene.[5]

PMR and the county deputies had a good working relationship. They had been working together on various SAR missions for years. The sheriff's department would defer to PMR regarding climbing aspects of search and rescue assignments. Law enforcement, in turn, had faith in McClure and Wright's ability to set up a command post, strategize, and execute SAR missions.[6]

Deputy Kennel informed McClure that the missing climbers were almost seven hours overdue. Kennel formally requested that PMR be activated.[7]

When the phone rang yet again, Wright was not surprised to hear that law enforcement had decided to activate the organization. He'd been involved in mountain rescue for many years.

McClure and Wright each called half of their organization's board members, bringing them up to speed on the pending operation. Wright made a few other calls, activating the PMR phone tree.[8] Like a communication waterfall, the series of telephone calls—*the call out*—would rally the highly-motivated, volunteer SAR workers on the mountain.[9]

Wright contacted the members on his specific phone tree. Of the twelve climbers he called, four stated they could roger-up, two were unavailable, while six calls went unanswered.[10] Wright hoped the other leaders, tasked with rallying the troops, were having better luck.

His immediate duties completed, Wright crawled back in bed to catch a couple of hours of sleep before a scheduled rendezvous with McClure.[11]

As a board member of PMR, Mike Craig had received a telephone call from Dave McClure.[12] Only thirty-one, Craig had already been a member of the organization for four years. His buoyant personality and impressive climbing resume had endeared him to the group.

His wife, Sue Shultz, was not a mountaineer but had considered herself an avid ski bum during her college years. She had participated in several PMR training evolutions, but in a support capacity, rather than on the front lines.[13]

Newlyweds, Craig and Shultz were chiropractors, working in separate clinics in Vancouver, Washington. They each left a message at their respective offices, informing the staff that they would not be seeing patients all day.[14]

They loaded Craig's climbing equipment into the bed of *Bivy*, their red Datsun pick-up. The dependable little rig had been nicknamed so, as Craig had spent many nights sleeping under her canopy during weekend climbing adventures.[15]

1:00 A.M.
CHALET ROOM
TIMBERLINE LODGE

Courtney woke with a start. There was knocking on the hotel room door. She hurried to the door and found that Deputy Kennel wished to speak to her.[16] Courtney told the deputy that the overdue climbing team had departed the lot around 3:00 a.m., Monday morning and that she had turned back with another girl, before the storm's arrival. Two young men in the room had also turned back. Courtney dutifully answered all questions; she was pleased with the response she saw from authorities.[17]

~1:00 A.M.
HENDERSON RESIDENCE
BORING

Startled awake, Rocky Henderson lifted the phone to his ear. On the other end of the line was Carl Harbour of PMR. Henderson, only half awake, had to clear his thoughts. He was recently divorced and felt as though he was floundering emotionally. Seeking a way to fill the void in his life, he had volunteered to serve with PMR. This was his first mobilization call.

Henderson was the raw recruit.

Being a self-employed furniture salesman, he didn't have to clear his schedule with any employer. He grabbed his Gore-Tex parka, snow trousers, and plastic Koflach climbing boots. After tossing his ice axe, backpack, and crampons into his vehicle, he began driving up to the resort. He was excited but wise enough to know that he had no idea what was in store for him.[18]

Atop the building's central Head House, the 750-pound bronze weathervane was trembling violently. Designed to turn freely, high winds were battering it. Below this was the steep, stately roof of the inn, with a pyramidal design resembling the mountain itself. Smoke is expelled from the colossal, stone chimney through open windows with round arches below the weathervane.

Following the hexagonal chimney down to the main floor leads one into the Main Lounge. Beside one of the three oversized fireplaces, Mar Goman and Diana Yates were sleeping on vintage couches, upholstered in crimson, hand-woven fabric. Mar and Diana had driven from their home in Portland, checked with the front desk, and had been advised that authorities were already working on the case. The women had opted to set up their personal headquarters in the lounge.

Deputy Kennel entered the room and walked across the white oak floor. There was very little light illuminating from the cast iron lamps overhead. Kennel had been told that one of these women was married to the leader of the missing climbing party. He woke Mrs. Goman and sat on a wooden coffee table.[19]

The deputy seemed to be focused on how much climbing experience Tom Goman had, especially on this particular peak. Mar told him that Tom had climbed Mount Hood around eighteen times.[20]

Only two months earlier, Hal Lillywhite had attended the accident management section of an intermediate climbing course put on by the Mazamas mountaineering club. Wright and McClure had been the presenters and had passed out applications for the PMR organization. Lillywhite not only filled one out, but he was also good friends with a serving member—Carl Harbour.

Now, Lillywhite was startled awake by a phone call from that same good friend.

"Would you like to help look for some lost climbers on the south side of Mount Hood?" Harbour asked, going on to provide further details.[21]

Lillywhite, like Rocky Henderson, was scheduled for his first day of SAR training during the third week of May. Harbour was now calling to round-up volunteers to participate in an actual operation, where children's lives were at stake.[22]

After graduating from the Air Force Pararescue School at Lackland Air Force Base in San Antonio, Texas, Rick Harder had moved to Portland, Oregon. At thirty-four, he was now a paramedic with the Portland Fire Department. Master Sergeant Harder continued serving as a reservist pararescue jumper for the 304th Air Rescue and Recovery Squadron (ARRS). He had co-created an intravenous warming bag, employed in Air Force SAR operations.[23]

In his first twenty-five SAR missions, Harder recovered twenty-four bodies. Most of these had been victims of the eruption of Mount St. Helens. This grisly statistic had earned him the nickname of *The Bagger*.[24] This was not intended as an insult, far from it. This moniker was bestowed on him in recognition of the difficult work he had performed during times of crisis.

Harder was receiving the call now, as he was also a member of PMR. After learning about the missing school children, he called the sheriff's office, who confirmed the basic facts of the case. Being a member of yet another mountain rescue team, the Crag Rats, Harder called Bill Bryan of that organization, to ask if they'd been notified. They hadn't. Harder received the same response when he contacted Master Sergeant Nesbit at the 304th ARRS.[25] He then telephoned his good friend, Ed Hall, also of PMR, who lived on the southwestern side of the mountain.

Hall and The Bagger had participated in several training exercises with the PJs and the Crag Rats. They worked well together while attending crevasse rescue courses and evacuation drills. They had additionally served together on two rescue missions. Harder asked his friend to meet him at Timberline Lodge.[26]

The Bagger began preparing for his trip. He gathered together his mountain climbing equipment as well as his medical bags and related paraphernalia. After adding a radio to his gear, he began driving to the mountain.

SNOW CAVE

Molly woke from a brief sleep. She was lying on her stomach with her face pressed against someone in the dark. She realized that she couldn't feel her legs. Others were sitting on her lower limbs, inhibiting circulation.

"I have to move," she remarked, very concerned.[27]

In response, Susan began shifting people about within the cramped chamber, one at a time. Goman said there might be a serious problem with Molly's legs.

Hearing this, Molly began to panic. She was soon hyperventilating, setting off a ripple effect among the group. Summers quickly crawled and wriggled his way over to Molly's side.

"Take slow, deep breaths," he whispered to her.[28] He soothed her fears, and she began to settle down. As a warmer, tingling sensation began to return to her legs, and while the consultant continued to monitor her breathing, Molly regained her composure.

Snowfall kept covering the entrance to the tunnel, and students took turns clearing away this accumulation.[29] One of the teens was outside performing this task. During the motion of tossing a shovelful of snow, a high gust of wind grasped the tool, and it went flying into the dark below.[30]

2:00 A.M.
MCCLURE-MASLEN RESIDENCE
PORTLAND

Wright called McClure to discuss the results of the call-out. Sixteen volunteers had promised to meet them at the designated site. Cheryl Maslen would remain in Portland, as the organization's in-town operations leader. Working from home, she would contact additional resources, attempting to mobilize them for the SAR operation.[31] Wright and McClure would share the duties of operations leader.[32]

McClure telephoned deputies up on the mountain, updating them on manpower developments. McClure was surprised when the deputy handed the receiver to someone. It was Mar Goman. From her, McClure was able to learn more about her husband's climbing experience, the make-up of the missing team, and the fact that two consultants from Outward Bound had accompanied the party. Mar assured McClure that the missing team was well equipped and mentioned that a few of the older students had successfully climbed the mountain on previous outings.[33]

SNOW CAVE

Pat was closest to the access tunnel leading to the outside world. The entrance was, yet again, attempting to seal itself with accumulating snow. To combat this, Pat started kicking at the entrance tunnel walls. He was clearing away ice and snow, which would allow for continued passage through the tunnel. Still not satisfied with the amount of fresh air within the shelter, students used an ice axe to poke more breathing holes through the roof of the chamber.[34]

Erin, also near the entrance, exited the cave for a turn outside. To get out this time, she had to stretch her legs down the tunnel first. With her boots sticking out into the elements, they became visible to students who were outside. Those teens banded together and pulled Erin out of the cave—backward.[35]

~3:30 A.M.
SKI PATROL OFFICE
WY'EAST DAY LODGE

When Rick Harder arrived, he found the ski patrol office at Wy'East Day Lodge empty. The Bagger left the building and walked uphill, across the street to Timberline Lodge. At the front desk, he spied the night auditor, Tom Jackson, and had a brief conversation with him.[36]

Harder discovered two women sleeping on couches near the fireplaces in the Main Lounge. Believing they were mothers of missing students, he roused them, seeking information. It was Mar and Diana, doing their best to get some sleep while awaiting any updates concerning the missing climbing party.[37] Diana told The Bagger that a handful of the students, who had turned back before the storm's arrival, were asleep somewhere upstairs.[38]

Harder did some investigating at the front desk and learned that Courtney, Mick, Lorca, and John were occupying a room within the resort.

Ed Hall found The Bagger. Due to his proximity to the mountain, Hall spent around 100 days of the year exploring her slopes and crags. Whether it was rescue work with PMR, backcountry skiing, or recreational climbing, Hall was familiar with the pending search sectors on the southern side of the peak.[39]

Mark Kelsey, also of PMR, and a climbing partner of Hall's, walked in and the men exchanged pleasantries. Kelsey was a professional cabinet builder and accomplished remodeler. Working with his hands had earned the 6'4" mountaineer an impressive physique and a definite presence. He had climbed the mountain over twenty-five times, by some of her more challenging routes. The principal skill set he brought to his organization was his navigation skills and abilities on extremely steep terrain.[40]

John Schneider, also of PMR, entered the room but soon departed with The Bagger.[41] Heading upstairs, the men encountered Deputy Krebs. After proper introductions, Krebs said he would wake the students and bring them to Harder for an interview.

Giles felt he should retrieve the backpacks under the tarp outside. It was his turn to stand outside, so he made his way out of the cave and over to the equipment cache. He managed to locate the cache but, as strong as he was, there was no way for him to lift the snow-covered tarp. Too much snow had fallen. The packs would remain out of reach.

After his designated time outside, Giles walked back to the cave's entrance tunnel. Dropping to all fours, he started crawling inside. Broad-shouldered, he noticed it was becoming more and more challenging to navigate through the narrowing aperture. There was a moment of panic as he had to physically wrench himself through the tunnel.[42]

3:45 A.M.
CHALET ROOM
TIMBERLINE LODGE

Mick stirred from his slumber. *Was that a knock at the door?* Courtney, being nearest the entrance, answered the summons. Gaining his bearings, he could see Courtney and what appeared to be a man in uniform, some type of authority figure.

Mick and Courtney stepped into the hall, gently closing the door behind them. Courtney informed the deputy that their friends—Lorca and John—were ill and shouldn't be disturbed. Krebs told the teens that one of the rescue leaders would like to speak with them. He took them to Rick Harder.

Krebs introduced the teenagers to Harder and Schneider, and this small band adjourned to a narrow hallway nearby.[43]

For Mick, what followed seemed surreal. He and Courtney were confronted with badges, tall and husky rescue personnel, and a battery of questions. Mick thought the searchers looked like firemen, as they were dressed in red.[44] For fifteen minutes, it was one question after another. It was intimidating. Mick and Courtney were as cooperative as they could be, talking about landmarks, clothing, equipment, and the last known position of the missing climbers.[45] Harder asked the majority of questions.[46] Finally, the rescue workers thanked the students for their time and departed the hall.

Anticipating a return to their room, Courtney and Mick suddenly bumped into Rich's dad and Molly's mom. These parents had noticed the break-up of the hallway meeting and began asking the students questions of their own. Everyone made their way toward a common area in the inn, where they could be more comfortable. As before, Courtney and Mick did their best to provide whatever information they possessed.[47]

The Bagger entered the office for the second time. Whereas the space had been unoccupied an hour earlier, it was now bustling with activity. Deputies Krebs and Kennel had already worked with Tom Jackson of Timberline Lodge, securing the services of a snowcat and driver. This vehicle would be used to transport SAR workers onto the upper reaches of the mountain as soon as dawn arrived. A request had been made to the Forest Service, to authorize the use of motorized transportation within the boundaries of the Mt. Hood Wilderness.[48]

The Bagger questioned a couple of PMR volunteers and then telephoned a doctor at Portland Adventist Hospital in Portland. Harder began discussing the need for medical practitioners to be placed on standby. He asked the doctor to contact colleagues at Providence Hospital. These medical providers were asked to prepare for the arrival of at least thirteen hypothermic patients.[49]

Rocky Henderson parked his vehicle in the lot, arriving nearly a half-hour early. Nervous, he headed toward the Lodge, confronted with heavy snowfall, visibility of around 500 feet, wind speeds of forty mph, and an ambient temperature of 28° Fahrenheit.[50]

Henderson wasn't sure how to proceed. Five months earlier, he'd been shopping in an outdoor supply store in Portland, when he spied a brochure from PMR. He filled out their application and submitted it for consideration. A month or two later, a letter arrived in the mail, welcoming him to the group. Before any training could occur, however, Henderson received this, his first mobilization call. *What do I do now?*[51]

A secondary weather front from the Pacific Ocean was rapidly moving in. Heavy cloud cover and scattered snow showers throughout northern Oregon were predicted. More snow was going to fall on the mountains, and the snow level would remain at 4,000'.[52]

Deputy Russ Williams had arrived and was doing an admiral job dealing with a handful of reporters, who had already arrived at the resort. He was feeling a bit overwhelmed when it came to the anxious family members. He scrawled a note in the sheriff's log, "Any parent calls—GET ED."[53] Deputy Ed Krebs would be the face relatives of the missing would come to know as the hours continued to pass.

Rocky Henderson passed the media, on his way into the ski patrol office. Once inside, he spied only two other men. Henderson couldn't be certain whether they were members of PMR. One of these men caught his attention. Roughly his age, dressed in cold-weather apparel, this stranger had an air of superiority about him. The raw recruit marked this stranger as a man used to authority in stressful situations. It was Rick Harder. Henderson walked up to The Bagger and introduced himself.[54]

CHAPTER 10
TALL GREY BEARD

The blue and white PMR Suburban rounded the final corner, pulling into the parking lot at Timberline. Dave McClure hopped out of the rig and quickly put on his bright red down jacket, zipping it up tight as the cold winds hit him. Wearing jeans, his legs immediately felt the chill.[1] Over four feet of snow had accumulated in less than twelve hours. McClure, a seasoned veteran of the Cascade Mountains, and of Mount Hood in particular, believed the seriousness of the situation was all too apparent to those making their way from the Suburban to the ski lodge.[2]

Barry Wright and Terry Swicegood, who had carpooled with McClure, looked up at what should have been the pristine slopes of the south side of the mountain. Wright could see nothing but curtains of ivory snow blowing across the slopes. As he had been born in Alberta, Canada, Wright had experienced scores of mountain storms. Knowing that school children were lost, somewhere in the blizzard above them, he shook his head, wondering who had led such a team.[3] He donned his dark blue ball cap, emblazoned with the PMR logo, and zipped up his jacket.

Entering the building, via a side entrance designated for use by ski patrol members, McClure, Wright, and Swicegood walked down the hall and into the patrol room. Here, they lined up communication devices on a table and unrolled their maps, pinning them to the surrounding walls. They prepped the SAR radio to communicate with the teams they were about to deploy into the field.[4] This office quickly became *Base Operations*.

McClure recognized The Bagger, as well as about a dozen other volunteers from their organization, all ready for assignments.[5] He greeted Deputy Krebs. The two had worked together for years.

A sergeant alerted Lt. Sherwood Stillman to the SAR operation unfolding on the mountain. Intrigued, Stillman asked who was overseeing the search. After learning that Deputies Krebs and Kennel were already up at Timberline, working with PMR, Stillman briefed Captain J.T. Grolbert.

The captain reviewed the situation and believed his deputies had things well under control. Should the operation need any additional manpower, or present any unique or difficult challenges, the captain could always dispatch more experienced officers to the scene.[6]

~5:20 A.M.
PARKING LOT
WY'EAST DAY LODGE

Mike Craig and Sue Shultz arrived up on the mountain without incident. Bivy, their trusty little truck, had plenty of sandbags and equipment in the back bed to keep the vehicle stable on the icy roads.

Shultz spotted several volunteers, trying to install an antenna outside Wy'East Day Lodge. Wanting to jump in and help, she quickly realized she had to get inside the shelter of the heated building. She couldn't believe how bitter-cold it was out in the wind.[7]

Nearby, four men piled out of a van. Carl Harbour, Jerry Janeck, Dave Rich, and Hal Lillywhite were all from PMR. They were members of the LDS church and lived and worked in the western suburbs of Portland. Harbour, Janeck, and Rich had climbed together for years, owned similar blue parkas, and were affectionately dubbed *The Three Amigos*. They had been members of PMR for several years.[8] Lillywhite, on his first mission, stayed close to his friends.

Jerry Janeck, a construction framer, had a considerable amount of experience climbing Mount Hood. At thirty-nine, he had seen his fair share of inclement weather over the years. He felt the existing whiteout on the mountain would hold terrible conditions, yet he wanted to get a team up onto her slopes—fast.[9]

Entering the facility, Lillywhite spied a couple sitting on a bench. Looking grief-stricken, these were clearly parents of one of the missing school children. This poignant scene was not lost on Lillywhite; he recognized the seriousness of the situation.[10]

Like Molly before him, Pat's legs went completely numb. Someone was lying across them in the dark. When he complained, Susan came to his rescue.

"You guys," she said, "we gotta take care of Pat. Please, move."[11] Susan set about organizing the reshuffling process that would allow Pat to move out from under the pile of climbers. Father Tom and two students volunteered to go outside, to provide more breathing space within the shelter.

"Is it light now?" Molly quietly asked of Summers.[12] The consultant had recently returned from another turn outside.

"No," he replied.

5:30 A.M.
BASE OPERATIONS
WY'EAST DAY LODGE

Sixteen volunteers from PMR mustered in Base Operations. Rocky Henderson felt like he was having a baptism by fire. The Three Amigos seemed eager and raring to go. There appeared to be no shortage of enthusiasm among the men; everyone seemed to know each other, yet Henderson was a stranger to them all. Fortunately, a seasoned member of the crew—Terry Swicegood—took him under his wing, providing him with some crucial guidance.[13]

Henderson quickly learned how jurisdiction was determined in SAR operations on Mount Hood. A borderline on the map runs down the southeastern side of the volcano, separating Clackamas County from Hood River County. Palmer Glacier falls in the former county while White River Glacier occupies the latter. For incidents west of the county borderline, the sheriff from Clackamas County would have authority. The majority of the 10,000 annual mountain climbers, ascending Palmer, were within his jurisdiction.[14]

The Sheriff was legally in command of the rescue operation, but he didn't have the manpower or mountaineering skillsets necessary to undertake such high-altitude SAR operations. PMR, the ski patrol, the Crag Rats, and other mountaineering rescue groups had the manpower and requisite skills, but they were powerless when it came to governmental and financial issues. The public looked to the sheriff's department for legal accountability and answers to harrowing questions, while law enforcement officials looked to the mountain rescue leaders for the raw data they needed to make the tough decisions.[15]

Direct, disciplined, and methodical, Dave McClure was considered the voice of PMR. A forty-nine-year-old associate professor of chemistry at Portland State University, deputies enjoyed working with him. McClure was intelligent and authoritative while maintaining an approachable and open-minded demeanor. In the official Sheriff's Department log, a description of McClure was written next to his name for easy identification, "PMR. Tall grey beard."[16]

The second man entrusted with SAR strategy and execution was Barry Wright. He had joined the Mountain Rescue Council of Oregon (MORESCO) thirteen years earlier, just as the organization was experiencing geographical and logistical issues. MORESCO had fractured into regional teams, leading to the formation of PMR. With a multitude of mountain rescues under his belt, Wright had transitioned from front-line searcher to a position of strategist and coordinator.[17]

Wright and McClure were confronted with an extremely difficult task. There were no specific facts that would indicate a probable location of the missing climbers. Fr. Goman's team was last spotted by two repairmen, who were working near the upper shack of Palmer chairlift.[18]

Wright and McClure agreed that the missing climbers—when confronted by the storm—would have chosen to descend along their original course. Hopefully, the team had left trail wands to follow during their retreat. Studying the map in front of them, McClure informed the deputies that they were looking at a triangular search area of about two square miles. The three points of this triangle included: the sheer cliffs of Mississippi Head to the west, White River Canyon to the east, and the summit itself.[19]

With the search parameters established, the question of where the SAR teams should be deployed became the next priority for discussion.[20] Experience came into play. PMR had been documenting their rescues for years and recognized that seventy percent of missing climbers had been found downhill from where they had last been spotted.[21] When confronted with a blizzard, or lack of visibility, climbers invariably descend the path of least resistance—the fall line.

As the deputies had done before them, Wright and McClure inspected the Forest Service document that Goman had filled out. McClure was pleased to read that the team had a sleeping bag with them, as well as a stove. He was alarmed, however, when he saw a blank space next to the word "altimeter."[22]

As the clock on the wall shifted to 5:40 a.m., PMR leadership knew that sunrise was occurring outside. With the storm still raging, sunlight would only slightly increase one's range of vision on the mountain.[23]

PMR wasn't the only regional organization with alpine rescue experience. The 304th ARRS is an Air Force unit whose peacetime mission centers on training for, and execution of, extremely difficult SAR operations. The men and women in their squadron are well respected for their history of humanitarian efforts and disaster relief activities since the unit's commissioning in 1957.[24] Assigned to the 939th Rescue Wing, and stationed at the Portland Airport, they employed seven different types of aircraft.[25]

Their pararescuemen, introduced to the squadron in 1961 and referred to as PJs, are specialists who train, organize and equip their men for personnel recovery missions. Known for their versatility, PJs are one of the premiere rescue resources in the Pacific Northwest. It was only natural that the sheriff's department would want to secure their services.

Captain William Moore, the spokesman for the squadron, received a call from one of the deputies up on the mountain.[26] Moore was told to stand by for the potential medical evacuation of thirteen climbers—four adults and nine children, adding that weather was appalling. The captain agreed as he was monitoring the weather and its resultant lack of visibility.[27]

Major Fred Stovel, the staff duty officer, was also hard at work. Knowing that several key people would be arriving for duty at 7:15 a.m., he telephoned them in advance to ensure they were properly equipped for a probable mission. Stovel also called the management of Timberline Lodge, to get a weather forecast for the mountain. Concerned with the response he heard, the major wondered if the first aircraft launched should act as a weather bird—*can we even get there from here?*[28]

Captain Moore called Jeffrey Youngbluth, one of his PJs, and brought him up to speed on the situation. Consulting the weather forecast, Youngbluth concluded that it would be impossible for aircraft to land up at the resort under such conditions. He gave the order to ready a Jeep. The vehicle was packed with heart monitors, sleeping bags, and enough medical supplies to tend to the needs of thirteen patients.[29]

McClure and Wright decided to dispatch two SAR teams, on separate missions, to targeted regions of the mountain. The first of these small bands, officially called Team 1, was dubbed *The Hasty Team*. Rick Harder would lead. His team would include Mark Kelsey, John Schneider, and Ed Hall of PMR.[30] Their mission would be to explore along the South Side Route. They would board a snowcat and be transported a mile up the mountain to Silcox Hut.[31] After checking to determine if the missing climbers were inside, the Hasty Team would then climb back aboard the cat and continue toward the upper shack of Palmer chairlift. There, they were to climb towards the summit, inspecting the crater region along the way. From the summit, they would work their way down around the base of Crater Rock and travel west to explore the upper reaches of Zigzag Glacier.[32]

Traveling in the same snowcat would be Team 2, led by Steve Glenn.[33] His team members would include Rich, Janeck, and Harbour, The Three Amigos of PMR.[34] They would also be dropped off at the upper shack of Palmer chairlift. Team 2 would then head west, towards the cliffs of Mississippi Head.[35]

Those cliff walls, shaped like the nose of a flatiron, are the dominant natural feature on the southwestern slopes of the mountain. Roughly halfway up the peak, scores of missing climbers had been discovered here, over the decades.

Deputy Kennell contacted Life Flight, based out of the town of Aurora.[36] This commercial medical emergency air ambulance network was apprised of the situation and told they'd be called back should the sheriff need their services.

Wright doffed his jacket. Underneath he had on his dark ski bibs, complete with suspenders, and a white sweatshirt. He was beginning to settle in. McClure, likewise, had removed his goose down jacket and clipped a speaker microphone to the collar of his long-sleeved t-shirt.[37]

Deputies were informed that transporting teams into the field was their next priority. Word had already gone out to recruit the services of a snowcat driver with significant experience.

~6:05 A.M.
MAINTENANCE SHED
RLK & COMPANY

Although John Young was not a member of PMR, he had so many friends in the organization that folks naturally called him for assistance when mobilizations were underway. Being able to safely control a snowcat, that can ferry search teams up a mountain in a snowstorm, was a skillset that was highly prized.

Sporting a dark, bushy beard, the burly man was an employee of RLK

& Company. He operated a 1967 Thiokol 1200B Spryte snowcat folks dubbed *Number 8*.[38] Powered by a six-cylinder Ford gasoline engine, this bulky vehicle had a four-speed manual transmission. The candy-red cat had a passenger capacity of nine. The driver and one passenger would sit up front, while the bulk of the team would fill in the bench seats in the back. RLK & Company owned two of these Spryte vehicles.[39]

6:10 A.M.
BASE OPERATIONS
WY'EAST DAY LODGE

When Barry Wright spotted Sue Shultz, he quickly ushered her to the main radio. She would man the unit while documenting the team's movements. Knowing that multiple team leaders—all male—would be communicating over the radio, the co-chiefs wanted a woman's voice emanating from Base.[40]

Shultz was given a pen and a stack of college-ruled paper. She made her first entry in PMR's official radio log: "6:15 A.M., Team 1 & Team 2 going to cat."[41]

6:15 A.M.
TIMBERLINE LODGE

The Hasty Team and Team 2 began boarding Number 8 in the lee of the inn.[42] Janeck donned a thick wool balaclava that covered his long hair and full-length beard. Differentiating between Harbour, Rich, and Janeck was difficult. The Three Amigos wore their nearly identical blue parkas.[43] It took three bystanders to close the rear door to the vehicle in the intense wind.[44]

Dressed in ski bibs, a Patagonia pile coat, and a Gore-Tex jacket. Mark Kelsey donned his unventilated, Joe Brown helmet. He looked like a motorcyclist.[45]

Steve Glenn, leader of Team 2, was a quiet and somewhat reserved man. He had a conservative, religious upbringing and seemed very cautious with his words.[46] He sat in marked contrast to the animated Amigos nearby. Glancing at the thermometer inside the vehicle, Glenn noticed that it was 26° F.[47]

It was going to be a long, cold ride.

CHAPTER 11
THE HASTY TEAMS

Seeking a status report on his missing son, Frank called the school. He was transferred to a man who appeared to be in contact with deputies up on the mountain. This man informed Frank that there was no sign of Fr. Goman's team, but the sheriff's office and PMR were on the mountain, organizing a search effort.

"Look, I'm going up," Frank stated.

"Well, the weather's dreadful," the man said. "The roads up there are pretty bad."[1]

"I don't care. I'm going up," Frank declared.

"Well, take care then."

Frank phoned his neighbor, asking if she would pick up his youngest son, Chris, after school. Next, he called his bookkeeper, John Bridges. Frank asked him if he would accompany him up to the mountain, not just as a driver, but as a friend. Bridges agreed.

SNOW CAVE

The crowded group was suffering significantly by lying down in the shelter.

"Let's try hunching-up," Summers suggested, "as this isn't working."[2] The consultant demonstrated what he had in mind. He sat with his back against the wall; his head almost touched the ceiling.

Molly followed his example, pressing her back against the wall of ice. As Summers began to help each of the students to upright positions, Molly quietly laid her head on Susan's shoulder.

Rich was having difficulty finding a suitable place to sit. Making his way over to Susan and Molly, he garnered a small space beside them, close to the exit.

Goman was outside in the elements, using his hands to clear snow from the cave's entrance.

The Hasty Team and Team 2 were ascending the slopes in Number 8. Although those monitoring radio traffic heard the voice of Steve Glenn in Base Operations, it was apparent that transmissions emanating from Base were not reaching the teams in the snowcat.[3]

Knowing an additional radio set was in the rescue Suburban outside, Wright ran out to the parking lot to test the extra unit. After conducting a radio check, communications with SAR teams resumed.

This unexplained equipment failure troubled Wright, and he discussed back-up plans with McClure. Recalling that the Mt. Hood Ski Patrol employed similar radios, PMR soon received authorization to borrow several handheld units.[4]

Shultz was not familiar with the topography of the mountain.[5] Whenever Wright or McClure mentioned landmarks or used technical terms, she relayed their words over the airwaves.[6]

McClure made a call to his wife in Portland.

"Cheryl, we need you up here," he stated.[7] Between directing the team leaders and handling SAR strategy, McClure and Wright were in desperate need of a base coordinator. They needed someone who could create experienced and balanced teams, supervise the distribution of communication equipment, and interact with sheriff's deputies. Cheryl Maslen packed a bag and climbed into her Volvo to make the drive to the mountain.[8]

McClure noticed they needed far more batteries for their radios than was in their supply cache. While Number 8 was still in transit, McClure jumped into the Suburban and drove thirty-four miles down to the town of Sandy. He spent $100 buying every battery in the store.[9]

Wright focused on the issue of transportation. Knowing that the average time for a snowcat to travel to the top of the Palmer chairlift and back was roughly ninety minutes, he called the maintenance manager for RLK & Company. *How much would it cost for the use of another cat?*[10]

Around 8,500', the snowcat driver announced that he wasn't sure of their precise location and, given the present conditions, he couldn't proceed any higher.

When the last man departed the cat, he dogged the rear door behind him and smacked the side of the vehicle, signaling the driver to begin his return journey to Base.

High winds buffeted Ed Hall. *This is pretty nasty.*[11] Hall and Harder were friends and co-workers. Before their careers, before their shared love of climbing, and before their work in mountain rescue—they were friends. Hall clapped The Bagger on the back, and the men assessed their surroundings. *Let's see what we can do.*

Harder radioed Base, asking the sheriff's department to provide him with a means of communicating directly with his ARRS squadron.[12]

Janeck, on Team 2, noted that temperatures varied from 30-35° F, and there was a considerable sheet of snow blowing.[13] Winds emanated from the west, traveling over the slopes at sixty mph.[14] The conditions were so foul that both teams huddled together in a tight circle. Janeck was unable to identify who was who amid the layers of wool and Gore-Tex. His balaclava had frozen, and the exposed portion of his beard was gathering frost.[15]

Janeck fully understood the importance of having teams positioned mid-way up the mountain in case there was a break in the weather. Although worthwhile to be brought to this location, if for no other reason than to verify the extent of the conditions, it appeared that it was time to abort their respective missions. Visibility was nearly non-existent. If there was nothing to be done, it was time to descend, regroup, and come up with alternative solutions to the problem.

A Marine during the second half of the 1960s, Janeck was no stranger to stressful situations and hazardous environments. Still, he bowed to the inevitable conclusion—there was nothing for them to do but wait out the storm.[16]

"This isn't working!" he called out through cupped hands.[17] Searching for lost climbers was next to impossible in these conditions and might place the rescue workers themselves in the unenviable position of calling for a rescue.

At 7:28 a.m., The Bagger chose to lead The Hasty Team north and began an ascent towards the summit.[18] Janeck, remaining in the huddle with Team 2, rolled his eyes in disbelief. The Bagger's men promptly disappeared into the storm.

~7:30 A.M.
JACKSON HOUSE
OREGON EPISCOPAL SCHOOL

A drowsy Amy Horwell walked into her living room. She was surprised to find a staff member, asleep on the couch. The woman awoke and spotted the girl standing beside her. She told Amy that the climbing party had not yet returned, and attendance at school today was optional. Missing class was so rare for Marion's daughter that Amy knew, whatever was going on, it was significant.

I'm not even sick.[19]

7:30 A.M.
304th AIR RESCUE AND RECOVERY SQUADRON
PORTLAND INTERNATIONAL AIRPORT

Major Charles Jones walked into the squadron offices, instantly recognizing that a mission was underway. The helicopter pilot learned there was a climbing party missing on Mount Hood. The major walked into the adjacent room to check the weather forecast, with its emphasis on flying conditions. There was a ragged, 100-foot ceiling at Timberline Lodge. Winds at the resort were forty-five knots. Jones departed the office, searching for Lieutenant Colonel David Mullen and Sergeant Ron Carpenter.[20]

7:40 A.M.
MT. HOOD NATIONAL FOREST SERVICE HEADQUARTERS
SANDY

Dick Hoffmann of the Forest Service received a call from a deputy in Base Operations. Rescue leaders were seeking authorization for helicopters, both military and civilian, to operate and land in the Mt. Hood National Forest. Hoffmann assured the deputy he would call back as soon as he had any information.[21]

7:40 A.M.
PALMER CHAIR LIFT UPPER TERMINAL
PALMER SNOWFIELD

After The Hasty Team had departed the scene, Steve Glenn led Team 2 to Palmer's upper shack. From there, they turned west as planned, headlong into the blizzard. The men continued as best they could, but their goggles started icing up.[22]

Glenn was soon frustrated. He understood this mission would not succeed. He radioed Base, providing Wright with a report of the conditions.[23] Their intended mission, to reach the cliffs of Mississippi Head, was aborted, and Plan B was set into motion. Team 2 arranged themselves four abreast and began exploring the terrain around the site where Number 8 had dropped them off. Wright asked for an estimate on the range of visibility.

"Five feet," Glenn replied.[24]

~7:45 A.M.
INFIRMARY
OREGON EPISCOPAL SCHOOL

As Sandy slowly woke, she realized she wasn't in her dorm room. Remembering that she had opted to sleep in the sick bay, she was suddenly wide awake, turning to look for Pat in the adjacent bed. He wasn't there. Confused, she rose and wandered into the hall, asking others if they had any information concerning Goman's climbing team. Sandy learned that a search and rescue operation was underway, and the missing climbers had been forced to spend the night somewhere on the mountain.

Returning to her dorm room, Sandy plopped down on her bed. Thinking of Pat, missing in a storm, fear took over. Her jaw clenched tight, her breathing quickened, her heart raced, and her muscles tensed. A painful migraine set in.

Her roommate, Chia, tried to assist by massaging Sandy's shoulders. Chia eventually persuaded her friend to call her mother in California.

"They're not coming back," Sandy cried into the receiver, her voice cracking with emotion.[25]

"You don't know that," her mother replied, doing her best to calm her daughter.

Nothing could sway Sandy's belief that a tragedy was unfolding.

SNOW CAVE

Molly and the others discussed Father Tom's physical condition. The teacher had endured more than his share of time in the elements during the night. He was out there now and had been for quite some time. He needed to come in and warm up. Tasha and Erin volunteered to go outside to relieve the man.[26]

A few minutes after the girls departed the shelter, Tom's voice was heard through the entrance tunnel, asking if he could enter. Those inside readily agreed.

The students near the tunnel saw an ice-encrusted pair of boots make an appearance. They seized hold of them and slowly, noisily, Goman squeezed into the cave. He was being pulled in on top of others. One of his boots grazed Molly's face before he finally came to rest atop Marion and a portion of Susan.

Molly, nursing the graze she had received, couldn't help but notice the teacher's appearance. His clothing was frozen, and he was shivering.[27]

7:45 A.M.
TIMBERLINE LODGE

Teams 3 and 4 began boarding Number 8.[28] Team 3 was led by Terry Swicegood, keeping Rocky Henderson under his wing. Jim Boucher was also on the team, and all three were members of PMR.[29]

Swicegood was a minister, who humorously balked at training exercises held on Sundays. As one of the most experienced climbers in PMR, he was a man who fit right in with the adrenaline-fueled, volunteer organization. His buddies loved to bring up the time he broke both ankles, rappelling off a cliff at Horsethief Butte.[30]

Swicegood heard that Team 4 would be dropped off at Silcox Hut, but he and his men would be transported to the elevation of the upper shack of Palmer chairlift. Their goal was to head east, toward White River Glacier on foot. Once there, they would head down the field of ice, searching for the missing students as they traveled.[31]

Mike Craig led Team 4. Whenever he teased Swicegood about his ankles, the minister always countered with two words—*poison oak*. Craig had once discovered a hidden cliff in the greater Portland area. To make the virgin route safe for rock climbing, he had borrowed a drill from Dave McClure and spent a day sinking bolts into the rock face.[32] Oblivious to the surrounding poison oak, he had returned home and got intimately affectionate with his new wife. Sue ended up in the hospital with a severe allergic reaction.[33] The tale never failed to provide a round of smiles and suppressed laughter.

Craig's colleagues on Team 4 included Mike Blailock, Marc Sellers, and Hal Lillywhite, all from PMR.[34] After being dropped off at Silcox Hut, they'd check the historic structure, to see if anyone had taken refuge inside. Next, they'd head east and enter the mid-level terrain of White River Glacier, hopefully rendezvousing with Team 3. Both groups would work their way back down the mountain, inspecting crevasses and caves along the way.[35]

Rocky Henderson approached Number 8. He walked around to the rear of the vehicle and reached for the door dogs. As he attempted to open the door, the force of the wind pushed it back, nearly knocking him over in the process.

One-by-one, team members started piling into the vehicle. Craig took a spot on the rear bench seat, as others dogged the door behind him.[36]

Although his friends considered him one of the most advanced climbers in the organization, Craig was nervous. He'd been having periodic panic attacks, shortness of breath, and an enhanced sense of anxiety ever since a skiing accident a few months earlier. He had suffered a head injury, and he knew he wasn't functioning at 100%. At times, Craig's thought processes felt downright foggy. A mere telephone call could easily trigger a panic attack. Craig continued to hold the radio, dreading the pending transmissions.[37] He didn't want to let his friends down.

Craig was wearing German leather hiking boots that had served him well for years. He wore blue ski bibs, a matching parka, and had a pair of glacier glasses tucked inside his breast pocket. The clean-shaven climber donned a balaclava that covered the majority of his face. He looked at his scratched, orange helmet. Next to his nameplate was a new sticker, added after he had suffered the head injury. It depicted a cartoon clown within a red circle, a diagonal line running through it. The label read, *NO BOZOS.*[38]

John Young manipulated the two steering clutches, slowly turning the vehicle around. Given the dreadful weather conditions, the snowcat could not approach its top speed of fourteen mph.[39]

Number 8 crawled up the slopes, the illumination from her four headlights barely piercing the falling snow.

7:46 A.M.
BASE OPERATIONS
WY'EAST DAY LODGE

Schultz monitored the radio communications coming in from teams up on the mountain. Word that The Hasty Team had hiked to the top of Palmer Glacier came over the radio, just as Teams 3 and 4 were heading for higher ground.[40] Schultz was not fearful as her husband, Mike Craig, was leaving for a mission. She had complete confidence in his mountain skills, head injury or no head injury.[41]

SNOW CAVE

The team could not remain in the shelter forever. Listening to the report of those who had just reentered the cave, Summers learned that the storm was not subsiding. It had intensified.[42] He knew that someone would have to depart the safety of the cave and descend the mountain to seek assistance. Using his flashlight, Summers could see that Goman was still shaking. Crawling over others to reach the man, Summers moved to a position near Tom's ear.

"Can you count to ten?" Summers asked quietly.[43] When the teacher was unable to accomplish this task, Summers knew Goman was in no condition to hike out.

The students were cold, damp, and concerned. Some of them had lost a mitten or a hat. No one seemed interested in even trying to locate these lost articles of clothing.[44] People were becoming lethargic. Molly and Brinton appeared to be the only exceptions. Brinton felt drowsy, but she was feeling fine.[45]

Summers made a mental note that most everyone appeared healthy, but he knew their conditions would only deteriorate in time. The moment for bold action had arrived.

"I think I'm gonna go try to find my skis and ski out of here," he said, loud enough for everyone in the cave to hear.[46]

"Yeah," Molly remarked, agreeing that the idea was a good one.

"That's a great idea," added Rich.

"I have to dig out my pack and my skis," Summers continued. "And, get my boots on." Once he had his equipment, he'd need to return to the cave to warm up for his journey ahead. "I'm going to walk out to get help," he repeated. "Stay in the cave and spend as little time outside as possible."[47]

As Summers crawled through the tunnel, he found himself struggling to fit through the ice-encrusted, claustrophobic corridor. The entrance to the snow cave had changed considerably during the night. The textbook entrance, he had constructed the previous evening, had sloped upwards to the sleeping platform inside the cave. Now, over twelve hours later, the slope of the tunnel had reversed. People standing outside, wanting to get in, now had to shimmy down a ramp to enter the shelter. The entrance corridor only managed to stay open by the periodic passage of personnel.

As soon as Summers emerged into the elements, he began to shiver; portions of his clothing were soaked from water that was pooling on the floor of the cave. With the wind howling, standing outside in his wet garments was excruciating, and he could feel himself losing strength.[48]

His skis were lashed to his backpack; the burden Giles had carried down from the crater region. The pack and the skis were buried under the group's tarp and a thick layer of snow. Summers looked to where the tarp *should* have been, yet all he saw was a smooth slope. Alarmed, he knew he didn't have the strength to dig out his pack by hand.[49]

Without the skis, he'd have to descend on foot. Wanting to take a partner, for safety reasons, Summers returned to the entrance of the cave and considered its occupants. Goman was out of the question. Pat had been tough during the ascent but had struggled with hypothermia. There was another hard-charging sophomore, that might fit the bill.

"Giles!" Summers yelled down the corridor. "You're pretty strong!"[50]

"Oh, no man!" Giles yelled back. "I don't feel very strong now. I've just been outside." Giles had only recently finished clearing away more accumulated snow from the cave's entrance, and he was exhausted.[51]

Summers stuck his head back down into the crawl space.

"Who in here feels strong?" he inquired.[52] There was a pause.

"I'll go if you'll take me," came a female voice.

"Who's that?" the consultant inquired.

"Molly," she replied, identifying herself.

"Okay," Summers called down, agreeing to the prospect. "Let's go!"

Although Molly had volunteered to accompany the man, she said she needed to obtain a hat and a dry glove before departing.[53] Giles offered her one of his gloves, which Molly gladly accepted.[54] Someone else provided her with a stocking cap. Just as she was about to leave, Molly crawled over to Father Tom, to tell him of her intentions and destination.

"Molly," he said, listlessly. "Goodbye."[55]

Molly's exit from the snow cave took some time to execute. A few students had to roll over and others had to shift position so she could reach the tunnel. She tried to exit the chamber head first, but her legs were crushing people. Her friends were protesting. She had to rethink her strategy.

"Can we have your spot?" Giles and Brinton asked, about Molly's recently vacated position against a wall.[56] At nearly the same moment, Rich made the same request. Molly ignored them all, as she was busy encouraging Goman to move to the space that Summers had recently occupied.

"I don't know where to go," came the teacher's faltering voice.[57]

"Move your legs a little to the left," Molly urged.

"I can't feel my legs," he replied.

"Come on!" Summers called down the tunnel. "We've got to start moving!"

Molly began backing out of the crawl space, calling out for Summers' assistance.

When the teen emerged, Summers helped her to her feet. Molly felt disoriented and off balance.

"I don't know," she said. "Maybe you'd better take someone else."

"No," Summers replied. "All we have to do is keep moving, or we're going to die."

"I don't know," she repeated. "I'm scared." Summers seized hold of her arm.

"Grab that axe," he instructed, pointing to Goman's ice axe, stuck in the snow near the cave's entrance.

"Do they have an axe inside?" she asked, but instantly recalled that there was such a tool within the cave. "Should we get something? look for our packs?"

"We have to go," Summers stated with a sense of finality. The consultant bent down and stuck his head back inside the tunnel. He offered some hopeful words of encouragement.

"We'll keep walking until we've found help," he said to the group, "or until we die."[58]

CHAPTER 12
DESPERATE GAMBLE

7:57 A.M.
BASE OPERATIONS
WY'EAST DAY LODGE

A constant stream of static dominated the radio. High winds were hitting the microphones of the searchers up on the mountain, causing another breakdown in communications.[1]

A garbled transmission came in. Everyone strained to comprehend what Steve Glenn was trying to communicate; Team 2 was near the upper shack of the Palmer chairlift, seeking authorization to stay put and wait for a break in the weather. They were recommending that other teams suspend their search operations as well, at least until visibility improved.[2]

~8:00 A.M.
SNOW CAVE

Molly followed Summers to the edge of the buried equipment cache.[3] At the base of the site was the steep slope that Pat had disappeared over the night before. Summers sat in the snow, motioning for Molly to sit behind him and wrap her arms and legs around him. Complying, she handed him Fr. Goman's ice axe.

"Hold on tight!" he instructed.[4] They glissaded down the embankment and into the unknown. Blowing snow prevented Molly from being able to see ahead at all; she entrusted the safety of the ride to her partner. Thankfully, the terrain eventually leveled out, the fresh powder acting as a braking mechanism.

Standing, Molly spied something off to her right, sticking out of the snow.

"Look, Ralph," she pointed. "The shovel."[5]

The Bagger strained to decipher Shultz's voice from Base. Not only were the winds interfering, but the radios The Hasty Team carried were freezing up. Two sets were attached to the men's packs, exposed to the elements. Harder, however, kept his unit inside his coat, nestled underneath his sweater and his jacket. This unit was faltering as well, and Harder was not surprised. He was wearing two stocking caps on his head, and both were freezing.[6]

The Bagger, who didn't have to think twice about bracing himself in rotor wash exceeding sixty mph, was staggering, attempting to maintain his position in winds that had grown in intensity.[7] The team decided to rope-up.[8]

Mark Kelsey was experiencing a flood of emotions and an overall imperative to continue, to press on, regardless of the conditions. Children were missing.

The entire left side of Kelsey's Gore-Tex parka—the windward side—was coated in super-cooled drops that created layers of rime ice. It felt like armor that was growing heavier and heavier with every passing minute. Periodically, he shook his jacket, shedding significant layers of fractured debris. He had to do the same with his balaclava and ski goggles.

They continued on, stumbling and being forced to their knees. They progressed, walking in the footsteps of the person in front, as breaking trail was an extremely arduous task. There was nothing to hide behind, to get a break from the tormenting winds. It was howling, and the men, experiencing the full fury of the storm, simply had to take it.[9]

Reaching 9,700', the team determined that they could go no higher. Placing their backs to the wind, they headed east, burdened with medical supplies and seven sleeping bags.[10] The Bagger reached for his radio.

"Don't bring the next team up here!" he yelled, "It's not worth it!"[11]

Harder was radioing this message to Wright and McClure. In Number 8, however, Teams 3 and 4 overheard this broadcast. The men in the snow-cat grew silent.

Wright and McClure mulled over their options. Finally, they directed the cat driver to drop Teams 3 and 4 at Silcox Hut. There, they were to seek shelter and await further instructions.[12]

Cheryl Maslen walked into Wy'East Day Lodge, after driving from Portland. She noticed that deputies had commandeered a space for their own media room. Wright brought Maslen up to speed on the situation and handed her the Forest Service document that Goman had filled out prior to climbing. She didn't find it very helpful.

Maslen's primary duties involved organization and documentation. She would issue the hand-held radio sets to rescue teams, help monitor and interpret incoming radio transmissions, and record as much as possible in the log. She would keep track of everything and everyone. She had access to the Sheriff's department's radio, but the PMR set appeared to have better clarity. This had not escaped the attention of the deputies, who preferred to use Maslen and Shultz's unit whenever possible.

Maslen would assign volunteers to specific teams. She knew the organization's members, knew their various levels of climbing experience, and even knew who fared better at higher altitudes than others.

A group of PMR members walked in, ready for a mission. Maslen took these climbers aside, knowing their skillsets. She knew she'd need their expertise later, so she put them on hold until the right time. The rescuers were frustrated, protesting at waiting when they were already raring to go.

"Look," Maslen explained. "We're going to wear others out at some point. They're going to have to come down, and I need you to be ready."[13]

Rocky Henderson peered out the side window of the snowcat, barely able to see the stone and timber structure they were parked beside.[14] Two of the men leaned heavily against the door, combatting the opposing forces of the wind.

Seven men emerged into the elements, taking heavy steps through the snow towards the southern side of the rustic cabin. Approaching the south side of the building, the men passed through a small breach in the wall.[15]

Once inside, they brushed the snow off of their parkas and took stock of their surroundings.[16]

Led by Jeffrey Youngbluth, six PJs from the 304th ARRS arrived in a Jeep. They made their way to Base Operations. They found Maslen and Shultz, manning the radio and doing their best to understand the garbled transmissions emanating from the mountain. Dave McClure leaned in, trying to help interpret the incoming communiqué.

Observing quietly, Youngbluth noticed that teams up on the mountain appeared unable to hear one another. The men on the peak were relaying their desired communication to Shultz, who repeated the message to the other team battling the blizzard. Recognizing the distorted voice of his colleague, Rick Harder, Youngbluth stepped closer to the radio. McClure was having trouble making out what The Bagger was attempting to convey. Youngbluth, who knew the various nuances of Harder's voice, was able to translate.[17]

Ed Hall was struggling to stay on his feet. Ground snow was blowing all around him. Small shards of rime ice were pelting The Hasty Team. Visibility was nearly non-existent. Hall didn't know if his next step would even land on solid ground. The men were cold.

Hall and Harder, wanting to communicate, stood face-to-face. They leaned forward and held one another, their foreheads touching, to hear one another over the howling storm.

"I've got to get more clothes on!" Hall shouted.[18]

The Bagger gave the order to dig a bolt-hole. By excavating a small burrow, or hole, into the snow, Harder and his team could temporarily escape the elements long enough to add more layers of undergarments.[19] Kelsey had a shovel, as did Hall.

Kelsey handed his tool to The Bagger and, accompanied by Hall, the men took turns digging in a snowdrift. Standing side-by-side, the men alternated throwing shovelful after shovelful of snow over their shoulders.

Hall's glacier glasses, which did not have leather side protectors, were collecting rime ice. Harder, ceasing his labor for a moment, leaned closer to his friend.

"This is a fucking survival situation!" he screamed, half serious, half in jest.[20]

"I know that!" Hall shot back. "Dig!"

~8:35 A.M.
MOUNT HOOD WILDERNESS

Molly couldn't believe the conditions they were battling. Winds were constantly whipping over the slopes, and wind gusts repeatedly knocked her over. It was difficult to see the terrain ahead. Summers led the way, continually looking over his shoulder to ensure his ward was close at hand. Each time Molly fell, Summers was there to offer support, be it physical, words of encouragement, or both.[21]

They took a short break and discussed their potential location.

"Last night," Molly began, "we were probably on Zigzag Glacier."[22]

"Yes," Summers concurred, "but there is Big Zigzag and Little Zigzag, and I don't know which one we're on." The consultant had his compass out and was doing his best to maintain a 160° bearing.

"Do you know this mountain?" Molly asked.

"Yes," Ralph replied. "I've spent a lot of time here."

"Do we have to walk very far?" she asked, her tone more serious.[23]

"It's the only thing that will keep us all alive right now. We will walk as far as we have to. At least with the compass, we will walk in a straight line."

Summers tucked the snow shovel away and handed his partner the ice axe. They decided to walk arm-in-arm, to combat the high winds.[24] Molly, again, felt the fear that she would never get home to see her mother again.[25] The pair continued to stumble and stagger. They glissaded down short sections of favorable snow when the occasion presented itself, and they somehow managed to avoid hidden crevasses.[26]

8:38 A.M.
BELL UH-1 IROQUOIS HELICOPTER
APPROACHING MOUNT HOOD

The first helicopter flight, launched from Portland International Airport, was approaching the mountain. Huey pilots, Lieutenant Colonel

David Mullen and Major Charles Jones, assessed their situation. Initial concerns over fuel consumption had dissipated. What was normally a thirty-five-minute flight had only taken eighteen, due to impressive tailwinds. The pilots had encountered the ceiling of an overcast layer at 4,500'. They had opted to climb to 9,000', where they could observe the violent clouds underneath. Now, on top of the overcast layer, they continued to approach the mountain.[27]

The pilots were violating standard operating procedures to respond to the call for assistance. Technically, the sheriff's office should have contacted the Department of Emergency Services to enlist the services of the squadron. Since this did not occur, a rescue coordination center division number had not been assigned to the mission. John Olson, of the 304th ARRS, was backtracking and taking care of the paperwork, while the pilots continued as if they had already been granted authority to proceed.[28]

Lt. Col. Mullen, Maj. Jones, and flight engineer, Sergeant Ron Carpenter, passed around the northern side of the mountain. Intending to land in the Wy'East Day Lodge parking lot, by approaching it from the east, the men aboard the helicopter watched in wonder as they paralleled the northern slope of the peak. The upper 2,000 feet of the volcano was covered in storm clouds. Individual portions of these atmospheric formations could be seen sweeping over the summit in a matter of seconds.

Rounding the northeastern corner of the mountain, alarms began sounding in the cockpit. The aircraft shuddered violently. Everyone felt the chaotic strains against their seatbelts and shoulder straps. The aircraft lost significant elevation in a series of instantaneous plummets. The Huey spun entirely around. Jones felt as if he was riding inside a spin dryer.

The pilots were forced to land the aircraft near the Cooper Spur Inn, a rustic mountain cabin, over twenty miles from Timberline Lodge. Safely on the ground, Jones looked up at the mountain. Clouds were screaming across the northeast face, like a freight train.[29]

~8:50 A.M.
PALMER CHAIR LIFT UPPER TERMINAL
PALMER SNOWFIELD

Team 2 noticed a significant shift in wind direction. The men had sought temporary shelter from the storm by remaining tucked in the lee of the upper shack of the chairlift. With the change in wind direction, however, they were once again confronted with the storm. Glenn learned, via radio transmission, that Number 8 was heading to their position, now that Teams 3 and 4 had been delivered to Silcox Hut. The driver had a set of keys in his possession that could unlock this building. Glenn welcomed the news. He welcomed any development that would get his men out of the elements.[30]

9:00 A.M.
BASE OPERATIONS
WY'EAST DAY LODGE

Craig Petrie, of the Mt. Hood Ski Patrol, had received a call from a friend, informing him that deputies were hoping to enlist the assistance of his organization. Petrie called Deputy Krebs to ascertain if this was true or not. The deputy thanked him, saying he didn't need their services at this time. Krebs was just about to hang up when Petrie added, seemingly as an afterthought, that the ski patrol had access to a snowcat. The news pleased the deputy, as a single cat could transport two teams of SAR personnel at a time.

Krebs accepted this offer. Petrie added that an additional snowcat might also be available.[31]

Finally! Some good news.

9:01 A.M.
PALMER CHAIR LIFT UPPER SHACK
PALMER SNOWFIELD

Seeing Number 8 emerge out of the white world below them, the four men of Team 2 breathed a sigh of relief. They'd been attempting to regain radio contact with The Hasty Team, without success.[32] Glenn aborted the plan to unlock the upper terminal, directing his men to pile inside the heated snowcat instead.

As they were helping one another into the rear of the cat, an incredibly powerful wind gust blew out the windshield.[33] Everyone in the vehicle was stunned, but no one was more concerned than the driver himself. With the understanding that he would only be required to drive rescue personnel up and down the mountain, Young had failed to dress appropriately should he be exposed to the elements. Snow began to accumulate inside the vehicle's cab as the men made a quick makeshift repair.[34] Glenn's men were concerned that the driver might grow hypothermic.[35]

McClure and Wright directed Team 2 to wait inside the cat, while they attempted to contact The Hasty Team. Young could potentially transport both teams back to Base. Communications with The Bagger's team had been spotty at best, but one transmission carried clearly over the airwaves. Harder indicated his men might be in trouble. He did not give a known position but said he was considering evacuation. It seemed wise for Number 8 to remain where it was, in case The Hasty Team needed her services.

Jerry Janeck, pleased to be out of the elements, shifted uncomfortably on one of the benches in the back of the vehicle. His fellow Amigos were rubbing their hands, trying to rewarm themselves. Janeck was irritated. If The Bagger hadn't ignored his recommendation for both teams to retreat, they could all be safe and warm. *Instead of looking for these kids*, Janeck thought, *now we're looking for one another.*[36]

~9:05 A.M.
SNOW CAVE

The climbing party was down to eleven. Giles was disturbed by the sound of shivering that seemed to permeate the chamber. He tried to stay busy in an attempt to stop thinking about their predicament. Keeping the tunnel open and free of accumulating snow occupied a considerable portion of his time.[37]

Giles, Alison, and Erik discussed the constricting entrance. Alison, being the smallest of the trio, wiggled her way through the tube to reach the outside. She intended to enlarge the diameter of the tunnel with her body as she exited. To a minor extent, she succeeded, yet the walls, coated in a layer of ice, barely budged. As the snow shovel had been blown away by the wind, Giles used the ice axe to help shave away the layers of ice from his side of the passageway.[38] Erik departed the cave, not long after Alison had made her exit. With his broad shoulders, the teen was having greater difficulty wriggling through the tunnel. He barely made it out. Erin was already outside the shelter, answering the call of nature.[39]

About fifteen minutes later, Giles could tell that one of the kids was attempting to return.[40] He looked through the tunnel, but could only see the sole of Erik's hiking boot, desperately fidgeting about within the confined space. Giles started using the axe again, trying to enlarge the hole. Frustrated with the lack of progress, he dropped the tool and grabbed hold of Erik's boot. Suddenly, the boot came off in his hands. Erik, on the outside of the cave, withdrew his leg from the tunnel, leaving Giles—inside—

holding on to the abandoned footwear.[41]

Giles looked down the seemingly telescopic scope of the tunnel, transfixed on its walls. Exhaustion, dehydration, and stress had all taken their toll. He felt neither terror nor peace.

They're out there, and we're in here.[42]

Molly and Summers could see the silhouette of a tree ahead of them, an exciting sight, as it indicated they were around 6,000' which is the highest elevation that trees grow at this latitude. They felt like they were in a canyon, and Summers said they should follow it down the mountain. It would most likely take them to the highway that encircled the peak. From there, they could hike to the town of Government Camp.

"We have a long walk ahead," Summers announced.[43]

"What's on the other side?" Molly asked, in regards to the eastern border of the canyon wall. "Can't we come out of this canyon and find Palmer?"

"Yes, but to climb out would take a lot of our energy and we'd no longer be following the bearing we set."

Continuing their downhill trek, the consultant felt confident that they were in Little Zigzag Canyon. After a few more minutes, Summers appeared to recognize how far they would have to travel down the canyon, as well as up the highway, to reach civilization.

"I know skiers who ski this in the winter," he remarked in resignation, "but, it's just too far to walk. Let's try to climb out."

Summers took the lead, post-holing up the eastern wall of the canyon.[44] Molly felt he was traveling too fast, even though the man was stomping his feet to make good steps for his partner. The terrain was steep, and they climbed straight up. Molly repeatedly removed her ski goggles, hoping to see the steps ahead of her. Visibility was so poor that she ended up creating many of her own steps in the snowbank.

At one point, Summers pulled far enough ahead that Molly lost sight of him in the alabaster pall. Upon reaching the crest of the canyon wall, she spied him standing beside a snow-laden tree.

"I'm sorry," Molly apologized, "I can't walk as fast as you."[45]

"I was watching for you," he reassured her, "but, I had to keep moving at a pace to keep warm."

Coming to a level section of terrain, Summers said the compass bearing was still pointing them to the left.[46] Molly understood, but she was busy fidgeting with her ski goggles again. They were bothering her, so she permitted them to hang loosely around her neck as she continued the descent. She started shielding her eyes with her gloved hands, as wind gusts dictated.

It had taken The Hasty Team forty-five minutes to create an adequate bolt-hole. Schneider was the first to enter the sanctuary, crawling in on all fours. Ed Hall was exhausted. It seemed that every time they excavated five shovelfuls of snow from the hole, the equivalent of two had blown back inside. Now, it was a never-ending task to keep the entryway free of accumulating snow. Schneider, Harder, and Hall took turns, using the bolt-hole to change into warmer clothing.[47]

Shultz and Maslen were monitoring radio transmissions emanating from the military helicopter. When it had been forced to make an emergency landing, Maslen raised an eyebrow. Had the Huey crashed on the peak, PMR did not have the resources to dispatch personnel on a second rescue.[48] It looked as if air operations were on hold. Snowcats would remain the only means of transportation up and down the mountain.

Summers strained his eyes. Was he seeing what he thought he was seeing?

"Guess what?" he called back to Molly. "A lift!"[49] Molly struggled up to his position and hugged him in celebration. The pair of exhausted climbers looked up at a ski lift tower.

"Oh, God, we're saved!" she exclaimed.[50]

"No, Molly," Summers countered. "We have to wait until everybody is with us to celebrate." The two stood there a moment, each alone with their thoughts. "I think this is the lift below Timberline," Summers guessed. "We have to climb up."[51]

They started climbing directly up the hill, but Molly said she was too exhausted. The pair turned to take on the incline diagonally, bringing them to a small grove of fir trees.

"This looks familiar," Summers remarked, somewhat puzzled. "We are going to have to go up."[52] They turned and began ascending once more. "This should come out real soon to the road by Timberline," he added. A rectangular object began to appear through the fog of snow ahead of them. Drawing closer, they were able to see that it was a sign. Summers approached, close enough to read the information it presented.

"Oh, no," he groaned. "I don't believe it. This is the Texas lift."[53] The significance of this revelation lost on Molly. Summers had to explain that they were actually near one of the chairlifts at Mt. Hood Meadows, a ski resort on the *southeastern* flank of the mountain. Summers worked here during the winter months. He and Molly had not descended a portion of Little Zigzag Canyon. They had been descending White River Glacier. They were over two miles from their perceived position.[54] Molly moaned.

"Come on," Summers sighed. "I'll keep your pace."[55] He gently grabbed her arm, and they began descending the mountain, following the ski lift cables overhead.

~9:30 A.M.
MOUNT HOOD WILDERNESS

Hall was the last of the team to utilize the bolt-hole, having changed into every stitch of clothing he had packed with him. *What's our next move?* he thought as he emerged into the fury of the storm.[56]

The group huddled and decided to head downhill, to Silcox Hut, where Harder's team could seek sanctuary.

"What route?" The Bagger shouted to the group, knowing that their descent would require compass work.[57]

Hall removed the overmit from his right hand and tucked it under his right arm. Having the expedition-grade mitten off enabled him to use his fingers—covered in a thin layer of polypropylene—to scrape the ice off his glacier glasses.

"From wherever we are!" Hall shouted, "a 180° heading will at least get us in the vicinity!"[58] Hall believed that, even in poor visibility, with this magnetic heading the team should at least come across the chairlift towers, Silcox Hut, or some other man-made structure that would assist them further in navigation.

Harder cupped his gloves.

"Kelsey," he shouted. "Man, navigate us down to Silcox!"[59]

Kelsey tucked his Thommen altimeter into his parka pocket and produced a compass and a map of the mountain. He studied his map, knew approximately where they were above the Palmer chairlift, and obtained his requisite azimuth.

The plan was anything but simple. Coming down the mountain in a whiteout, Kelsey would deliberately skew the traditional azimuth to the west of the ski lift. He would also ensure they aimed for a position 200 feet below the top shack of the lift. At that point, if still enveloped in the blinding storm, they would turn east and monitor their surroundings as they hiked. They'd surely spot the lift towers and follow them down to Silcox Hut.[60]

As Kelsey put away his map, an incredibly powerful gust of wind suddenly knocked Ed Hall off his feet. Hall watched in horror as his overmit, tucked under his arm, flew away and disappeared into the storm. He looked down at his exposed right hand, covered in only a thin layer of polypropylene.

Oh, no.[61]

~9:35 A.M.
BUTTERCUP
MT. HOOD MEADOWS

Molly dutifully followed Summers. They had reached the gentle bunny slope, packed with novice skiers on sunny days. They stayed close to the left-hand tree line, using it as a guide for the final portion of their journey.[62]

~9:45 A.M.
PALMER CHAIR LIFT UPPER TERMINAL
PALMER SNOWFIELD

Team 2, trying to stay warm in the stationary snowcat, finally established contact with The Hasty Team, informing them that they were waiting for them at the top of the Palmer chairlift.[63] Harder thanked Glenn but stated Team 1 would be heading down to Silcox on foot.[64]

Janeck, overhearing this transmission, was floored. If The Bagger intended to seek shelter for his men, Number 8 stood ready to provide such protection. *Why have your men trudge over 1,500 feet down the mountain, in a blizzard, when they don't have to be exposed to the elements?* This seemed like an unnecessary risk to Janeck.[65]

Hall was well aware that ice had started accumulating on his polypropylene inner glove, but his hand appeared okay. He believed that the ice was actually protecting him. A slim, sliver of bare skin—between his parka and his inner glove—was exposed to the elements. *That could be problematic.*[66]

Kelsey was navigating The Hasty Team down the mountain. The Bagger was out ahead, turning around now and then to make sure he was staying on course with the navigator. An intense storm gust blew so much snow the men temporarily lost visual contact with one another. They waited, stomping their boots. When their hazy silhouettes once again rematerialized, Kelsey used hand signals to direct The Bagger to the left. When the man was perfectly lined up with the azimuth, Schneider, Hall, and Kelsey advanced to Harder's position, and the entire leap-frogging maneuver repeated.[67]

Inside the warmth and comfort of the Ski School Office, a handful of employees were busy tending to their various responsibilities. The door to the building suddenly opened. The staff turned to see two snow-covered figures framed in the doorway. A weary man, with icicles festooned in his mustache, stepped forward.

Ralph Summers identified himself.

CHAPTER 13
ANT COLONY

The mountain highway had been clear all the way to Government Camp. Not wanting to stop to don chains, Frank McGinness took the risk, driving a white Pontiac Catalina up the six-mile road that leads to Timberline Lodge. John Bridges was with him. The final stretch of their journey was over compacted snow and ice.

Snow was coming down heavily as they pulled into the parking lot. Frank was in a mental fog, desperate for information concerning Patrick. There was a multitude of activity in the lot. SAR volunteers were scurrying about, and shouts rang out from one colleague to another, the clarity lost amid the high winds.

As soon as Frank and John emerged from the car, they were flagged down by a state police officer, sitting in a nearby patrol car.

"Do you know anything about this Oregon Episcopal School climb?" the officer inquired.[1]

"Yeah," Frank replied. "I'm here . . . I'm one of the parents."

9:48 A.M.
BASE OPERATIONS
WY'EAST DAY LODGE

Deputy Krebs was shocked to hear the voice of Ralph Summers, calling from Mt. Hood Meadows.[2] Summers relayed that the missing climbers were holed-up in a snow cave. It was difficult to say how far he had traveled during the trek to safety, but he was certain that he and Molly had descended several thousand feet in elevation.

While Krebs was speaking with Summers, another deputy requested that McClure and Maslen prepare to communicate with the media. With nearly a dozen children lost in one of the most brutal mountain storms in decades, the level of press coverage would be unprecedented.[3]

Frank, a member of the Friends of Timberline's restoration committee, had been to the resort two weeks earlier to meet with their curator, Linny Adamson. Making his way through the familiar interior of the historic head house, Frank was looking for anyone who knew where the rescue authorities were located.

A large corporate conference was in progress at the inn, and Frank found himself wading through a sea of attendees and tourists, weaving in and out of various knots of humanity. Everyone seemed bathed in the soft light of the linen-covered chandeliers. It was a cheerful, yet chaotic environment, and Frank felt completely out of place.

"Do you know anything about the Oregon Episcopal School climbers?" he asked a woman.[4]

"No," she replied. "What's this about?"

"Well, there's a school up here, that's got their kids on a climb, and they're lost up on the mountain."

"Oh, my," she exclaimed.

"I'm one of the parents."

"I hope it works out for you," she replied sadly, disappearing into the crowd.

Frank was growing increasingly frustrated when he suddenly ran into Linny.

"Oh, Frank," she cheerfully greeted him. "Did we miss a meeting?"

"No," he replied to the dark-haired curator. "I'm here for my son."

"Oh, my God," Linny exclaimed, recalling that Pat attended OES. Tears welled up in her eyes.

An announcement interrupted them. *Anyone seeking information regarding the missing climbing party should proceed next door, to Wy'East Day Lodge.* For Frank, this was manna from heaven.

Elsewhere in the building, Diana Yates and Mar Goman overheard a passing rescue worker cry out, "We found them! We found them!"[5] Overjoyed, the women hurried over to the public telephone and called Tom's mother. Mar reported that Tom was alive and would be down the mountain shortly. Only a few minutes after this call, Diana learned that Tom was still missing and only two members of the party had hiked out to safety. Diana and Mar agreed to be more cautious when it came to future updates.

Hearing that information was being shared across the street, the women opted to remain where they were. They had noticed that rescue workers, deputies, hotel employees, and reporters were all using the public telephone. By remaining where they were, the women could overhear telephone calls that contained vital information.

Branching out, the women started asking journalists questions. The reporters, in turn, asked Mar for facts concerning her missing husband. *How old is he? How many times had he climbed the mountain?* They even asked her how to spell "Ralph Summers."[6]

In the Cascade Dining Room, Mick, Lorca, Courtney, and John were being treated to a breakfast buffet by members of the OES faculty, who had driven up to the resort. Lorca and John had risen around 7:30 a.m. Mick and Courtney had been up since 3:45 a.m. Sue Schula, Molly's mother, sat with the kids.

John was itching to return home. He had roamed the halls of the resort and stopped to pet the resort's mascots, two St. Bernards named Heidi and Bruno. *What to do now? Let's get this show on the road.*[7]

A message was delivered to the table. Summers and Molly had hiked from a snow cave, down to Mt. Hood Meadows. Mrs. Schula was visibly relieved. Mick looked at the faces of the adults and realized the situation on the mountain was worse than he and the others had believed. *What is this business about a snow cave? What is Meadows? If Ralph and Molly are safe, what about the others?*[8]

~10:07 A.M.
WY'EAST DAY LODGE

Reporters gathered around Deputy Krebs, as he entered the covered area, outside of the Lodge. As cameras rolled and voice recorders were activated, all eyes turned to the deputy.

"At this point," Krebs stated, "we do have a location on the students and on the four adults who were with them. Everybody is all right. They're cold. They're dug in. We have fifty to sixty mph winds up there. The weather is severe, but everybody is in good medical condition."[9] Krebs added that two climbers had managed to hike down to Mt. Hood Meadows—one of the adults and one of the students. Transportation was being arranged to bring them to Base and, just as soon as there was a break in the weather, authorities would head up the mountain to retrieve the missing team.

"You actually reached them?" a reporter inquired. "You actually got to the point where they were?"

"No," Krebs conceded. "We only have the area pinpointed."

"How do you know that?" the man asked.

"Because of the people that came down. They gave us the location."

"Where are they located now?" came another reporter's question.

"Well," Krebs thought for a second, "They're dug-in down off of White River...a Glacier."

"How far down on the mountain?" asked the first reporter. Krebs paused, looking skyward as if he was mentally replaying the phone call with Summers.

"I'm guessing about 9,000', but I can't tell you for sure. I'd have to go back and check the maps to give you the exact location."

Families of the missing climbers were quick to pounce on this news. Two members of Fr. Goman's party had made it out, and it sounded as if everyone was warm in the cocoon of a snow cave. Relatives breathed a sigh of relief. Uncertainty seemed to melt away, replaced with the hope that, once a window of fair weather presented itself, their loved ones would be led down to safety.

~10:12 A.M.
TIMBERLINE LODGE

Frank and John were walking through the Quonset hut tunnel, which led from the Lodge's front door down to the parking lot. Frank's frustration had flared into outright anger. Instead of turning left and walking over to the ski lodge, he turned right, walking quickly through the frigid winds. Passing the fenced-in swimming pool, they rounded the corner of the building and started heading towards the ski-slopes. Frank was mad at the mountain and wanted to take on the weather.

"F-it!" he said. "I'm going up. I'm going to find Pat."[10]

"You're nuts," John replied. "Look at it out here!"

"I don't care!" Frank shouted back, already advancing into the storm. He looked uphill to where Silcox Hut is typically seen in the distance. Nothing. He couldn't see anything beyond thirty yards. He wouldn't fight the nearly-irresistible paternal urge to continue on, to battle his way through the elements towards his oldest son.

Sinking up to his knees in snow, Frank struggled to stay on his feet in the blistering winds. Snow was striking the left side of his face, feeling like a hundred shards of subzero glass.

He had minimal protection for this kind of weather; polypropylene underwear under khaki slacks, insulated socks, and a pair of Timberland boots with only a few miles on them. He wore a polyester cap and a down-filled, bright orange jacket. He had neither glacier glasses or a balaclava.

In spite of his clothing, Frank was internally raging, and his heart demanded that he continue ascending. About 100 yards into his trek, he found himself looking deeper into the storm. He had never seen anything like this. It was a black hole. Sheets of snow were swirling all around him, as if he were in a Sci-Fi movie, walking into a time-warp. He suddenly stopped. A little bit of reality sank in. Christopher was at home. Patrick was up on that mountain . . . somewhere. His boys would need their dad.

Wow, not a good idea.

Distraught, Frank turned and began his trek back down to safety.

Below, John watched as his friend's ethereal figure reemerged from the storm. He had known he couldn't sway his friend, once his mind was set. John had simply waited for Frank to learn his lesson. Knowing his friend was emotionally drained from the burdens of the day, John tried to think of something comforting to say. As Frank returned to his side, shivering and despondent, John merely clapped his friend on the back.

"Smart move," he remarked.[11]

10:13 A.M.
UPPER TERMINAL, PALMER CHAIRLIFT
PALMER SNOWFIELD

The driver of Number 8 radioed Base. The battery in the snowcat was dying, and the transmission was freezing.[12] He was asking if he could return the cat to Timberline and have McClure dispatch a different vehicle up the slopes. Mid-conversation, the driver sighed heavily. The battery in the vehicle just died. Discouraged, McClure advised Team 2 to assist in any way they could; attempt to get that cat started again.[13]

As the vehicle transporting Summers and Molly arrived, a handful of reporters swarmed to their side. Journalists cornered Molly as soon as she exited the car. Her hair was disheveled, and her ski goggles hung lazily around her neck. Reporters bombarded her with questions: *what were the conditions like up on the mountain? How were the students coping with the storm? How long had it taken her and Summers to descend from the snow cave?* She did her best to answer these queries politely but stated that she felt she should be speaking to the sheriff.[14]

Frank walked into the upper floors of the Lodge, hoping to find someone in charge of the search efforts. He bumped into a haggard looking man, with water dripping from his mustache. Frank thought this man looked wasted, with a dazed look on his face.

"Do you know anything about what's going on up there?" Frank inquired.[15] Seemingly confused, the man didn't reply. "My name is Frank McGinness, and I'm looking for my son, Patrick."

"Oh, my God," the stranger exclaimed. "You're Patrick's dad? I have never seen anybody recover from hypothermia like your son." Frank had just bumped into Ralph Summers, without even knowing it.

Frank had to think for a moment and acknowledge that he didn't really know anything about hypothermia. He didn't know how important or significant recovering from it was, to a mountain climber.

Summers explained that Pat had been assisted into the snow cave after dark, but by this morning, the teen had helped Ralph and Molly dig out the entrance to the snow cave.

In just a single minute with Summers, Frank learned that his son was alive, he had experienced some kind of medical condition on the mountain, but he had rallied enough to be of great assistance to the team. Frank beamed. Pat was alive.

Frank saw Molly walking into the building. She appeared flushed and exhausted. The reporters followed her and Summers inside, leaving Frank alone in a crowd of bystanders. There were people passing one another in the doorways. The place seemed to be crawling with SAR volunteers and relatives of the missing. People seemed to be harboring the same questions: *who was in charge? Where should we be congregating? Who will be disseminating information?* Frank felt as if they were all struggling and crawling over one another, like a chaotic ant colony.[16]

~10:20 A.M.
BASE OPERATIONS
WY'EAST DAY LODGE

The Bagger radioed that The Hasty Team was descending, east of the Palmer chairlift, around 8,500'. McClure, in turn, brought Harder up to speed on the sudden appearance of Summers, the dead battery in Number 8, and Teams 3 and 4 who were holed-up in Silcox Hut.[17]

After McClure conversed with The Bagger, he radioed Team 2 in Number 8. A secondary asset was being dispatched up the mountain to retrieve them.[18]

Summers had deftly avoided reporters. He made his way to a chair in Base Operations, near a wall of shelves, filled with office equipment. He began changing out of his wet clothes. Seeing how exhausted he was, Sue Shultz pitched in and started helping him with his boots. She knew that the poor man might be headed back up the mountain to help with the SAR efforts, and would need his boots as dry as possible.[19]

The consultant's drenched, blue parka came off just as Deputy Krebs leaned in to ask him a handful of questions. When Krebs was drawn aside by a colleague, McClure stepped forward with a few questions of his own. Summers changed out of his soaked shirt.[20]

Shultz saw a teenage girl standing idle, off to the side.

"A little assistance?" Shultz called out to her.[21] The teen stared back at Shultz, with a look of disbelief. Shultz took a better look at the girl—her clothing, her age, and her disheveled hair. "Oh, my gosh, you're Molly," Shultz apologized, putting two-and-two together. She returned to her work with further intensity, trying to figure the best option for drying the soaked climbing gear.

Several network news cameramen entered the room and fanned out to film the action in Base Operations. One of these men, from KGW News, trained his camera on Summers. The bare-chested consultant's hair was unruly, his lips were swollen, and his face appeared wind-burnt. He wore a pair of large, prescription eyeglasses and was clearly in need of rest.[22]

Summers informed authorities that the missing climbers were out of food and water and that Pat had already displayed signs of hypothermia. He added that the physical condition of the students had deteriorated somewhat during the course of the night.[23]

Before Summers had time to finish changing, one of the PJs, Jeffrey Youngbluth, led him over to the wall where a map of the mountain was displayed. The PJ noticed that the consultant was exhausted and probably hypoglycemic and dehydrated. Summers seemed to be moving slowly, physically and mentally, but the location of the snow cave was of paramount importance.[24]

When asked the location of the cave, Summers stated that he believed it to be on the east side of a moraine inside White River Canyon.[25] It was near a crevasse he estimated to be thirty feet deep, and up to five feet across. The cave's entrance was below a 20° rise, yet above a 50° slope. A yellow rain parka marked the entrance to the cave.[26]

When asked for his estimate on the elevation of the cave, Summers paused.[27] The climbing party did not have an altimeter, so, a guess was the best the consultant could provide. Summers pointed to a spot on the map, at 7,200'.[28]

If Summers was correct, all four SAR teams were currently deployed on the wrong glacier. The adjacent glacier would need to be searched.

Summers was fielding requests for information as best he could. Occasionally, someone would ask him a question that he had already answered. It seemed to him that individuals would get a snippet of information, and then depart to share it with colleagues.[29]

Barry Wright was deeply troubled, feeling that there was too much ambiguity in Summers' statements. His descriptions of terrain features, as detailed as they were, shed no light on the cave's specific location. Wright left the room with the distinct impression that Summers had no clue what path he had taken to Mt. Hood Meadows. By his own admission, the consultant had thought he was in Zigzag Canyon, on the far west side of Palmer Glacier, until he and Molly had emerged at the Meadows.[30] *Why hadn't he carried an altimeter and taken a reading at the cave?*[31]

Members of the press had been told that the location of the cave had been pinpointed. Knowing now that this was inaccurate, Wright was uncomfortable. He knew the public had no concept of how much terrain would need to be covered, or how many man-hours would need to be expended, to locate the entrance to a solitary snow cave. They were looking for a needle in a haystack—a haystack engulfed in a blizzard.

Maslen, who had been taking notes during the debriefing, noticed Summers' uncertainty as well. After Krebs, McClure, and Youngbluth had questioned the consultant, Maslen took him aside. They spoke privately in a nearby alcove; it was an attempt to coax further information out of him.[32]

Through a radio transmission, Team's 3 and 4 learned that Summers and Schula had hiked out to safety.[33] The missing climbers were holed-up in a snow cave, possibly around 7,200' on White River Glacier. When Swicegood, Craig, Henderson and the other men in the cabin heard this elevation figure, they started gathering their gear. If they were at 6,950', and the missing students were only 250 feet higher up in elevation, and just to the northeast, then they were the closest SAR workers to the cave. Henderson couldn't believe how close they were, envisioning a quick rescue.[34]

The men pulled out their compasses and a map of the mountain. To intercept the White River Glacier at 7,200', they'd have to set a bearing of 43°.[35] Swicegood radioed this plan down to Base for approval.

Wright, who had been plotting the proposed mission on a map, confirmed Swicegood's findings and approved the plan.[36]

When Molly Schula entered the room, Mick and the other members of the breakfast party were elated. Still dressed in her climbing clothes, she answered as many questions as she could. The conversation soon turned to the search parties.

While everyone else was engaged in various conversations, Molly leaned toward Mick, confiding that she was concerned about Father Tom. The man had been outside the cave for extended shifts during the night, howling and screaming.[37]

Following the extended breakfast, the students went their separate ways. Chuck Reynolds, from OES, would drive John back to the school.[38] Lorca would ride with a different teacher.[39] Courtney's parents had arrived and decided to take her home, to more familiar and supportive surroundings.[40]

Courtney felt extremely confused. Several of her classmates were still missing on the mountain. She was departing the resort with far more questions than she had answers.[41]

In the parking lot, a cameraman from KGW News filmed the exterior of the yellow school bus. It seemed isolated from the rest of the nearby vehicles. The wind buffeted its mud flaps.[42] Mick Garrett, feeling like the odd man out, stepped aboard the bus for his return journey to civilization.[43]

SNOW CAVE

Brinton and Giles noticed that the entrance to the snow cave was becoming smaller and smaller. It was like looking through a telescope. Rich was nearby, and the three teens did their best to comfort one another.

Giles began hallucinating.[44] As the winds continued to wail outside, the teens were thinking about the inevitable question.

Are we going to die?[45]

CHAPTER 14
RESCUERS RESCUING RESCUERS

Jeff Hicks and Susan Lekas, employees from OES, wandered about looking for the four students who had turned around before the storm.

Jeff had driven a school-owned Suburban up to the mountain. He had been a chaperone on several previous climbs up Hood. When people in the Lodge told him not to worry, things were going to be alright, he couldn't take their advice to heart. He had broken his ankle on one of the school-sponsored ascents—glissading. Accidents can happen in broad daylight. Looking out a window, he wondered what could go wrong in a raging storm.

A couple of years back, Jeff had come up to the resort with Father Tom and a busload of teens. Tom took one look at the conditions and directed the driver to turn around. The mountain would wait for another day.

On another climb, Jeff had stood on the summit of Mount Hood in inclement weather. To him, it was like standing in the center of an all-white room. He had joked with Tom, that—fortunately—they had left trail wands in the snow during their ascent. They had followed these "bread crumbs" down to the lower slopes, where fairer weather prevailed.[1]

A flatbed snowcat, dispatched to assist Number 8, arrived at the upper shack. After a jump-start, Number 8 sparked to life again. The chilled occupants were relieved.

While the battery charged, McClure's voice crackled over the radio, assigning Team 2 a new mission. Glenn and his team were to head southeast to find safe passage onto White River Glacier, around 7,400'. From there, they were to link-up with Teams 3 and 4.[2]

There was a pause, as Team 2 calculated the necessary equipment for the new mission. White River Glacier is riddled with visible and hidden crevasses. Taking those hazards into consideration, Glenn informed Base that Team 2 did not have any ropes.[3] Discouraged, Wright and McClure directed Team 2 to return to the Lodge.

In response, both snowcats began a cautious descent of the mountain. The flatbed assumed the lead position, while Number 8 followed about ten feet behind. In the whiteout, Janeck and his Amigos lost sight of the flatbed ahead of them, multiple times.[4]

~11:20 A.M.
WY'EAST DAY LODGE

Meandering around the halls, Frank approached a small group. Through introductions, he found himself talking to George O'Leary, Erin's father. George invited Frank to have lunch with him across the street.[5]

The two fathers ate quietly, saying very little. Although he was pleased to have discovered someone who shared his deep concern, Frank found the somber atmosphere distinctly unnerving.

When would they have answers?

Frank spied a deputy walking by, and then another. The sight of law enforcement officers flooded him with thoughts of Patrick.

Years earlier, Frank had come home from work and found his home empty. Looking out his bedroom window, Frank spied Pat chopping wood in the neighbor's yard.

Raising his ax, Pat caught a glimpse of a man in the window of his own home. Panicked, the youth bolted into the neighbor's house. Minutes later, Frank heard muffled voices outside his house. Curious, he opened his front door.

"Freeze!" demanded one of the half-dozen police officers, casting flash-lights in Frank's face. Their weapons were drawn.[6]

Explaining that he lived at the residence, and this was all just a misunderstanding, Frank looked at his neighbor's house and saw his sons peering back at him from the door. Patrick had been convinced he had spotted a burglar in his home and, to protect the family, had called the cops on the mysterious intruder.[7]

Swicegood directed the men of Teams 3 and 4 to divide into two rope teams.[8] Breaking out their 9mm kernmantle lines, they roped-up and made a final equipment check.

Swicegood emerged from Silcox Hut and headed uphill in a northeasterly direction. About seventy feet behind him came Lillywhite, charged with manning the compass and keeping the first team on course. Jim Boucher would serve as anchorman.[9]

Lillywhite was experiencing his first whiteout. There was a complete absence of shadows or signs of contrast. Terrain features, even those directly under his feet, vanished. He had a cap, glacier glasses, and well-worn climbing boots purchased from a second-hand equipment sale. His long underwear, wool pants, wool shirt, and reasonably decent coat were not keeping him as warm or protected from the elements as he would have liked.[10]

As navigator, he was shocked at how quickly the wind gusts blew the team off course. Whenever there was a momentary lift in visibility, he used hand signals to communicate with Swicegood. The cold, the wind—the whole experience was beyond anything he could have imagined.[11]

Mike "No Bozos" Craig, now in charge of the secondary rope team, followed in the footsteps of Swicegood's men. His glacier glasses were icing up, not only on the outside but on the inside as well.[12] Behind him came Henderson, Blailock, and Sellers.

Henderson kept glancing back over his shoulder. The raw recruit was being introduced to full whiteout navigation. Blailock yelled out compass bearings, using his ski poles to point to the left or the right. At times, whistle signals proved inaudible at only twenty feet.[13] The men placed wands, in case the teams had to return along their original course.

Craig was also forced to look back, constantly, to see these visual navigation commands.[14] The high winds were pushing him off to the right, and he was finding it difficult to maintain his course.[15]

Though Swicegood was the man-in-charge, he was experiencing a sense of apprehension. He was pleased that the intense winds were at their backs, but merely leaving the sanctuary of Silcox Hut was unsettling.[16]

Lt. Col. Mullen, Maj. Jones, and Sgt. Carpenter had been monitoring the weather for nearly three hours. Since they had been forced to land their Huey, the team had been periodically checking-in with authorities in Base Operations. Mullen learned that an adult and one of the students had reached safety by hiking through White River Canyon. Recognizing that the canyon was on the way to Timberline Lodge, Mullen gave the order to initiate aircraft start-up procedures.[17]

Status reports were coming in from the teams in the field. Maslen and Shultz had been making sure that everything was documented in the log. The Hasty Team was still descending on foot, following underneath the Palmer chairlift. Team 2, being transported in Number 8, was nearly back to Base. Teams 3 and 4 were roped-up, heading northeast on a 43° bearing towards White River Canyon.[18]

The snowcats returned to Base.[19] Visibility was so poor in the parking lot that rescue workers couldn't see Timberline Lodge, even though it was just across the street. Harbour, Janeck, and Rich—The Three Amigos—still felt strong. They decided to find Cheryl Maslen and advise her that they were available for another mission.[20]

The sheriff's department was being bombarded with requests for information. Telephone calls were redirected up to Wy'East Day Lodge, but reporters continued to walk into the sheriff's office or contacted them via FAX. Sheriff Brooks, legally in charge of the operation, had his deputies share as much information as they possessed, including a list of the missing climbers.

Reporters began calling colleagues, who were already up at the inn, plying them for information. *One climber was diabetic? An adult and child had hiked out in a blizzard? Valiant volunteers were battling the elements to reach a hidden snow cave?*[21]

Reporters knew this story would capture the nation's heart.

12:05 P.M.
MOUNT HOOD WILDERNESS

Swicegood contacted Base with a status report. One of his gloves had blown away in the high winds; he needed a replacement. His men were at 7,200', and they weren't making much headway.[22]

Minutes later, Harder was reporting that The Hasty Team had descended to 7,000' and were fanning out to try to locate Silcox Hut in the blizzard. When asked if they needed anything, The Bagger replied, "Stocking caps and food."[23]

12:20 P.M.
WEST MORAINE
WHITE RIVER CANYON

Stumbling over snow-covered rocks, Henderson was doing his best to maintain position within his rope team. He saw that something was occurring up ahead. Lillywhite had stopped and appeared to be struggling with a rope. Henderson turned around and waved for his colleagues behind him to rally at his position.[24]

Facing whiteout conditions, Terry Swicegood had blindly walked right off a cornice, and was tumbling down into White River Canyon.[25]

12:20 P.M.
LANDING ZONE (LZ)
WY'EAST DAY LODGE SOUTH PARKING LOT

The first helicopter from the 304th ARRS approached from the east.[26] Around 11:50 a.m., this Huey had managed to lift off from the Cooper Spur region and flew at low levels, clockwise, around the mountain.[27] The pilots had hoped to fly over White River Canyon, but everything above 6,500' was engulfed in storm clouds. The aircraft was only able to climb to 6,000'.

Frank McGinness, in the parking lot, heard the helicopter approaching, long before it finally appeared.

After the Huey landed, Lt. Col. Mullen emerged and made his way towards Base Operations.

"You can't get any worse conditions for flying a helicopter," he remarked to reporters.[28] As the pilot continued walking, Frank sidled up to him.

"Do you know anything?" he asked. "I'm one of the parents."[29]

"I'll tell you this," said the colonel, "I flew in Vietnam—many, many missions—under gunfire, but that was the most scared I've ever been in my life. We hit a wind gust that flipped our chopper 360°. That's when we came down."

~12:21 P.M
WEST MORAINE
WHITE RIVER CANYON

Swicegood could vouch for the abysmal lack of visibility. He had been following a compass bearing of 43° when he walked, blindly, right off a cornice that divided Palmer Glacier from White River Canyon. He tumbled about fifty feet down the slope.

Lillywhite had checked Swicegood's fall.[30] Boucher, directly behind Lillywhite, had seen his friend go into arrest mode and mirrored the maneuver, stopping Swicegood's continued descent.[31] As the two remained fixed in place, climbers from Craig's rope team came to render assistance.

Henderson and Craig carefully walked to the edge of the cornice and peered over the brink. From Henderson's perspective, it looked as if Swicegood had tumbled down a portion of the canyon wall, into a large pile of wind-blown snow.[32] As Lillywhite and Boucher remained in their positions, the others set snow anchors, tied a secondary line into Lillywhite's, and began hauling Swicegood back up the slope.[33]

Back at Silcox Hut, Craig had quietly confided to his team that he had been having some trouble in recent months. Worried about having a panic attack, and not wanting to be a burden or hindrance, he had pawned the radio off on another member of his team. Members of Team 4 joked that they were in possession of a "Dysfunctional Mike."[34] Their radio and leader were both malfunctioning. Craig took the joke in stride but now, while assisting Swicegood, he was feeling useful at last.

Well, he thought to himself, *now we gotta go to work.*[35]

Code 1244   135

Looking down at the terrain surrounding his snowshoes, Henderson experienced a peculiar illusion. *Where's the edge?* he thought, in regard to the cornice. *Oh! There it is. No. Where'd it go?* He immediately understood how Swicegood had managed to walk clean off the cliff.[36]

~12:25 P.M.
LANDING ZONE (LZ)
WY'EAST DAY LODGE SOUTH PARKING LOT

Some of the PJs took notice of how ill Frank McGinness looked as he walked past. When they learned he was a parent of a missing student, they offered medical assistance. Frank politely declined, stating that he simply needed to lie down and get some sleep. He walked away, trying desperately not to slip on the ice and snow.[37]

12:35 P.M.
SILCOX HUT
PALMER SNOWFIELD

The Hasty Team found the small breach in the drafty wall of Silcox Hut.[38] Harder, Hall, Kelsey, and Schneider passed into the structure to get out of the wind. They stomped their boots on the glacial sand floor, scaring the ever-present mice.[39]

The group had taken three hours to descend 2,000 feet, and they were exhausted. Their goggles had iced over, cracked, and a couple had broken out of their frames. Hall had lost his overmit, and his exposed hand was pale. Schneider's coat had ridden up a little, and there was some frostnip visible along his lower back.

Kelsey was experiencing a slight burning sensation around his forearms and wanted to investigate. He removed his gloves and his inner polypropylene layer. Pushing up the sleeves of his parka, he could see rings of marble-colored skin just above his wrists. He tried to piece the puzzle together. His gloves had been pulled over the top of his parka sleeves, but while moving and helping to dig the bolt-hole earlier in the morning, his gloves had scrunched down, somewhat, permitting ice to accumulate around his wrists. Kelsey recognized what the burning rings meant—frostbite.[40]

Kelsey's stove was found in his pack, so they set about brewing some hot tea.[41]

Their headgear was so frozen that Harder and Schneider could stand theirs up in the corner of the hut.[42]

Safely extracted from White River Canyon, Swicegood gathered his thoughts and sought a parley with his rescuers. There was some debate over whether they should continue on to White River Glacier or return to Silcox Hut. Some in the group wished to descend the slope in which Swicegood had taken his tumble. Swicegood noted that the western edge of the canyon was heavily corniced and that the threat of avalanche was extremely high.[43] It had been impossible to tell, from his vantage point, where the floor of the canyon was located. He recommended returning to Silcox. The team agreed, seeking authorization from Wright and McClure.[44]

The members of Team 2 congregated around the entrance to the office spaces, waiting to see if Maslen would assign them another mission. Glenn, Harbour, Janeck, and Rich, had endured the full fury of the blizzard. Even when they sought shelter inside Number 8, the windshield had blown out, necessitating repairs. No one would have blamed them for wanting a break, but the Amigos were eagerly seeking another mission.

Janeck noticed a deputy was debriefing Summers. The consultant was explaining how the snow cave had been constructed.

"What equipment did they have?" Janeck interjected.[45] Summers answered the question. "So," Janeck continued. "They have a snow shovel?"

Summers explained that the shovel had blown away in the wind. He and Molly had come across the shovel after their sitting glissade and packed it out.

This revelation was met with some confusion and disdain from Janeck. The tool could have been used to keep the entrance tunnel clear, to dig an additional cave, and to help alleviate the cramped conditions in the primary shelter.[46]

The conversation turned to the hazards of descending Hood's South Side Route in blizzard conditions. In fair weather, it is easy to return to Timberline Lodge under a bright canopy of cobalt blue sky. The hotel is visible to climbers throughout the descent. In a storm, it is only natural to follow the fall-line down the mountain. This takes mountaineers on a southwesterly course, leading directly over the cliffs of Mississippi Head. Climbers know that the Lodge is due south—180°—from Crater Rock.[47] During foul weather, climbers deliberately compensate to the east during their descent. This is done to maintain a 180° heading as best as possible. Over-compensation during such a maneuver can send a team too far east, leading down onto the crevasse-strewn White River Glacier.[48] Since Goman's team was following a 160° bearing, rather than 180°, their direction had shifted to the southeast.

Janeck was discouraged. Rick Harder had made decisions up on the mountain that had confounded him. He was also not impressed with the consultant OES had hired.[49] Within minutes, however, Janeck received news that boosted his spirits. Jeffrey Youngbluth had agreed to add The Three Amigos to his team.

Team 5 was suited-up and awaiting mission tasking in a hallway.[50] In addition to Youngbluth, the team included: Jon Swails, Jan Nesbit, David Bourland, and David "Big A" Armstrong.[51] His nickname derived from the sheer size of his arms.[52] All five were PJs from the 304th ARRS. Maslen authorized the combined forces and Wright directed them to resupply The Hasty Team at Silcox Hut.

The men walked out of the building together, as cameramen filmed their progress. The PJs were dressed predominately in olive, while the Amigos remained easily recognizable in their blue parkas. Cameras continued filming as each volunteer climbed onto the back of the flatbed snowcat.[53] Amid a pile of supplies were backpacks, stocking caps, ski goggles, gloves, and food.[54]

Maneuvering himself over the pile, Janeck hunkered down with his back to the cab of the snowcat. He made room for his companions and their equipment.

Janeck had observed the Flyboys—helicopter pilots—interacting with the press, team leaders from PMR debating search strategies, and deputies trying to coordinate the unprecedented alpine circus. To Janeck, the chaos appeared to be the ultimate gathering of Type-A personalities, all jockeying for position and attempting to determine who was number one.[55]

Four PJs piled into the back as well. Youngbluth walked around the side of the cat to occupy the passenger seat. As soon as he closed the door, the tracked vehicle sped off and disappeared into the storm.[56]

With Harder's men already at Silcox Hut, Teams 3 and 4 to return there shortly, and Team 5 and The Amigos en route via a snowcat, all rescuers on the mountain would soon gather in the decrepit cabin.

Craig Petrie, of the Mt. Hood Ski Patrol, delivered the additional snowcat to Deputy Krebs. Wright and McClure were thrilled and wasted no time putting the new asset into operation.[57]

A break in the weather would need to occur for any real progress to be made. Maslen was concerned. Continuing to deploy teams, under present conditions, could result in rescuers rescuing rescuers...again.[58]

CHAPTER 15
THE THREE AMIGOS

The whiteout conditions had caused the termination of five SAR missions within seven hours. Two military helicopters had made it to the mountain, and both were currently grounded. McClure said to his colleagues that, once these Hueys were able to participate in the operation, some of the PJs would need to be aboard those aircraft.

He relayed this message over the radio, as five of the PJs were en route to Silcox Hut. The Bagger, who had arrived as a PMR volunteer, quickly shifted into his role as a military senior enlisted advisor. He volunteered to return to Base, along with David Armstrong. The two PJs would be on standby for Huey missions.[1]

~1:22 P.M.
SILCOX HUT
PALMER SNOWFIELD

The snowcat delivered The Three Amigos and Youngbluth's Team 5 to Silcox Hut, stopping only long enough to offload the provisions that were brought up to resupply the men within the cabin.

The driver turned his vehicle and headed northeast, slowly following the trail wands that Teams 3 and 4 had placed during their journey to the edge of the canyon.[2]

Rocky Henderson was trying to spot the next wand ahead when he spied the headlights of the snowcat, emerging through the storm. Some of the men rushed forward, waving their arms, to warn the driver to stop where he was; the men would come to him.[3]

Teams 3 and 4 boarded the vehicle, thankful to hitch a ride back to the safety of Silcox Hut.[4]

Harder and Armstrong had grabbed their gear and were headed out of the cabin, just as the men of Teams 3 and 4 entered the structure, exhausted and dehydrated. Boarding the cat, the two PJs began their return journey to Base.[5]

Inside the shelter, Youngbluth began strategizing. He understood where Swicegood had taken his unexpected tumble. If the PJs could board a cat and head 1,200 feet higher up than the fall site, there should be a safe passage down into White River Canyon from there. Once they were on the glacier, he and his men could search for the snow cave while descending the river of ice on foot.[6] Three men asked to join this line-up.[7]

Wright authorized Youngbluth to take these volunteers with him in a cat, but he had a separate mission for The Three Amigos.

When the second snowcat arrived, Youngbluth, his group of PJs, and Schneider, Swicegood, and Henderson climbed aboard. These men were now part of Team 5.

The Amigos—Rich, Janeck, and Harbour—were directed to head east, on foot. They were to travel along a 40° course, which would take them slightly higher up, to the moraine that separates Palmer from White River Canyon. There, a hopeful passage could be found down to the glacier. Only then could they begin looking for the snow cave.[8]

Mike Craig sat down in the hut, pleased to be out of the elements. His face was hurting.[9] His cheeks were pale, and he was feeling an intense tingling sensation. Between the bottoms of his glacier glasses and the top of his balaclava, ice crystals had formed on the tiny strips of exposed flesh. Those strips had frostnip as a result of exposure. His hands were warm, so he held them up to his cheeks, cautious not to rub the affected area.

Ignoring the pain, Craig did his best to participate in the discussion of various strategies. Given the head injury he had sustained months earlier, Craig believed he was doing alright and that no one, outside Team 4, had any inkling that he was experiencing decision-making difficulties. He could do really well with tasks he had been trained to do, but making quick decisions seemed an elusive endeavor.[10]

If he couldn't be out on a mission, he could at least entertain the troops with stories of his life. He was quite the charmer. His parents had taken his kid sister out of high school, and the trio had run away to join a circus. His sister sold cotton candy, his mother played the organ, and his father stayed just ahead of the circus, promoting the event and securing venues.[11] Craig had been left to run the family farm in Ridgefield, Washington.

~1:57 P.M.
BASE OPERATIONS
WY'EAST DAY LODGE

Deputy Krebs announced that a third snowcat was now available at the base of the Glade Trail, an old backcountry ski trail leading from Government Camp to Timberline Lodge. The driver, Scott Russell, would ascend 1,992 feet up the ski run, scanning the corridor for any sign of the missing climbing party.[12]

Deputies discussed activating the Crag Rats, a mountain rescue organization in the Columbia Gorge.[13] Policies and procedures concerning their potential activation were debated, but, in the end, PMR leaders advised that more resources were not the answer. Putting more people into the field, during a whiteout, would merely be placing more people in danger.[14] The deputies opted to keep the Rats tucked up their sleeve, as a wild card if needed.

~2:05 P.M.
WEST MORAINE
WHITE RIVER CANYON

Formed over the centuries, the areas bordering White River Canyon are comprised of boulders, rocks, and sediment pushed up laterally by the advancing White River Glacier. These moraines overlook the canyon, far below. Number 8 turned uphill, maintaining a safe distance away from the edge of the moraine.

With visibility hindered by the snowfall, Schneider volunteered to get out and hike ahead of Number 8. Snowshoeing in front of the cat, he acted as a scout for the driver, who maneuvered past the snow-covered rock outcroppings.[15]

Riding shotgun, Henderson could barely make out Schneider's figure. Part of the team's mission was to report back to Base what they could see down on White River Glacier, but Henderson could barely see outside the vehicle.[16]

As the cat crawled up the mountain, the PJs discussed details of Sum-

142   Ric Conrad

mers' debriefing. The elevation figure of 7,200', where the consultant estimated the snow cave to be, came into question. Since Fr. Goman's team had not carried an altimeter, it seemed odd to create SAR strategy based on one man's guess.[17]

2:20 P.M.
WEST MORAINE
WHITE RIVER CANYON

The Three Amigos reported that they were at 7,350'. They were maintaining their 40° course as best they could, and they had discovered a "first valley" nearby.[18] Confused as to what this could mean, McClure asked if they had dropped down into White River Canyon. The three men were standing near a cornice, with a significant drop-off, looking down to the glacier. They were advised to proceed with caution.

At last, a team was poised to explore the terrain hiding the snow cave.

~2:20 P.M.
WEST MORAINE
WHITE RIVER CANYON

Number 8 came to a halt, and Youngbluth directed the team to survey the area surrounding the vehicle. The weather was only growing worse.[19] *How was this possible?* Recent snow deposits were cast up into the air by heavy winds, periodically decreasing visibility even further.

The group agreed that visibility was so limited, there was no way for them to locate a passage down to the glacier.

Resigned, they climbed back aboard the cat and reported that they were beginning a retreat to Base. They would proceed along a southwesterly course until they intercepted Palmer chairlift and follow the cable lines downhill.[20]

2:33 P.M.
MEDIA ROOM
WY'EAST DAY LODGE

The Sheriff's department met briefly with the press.

"The weather is so bad," Deputy Krebs informed reporters, "that the teams can move only a few feet at a time. They are running into dangerous obstacles all the time. They have to be extremely careful, because the risks are really high."[21]

Wright listened carefully as Harbour provided a status report on the Three Amigos. For over thirty minutes, the trio had been encountering grueling conditions. They were forced to accept defeat. Visibility was fifteen feet, at best. They had very nearly fallen off a cornice.[22]

Wright studied the topographic map on the wall, wondering how far the drop-off was to the canyon at their elevation. He was not pleased with his findings—*400 feet*. He had to take a moment to absorb this disappointment. Bending to the inevitable, he directed the Amigos to retreat to Silcox Hut.[23]

A report from the Hut stated the storm's ceiling was beginning to lift.[24] The sheriff's department lost no time in coordinating with officials from the 304th ARRS. *How soon could we have birds in the air?*

As Team 5 arrived back at Base, Youngbluth learned he would be one of two PJs assigned to a preliminary helicopter flight over White River Glacier. Youngbluth debriefed with Krebs, McClure, and Wright before readying himself for the next mission.

Deputy Krebs, Lt. Col. David Mullen, and Maj. Charles Jones walked outside. Looking up at the mountain's southern slopes, they noticed visibility had, indeed, lifted. They could even see Silcox Hut.[25] Krebs authorized the pilots to begin start-up procedures while he tracked down the whereabouts of Ralph Summers.

The pilots knew the momentary window of clear visibility wouldn't last long. Any information Krebs could provide would greatly assist them in determining where to hover and scan for signs of life.

In a nearby office, Harder contacted Dr. William Long in Portland, to discuss what to do with any patients they discovered.[26]

"I want them to be brought here," the doctor remarked, referring to Emanuel Hospital. "I don't care if they look like they are dead. I want to give them a try."[27]

The Bagger also called the disaster unit at Providence Hospital, notifying them that they were going to be receiving hypothermic patients, and these patients would require bypass rewarming.[28]

The cold and exhausted Amigos entered the shelter, to a warm reception from other SAR teams inside. Harbour noted that visibility, at these lower elevations, was lifting. Winds had dropped, mercifully, down to around twenty-five mph.[29]

The Amigos were discouraged. They had been battling the elements all day, with nothing to show for their efforts. Even while removing their gear, they were trying to think of ways to make a further contribution.

Miles away, Dee Zduniak had been oblivious to the search and rescue efforts occurring up on the mountain. She had left the school's climbing team above Palmer Glacier and had driven home. Now, her boyfriend informed her that the team she had accompanied was missing. Zduniak immediately volunteered to participate in the SAR efforts.[30]

Rich and Janeck fell into conversation with Mark Kelsey, who'd been on The Hasty Team. Kelsey had been waiting in the cabin for over three hours. The men discussed the breaks in the ferocity of the wind. There were glimpses of fair visibility.[31] If they could just be in a position, overlooking the White River region, during such a moment of clarity, they might be able to provide Wright and McClure with some detailed observations. To do this, they'd need to remain idle for a while, and it would be wiser to maintain such a vigil in the safety and warmth of a snowcat with a functioning heater.

The men radioed Base with their proposal, which was readily approved.[32] Number 8 was already en route back to Silcox Hut. McClure authorized the Amigos and Kelsey to deploy as soon as the snowcat arrived.

Aboard the Huey were pilots, Mullen and Jones, and flight engineer, Sgt. Carpenter. Directly behind them came two PJs, Jeff Youngbluth and Jan Nesbit.[33] Deputy Krebs requested that Ralph Summers board the aircraft as well.[34] To make room for him, military personnel removed a hoist, leaving it in the parking lot.[35] Visibility appeared to be improving, but wind speeds remained unpredictable.[36]

Rocky Henderson watched the helicopter taking off from the LZ. The raw recruit was heading home to get some sleep. Starting his truck, he realized that if this helicopter mission failed to turn up any new leads, the students would spend a second night in the snow cave. Henderson was deeply concerned.[37]

The helicopter flew east to White River Canyon, proceeding up the eastern moraine. The pilots encountered whiteout conditions at 7,000'. Cautiously, Mullen maneuvered the Huey, nudging it up the mountain. Exposed rock clusters, along the ridge, came in and out of view. Mullen used these outcroppings like makeshift trail wands. He kept the aircraft as steady as possible, given the wind conditions, so Summers could inspect the terrain below.

Around 7,600', colossal snow cornices came into view, clinging to the edge of the canyon wall. Around 8,400', Mullen was unable to spot any more rock outcroppings, making it extremely difficult to gauge the distance between his aircraft and the mountain itself.[38]

Mullen slowly backed sideways down the ridge. He performed this maneuver gently until the aircraft emerged below the whiteout.

Maneuvering to the west side of the canyon, Mullen inched his way up this ridge, once again using rock outcroppings along the moraine as a guide. Only reaching 7,600' this time, the pilot recognized the reality of the situation. There was simply no reliable method of determining a safe reference point. Turning his aircraft south, he retreated from the slopes and returned to the LZ.[39]

CHAPTER 16
VOICES IN THE DARK

4:30 P.M.
LANDING ZONE (LZ)
WY'EAST DAY LODGE SOUTH PARKING LOT

The Huey returned to the LZ. As the main rotor blades began to slow, the cargo door swung open. Summers, Youngbluth, and Nesbit exited the aircraft and made a beeline for Base Operations. The men knew they owed Wright an assessment of what they had seen from the air. The consultant now believed the snow cave was situated on the west side of the canyon, instead of the east. With so much snow accumulation, however, the terrain had changed considerably since he and Molly had departed the shelter.[1]

This helicopter flight had returned at the optimal time. The 304th ARRS had determined that weather conditions were too poor for flying and grounded their birds.[2]

4:42 P.M.
WEST MORAINE
WHITE RIVER CANYON

The snowcat carrying Kelsey and the Amigos had reached 8,100', on the west moraine.[3] Kelsey reported limited visibility as the men looked out over the canyon. It seemed as if a clear picture of the area was never going to materialize. Wright advised the group that the missing climbers might be holed-up on the western edge of White River Glacier, just below the men, rather than across the canyon. Acknowledging this update, the cat was used to grade off a level platform in which to park the tracked vehicle.[4]

Craig Petrie delivered another snowcat to Deputy Krebs. PMR planned to ensure at least four or five SAR teams were always operating in the field. With five tracked vehicles employed, additional resources would be dispatched up the slopes as weary workers retreated.[5]

Entering Base Operations, Petrie informed McClure and Wright that some of White River Canyon was visible from the parking lot. The men discussed options, focusing on answering the critical question, *what can be done before sunset?*[6]

Ouzel Outfitters had invited about a dozen staff members of Timberline Lodge to spend the day rafting on the Deschutes River, hoping the employees would enjoy their experience and promote river rafting to patrons of the Lodge. The weather had been relatively rainy all day, and even when the sun did emerge, it had been cold. The group walked into The Rainbow Tavern, a rustic establishment just a few blocks from the river.

Scooting around the red seats in a spacious booth, the group was soon enjoying a meal and a round of drinks.

A television was mounted on the wall, and the news came on. A major network news anchor was informing the nation that a group of school kids were holed-up in a snow cave, somewhere on Mount Hood.

Jon Tullis, Judy O'Regan, and their colleagues watched the broadcast intently as an overview of the SAR operation was explained. The staff was stunned. It wasn't unusual to see their inn on the local news, but this was national. The story was big, and the whole country was now following it.[7]

We shouldn't be here, O'Regan thought to herself.[8]

The parking lot came into view, and his first thought was—*pandemonium*. Ky Krank cautiously maneuvered his Volkswagen around knots of reporters, cameramen, news trucks, and rescue workers. The south end of the lot had been turned into a landing zone, and two military helicopters dominated the scene.

Locating an available parking space, Krank exited the vehicle and headed through the chaos. At forty-four, he was a program manager in the avionics division of Tektronix in Beaverton. He had left work as early as he could and drove up to the mountain, filled with energy and hope.

Walking through the front entrance to the Lodge, he passed a couple, clearly parents of a missing teen. Though Krank had been in PMR for over five years and had been a team leader for four, encounters with relatives of the missing never ceased to be emotionally wrenching.

As he arrived in Base Operations, Krank checked-in with McClure. "I might have a team for you," said McClure, "real soon."[9]

5:43 P.M.
WEST MORAINE
WHITE RIVER CANYON

Kelsey and the Amigos had been waiting patiently in the snowcat for an hour, perched on a crest that could provide a fair view of White River Canyon. Hopes that a moment of clear visibility would materialize eventually evaporated, so the cat turned around and began the journey down to Base.[10]

6:00 P.M.
PARKING LOT
WY'EAST DAY LODGE

Deputy Mike Hattan pulled his patrol car into the parking lot. Putting on his coat, he noticed large snow berms surrounding the lower section of the lot. An ODOT snowplow had cleared the site, transforming it into a landing zone. Looking up at the mountain, he had mixed feelings. When he first learned of the lost climbing party, he had feared the worst. Teenagers, ill-equipped and exposed to the elements, would surely perish. When he heard there was a snow cave, a wave of relief had washed over him. There was hope.

Hattan's training as a SAR coordinator had begun eight years earlier when he was only twenty-six. Since that time, he had gained a considerable amount of experience. He had been instructed to meet Lt. Hanners, at the Lodge, at 6:00 p.m.[11]

Hanners and Hattan entered the building and made their way upstairs to Base Operations. They were brought up to speed on weather forecasts and manpower reports.

Lt. Hanners assigned Deputy Krebs as the official liaison with the families of the missing climbers, a job he'd been performing all day. Krebs was to see to it that families were provided food and lodging and that they were not to be bothered by members of the press.[12] Next, a deputy was assigned to man the entrance to Base Operations, ensuring only authorized personnel were granted access.[13]

Deputy Hattan secured more telephone lines for the office, as well as for the designated media room, one floor below. He helped prepare a briefing room, conveniently adjacent to Base, for all incoming SAR volunteers.[14]

McClure wanted to send a group up the far side of the canyon.[15] Team 6 was formed, and their mission was to get as high as possible along the eastern ridge of the canyon, in the hopes that they could peer over the edge and survey the glacier. If they could find safe passage down to the ice, then they were instructed to do so.[16]

Ky Krank would be joined by Matt Nauman and Jim Wright, both of PMR.[17] Ralph Summers asked to join their ranks. He had volunteered to be on several teams throughout the day, but each request was denied.[18] Leadership knew this was a specific, all-night mission, and they wanted Summers close at hand.

Craig Petrie volunteered to drive Team 6 to Mt. Hood Meadows in the PMR Suburban.[19] There, they'd be picked up by a snowcat driven by Lew Russell.

Russell, founder of Tidewater Barge Lines, ran a family business renting snowcats. Lew and his son, Scott, were not members of PMR nor employees of RLK & Company, but they were called when traction vehicles were needed in high-altitude rescue operations on the mountain.[20]

7:00 P.M.
BASE OPERATIONS
WY'EAST DAY LODGE

McClure was scheduled to provide a chemistry lecture at Portland State University in the morning. Confident that the snow cave would be found by then, he handed PMR's full operational reins over to the capable hands of Barry Wright. Saying his goodbyes to his wife, who chose to stay, McClure walked out of the building and caught a ride back to Portland with Steve Glenn.[21]

John Bridges roused Frank McGinness from slumber. John prodded his friend to go downstairs to eat before the dining room closed for the night. Frank, still feeling under the weather, tried to brush off the request, but John was adamant.

Relenting, Frank rose, ran his fingers through his hair, and walked down to the dining facility. As soon as he walked in, he was flagged down by half a dozen men, seated at a table. Frank recognized them as the PJs who had asked him if he required medical attention. They invited him to join them for dinner.

As a former staff sergeant, Frank was glad to hear some of the military stories and rescue tales the men shared at the table. It fed his hope that the operation, currently underway, would have a happy ending as well. Following the meal, one of the PJs invited Frank to accompany them so that they could show him the grid coordinates for tomorrow's search operation.

"You know how to read a map?" the PJ teased.[22]

"Oh, yeah," Frank replied. "I can get lost, too," he said. This bit of humor brought a round of laughter from the assembled men.

Lew Russell and his snowcat arrived. Without hesitation, Naumann and Wright began loading their packs into the back of the cat.

Krank was not happy. He and his Team 6 had been waiting at Meadows for around ninety minutes. The men knew the sun would set at 8:26 p.m., so they didn't have much time to climb to the eastern rim of the canyon safely. They'd still have to find a suitable location in which to peer down onto the glacier, hoping for a window of fair visibility.[23] Krank climbed into the shotgun seat and secured his lap belt, just as the vehicle lurched forward.

If weather conditions proved too brutal, they could remain sequestered inside the cat. If the weather improved, they were prepared to spend the night outside.[24] McClure had been very specific with this team. He wanted men that could stay out until the following morning, a team that could remain autonomous and move quickly if needed.[25]

Krank couldn't have asked for better teammates for such a mission.

Naumann and Wright had recently returned from climbing Aconcagua, the highest mountain in South America. Krank was optimistic about his team and its mission. He was with men he could trust, climbers who were extremely focused and experienced.[26]

Deputies Krebs and Kennel's shift ended, but they chose to remain at the resort to continue working. Lt. Hanners and Deputy Hattan, who had arrived two hours earlier, now became the officers-in-charge of the search efforts.[27]

The lieutenant publicly called off the ground search for the night.[28] PMR personnel continued to work quietly, avoiding members of the press.

Lt. Stillman telephoned Lt. Hanners. Captain Grolbert had directed Stillman to relieve Hanners by 8:00 a.m.

Hanners informed his counterpart that the precise location of the snow cave was still unknown. Although search efforts for the night had been halted, he intended to remain on the mountain until the missing party was found. It was unnecessary, in Hanners opinion, for Stillman to proceed to the mountain. Stillman agreed, indicating he'd keep an eye on ongoing developments.[29]

Hanners contacted Captain Grolbert, providing a status report. The captain advised his subordinate to contact him, should any more resources be required.[30]

Grolbert phoned Chief Deputy Bradshaw. The two agreed to meet at Wy'East Day Lodge in the morning.

As the sun set, it became apparent that the operation would take longer than anyone anticipated.[31] *How am I going to feed these guys?* Cheryl Maslen wondered. To her immense relief, Casey Marley, manager of Clackamas County Emergency Services, indicated that this was no problem.[32]

Marley began working with the director of public affairs for Timberline Lodge, to ensure lodging and meals were provided for all the rescue workers. The Lodge would, of course, do everything they could to accommodate a successful rescue operation. Marley also contacted the Red Cross, who agreed to dispatch a food van to the parking lot.[33]

8:45 P.M.
EASTERN RIM
WHITE RIVER CANYON

The sun had set, and Krank was feeling anxious. Light was fading, and he desperately wanted a view down into that canyon. During a break in visibility, he directed Russell to stop the vehicle. The team glanced at the altimeter—7,400'.[34]

"Let's give it a shot," Krank exclaimed. "Jump out, and we'll go take a look."[35]

Forgoing roping up, Team 6 hiked west, directly into the wind. No snow was falling, but gusts of wind kicked up snow all around them. Even though Krank had a hat, helmet, balaclava, and eye protection, his face grew cold quickly.

The team inched towards the edge of the canyon. Naumann approached first. Krank and Wright followed but fanned out cautiously. Falling through a cornice was a genuine concern.[36] Krank used his ski poles to help brace himself against the wind. A decent view of the canyon was not forthcoming.[37]

Krank retrieved his radio from deep inside his clothing, seeking authorization for his team to rappel down the canyon wall. With the high risk of avalanche, this request was denied.[38]

Disappointed, Krank directed the team to return to the snowcat. They'd have Lew Russell transport them a little higher.[39]

On the opposite side of the canyon, Scott Russell halted his snowcat at 8,100'. Team 7 was on board, led by Larry McDaniels of PMR.[40] His colleagues included Les Hedquist, a recent addition to PMR, and Pete Rue, a member of the Mt. Hood Ski Patrol.[41] Russell kept the engine running, as this team had been told to spend the night in the cat.

Teams 6 and 7, poised on opposing sides of the canyon, began providing Barry Wright with hourly updates.

Don Penater and his mother were watching television news updates. Marion was still holed-up in a snow cave, somewhere on the mountain. Although their mother was upset, Don privately chuckled. *Everyone in the cave will be somewhat cold and undoubtedly wet. Might teach em' a lesson,* he thought. It was getting late, his sister was safe in a shelter, so Don hugged his mother before heading back to his own home.

"I'll come down here bright and early tomorrow morning," he assured her. "We'll have coffee and figure out what we're going to do."[42]

True to their word, the PJs that had treated Frank to dinner, had adjourned to the lounge for a drink and conversation. There, they outlined their search patterns for the following morning. Frank observed as one man traced his finger over a map of the mountain. Grid coordinates were provided, weather forecasts were discussed, and hopes were abundant.[43]

When the men finished their informal briefing, Frank shook their hands and thanked them for their time and information. Frank's stomach cramps, which he had been enduring since Sunday night, outright disappeared.

Deciding to stretch his legs, he walked out the main doors of the inn. He was suddenly accosted by a handful of reporters, pressing him for information concerning the search operation.

"Hey, guys," Frank replied. "Leave me alone. I don't know anything. There is no information at this point."[44]

Team 6 was traveling up a particularly steep section of deep snow when the snowcat suddenly got stuck. Lew Russell tried to back the vehicle out, but this, somehow, only managed to make things worse. Backing again, while simultaneously turning slightly, the cat began to tilt to the right. The driver cautiously maneuvered the vehicle, which leaned even farther.

Krank, riding shotgun, found himself in an unenviable position. *Are we going to tumble?* he thought. *I'm on the downhill side of this thing.* He checked to ensure his belt was secure but didn't want to say anything, for fear of disturbing Russell's concentration. As the snowcat slowly leveled out, achieving the necessary traction, Krank found himself very impressed by the driver's skills.[45]

The altimeter read 7,600'. Team 6 had been transported as high as Russell could take them. The men exited the vehicle, thanking their driver for the ride. Russell began his descent to Meadows.

11:00 P.M.
BASE OPERATIONS
WY'EAST DAY LODGE

Hanners, Hattan, Krebs, and Wright were planning the following day's search strategy. The Hueys were scheduled to lift off—weather permitting—at 5:00 a.m. PMR Teams 6 and 7 were already positioned on opposing sides of the canyon.

Reporters had found Rick Harder, who was confident that the weather would turn in their favor. The Bagger informed the press that, come tomorrow morning, he and his team would have the students rescued by 7:00 a.m., and throw "a hell of a party by 7:30."[46]

After Harder departed, Deputy Hattan had a task for the press.

"I want Phil Volker," said the deputy, referring to a specific meteorologist he trusted from Portland's Channel 6 News.[47] One of the reporters contacted Volker, who agreed to speak with the deputy over the phone.

"I need to know what the weather's doing," Hattan said. "Tell me what's going on."

~11:14 P.M.
BASE OPERATIONS
WY'EAST DAY LODGE

Family members met with Deputy Krebs to hear about search plans for the following morning. When asked about the weather forecast, Krebs relayed what the meteorologist had explained. Predictions meant nothing. A mountain the size of Mount Hood can often alter the environmental conditions—creating its own weather.[48]

"If we could get a hole in the weather, so I could leave overnight clothes and food, I would not feel alarmed," Krebs explained, talking about dropping supplies to the missing climbing party. "Under the circumstances, it's going to be tough, in or out of the weather. Remember, you're talking about sitting in lukewarm water for two days. Outside, it's a hundred times worse."[49]

He was asked about a safe return of the students.

"I can't promise you anything," Krebs confessed, "but if everything is done right, and we believe it is, they're going to stay in that cave. They're going to be cold, but they're going to be safe. They're going to be shivering, but they're going to be alive."[50]

A break in the weather finally arrived. Skies began to clear.[51] Wind speeds dropped, and a glimpse of the upper slopes, illuminated by starlight, could be seen from Timberline Lodge.

Team 6 was hiking along a ridge at 8,500'. The air was crisp. Passing behind natural windbreaks, there were moments of complete silence.[52]

Making his way around a snow hummock, Krank stopped in his tracks. From somewhere in the darkness, he heard cries for help—faint pleas for assistance, accompanied by the sound of someone beating tin cans.[53] He waited.

There it was again.

A male voice, faint and muffled, down in the canyon. The breeze was coming from the west, so it seemed plausible that voices were carrying on the wind.[54] Krank trotted over to his companions.

"Did either one of you hear anything?" he asked.[55]

"Yeah, we heard something, said Wright. "We don't know what it is."

"Probably one of the other crews down there," Naumann added.

"Well, I don't know," Krank turned towards the canyon. "I thought I heard banging."

Although Wright and Naumann heard voices, only Krank had heard the banging. Team 6 informed Base Operations.[56]

Making their way over to the precipice, the men peered down into the canyon.[57]

Nothing but darkness.

Maslen, Wright, and Deputy Hattan greeted Krank's transmission as good news. Hattan felt a rush of adrenaline. *Okay*, he thought. *We've got something! Let's wake people up!*[58] Maslen felt, for the first time, that they had a clue that somebody was out there, alive. Recognizing that winds can carry voices, PMR would need to create new teams to investigate this promising lead.[59]

~11:40 P.M.
CHALET ROOM
TIMBERLINE LODGE

In a basement room, filled with bunk beds, Lillywhite and nine other rescue workers were trying to get some sleep.[60] The phone rang, startling the group. Wright was on the other end of the line, informing the men that the weather was clearing, cries for help had been heard, and two more teams were to be dispatched up the mountain.

Wright made one thing perfectly clear. Only experienced SAR personnel were to be permitted on these two teams. As the newest trainee in PMR, Lillywhite would have to remain behind. Lillywhite accepted this fact but headed across the street to make himself available.[61]

11:44 P.M.
BASE OPERATIONS
WY'EAST DAY LODGE

Wright contacted Larry McDaniels, who was on the west side of the canyon. *Is there any chance members of Team 7 are making noise?*

McDaniels confirmed that he and his team had been quiet. If Team 6 was hearing voices in the dark, they were not emanating from Team 7.[62]

WEDNESDAY

May 14, 1986

Ric Conrad

CHAPTER 17
FIREFLIES

Not wanting to disturb his roommate, Frank McGinness had been quietly staring into the darkness. Suddenly, something caught his attention. He rushed to the window, surprised that he could see pretty far up the mountain.

"John," Frank called out to his slumbering friend. "I think I see a snowcat."[1]

"You can't see a cat," John mumbled, rolling over. "You're imagining things."

Frank roused his friend, dragging him to the window to see for himself. Pointing up the mountain, Frank asked him to verify what he was seeing.

"I'll be damned," John agreed. "It is a snowcat."

The men were observing Team 7, exploring the western rim of White River Canyon. Frank and John watched for some time. The vehicle's headlights resembled fireflies slowly floating in space.

Although interested in what he was seeing, John pleaded with his friend to get some sleep.

In Room 8, Mar Goman and Diana Yates were exhausted, yet unable to sleep.[2] Mar's thoughts were racing. She kept thinking about mountains she and Tom had climbed together, early on in their marriage. Mar still enjoyed hiking, but her mountaineering pursuits had ceased years ago.[3] She was no stranger to exhaustion and had recognized it in Summers. He was obviously drained. Diana and Mar had offered to share their accommodations so that Ralph could get some rest.

The room contained one queen-sized bed, and they took turns sleeping in the room.[4]

~12:05 A.M.
BASE OPERATIONS
WY'EAST DAY LODGE

In addition to their standard climbing equipment and provisions, Team 8 carried five climbing ropes, sixteen wool blankets, six tarps, and several flares.[5] Consisting of Harbour, Janeck, Rich, Kelsey, and Blailock, Team 8 asked if snowshoes were needed at higher elevations. Teams 6 and 7, the two groups that were already up the mountain, recommended crampons instead. Skies were clear, wind gusts had dropped to 30 mph, and temperatures remained below freezing.[6]

Lillywhite's willingness to be available, even though he'd only had one day of experience with PMR, didn't go unnoticed. He was being assigned to Team 9, under the leadership of Mike Craig. Marc Sellers and Dave McNeil were also added to the team.[7]

In response to reports of overhearing voices in the dark, Wright had created Teams 8 and 9. Both groups were to meet at Mt. Hood Meadows. Once there, they'd be transported up the eastern rim of White River Canyon.

Loading up the PMR Suburban with a couple akja sleds, meant for transporting injured climbers, Team 9 piled into the vehicle and began their twenty-minute drive to Meadows.

Mike "No Bozos" Craig had been awake for nearly twenty-four hours. He closed his eyes for a quick catnap during the drive, feeling the burn of frostnip on his cheeks.[8]

~12:15 A.M.
EASTERN RIM
WHITE RIVER CANYON

Team 6 spotted boot prints around 8,200', near the eastern border of White River Canyon. They would investigate these tracks, hoping they could lead them to the snow cave.[9]

Team 7, higher up and on the opposing side of the canyon, confirmed that they could see the headlamps of Team 6.[10]

~12:25 A.M.
TIMBERLINE LODGE

Deputy Hattan, like others, was suffering from insomnia. His shift had ended at midnight. After a quick shower, he tried to get some much-needed sleep. He stared up at the ceiling. Minutes passed.

Recognizing that he wasn't going to be able to fall asleep, he got up, put his uniform back on, and headed back to Base.[11]

Although he had three years of PMR experience under his belt, Tom Stringfield still considered himself fairly new to the organization. A thirty-nine-year-old civil engineer, he was now being asked to join the SAR effort.

He'd started climbing mountains over ten years ago, viewing Oregon from the top of The Three Sisters, Broken Top, Mount Washington, and Mount Hood.

After preparing a few easy meals to add to his backpack, he loaded his equipment into his Mercedes and headed up to the mountain.[12]

The headlamp batteries were having difficulty in the intense cold, causing frequent swap-outs as their illumination continued to dim and flicker like fireflies. Team 6 finally decided that only the man in the lead position would employ a headlamp; the rest would merely follow their companion. This would save both time and battery life.

Ky Krank looked up, catching a glimpse of stars. He commented that it would be nice to be inside a snowcat, even if it *didn't* have a windshield. The men all chuckled.

There was no talk about digging a snow cave or erecting a tent. After hearing the voices in the dark, Team 6 was motivated to keep moving.[13]

The front end of Scott Russell's snowcat lurched forward and came to an abrupt stop.[14] Russell radioed Deputy Hattan and Barry Wright, informing them of his predicament.[15] Around 8,300', along the eastern edge of Palmer Glacier, the cat had suddenly broken through a hidden crevasse.[16]

Team 7 stood at the western edge of the upper region of White River Glacier.[17] Here, at 9,000', McDaniels could look up and see the mammoth snow cornices along the canyon's western border.[18] Finally, a team had found safe passage down to the ice. The men began descending the glacier in a lengthy, zigzag pattern.

Wright and Maslen were consulting the map of the mountain on the wall, shifting colored pushpins and using grease pencils to match the elevation marks to SAR teams' locations. Team 8 was directed to aim their headlamps uphill to allow Team 6 to get a fix on their position.[19]

Team 7 wanted to know if Summers and Schula had encountered any vegetation during their trek from the snow cave to Mt. Hood Meadows. A deputy departed to wake the consultant.[20]

While they waited, Maslen informed Wright that Scott Russell had managed to safely extract the front end of his snowcat from the hidden crevasse.[21]

When Summers arrived in the office, he recalled seeing lichen on some rocks, roughly forty-five minutes after departing the snow cave. An hour or so after his departure, he and Schula had encountered trees. Summers reasoned they must have been around 5,800' to 6,000' at that time. Recalling his journey through dangerous conditions once more, he now believed the snow cave was situated between 8,400' and 8,800'.[22]

Team 8 found an ideal position around 8,600', along the eastern edge of White River Canyon. It was a small spur of rock and ice, jutting out from the canyon wall. Once sunrise illuminated the canyon, it should be the perfect perch in which to view a large swath of the glacier.[23]

Kelsey, Blailock, and the Amigos began discussing possibilities. If any of the missing students and faculty took a turn outside the snow cave, they would be unable to see the SAR workers in the dark. Team 8 had five hand-held illuminating parachute flares in their possession. These could serve as a beacon for the missing climbers.[24]

A flare can shoot high—over 700 feet—into the cold mountain air, producing a brilliant white flame. The beacon will burn for about thirty seconds, slowly descending by means of a parachute. It can illuminate the surrounding terrain while traveling aloft with the prevalent winds.

Harbour took a few steps away from his companions to ignite one of the flares. He held it in one hand and prepared to pull its cord with the other. He yanked on the string.

Nothing.

The team produced another flare and Harbour repeated the procedures.

Nothing.

They either had faulty flares, or the wind affected the ignition process.

The radio waves started crackling with transmissions as several messages were aired, one after the other. Team 7, exploring the upper western reaches of the canyon, thought Team 8 had discovered the snow cave and began heading towards their position.[25]

2:45 A.M.
EASTERN RIM
WHITE RIVER CANYON

Team 6 had finished sweeping the eastern rim of the canyon, from 9,000' down to 8,000'.[26] Their mission was considered complete, and the team had a set rendezvous time with a snowcat. Knowing that his radio would soon lose power, Krank radioed Base Operations with a final summary of what they had experienced. Authorities thanked Team 6 for their information and requested they check-in upon their return.[27] Krank, Nauman, and Wright, cold and tired, headed to their designated rendezvous point.[28]

3:00 A.M.
BASE OPERATIONS
WY'EAST DAY LODGE

Wright and Deputies Krebs and Hattan understood that some members of PMR had business commitments and would need to head home soon. Maslen added that many volunteers were coping with exhaustion. There was still a vast amount of surface area needing to be searched after sunrise.[29]

Seattle Mountain Rescue (SMR), the Crag Rats, the Alpinees, and other mountain rescue organizations were discussed: their capabilities, specialties, limitations, and geographic headquarters.[30] Because of SMR's certifications with the Mountain Rescue Association, Maslen held the organization in high regard.[31]

Following this meeting, Krebs contacted the Alpinees as well as the Crag Rats. Both organizations are based out of Hood River. Both groups were asked to have their volunteers muster at Wy'East Day Lodge at 5:00 a.m.[32]

Deputy Hattan contacted Clinton Peterson of the Mt. Hood Snowmobile Club, asking him if he had access to a Tucker Sno-Cat.[33]

3:05 A.M.
WHITE RIVER GLACIER

Using the light from their headlamps, Team 7 came across tracks emanating from above and headed downhill.[34] McDaniels alerted Wright. *What elevation are you at?* 7,300'. *How many distinct boot prints are visible?* Two. *Are these the same prints Team 6 discovered earlier?* No. *Using a compass, does the bearing of these prints match the one Summers used after exiting the snow cave?* Yes.

Summers, who was in Base Operations, overheard these transmissions and felt positive these were the tracks he and Molly had created during their descent from the snow cave.[35]

Wright, Maslen, Summers, and the deputies congregated around the radio and waited, as Team 7 followed these tracks uphill.

3:28 A.M.
UPPER TERMINAL, TEXAS CHAIRLIFT
MT. HOOD MEADOWS SKI AREA

At 7,300', Team 6 had their headlamps on, facing south. They were waiting for Lew Russell to appear in his snowcat, to transport them down to Meadows. Twin pinpoints of light below grew steadily in size. It was Russell's headlights.[36]

As soon as Krank entered the vehicle, he realized there were two passengers inside—Craig Petrie and a reporter. Krank was not pleased to see a reporter. On many occasions, Krank had witnessed journalists providing the public with inaccurate information.

Petrie began asking several questions. *Where had the team searched? What did they find? Tell us more about these voices in the dark.*

As a former pilot in Vietnam, Krank's military training was kicking in. He felt his team needed to keep their facts, thoughts, and impressions clear and unfiltered, for their final debriefing with authorities in Base Operations.[37] It was best to remain silent.

"No comment," Krank replied impassively.[38]

3:33 A.M.
WHITE RIVER GLACIER

The boot prints Team 7 had been so diligently tracking disappeared at 7,700'.[39] McDaniels' teammates gathered around him, their collective headlamps illuminating the terrain ahead.

The men were instructed to continue following the last known heading and hope for the best.[40]

3:58 A.M.
EASTERN RIM
WHITE RIVER CANYON

Team 8 was unable to contact Team 7. Both groups were able to communicate with Base. Team 8, at 8,600' on the eastern rim, blew their whistles, asking if Team 7 could hear sounds. They could not. Team 7, down in the canyon, inquired whether their counterparts could see their headlamps. The answer, again, was no.[41]

Mark Kelsey and his colleagues on Team 8 huddled together and stomped their feet to remain warm. They were still on the spur along the eastern rim of the canyon, their arms crossed across their chests, their backs to the wind. Their ice axes and ski poles were stuck in the snow nearby. They could communicate, but in elevated voices, just enough to hear one another over the din of the wind.

In the darkness, they heard it. A voice? *Help!* Popping their headlamps on, team members looked at one another. With their faces obscured by balaclavas, only their eyes were visible behind ski goggles. Kelsey studied the questioning eyeballs of Harbour, Janeck, Rich, and Blailock. Everyone appeared to have heard the sound.[42]

Team members fanned out and searched the nearby area. As Janeck rounded a snow hummock, he sank his ice axe into the snow and lurched forward a bit. The noise this movement created was eerily similar to the *scream* in the distance. Janeck removed the axe and repeated the motion, in an effort to recreate the sound. *Yes, that does resemble a scream.* He wondered if such sounds had been interpreted as voices.[43]

Regrouping on the prominence, Team 8 compared notes. Kelsey believed he came up with the most feasible explanation for the cry for help. He showed the group his ski poles, which had an inner and outer tubular shaft. They were lined with boreholes, with a push-button detent mechanism that enabled the user to lengthen or shorten the pole's length. Kelsey stuck his poles in the snow and began slowly rotating them. As the winds, whipping over the slopes, passed through the open boreholes, the sound it created resembled anything from a piccolo, to actual voices.[44]

4:00 A.M.
SKI PATROL HALLWAY
WY'EAST DAY LODGE

Family and friends of the missing climbers began to gather and share what little information they had concerning the weather. They congregated near the entrance to Base Operations, sipping coffee while straining to overhear conversations between rescue workers. People were desperate for information—reliable intelligence.

The weather forecast called for partly cloudy skies on Wednesday, with a scattering of snow showers in the northern parts of the state. Winds would be coming from the west to northwest, 10 to 20 mph. The freezing level would be around 3,500 feet.[45]

Authorities in Base felt confident that the weather was relenting, and once the helicopters were airborne, the snow cave would be discovered. This would end the search portion, and workers could then commence with the rescue itself.

Deputy Hattan had been fielding questions by the growing crowd of reporters. *Would the weather hold? Would the children be rescued?* With kids of his own, the deputy suddenly had difficulty separating his duties from his emotions. At some point, the emotions took over. Tears stung his eyes, his ability to speak became strained, and the deputy quickly excused himself from the room.[46]

Mike Craig's Team 9 was at 7,500', on the eastern side of the glacier. Upon reaching 8,000', they would turn left and begin crossing the ice field.[47]

4:15 A.M.
BASE OPERATIONS
WY'EAST DAY LODGE

Deputy Kennel officially began another duty shift. He glanced around to get a better understanding of what assets were available. The officer in charge was Lt. Hanners. Deputy Krebs was Hanner's principal assistant, Deputy Hattan was serving as a liaison officer, while Kennel was tasked with manning the radio.[48]

Kennel learned that PMR Teams 6 through 9 had been working through the night, and others were suiting up to join in the effort. Some teams would depart from Mt. Hood Meadows while others would leave from Timberline.[49] Skies were, mercifully, continuing to clear.[50]

CHAPTER 18
THE FOG OF WAR

Al Radys had joined PMR years earlier, served as the organization's president, and had seen his share of troubles on the mountain. He had witnessed novice climbers, insufficiently dressed for the elements. Once, he witnessed a climber employing a tire iron as an ice axe.[1]

He assembled a small crew of men that were soon dubbed Team 10. This trio of volunteers consisted of himself, Tom Stringfield, and Allen O'Bannon.[2] They were asked to scout an upper bench above White River Canyon.[3] Team 6 had recommended this ramp be inspected as it matched the description of the steep snow slope in which Summers had dug the snow cave.[4]

Team 10 boarded a snowcat and departed Base, heading up to 9,000' or higher. Because of the ceaseless droning of the engine, very little conversation was held during the journey.[5]

As the long night was coming to an end, Base Operations started buzzing with activity.

Lt. Hanners contacted the command staff at the sheriff's office, requesting supplemental personnel to assist in the operation. He asked that the medical examiner be placed on standby.[6] The pilots from the 304th ARRS were ready to fly at first light.[7] Senior leaders stood with their arms crossed, leaning in towards one another, quietly discussing strategy.

Three members of the Alpinees walked in and were greeted by Wright. Gerald Donahue, Scott Walker, and Jim Holloway were well-rested and eager to contribute to the cause. Their organization had been formed in 1947 by four veterans of the 10th Mountain Division. After their duty in the Italian Alps, these regional heroes had returned home and created a rescue organization to serve the north side of Mount Hood. Wright, knowing these men were accomplished cross-country skiers, began studying the maps on the wall. *Where could the Alpinees be of assistance?*[8]

Not far behind this group, four members of the Crag Rats also reported for duty. They were all wearing their signature black-and-white, buffalo plaid wool shirts, a trademark of their organization since 1926. They stated that more of their troops were on the way.[9]

In the adjacent First Aid room, Harder had begun organizing a triage center. Cardiac medication, extra life packs, and stimulators, which he had requested from Providence Hospital, had arrived on site. Three PJs were prepared to man the triage center. The Bagger, sporting a five-o'clock shadow, excused himself to prepare for flight operations.[10]

~5:10 A.M.
TIMBERLINE LODGE

Frank McGinness had showered and dressed for the day at 3:30 a.m., unable to get more than a couple of hours of sleep. Now, he was surprisingly hungry. He hadn't eaten much at dinner with the PJs.[11]

Frank and John Bridges emerged from the inn. The morning stars flickered as the first signs of dawn lit the sky in soft pastels. He was amazed at how clear the weather had become.

John spied the Red Cross van in the parking lot, so the pair wandered over to see what options they had for an early breakfast. Soon, Frank's stomach was satisfied.

"Coffee and donuts never tasted so good," he remarked.[12] As Frank sipped his coffee, he grew concerned that the moisture in the outlying valleys might rise to form fogbanks. This might hamper the search efforts as much as yesterday's whiteout.

Barry Wright had fetched a hot cup of coffee from the van. He had been a long-time member of the Red Cross Damage Assessment Group and knew some of the volunteers that were handing out pastries.[13]

Cheryl Maslen took a trip out to the van as well. She procured a box of bologna sandwiches and small containers of spaghetti and beef stew, which had been warming under a heat lamp. She returned to Base Operations and distributed these meals. The heated, pressurized cans of food began exploding as the hungry volunteers opened them. Hearing this commotion, Maslen turned to see rescue workers, splattered with milled-wheat shrapnel. She glanced over at Wright, and the two shared a much-needed moment of stifled laughter.[14]

~5:15 A.M.
LANDING ZONE (LZ)
WY'EAST DAY LODGE SOUTH PARKING LOT

Mike Moffitt could see three military helicopters on the ground, side-by-side, on the uphill portion of the lot, while news helicopters were situated at the southern periphery of the marked-off landing zone. The twenty-eight-year-old landed his Bell 206 JetRanger helicopter at the southern-most edge of the parking lot.[15] His single-engine, two-bladed aircraft was owned by Hillsboro Helicopters, and Moffitt was their chief pilot.

KOIN 6 News had chartered the helicopter and its pilot, to gain aerial coverage of the search operation. Moffitt had picked up the KOIN crew from the downtown heliport. He'd meet reporter, Sandy James, with a ground crew, in the parking lot.[16]

Moffitt climbed out of the aircraft and straightened his shirt and tie.

5:15 A.M.
TRIANGLE MORAINE
PALMER GLACIER

Team 10 arrived at 9,800', ready to scout the upper bench above White River Canyon. The snowcat had taken the team much higher than anyone had expected. Stringfield exited the vehicle, glad to see that the winds had backed off. There were still some stars out, but the sky was getting lighter by the minute, preparing the mountain for the first beams of the morning sun. Radys, Stringfield, and O'Bannon began ascending even higher.[17]

5:20 A.M.
BASE OPERATIONS
WY'EAST DAY LODGE

Ed Hall was fed and fully rested, having received a good night's sleep at his home in the nearby town of Welches. He arrived in the lot for a second day of SAR work and bumped into Rick Harder, making his way out towards the landing zone. The Bagger was wearing his scarlet down jacket.

"Where are we going?" Hall asked his friend.[18]

"Hey!" The Bagger replied. "Hook up with the Crag Rats, and we'll fly you guys up."

It didn't take long for Hall to link-up with Bruce Hukari and his cousin, Ken Hukari, members of the Crag Rats. Armed with a new overmit, courtesy of Sue Shultz, Hall and his friends walked out towards the LZ, filled with energy and optimism.

Coming down the staircase was a man feeling anything but energetic. Ky Krank was exhausted. Team 6 had just returned from their overnight mission, drained and drowsy. After being debriefed by Wright, and being assured that they had done all they could during the night, their mission was finally concluded.

As a military pilot, with three tours in Vietnam under his belt, Krank recognized *the fog of war* as he descended the stairs. In his exhaustion, he had to maneuver through the chaos of volunteers, deputies, military personnel, anxious parents, and members of the press. There were disagreements, some fairly heated, but everyone was doing their best with the same goal in mind.

Passing an open door, Krank did a double-take. He had seen an available bunk inside the small room. Through his weary eyes, no Presidential suite could have been more inviting. He approached the bed and collapsed like a house of cards, his cap, scarf, and gloves flying in different directions.[19]

5:25 A.M.
LANDING ZONE (LZ)
WY'EAST DAY LODGE SOUTH PARKING LOT

Ralph Summers emerged from the building and started walking towards Maj. Stovel's aircraft. Deputies had asked Summers to board one of the Hueys, to assist in pinpointing the location of the snow cave from the air.[20] Dozens of people watched him pass by, some following him through the lot, offering support.[21]

"Go with God, Ralph! Go with God!" came encouragement from the crowd."[22]

Frank and John had been observing the helicopter pre-flight procedures.[23] Aboard were pilots Major Fred Stovel and Major David Schildmeyer, and flight engineer, Sergeant Wes Lohman.[24] Also climbing into the aircraft were PJs: Rick Harder, Jeffrey Youngbluth, Jan Nesbit and Charlie Ek.[25]

"Go, baby, go!" one of the father's encouraged, as the helicopter lifted off the ground.[26]

"I've never seen real heroes before," another parent remarked to a nearby reporter, "but these men certainly are."[27]

The small crowd watched as the helicopter made its way up White River Canyon. The Huey was passing over the mountain slopes under fair skies.

As Maslen watched the helicopter ascend the mountain, a deputy came up beside her. Frustrated with the media's repeated requests for information, the sheriff's department was asking Cheryl to meet with journalists. *Could she provide the community at large with a status report on their SAR efforts?* Maslen agreed.[28]

5:32 A.M.
WHITE RIVER GLACIER

Mike Craig's Team 9 discovered boot prints on the east side of White River Glacier, at 7,200'. These were made by two climbers, led downhill, and veered to the west.[29] Craig's team began following these tracks uphill to trace their origin.

~5:37 A.M.
BELL UH-1 IROQUOIS HELICOPTER
OVER WHITE RIVER GLACIER

Aboard another military Huey, were pilots, Lt. Col Mullen, Maj. Jones, and flight engineer, Sgt. Carpenter.[30] The pilot maneuvered the aircraft so that it slowly skimmed above the surface of the glacier. Mullen and Jones scanned the terrain below.

There!

Visible in the snow were two sets of boot prints—mute evidence to the erratic course and periodic stumblings Summers and Schula had endured in the previous day's appalling weather. The Huey slowly followed this path up the mountain. Around 7,600', the tracks vanished, obscured by drifted snow.[31]

A reporter from KATU News sat in his blue Chevy Impala. The windows were down, and he propped the door open with his leg.

Frank and John, walking by, thought the reporter was listening to a talk show. The duo stopped short as they noticed a police scanner and a short-wave radio in the car. The reporter was picking up radio traffic between rescue authorities and the military pilots.[32] Here was the type of information Frank had been so desperately seeking, *unfiltered truth.*

Soon, others joined Frank and John around the reporter's vehicle, listening intently to the transmissions. The reporter didn't seem to mind the gathering ensemble, as long as everyone remained quiet enough. He even turned the volume up, to accommodate his new companions.

5:39 A.M.
EASTERN RIM
WHITE RIVER CANYON

Harbour, Janeck, Rich, Kelsey, and Blailock were huddled together around 8,600', still perched atop the small spur jutting out from the canyon wall.

Come on, sun, Kelsey thought, just as it burst over the horizon.[33] The men turned west, scanning the entire western flank of White River Glacier, from around 9,000', all the way down to 6,000'.[34] Five sets of trained eyes were receiving the first clear view of the icefield.

Using binoculars, Rich and Kelsey trained their vision on two objects to the southwest, on the other side of the canyon. They both believed the objects were rocks, but as the light intensified, something about these objects captured their attention. *Is that a red sleeping bag?* Kelsey motioned to Harbour who, likewise, tried to determine what they were seeing. There didn't seem to be any movement.[35]

Kelsey grabbed the radio and informed Base of a potential discovery.[36] A military Huey was simultaneously approaching the location in question.[37]

Maslen watched as the first rays of sunrise illuminated the edge of Steel Cliff in the Devil's Kitchen region of the volcano's crater. With a mixture of yellow and orange light illuminating the upper crags and the pristine snow slopes, witnesses in the parking lot were filled with renewed optimism. Maslen, however, had mixed emotions. She could see how much new snow had fallen. The mountain was breathtakingly beautiful, but the sheer volume of snow that had fallen was concerning.

Clear visibility and a reduction of wind had raised her hopes. Her experience with SAR operations, however, brought home the harsh reality that it could be too late to save the missing climbers. *If PMR personnel, who were well-equipped and well-trained, had struggled in the whiteout, how well had the kids endured such conditions?*[38]

Drifting between hope and despair, Maslen turned and headed back towards Base Operations.

Rick Harder, Ralph Summers, and several PJs were aboard the Huey, passing over the seemingly endless river of ice. Investigating the sighting of what could be a red sleeping bag, they spied something below. Summers peered down at the glacier and observed a couple of objects, but he couldn't identify them.[39]

Master Sergeant Charlie Ek, a thirty-eight-year-old PJ with seventeen years of experience, spotted the objects as well. He knew what he was seeing. Knowing how powerful the two-day storm had been, Ek wasn't sure how any of the missing climbing party could have fared out in the elements. Still, he hoped for the best as the helicopter banked to the side.[40]

The Bagger also recognized what he was seeing and communicated his observations to rescue coordinators down in Base Operations.[41]

Maslen walked back into Base, just in time to overhear Harder's voice on the radio. Her heart jumped in her chest.

Did he just say, survivors?[42]

The precise wording was jumbled, but The Bagger appeared to be informing authorities that survivors had been spotted below, on White River Glacier.[43] Instead of experiencing a feeling of euphoria, Maslen felt confused. She was sure there was a mistake. Surely Harder was referencing bodies?[44] The Bagger's voice came over the airwaves again, requesting Life Flight backup.[45]

A group, who had congregated in the hallway right outside of Base Operations, plied Deputy Krebs for information as he emerged from the office. Krebs informed them that survivors had been discovered, but he had no further details at the moment.[46]

~5:46 A.M.
WHITE RIVER CANYON

Team 9 was at 7,340', on the east side of the canyon, tracking boot prints they believed to have been made by Summers and Schula.[47] When Craig's men overheard The Bagger's radio announcement, that survivors had been spotted around 7,700', Team 9 started moving.[48]

~5:46 A.M.
LANDING ZONE (LZ)
WY'EAST DAY LODGE SOUTH PARKING LOT

The group huddled around the reporter's Impala overheard the radio transmission, indicating the helicopter crew had spotted survivors. Frank McGinness and the others erupted into cheers.[49] Strangers congratulated one another, exchanged hugs, and shared handshakes.

Family members telephoned relatives and friends, sharing the good news. Mrs. Haeder imagined a quick reunion with her son, Rich, picturing him arriving safely on a stretcher.[50]

Several minutes later, this group watched as the Huey containing Harder and his PJs landed in the parking lot. Summers suddenly emerged and trotted away from the helicopter. The aircraft immediately lifted off and returned to the glacier.[51] Bystanders were baffled as to why this had occurred.

Maj. Stovel landed his Huey on the ice at 7,700'. Harder, Youngbluth, Nesbit, and Ek jumped out. Mindful that Summers had reported a sizeable crevasse near the snow cave, the four PJs roped-up. With this safety procedure tackled, they made their way toward the dark objects at the foot of a steep slope.

Using a lengthy ice axe, Youngbluth probed the ground as he drew closer.[52] He could see he was approaching an adolescent, curled-up in the fetal position in the snow. Vital signs were checked. There was no sign of breathing, and Youngbluth couldn't find a pulse. The teen was missing one glove and one boot.[53]

~5:55 A.M.
BELL UH-1 IROQUOIS HELICOPTER
OVER WHITE RIVER GLACIER

In another Huey, the pilots observed the PJs on the glacier below. Gaining altitude, they spotted another figure, lying prone in the snow. This was near the top of the western moraine, directly along the rim that divides Palmer Glacier from White River Canyon.[54] The estimated elevation of this discovery was 8,200'.

~5:59 A.M.
LANDING ZONE (LZ)
WY'EAST DAY LODGE SOUTH PARKING LOT

The crowd in the parking lot could see the second Huey up the mountain. It appeared to be hovering. Witnesses spied a red flare, dropped from the aircraft to the snow below. The glow from this flare looked like a beacon. Parents noticed that the helicopter continued to hover.

"Come on," one of the fathers said in regards to the missing students. "Why don't they get out and wave?"[55]

Wayne Litzenberger, Alison's father, was amid the crowd, observing the proceedings.

"What I don't understand," he said, within earshot of a reporter, "is how they got into this pickle."[56]

Youngbluth, Nesbit, and Ek turned their attention to the red sleeping bag in the snow. Youngbluth used his ice axe to probe around the bag. Nothing. Approaching the third object, the group found a second climber.[57] This youth was also lying in the fetal position.[58] As before, the PJs found no vital signs.

Probing of the area, with axes, continued while Harder reached for his radio. Contacting Base, he requested the Crag Rats. They were to bring two or three ropes and snow anchors.[59]

The Bagger had been instructed to avoid announcing any discovery of deceased climbers over the airwaves, protecting relatives of the missing from overhearing such a transmission. Recalling this instruction, Harder pulled out his Air Force radio instead of the one PMR had provided him. He contacted Sergeant Swails down at Base, reporting that they had two Deltas—a code word for bodies. Harder directed Swails to quietly alert the sheriff's department of this development.[60]

Soon, Team 8 arrived on the scene and encountered PJs standing over the two teenagers. Jerry Janeck instinctively approached one of the victims, hoping to see signs of breathing, but The Bagger rebuked him.

Harder said the two victims were deceased and he didn't want anyone disturbing them.[61] He then directed the military helicopters to continue the SAR missions that had been assigned to them.[62]

Mark Kelsey approached the bodies but did not receive the same rebuke that greeted Janeck. Perhaps it was because of their previous history, but The Bagger permitted his friend to draw closer. Kelsey began reading the clues. Both teens were in the fetal position, at the base of a moderately steep hill. The students were flush with the surface of the accumulation, indicating that the snow, driven by the wind, had blown around them and filled in all the nooks and crannies they presented. They had been there a while.

Kelsey turned his attention uphill. To his trained eye, he recognized a fall line when he saw it. To him, there was no doubt that these two youths had originally been atop the ridge. They had either hiked down or slid down, but they had come to rest at the bottom of the hill. Then, lost and battered by the elements, they instinctively pulled themselves into the fetal position to preserve body temperature.[63]

The Bagger advised Team 8 that he was waiting for the arrival of Crag Rats. Janeck was surprised, offended, and confused all at the same time. Why seek the assistance of the Crag Rats when Team 8—PMR—was already on the scene, more than willing to lend a hand? Another thought entered Janeck's mind.

Does Harder even have the authority to declare these patients dead?[64]

CHAPTER 19
VITAL SIGNS

Team 10 gathered in a huddle to discuss the radio traffic. They had heard that survivors had been located. They could clearly see helicopters exploring farther down the mountain. If climbers had been found at lower elevations, that is where they thought they should proceed. It most likely meant the snow cave was somewhere in that vicinity. The men started descending the slopes.[1]

Teams 9 and 10 were en route to converge on the discovery sites. The PJs wanted to make sure the Crag Rats brought two or three ropes as well as snow anchors. Operating one of the snowcats, Scott Russell overheard this transmission and advised that he was at 9,100'. He had a rope, several anchors, and would descend to the Lower Discovery Site.[2]

Deputy Kennel picked up the telephone and placed a call to the Alpine Ambulances and Advanced Lifesaving Ambulance Services.[3]

The Bagger had instructed Team 8 to keep away from the scene and continue looking for the rest of the missing climbers.

Mark Kelsey radioed Barry Wright, requesting the presence of Ralph Summers.[4] If the consultant were to inspect the discovery sites, perhaps he could recognize specific terrain features that could help them locate the hidden snow cave.

PJs on the scene stated they did *not* want Summers up on the mountain.[5]

Kelsey turned his attention back to the slope. He and three teammates screwed their ski poles together to create probes. Forgoing roping-up, Kelsey and his friends began a cursory probing of the canyon wall. It was arbitrary, no direct planning applied. They just started moving up the slope in a northwesterly direction, randomly probing the terrain as they advanced.[6]

~6:15 A.M.
BASE OPERATIONS
WY'EAST DAY LODGE

Questions Deputy Krebs posed to PJs over the radio were not being answered to his satisfaction. Of crucial importance was the question of the precise location of the Lower Discovery Site.

"Well..." someone on the mountain replied over the airwaves. "You don't need that right now—we'll get back to you."[7]

One of the men from the Hoodland Fire Department observed that decisions that were being made at the Lower Discovery Site were not being transmitted to Wright and Krebs.[8]

It had been over ten minutes since Harder's last transmission. Where was the follow-up report? Where were the details?

Military PJs are accustomed to a different chain-of-command and are more comfortable following their own policies and procedures. Still, Maslen expected some level of communication with local authorities.[9] What was happening up on the mountain?

The radio crackled.

Authorities were puzzled. Messages from the PJs were reaching Base, but requests for further information to the military appeared to be ignored.

~6:15 A.M.
LANDING ZONE (LZ)
WY'EAST DAY LODGE SOUTH PARKING LOT

Word that rescue workers were now asking for ropes, as opposed to stretchers, flared up.[10]

"That has to mean everyone can walk out, and nobody is injured," someone speculated.[11]

Mar and Diana stayed off to the side. Rescue workers were walking in all directions, deputies were fielding questions from journalists, and the landing zone was the epitome of pandemonium. It was chaos. *Who's in charge?* Diana wondered. The two women watched reporters sequester PMR personnel as they passed through the landing zone. Employing the technique that had worked so well for them within the halls of Timberline Lodge, Mar and Diana edged closer, trying to overhear conversations. Although each rescue worker appeared to have his own take on the operation, it became evident that something was very wrong up on the glacier. The women couldn't piece together what had happened, but it was clear that something unexpected had occurred.[12]

With his military background, Frank knew that if survivors had been found, rescue workers would be reaching for ropes and stretchers. Frank could see such equipment in the parking lot, ready for use. When one of the helicopters returned to the parking lot, he watched intently to see what her crew would do upon landing.

As the Huey touched down, a sergeant exited the aircraft. This PJ immediately mustered-up more SAR personnel. Frank was mentally imploring these men to take the stretchers with them, but the equipment remained where it was, idle and useless.

That's not a good sign, he confessed to himself.[13]

He turned his attention back to the Chevy Impala. The group surrounding the reporter's car continued to eavesdrop on the radio traffic.

A request from the sheriff's department came over the airwaves. *Could everyone switch over to the Search and Rescue Interagency Frequency?*[14] This high-frequency channel, though not encrypted, would mean more privacy for all official parties. More importantly, rescue organizations could communicate without outside interference.

Frank overheard a specific transmission; rescue workers had reached one of the victims. Suddenly—the radio went dead.[15]

"They just said they reached one of the victims," repeated the grandfather of one of the missing students. "What do you suppose that means?"[16]

"What's going on?" Frank asked.[17]

"They've switched," replied the reporter. "A military channel, no doubt."

Frank looked down at the ground. He had served in the Security Agency, a signal intelligence branch of the Army. Their responsibility had been the security of military communications. Frank realized this frequency change meant that authorities had discovered something that they didn't want broadcast on an open channel. That, he reasoned, could only mean bad news.[18]

Unlike the bystanders around the Impala outside, Wright and Krebs could now continue to hear the communications of the various SAR agencies. Team 7 was heading down the mountain. Scott Russell, in his snowcat, was unable to locate safe passage to the Lower Discovery Site. Team 8 had already been to the site and was now busy probing as they ascended toward the Upper Discovery Site. Teams 9 and 10 were in transit as well.

The pilot of the incoming Life Flight helicopter remained on a different channel. Shultz had to relay messages between him and the PJs on the mountain. The civilian pilot asked if there were nurses on site.[19] There were indeed.

Many medical personnel were on the premises, anxiously awaiting news. Lane Wintermute, fire chief for the Hoodland Fire District, was among those present in the offices. From his department was Neale Brown, David Summer, and Richard Curtis, serving as paramedics or logistics support. Jon Swails, who had been on Team 5, and was a liaison officer with the 304th ARRS, was on hand as well. Life Flight nurses, JoAnne Fairchild and Sarah Evenson, waited patiently.[20] They were all waiting for an update from the PJs on the mountain.

What in the world was taking so long?

The blue and white Life Flight helicopter touched down in the parking lot. Crew members emerged from this aircraft and walked towards the Lodge. They didn't run as if anyone's life was on the line. This observation brought family members some measure of comfort.[21]

Lt. Hanners pressed his deputy to determine the condition and location of the three survivors. The deputy continued with his efforts to contact the squadron members, but there was no reply.

The silence over the airwaves was perplexing.

The PJs up on the mountain could tell that the sheriff's Federal Aviation Administration (FAA) radio was malfunctioning. Bound by specific procedural prohibitions, they refused to relay any sensitive information to civilians, even the leadership of PMR.[22]

Wright, like the deputies, was unaware of the equipment malfunction and continued his efforts to communicate with the PJs. He demanded to know the precise location of the Lower Discovery Site. There was no reply.[23]

John Schneider of PMR and John "Gabby" Harkness, a PJ, climbed out of a helicopter. The Bagger had directed the duo to land atop the canyon wall, to determine for themselves, what was on that ridge. Schneider began approaching a prone figure in the snow. There were no vital signs.

The men could see boot prints in the snow, originating from somewhere higher up the mountain.

Having only their ice axes, they went to work probing the snow surrounding the third victim.[24] Although the precarious location of this patient was not ideal for snow cave construction, Schneider and Harkness knew that the shelter had been constructed amid a whiteout. Finding nothing, they climbed back into the Huey.

The Bagger, believing he and his men were working with deceased patients, saw no need to interrupt the SAR operation that had been underway for over twenty-four hours. He and Barry Wright had planned for six teams to be deployed into the field by helicopter: two teams of Crag Rats, one from PMR, and three consisting of PJs. This air deployment plan had already been approved, and Harder believed he was executing the existing SAR strategy.[25]

The Bagger wanted the Crag Rats to transport the three victims down the mountain.[26] Although Team 8 had volunteered to perform this duty, Harder believed they should continue the search for the rest of the missing party members.

Youngbluth assessed the situation. They had discovered three climbers, most likely all teenagers, that must have departed the snow cave. Harkness and Schneider had reported seeing tracks leading uphill from the Upper Discovery Site. With these clues, it appeared as if three students had departed the cave and descended. At some point, they veered eastward, down into White River Canyon, perhaps to get out of the wind. The PJs wanted to shift their attention to higher ground.

Youngbluth understood that authorities were now faced with the possibility that the students and faculty members could be scattered all over the south side of the mountain.[27]

6:33 A.M.
UPPER DISCOVERY SITE
PALMER GLACIER

Team 10, consisting of Radys, Stringfield, and O'Bannon, had jog-trotted down Palmer Glacier, losing over 900 feet in elevation during their journey. They were approaching the Upper Discovery Site, at 8,200', just as Schneider and Harkness were flying away in a Huey.

The team came upon the lone climber, prone in the snow.[28] One of Radys' men approached and checked for a pulse. It was difficult to determine the gender of the climber, as there was an accumulation of ice on the skin. They could tell this person was not a fully-grown adult.[29]

Fresh boot prints were visible. These had been made by grown men, and recently. Stringfield reasoned that the men in the helicopter had approached the fallen climber and checked for vitals.

Radys got on the radio, identified his team and their position, and asked for orders. Harder replied to this immediately, stating that he didn't want mountain climbers—*send the Crag Rats*.[30] This stunned Radys. He and his men were trained. Radys was the president of PMR. His men were properly equipped and were on the scene. Why send others to their destination? Radys, again, sought direction. He received the same response from The Bagger.

Discouraged, Team 10 focused on the secondary set of tracks. There were three sets of boot prints, originating from somewhere uphill. Placing a trail wand next to the prone climber to mark the location, Team 10 began tracking the mysterious set of prints.[31]

As the men made their way back uphill, Stringfield turned to see a helicopter returning to the scene. A military smoke grenade was tossed near the site. After the small steel cylinder struck the snow below, a colossal stream of yellow smoke emerged from emission holes in the top of the device. The prevalent winds bore the smoke along, and the display resembled a mustard-colored streamer.[32] Team 10 turned and continued ascending the mountain.[33]

~6:40 A.M.
LOWER DISCOVERY SITE
WHITE RIVER GLACIER

Team 9 arrived at the Lower Discovery Site, encountering Harder and a couple of PJs on the scene. Mike Craig could clearly see the two adolescents, curled-up in the snow. There was a missing glove, a missing boot, hats were off, and parkas were unzipped.[34] The chiropractor had the impression that these young people must have been confused, scared, and suffering from hypothermia.

"We've got two bodies," Craig said to The Bagger. "Probe the fall line. We've got them."[35]

"We're on it," Harder replied. "Go on down and get another mission."

Hal Lillywhite, still roped to his companions on Team 9, stepped towards one of the teens. He saw a girl, lying on the snow. Her face was covered with a thin layer of ice, but he could see that she was somebody's beautiful daughter.[36]

The Bagger directed Craig and his team to focus their search farther down the canyon.[37] Like Teams 8 and 10 before them, Team 9's offer to assist was declined.

6:47 A.M.
BASE OPERATIONS
WY'EAST DAY LODGE

Sixty-two minutes after their initial announcement of finding survivors, PJs at the Lower Discovery Site were requesting a military helicopter. Team 10 was reporting red and blue-flagged trail wands, high above

Code 1244   185

them on Palmer Glacier. Radys asked Wright if another team could investigate.[38]

A separate helicopter was being dispatched to investigate the area, up near 9,200'.

The facts were still not in, but personnel in Base Operations continued with their efforts to contact Medical Examiner, Doug Pratt.[39]

~7:15 A.M.
PALMER GLACIER

Team 10 would occasionally lose sight of the tracks they were following. New snow drifts concealed signs of the original prints. The team had been trained in tracking, however, so they pressed on.[40]

These men had also been instructed to investigate any significant crevasses they encountered.[41] As Stringfield was of a slightly thinner build than Radys or O'Bannon, he volunteered to be lowered into these yawning traps.

After proper anchoring, Stringfield was lowered into each crevasse they found. Several were so large that he was unable to stem and use the walls to assist him. While dangling in mid-air, sometimes as far as thirty feet below his teammates, he would holler and blow his whistle. On each occasion, as he waited between colossal walls of ice, his calls were met with silence.

Employing a climbing ascender, Stringfield would return to the surface of the glacier, and the team would advance to the next objective.[42]

7:20 A.M.
BASE OPERATIONS
WY'EAST DAY LODGE

Team 7 returned to Base, dog-tired from working through the night. They turned in the hand-held avalanche transceivers they had checked-out and advised Maslen that their snowshoes were still strapped to the back of Scott Russell's snowcat.[43]

Noting how much time had passed since the discoveries, Deputy Kennel scrawled an entry in the sheriff's log, "Poss 1244 X 3 in Hood River County."[44] This code, used by the sheriff's department to indicate a deceased person, was multiplied by three, and it marked the moment that Kennel lost hope that all three climbers were found alive. Lt. Hanners, Deputy Krebs, and Barry Wright did not see this entry in the log.

While Team 10 was communicating with Base, yet another set of boot prints were discovered by Stringfield and O'Bannon. Radys relayed this information to authorities, stating that two of the sets had clear indications that crampons had been strapped to the boots, while the third set was devoid of such traction devices. The men were not surprised when they were asked to follow these tracks to their source.[45]

A Huey landed in the lot. The five members of Team 8 were its passengers. As they had been searching the snow slope that separated the two discovery sites, a PJ had directed them to catch a ride with an approaching Huey. Kelsey, Blailock, and the Amigos had agreed to return to Base, ready to confront someone in authority.

Kelsey climbed out of the aircraft and started walking away amid the rotary downwash. A crowd was moving in towards him. Kelsey saw the looks on their faces—hope and desperation. *Give us something, please,* their expressions seemed to say. He wanted to tell them what they had found. He wanted to hug the parents waiting for their children, do something, but he knew he wasn't allowed to divulge any information.

A woman ran up to him and identified herself as a mother of one of the missing students.

"I hear you found someone," she said.[46]

"I can't say anything," Kelsey replied, emotionally torn. "There's someone whose job is to give that information. I'm sorry." On the mountain, the seasoned SAR volunteer had kept his mind occupied with the tasks at hand. Here, feeling alone, he was suddenly confronted with raw emotions.

John Schneider had descended the mountain with Team 8. Rich, Schneider, and Janeck approached the first deputy they saw, adamant that Ralph Summers should board a helicopter and visit the Lower Discovery Site. Perhaps he would recognize the area.[47] Nearby, Summers listened, anxious to assist in any way he could, but his movements were subject to the will of the sheriff's department.

This plan was presented to Rick Harder up on the mountain. Did he want Summers up at the site? Bagger's response was clear.

Absolutely not.[48]

When pressed for an explanation of why the consultant should not be flown up, the men learned Harder had declared it was too dangerous. This response infuriated Janeck, and he wasted no time in voicing his opinions. Wasn't Summers an employee of Outward Bound? Hadn't he survived a harrowing walk-out in a blizzard? Surely, he could handle blue skies and a moderate breeze.[49]

Fr. Tom Goman

Pat McGinness, Alison Litzenberger, and Erik Sandvik at Oregon Episcopal School, November 1985.

Richard Haeder, Jr at the start of the climb, May 12, 1986.

Ric Conrad

The OES team, near the Palmer chairlift, May 12, 1986

The last photograph, May 12, 1986

The school bus, Tuesday morning, May 13th 1986

(L to R) Mike Blailock, Unidentified, Hal Lillywhite, and John Young, Boarding #8, May 13, 1986

Terry Swicegood and Rocky Henderson, May 13, 1986

Teams 3 and 4, aboard Number 8, heading out on their missions, May 13, 1986

Dave McClure,
Co-Chief for Portland Mountain Rescue

Barry Wright,
Co-Chief for Portland Mountain Rescue

Ed Hall and Mark Kelsey

Mike Craig, leader of Teams 4, 9, 19 and 5

Ralph Summers and Molly Schula

The chaotic landing zone in the parking lot, May 15, 1986

(Front row) Deputy Hattan, Deputy Serafin, and Rick "The Bagger" Harder, May 15, 1986

One of four Bell UH-1 Iroquois Helicopters, 304th ARRS, May 15, 1986

Ric Conrad

Deputy Mike Hattan and Deputy Lou Serafin

Pat McGinness

Ric Conrad

CHAPTER 20
CODE 1244

Jon Tullis was looking for somewhere to park amid the myriad of vehicles. ABC, CBS, NBC, CNN, and several local news stations had their trucks lined up like a brightly colored Gypsy caravan.[1] He had never seen so many national news agencies ascend on the resort. The horrific whiteout had been keeping most reporters off the mountain. Only four to six journalists had managed to make it to the resort on Tuesday. This morning, the number of reporters had already tripled.

When Timberline Lodge Public Relations Director, Bill Conerly, spotted Tullis in the building, he asked for his assistance with the media.[2] Tullis was ready to jump right in.

Deputies were overwhelmed with the sheer number of inquiries from reporters. Because she was in a better position to provide details concerning mountaineering techniques and procedures, Cheryl Maslen had been asked to assist the deputies.[3]

Tullis was struck by the chaos in the designated media room. Phone lines had been dragged across the floor and patched into Base Operations, upstairs on the second floor. Deputies were fielding questions from reporters, about everything from their relationship with the 304th ARRS to search strategies above timberline.[4] Cameramen, with shoulder-mounted RCA Hawkeye or TK-86 self-contained portable units, would turn suddenly, and anyone standing too close had to duck.

As Tullis headed upstairs, he noticed that Conerly had the cafeteria cordoned-off, as a space designated for family and friends of the lost climbers. A crowd was gathering there now as word had spread that an announcement was forthcoming. Tullis passed through the busy cafeteria and into a congested hallway.

It was a media zoo.

Team 10 had been backtracking three sets of boot prints up Palmer Glacier, hoping these would lead to the snow cave. At 9,200', Radys radioed Base, thinking an aerial reconnaissance might be faster.

The Bagger was told to have one of the military choppers redirected to the Triangle Moraine region to investigate.[5]

Team 11 was comprised of David Allen and Richard Ernst of PMR, and Ken Hukari and Don Pattison of the Crag Rats.[6]

PMR's Gary Uhland, Terry Swicegood, Gary Salberg, and Steve Belding made up Team 12.[7] Their mission was to hike Salmon River Canyon and explore it all the way downhill to Highway 35.[8] This would involve a descent of 2,400 feet in elevation, investigating if any of the missing climbers had descended the canyon in the whiteout, inadvertently passing the resorts altogether.

Teams 8 and 9 were off the mountain and in need of some well-deserved rest. These men had all been turned away from the Lower Discovery Site. They had no idea that several deputies, as well as Barry Wright, were in the dark about the condition of the frozen climbers who had been found on the mountain.

Jerry Janeck felt the exhaustion, physically and emotionally. He had received no sleep since Monday night and had battled the elements on several missions during that time. He couldn't comprehend why The Bagger had cordoned off the site and refused to allow Summers to be flown up to the scene. The sheriff's department seemed to acquiesce to The Bagger's direction as well, which made no sense to Janeck. With a heavy heart, his thoughts drifted back to the two children he had seen in the snow. He believed the other lost climbers might be discovered farther down the glacier, and he mentioned this to his Amigos as they all climbed into Harbour's van for the long drive home.[9]

Sue Shultz, who felt confined after so many hours in Base, opted to meet her husband as his team came off the mountain.[10] Finding Mike in the parking lot, she listened as her husband privately divulged what he had seen and experienced at the Lower Discovery Site.[11] Fighting back tears as she processed the information, Shultz carefully steered away from the news vans, avoiding reporters.[12]

Mark Kelsey, who had worked long and hard, was equally exhausted. As he walked through the lot towards his truck, he looked around and was well-pleased with the manpower that now appeared to be available to the search effort. As he climbed into the driver's seat of his rig and closed the door, he wondered how valuable he would be, now that there was unlimited visibility. The man who had served as the Hasty Team's navigator through a blizzard, and worked with Team 8 throughout the night, didn't have to think too long. He leaned his head against the door, merely wanting to close his eyes for a few minutes. He was comatose for hours.[13]

~8:21 A.M.
BASE OPERATIONS
WY'EAST DAY LODGE

In response to the request for a military helicopter to investigate tracks farther up the mountain, one of the PJs asked to speak to the man in charge of Base Operations. Lt. Hanners grabbed the radio and identified himself. The lieutenant was asked to drive to Government Camp, six miles down the road. PJs would land there with a load of *important equipment*.[14]

There was a pause in the conversation. Hanners knew he wasn't receiving all the information but deduced that the PJs didn't want to discuss details over the airwaves. Hanners stated he and Deputy Krebs would meet the helicopter as requested.[15]

Handing the radio back to Maslen, Hanners looked around to see if he could spot Krebs. The deputy had just departed to meet with relatives of the missing climbers.

8:23 A.M.
CAFETERIA
WY'EAST DAY LODGE

Family, friends, and a few OES staff members had congregated in the cafeteria, anticipating a major announcement about the three survivors. Someone from the school approached Frank and asked him what hospital he would prefer Patrick be sent to, once the boy was rescued. Recognizing that every member of the climbing party would have to be seen by a medical specialist, after two nights on the mountain, Frank was not alarmed by the question. He knew the query was geared towards geography; what would be the closest hospital to your residence, so that you don't have to travel far to be with your son?

"I suppose Providence is closest to us," Frank replied.[16]

Jeff Hicks shifted in his chair. The resident advisor from OES had stayed the night in Timberline Lodge, unable to bring himself to return to the campus just yet. Father Tom's team was still on the mountain. Nothing like this had happened in the six years Jeff had worked at the school.[17] Nothing like this had ever happened in the history of the Basecamp program.

"Ladies and gentlemen," announced a loud voice. "Please take your seats, and we can begin."[18]

Deputy Krebs walked into the room, carrying a piece of paper. He walked to the front of the room and introduced himself to the assembled crowd.

"I don't know what's going on," Krebs acknowledged. "I'll give you as much information as I can. I promise to level with you."[19]

A middle-aged man, wearing a blue sports jacket and a tie, suddenly entered the room. Offering an apology for interrupting the proceedings, he walked up to the deputy. The two held a private conversation as parents leaned forward, straining to overhear any snippet of what was being whispered.

"I don't know what's going on," Krebs repeated to the crowd. "But...I've been told that I have to end this meeting right now and that my presence is requested down in Government Camp. I have no idea why. As soon as I find anything out, I will let you all know."[20]

Incredulously, Frank and the other relatives watched as Krebs walked out of the room. The one man who appeared poised to release coveted information was exiting the scene.

Hanners and Krebs walked outside and found themselves wading through a small crowd. The lieutenant, ignoring the approach of any reporter, informed Krebs of the cryptic radio message he had received. The pair climbed into a Toyota pick-up and sped off down the highway.[21]

There was general confusion back in the cafeteria. The man in the suit stayed at the front of the room. Eventually, he addressed the crowd himself. He broke the unbearable news. The three survivors were, in fact, deceased.

Jeff Hicks joined in the collective *gasp* that followed. He watched as two of the parents collapsed to the floor. A hush swept across the room; family members fought to absorb the magnitude of this announcement.

Oh—my—God.[22]

Frank felt as though someone had just pulled his heart out through the soles of his feet.[23]

Barry Wright had escaped outside to try to clear his thoughts. He was baffled as to what was taking the PJs so long to get three survivors down the mountain. Just like Hanners and Krebs, the word "deceased" had not yet made it to him.

His thoughts shifted to the survivors themselves. Why were they out in the elements? There were a handful of possible explanations, he reasoned. Frustrated with waiting for a rescue, the three climbers may have struck out on their own, following the example set by Summers and Schula. The snow cave itself might have collapsed. This could have forced whoever was outside the cave to seek new shelter. A perfectly plausible explanation was that the trio was so affected by hypothermia, they wandered off.[24]

Wright was frustrated for another reason as well. By reviewing team movements, he had concluded that the boot prints, which Team 10 had been following with such high hopes, had been created yesterday by other searchers. Another lead evaporated.

Gerald Donahue, Scott Walker, and Jim Holloway—Team 13—began boarding a nearby chopper. Accompanying them was Dee Zduniak, the technical consultant from Outward Bound who had been on Fr. Goman's team two days earlier.[25]

Deputy Russ Williams, public information officer, stepped forward and introduced himself.[26] He stated that the three victims had been spotted from the air, around sunrise. Two were located at the foot of a steep slope around 7,700', while the third was found near the top of the western moraine, 500 feet higher up the mountain.[27] Two of the climbers had removed boots. One was missing a parka. Another was barehanded, with no set of gloves to be found.[28]

Parents began clamoring for identification of the bodies.

"Were they boys or girls?" someone asked.[29] "How many of each?"

"It's impossible to tell," Deputy Williams replied. "Their faces are too swollen to identify them."

"Were they students or adults?" another asked.

"We can't determine that either," Williams conceded.

Diana wondered what question she could pose to authorities that would help exclude Tom.

"Did any of them have facial hair?" she asked.[30] Only two members of the climbing party had beards—Summers and Goman. Williams paused.

"No," the deputy replied.

Diana felt a wave of relief wash over her. Tom was not among the bodies.

For Mar, however, this revelation did not bring any measure of comfort. She had already given up hope of ever seeing her husband alive again. *If Tom were alive or had any type of control, this wouldn't have happened. If any children are dead, then he's dead too.*[31]

~8:30 A.M.
PARKING LOT
GOVERNMENT CAMP

Turning west on Highway 26, Lt. Hanners and Deputy Krebs quickly turned, yet again, onto Government Camp Loop Road. They pulled into a spacious parking lot, designated as the landing zone for the inbound military helicopter.[32]

They waited.

Important equipment?

8:30 A.M.
BASE OPERATIONS
WY'EAST DAY LODGE

Wright walked back into Base, just in time to hear a radio message from Al Radys. Team 10, high up on Palmer, was observing a handful of climbers above the Hot Rocks. This mystery party appeared to be descending the crater. Could they be some of the missing students?

Teams of Crag Rats began relaying their current locations.[33]

Maslen was frustrated. She just discovered that a couple of these teams were on the mountain. They had not been assigned a number by her, nor were they given a specific mission by Wright or Krebs. She was in a difficult position, tasked not only with creating SAR teams but ensuring they were qualified to perform the necessary tasks at hand. She had already turned away regional climbers who had volunteered their services.

Random mountaineers from Oregon and Washington had been showing up at Base, volunteering to join in the effort. Although they had the most honorable of intentions, they were not certified by the Mountain Rescue Association. Likewise, some familiar names from the ranks of the Mazamas offered their services. Maslen had to turn down their kind offers of support for the same reason. Unless the individual was certified, or if Maslen personally knew of the climber's skills and resume, she could not authorize their involvement.[34] The extra teams up on the mountain were surely experienced climbers, but their presence on the mountain had not been authorized by anyone in Base.

As Wright considered the map on the wall, he overheard Radys on the radio, making contact with the Crag Rats.[35] So engrossed in the conversation was Wright, that he did not hear a telephone conversation that was occurring nearby.

Deputy Kennel was on the phone with the Hood River County Sheriff's Office. Kennel informed them that at least one of three Code 1244s had been discovered within the boundaries of their county.[36]

~8:40 A.M.
FRONT DESK
TIMBERLINE LODGE

Seeing how distraught family members had been in the cafeteria when confronted with the terrible news, Jeff Hicks thought he should be the one to contact folks back at OES.

As the pay phones in Wy'East Day Lodge were in use, he crossed the street and asked employees of Timberline Lodge if they had a phone he could use.

"Use this one," the front desk attendant offered.[37]

Jeff knew who he had to call but was hesitant to be the bearer of such news.

Sam Dibbins was not only a popular history teacher on campus, but he was also in charge of the Basecamp program. The teacher had three sons, two of whom attended OES.

Jeff paused. He had never really been confronted with death or the process of grieving. He dialed the number.

"Sam," he said quietly. "It's Jeff. You need to sit down."

Lt. Hanners and Deputy Krebs watched as the military helicopter slowly came to rest in the parking lot. A PJ emerged from the aircraft and raced over to the deputies.

"We've got two deltas," yelled the PJ.[38]

"*What* type of equipment are you turning over?" Hanners questioned, not able to hear over the noise of the aircraft.

"Two bodies!" the PJ called out.

Shocked, Hanners watched as PJs unloaded one body bag, and then a second from the aircraft. With great care, these were placed on the pavement next to the Toyota.[39] Hanners was utterly taken by surprise.

"I thought the climbers were alive!" he remarked to the PJ.

"All three were dead!" came the reply.

Deputy Kennel informed Wright that he had telephoned Mt. Hood Meadows, asking if their staff had any cross-country skiers that could assist in the SAR operation?[40]

Wright merely nodded in acknowledgment, lost in his own thoughts. Why were Crag Rats requested at the discover sites when PMR was already on the scene? What was happening? Where was the necessary data, in which to make command decisions?[41] Unknowingly, he had been in the wrong place at the wrong time on multiple occasions. Word was circulating that the three victims were deceased, and everyone assumed that the people in charge had already been privy to this information.

The sheriff's log was open and ready for continual, real-time entries by deputies. Wright was busy overseeing the teams on the mountain and hadn't seen a crucial entry in this document. Four numbers had been scribbled on the page. Four numbers that would have told Wright everything he needed to know—*1244*.[42]

Hanners and Krebs were stunned. The three "survivors" reported over the airwaves, were deceased. There had been six radios at the two discovery sites. *How had this crucial piece of information not been transmitted?*[43]

PJs handed Krebs a hat and a ski glove, stating the articles had been found beside the bodies.

Krebs was nearly speechless. With no warning, he was confronted with two climbers, presumably dead, who would have to be transported to a hospital for that call to be made.[44]

Thinking quickly, Hanners directed military personnel to transport the third victim, still on the mountain, directly to the LZ at Wy'East Day Lodge so proper protocol could be followed.[45]

Hanners and Krebs unloaded the contents of their vehicle to make room for the *important equipment*. Carefully, they loaded the two body bags into the bed of the rig. They drove away, leaving a pile of tools and equipment abandoned in the parking lot.

Krebs manned the wheel while Lt. Hanners radioed the Media Room.[46]

Team 13 was exploring White River Canyon. The Alpinees were slowly weaving their way through the forest of snow-laden mountain hemlock and stunted scrub pine. Team members remained vigilant, scanning the terrain for any sign of the missing climbers. As the entire canyon was covered in a heavy layer of fresh snow, they hoped that any disturbance in the pristine ivory blanket would be spotted, even at a distance.

Deputy Hattan grabbed the handset. Lieutenant Hanners explained the unexpected delivery of climbers in body bags and demanded to know why they had been flown to Government Camp instead of Timberline. Hattan was as surprised as his superior. He'd assumed the missing climbers would be brought directly to his location.[47]

Knowing he needed to see if Barry Wright knew more than the Sheriff's department, Deputy Hattan walked down the hall towards the staircase. Passing an open door, he spied a gathering taking place inside a storage room. Stepping back for a second look, Hattan recognized Rick Harder, engaged in conversation with a Life Flight nurse. Behind them, a PJ and a couple of other bystanders stood next to a stack of folded chairs.[48]

Hattan couldn't believe what he was hearing. The Bagger was telling the nurse that he had been in contact with Dr. William Long at Emanuel Hospital, and the doctor wanted the bodies flown to his facility.

"What the hell are you doing?" Hattan asked sharply. "What's going on?"[49]

Harder stated that he didn't want family members to see their loved ones arriving in body bags in the parking lot, so he had ordered them flown to Government Camp. The Bagger was now coordinating with civilians to have the bodies transported to Portland.[50]

At that moment, Hattan realized Harder had been in contact with agencies outside the sheriff's office and was making decisions on his own. The deputy and the PJ were soon engrossed in a heated debate. Hattan reminded Harder that any movement of bodies was contrary to state law.

"You can't take a body across county lines," Hattan noted, recognizing that The Bagger proposed to move bodies from Clackamas County to Multnomah County. "You can't even *move* a body without the permission of the medical examiner. Pratt has the ultimate authority."

Hattan and Harder had worked together during previous SAR operations. From Hattan's perspective, he believed Harder knew what he was proposing was superseding his own authority. The deputy respected The Bagger's abilities, yet he expected everyone to adhere to established protocols and standard operating procedures.

This isn't going to cut it, thought Hattan.

The deputy departed the scene and began climbing the stairs, toward Base Operations. Hattan knew he had to make some calls. Harder was ignoring the established chain of command. Oregon State law was very explicit. The sheriff in a given county oversees SAR operations within his county—period. The sheriff's authority even supersedes state and federal.[51]

Lt. Hanners radioed his superiors in Clackamas, inquiring whether they had managed to reach Doug Pratt, the medical examiner. *No*; there had been no such contact. Hanners requested that ongoing efforts be made and, once contact was established, inform the man that his services were needed at the Oregon State Police field office in Government Camp.[52]

Next, Hanners contacted Hood River County Sheriff Richard Kelly and informed him of the discovery of the three deceased persons on Palmer and White River Glaciers. Two of the victims may have been discovered within the boundary of Hood River County. As a result, Hanners was making the required telephone call to his counterpart. Hanners learned that a deputy at the Lodge had already telephoned with the news.

Although Clackamas County would continue to head the SAR operation, Hanners asked if Hood River authorities would like their medical examiner dispatched to Government Camp as well.[53]

Hanners soon learned that medical examiner from Clackamas County was unavailable, but the department had authorized a local funeral home to pick up the bodies for transport to the City of Roses.

Wright received a telephone call from Mt. Hood Meadows. They stated they would be sending skiers over shortly, along with additional avalanche probes. No sooner did Wright return the receiver to its cradle when the telephone rang again. It was Dave McClure, advising his friend and counterpart, that he was gathering his things and would be returning to Base as soon as possible.[54]

Deputy Hattan suddenly stuck his head in the office.

"We have a problem," he announced.[55]

CHAPTER 21
COMMAND AND CONTROL

Clearly angered, Deputy Hattan explained to Barry Wright how he had come across The Bagger, conducting a private meeting in a storage room. The content of his conversation with Lt. Hanners was also relayed. The deputy could tell by Wright's reaction that PMR was, likewise, in the dark. Both men had been left out of Harder's information loop.[1]

Learning that two deceased climbers had been transferred from the glacier to a parking lot down the mountain, was news that Wright had to take a few moments to process. He soon understood why confusion had reigned.[2] The PJs had intentionally avoided anything that would relay the message, *we've discovered bodies,* over the airwaves, knowing that such transmissions might be overheard by loved ones.[3]

Among rescue workers, there was an unofficial understanding. If a person is declared "deceased," they must be evacuated by ground forces, because there is no longer a need for medical expediency. If a person is proclaimed to be a "survivor," however, priorities remained high. Aircraft could continue to be employed, and additional resources could be put into service.[4]

The Bagger had followed protocol by asking for Crag Rats with sleds, which would have allowed for the proper transport to the Lodge. He continued to employ the aircraft in their pre-assigned search sectors.[5]

Wright was confused as to why the helicopter was eventually used to move the victims to Government Camp. He certainly couldn't explain why The Bagger was communicating with a civilian physician on his own, nor why he was attempting to transport bodies across county lines. Wright had his hands full overseeing the deployment of multiple SAR teams. The Sheriff's office would have to take the lead on regaining command and control.[6]

~9:15 A.M.
PARKING LOT
OREGON STATE POLICE FIELD OFFICE
GOVERNMENT CAMP

Observing the funeral home employees' procedures, Lt. Hanners received a transmission from Deputy Hattan in Base Operations.

"Something's got to be done," said the deputy. "We're out of control."[7] Hanners asked Hattan to elaborate. The deputy brought his lieutenant up to speed on what he had overheard in the storage room. Hanners and Hattan discussed The Bagger's plan and its implications. The lieutenant stated that, once he'd return to Timberline, he'd ensure that procedures and regulations would resume. Hanners finished his call and returned his attention to the parking lot.[8]

A Life Flight helicopter landed near the officer's Toyota pick-up. News crews had shown up to capture the event.

Deputy Krebs, wearing a dark blue down jacket, assisted two paramedics in loading the first victim into the rear of the aircraft. As the rotor blades on the helicopter continued to drone, Krebs and the two funeral home workers carefully loaded the second victim. Once the helo departed, the deputy strolled over to reporters.

"These people here," Krebs spoke into their microphones, "are two of the subjects that earlier, were described as fatalities. They're being rushed, in their state—"[9]

"Which is?" a reporter interrupted.

"Frozen, at this point," Krebs replied, "to the hospital, for a doctor who is awaiting them, to give them emergency care." The deputy was doing his best to avoid assigning a label to the climbers' conditions.

The civilian aircraft began its flight from Mount Hood to Portland, sixty miles to the west.

~9:25 A.M.
KOEBER RESIDENCE
PACIFIC CITY

Don and Tara Penater watched news updates concerning the events transpiring up on the mountain. They were keeping Don's mother company at her house. Still under the belief that the missing climbers were safe in their hidden snow cave, they all sipped coffee and discussed the pros and cons of being in such a cocoon.

Don suddenly lurched towards the television. He had just seen a body bag being loaded into the back of a Life Flight helicopter.

"Okay," Don roared, leaping out of his chair. "We're moving!"[10] He now understood that his sister—Marion Horwell—was involved in a much more severe situation than he had imagined. He directed his wife to retrieve their daughter from school and head to OES to take care of their niece, Amy. Don stated he would take a separate car.

"I'm going right now," he said, "because I'll probably end up on Mount Hood."

10:03 A.M.
EMANUEL HOSPITAL
PORTLAND

The Life Flight helicopter touched down at Emanuel Hospital.[11] Medical specialists raced to offload the patients. A UPI reporter pressed David Long for answers. Long, director of the hospital's helicopter service, was careful with his words.

"It is difficult to know their condition," he said. "They have to be warmed up first. The doctors have to take it step by step and very slowly. And, warm them up and hope that their life-lines will follow."[12]

Dr. William Long, chief of trauma service, would lead a team of forty cardiac and trauma specialists in an attempt to stabilize the patients. He was optimistic, partially from his own experience with treating hypothermic patients.

He knew of a case where doctors had treated three mountaineers who suffered several hours of hypothermia and failed to register any heart activity. All three climbers had not only been rewarmed and had their hearts restarted, but they appeared to suffer no discernable neurological damage.[13]

Perhaps there was still hope for the incoming patients.

10:05 A.M.
BASE OPERATIONS
WY'EAST DAY LODGE

The discovery of three missing climbers failed to shed any light on the location of the snow cave. The nearby boot prints indicated that the victims had descended from somewhere higher up on the glacier. Ralph Summers had been flown over the terrain in a Huey, but the region was blanketed with so much new snow that he was unable to assist in identifying his earlier route down the mountain. Wright knew, all too well, how much territory his teams still had to cover.[14]

Thankfully, resources continued to arrive in the office spaces. Brandy Johnson, Martin Johnson, and Warren Johnson—respected skiers from Mt. Hood Meadows—volunteered their services. Cheryl Maslen dubbed them Team 15 and scheduled them for a Huey flight, clear up to 10,000', above Triangle Moraine.[15] From this elevation, they were to ski down the mountain, searching along the way.

~10:10 A.M.
EMANUEL HOSPITAL
PORTLAND

The core temperatures of the two patients seemed unbelievable. By employing indwelling catheters, the temperatures of these two girls registered at 43° and 45° F.[16]

Dr. Okies received a patient who was still curled up in the fetal position. Being unable to extend her legs to gain access to the femoral artery, a sternotomy was performed.[17]

Trauma teams connected the patients to cardiopulmonary bypass machines and undertook the methodical rewarming process. Doctors would use the device in an attempt to warm their patient's blood while *not* stopping their hearts. In marked contrast to open-heart surgery, doctors would return this blood directly to the patient's heart. It was hoped that this process would not only assist in warming their vital organs but in meeting the output demands of the rest of their bodies.[18]

~10:15 A.M.
PARKING LOT
WY'EAST DAY LODGE

Jeff Hicks and Susan Lekas made their way through the parking lot, doing their best to avoid reporters. As employees of OES, they would have been considered media commodities if their identities were disclosed.

They had been sent to retrieve Mick, Lorca, John, and Courtney, but all four students had left with other adults. Jeff had been functioning as the liaison for Sam Dibbins but, with the situation becoming critical, the resident advisor knew he should be back in the dorms. With heavy hearts, Jeff and Susan climbed into the Suburban to begin their return journey to the campus.[19]

Cheryl Maslen was also weaving her way around the tangle of news vans. The vehicles were originally parked near the southern edge of the lot, but they had slowly migrated as the morning unfolded. The space needed for the helicopter LZ kept expanding, nudging journalists and bystanders farther north.

By now, the reporters recognized Maslen's face. She'd helped the deputies by fielding questions from the press. Recently, she had several mountaineers conduct a mock probe line, to demonstrate what the searchers were doing up on the slopes.

Another reporter was requesting an interview. Maslen stood still with the backdrop of the Lodge featured prominently. As the reporter began asking questions, his cameraman suddenly slipped on a patch of ice and fell to the pavement. Maslen was astonished but impressed. The cameraman had protected his equipment from damage.

"It's a $60,000 camera," the man winced, obviously feeling the impact of the unforgiving pavement.[20]

10:18 A.M.
BASE OPERATIONS
WY'EAST DAY LODGE

Captain J. T. Grolbert and Lt. Sherwood Stillman walked into the office spaces. The officers wanted an update from the mountain rescue leaders at the center of communications.[21]

Wright and Hattan provided the necessary briefing. Team 10 had spotted a lone climber high up on Newton Clark Glacier. That report was investigated without yielding any results. Team 11 was with the Crag Rats. Team 12 was around 5,100', hiking down Salmon River Canyon. Team 13 hadn't checked-in for a while. Team 14's mission had been canceled. Team 15, comprised of the three skiers from Mt. Hood Meadows, was set to explore from about 10,000' on down the mountain.[22]

Two of the OES climbers were currently being treated at Emanuel. A third was on a military helicopter, heading to the same facility.

The squadron Huey, bearing the climber who was found at the Upper Discovery Site, landed on the roof of the hospital.[23] The patient was transferred to a waiting gurney.

This climber, like the previous two, had no identification.[24] There had been an initial report of two boys and a girl.[25] That had to be corrected, to note two girls and one boy.

There was an operatory for each of the three patients, with at least nine specialists in each room. One staff member was assigned the task of passing from room to room, keeping physicians and nurses updated on the status of all three patients.[26]

The boy's temperature was 46° F.[27]

Deputy Hattan and Wright discussed current operations as the latter updated the wall map with the movements of their personnel.

Team 11 joined the Crag Rats. It was decided to label these men as 28A and 28C. Maslen had not formed these teams and had no idea who was in each group. Team 28A was high up on the east rim at the head of White River Canyon. Team 28C was exploring the western rim of White River Glacier, 400 feet below Team 10.[28] There were about ten Crag Rats and three PMR members in these two units.

Lew Russell and Craig Petrie were aboard a snowcat, departing Base. The plan was for Petrie to drop Russell off at the top of Sand Canyon. From there, Russell would slowly ski down the canyon, to determine if there were any signs of the missing climbers. While Russell was skiing, Petrie would maneuver his snowcat around, descend to the base of the Glade ski trail, and pick his colleague up at the base of the canyon.[29]

Hattan was pleased. Sections of terrain were being covered, explored, and even flagged. Though there was still no sign of the snow cave, teams were checking-off large areas of terrain that did *not* contain the cave.[30]

An information center was erected within the school administration building. From here, updates on the search efforts were provided to family, friends, the student body, and the general public.[31]

Courtney, one of the students who had turned around before the storm, was impressed that the school was implementing various support services and had declared that final exams were optional.[32]

Lorca, whom Courtney had escorted down the mountain, was also pleased with the school's response. Class attendance was optional, yet teachers could still be found within their assigned classrooms. Students were told they could forgo the standard curriculum and speak directly with their instructors about the events on the mountain. Lorca declined to attend class but appreciated the fact that some type of counseling was provided.[33]

John Whitson found himself embroiled in a conversation concerning the missing students. Some of his classmates were pondering the situation and pressing him for information.

"Well, you were there," someone pointed out. "Who do you think is alive?"[34]

"I don't know," John replied, honestly. "I don't know these people well enough to speculate on what they would do in this situation."

Chia was dealing with a wide variety of emotions. She was assigned to a climbing team that was to make an attempt in just a couple days.

"All we can do," she informed reporters, "is just pray to God and hope. I have mixed feelings about it. I'm scared. But any of us would go."[35]

"Yeah, we'd all go," several of the students nearby her agreed, referring to future attempts on the mountain.

Sandy had not attended classes all morning, preferring to remain alone with her thoughts. A few months earlier, she had been performing community service at a local women's shelter with Alison. They had been washing sheets and blankets when one of them noticed a door that led to the roof of the building. A sign was visible; an alarm would sound if the gate was opened. Unable to resist, the girls carefully opened the door. No alarm sounded. Excited, they ascended to the roof. There, the girls found a place to sit and talk. The topic focused on what they thought their lives would be like when they grew up.[36]

Reporters stated that a couple of helicopters had flown three patients to Emanuel Hospital. Sandy found a friend, Greg Crawford, and asked if his mother could drive them all to the hospital.

As a spokesman for the school, Mariann Koop was used to interacting with members of the press, but nothing could have prepared her for the questions she was now receiving.

"We prayed together as a group," she stated to reporters, "for the safety of our friends and classmates."[37]

Reporters were mixing with members of the faculty. There were scores of photographs on the walls. Many pictures from the school's Basecamp program were on display: teens on Mount Hood, students practicing climbing techniques, and kids learning knot-tying techniques.[38]

Koop did not disclose that Hollywood was already considering making a film concerning the unfolding calamity. OES Board members had advised the producers that they would not assist in commercial exploitation of the tragedy.[39]

11:00 A.M.
BASE OPERATIONS
WY'EAST DAY LODGE

Shultz was busy scribbling mission updates into PMR's radio log. Team 10, at 9,000', was working in conjunction with the Crag Rats.[40] That meant that all teams up on the mountain were working together, in two large groups.

Team 13 had reached Highway 35. They would hitchhike back to Base to be assigned another mission.[41]

~11:10 A.M.
EMANUEL HOSPITAL
PORTLAND

Doctors were confronted with three cases of profound hypothermia. The conventional treatment, for patients with body core temperatures between 83° and 95° F, would include a warm bath, warm blankets, or introducing heated, humidified air into the patient's mouth. One could even introduce warm fluids into the abdominal cavity itself.[42] Technically, if a patient had a functioning circulatory system and the cold temperatures had managed to preserve vital functions, hope was a possibility.

Dr. William Long recognized that there was no standard method for reviving patients suffering from profound hypothermia. Cardiopulmonary bypass appeared to be the only option.[43] Still, how rapidly should patients be rewarmed? Should kidney-dialysis also be performed? Should that be done at the same time as the rewarming with the heart-lung machine? What drugs, if any, should be administered? Would a patient's circulatory system be damaged? Was there already clotting? There were scores of questions, yet few answers.[44]

Doctors had no way to identify their patients. Upon their arrival at the hospital, the victims might have been identifiable to family members, but none were present at that time.[45]

The bypass procedures had shown progress. Doctors managed to raise the body core temperatures of the girls to 68° F.[46] The side effect of this rewarming procedure, however, was a significant excess of watery fluid collecting in the tissues of the patients. Severe edema had changed their facial features as the procedure progressed. They were no longer recognizable.[47]

Accompanied by Greg and his mom, Sandy walked into the hospital, went straight to the information desk, and explained why she was there. They were ushered into a waiting room where the hospital staff brought water, soda, and even a chaplain.

Sandy slumped down into a chair, her thoughts drifting to her friend, Alison. The two were best friends. Even when Sandy had moved to California for their freshman year, the girls constantly called and corresponded with one another. When the Douthit family took a family vacation to Canada, Alison went with them. When Alison's parents divorced, she spent a few weeks with Sandy's family in California.

Sandy needed information, even if it was bad news. Emboldened, she stood and walked to the nurse's station.

"May I identify the bodies?" She asked.[48]

CHAPTER 22
BROTHER

A tall rugged man emerged from a beige Porsche 911 and trotted toward the student dorms. Encountering a group of teary-eyed girls along the way, he asked if they had heard any updates on the identities of the climbers that had been flown to Emanuel Hospital. Not yet.

Entering his sister's apartment, Don embraced his niece, Amy. She appeared to be handling the situation bravely, and she was surrounded by caring OES staff.

"Listen, sweetie," he said. "Aunt Tara, Lesley, and your grandma are on their way up here, so you'll be fine. I have to leave. I've got to find out whether I have to go up to the mountain or not."[1] Amy nodded but said nothing.

~11:15 A.M.
WHITE RIVER GLACIER

It was warming up, so Ed Hall removed his gloves. His right hand, which had been exposed to the fury of yesterday's storm, fared far better than he had anticipated. He had some blisters around his wrist, but otherwise, his hand was recovering nicely.

Hall and several Crag Rats had been flown up to Lower Triangle Moraine several hours earlier, at the request of The Bagger.

Hall, accompanied by Bruce "Lightning" Hukari and Ken Hukari had screwed their ski poles together, creating makeshift avalanche probes. Declining to rope-up, they conducted their own mini-probe line. They explored areas that seemed to match Summer's description of the snow cave site. They had carefully searched for any tactile anomalies beneath the snow.

Around 8,000', on the eastern side of the glacier, the trio removed their packs and retrieved what food they had brought from home. It was time for lunch.

Hall popped some dried fruits and nuts into his mouth as he fished a potato from the bottom of his pack. At home, he had baked the potato, opened it up, slathered the interior with butter, and wrapped it up tight for safekeeping. Now, hours later, it had gotten mashed-up a bit but remained a good source of carbohydrates. It was his go-to mountain food.

"My Irish heritage lends me to potatoes," he chuckled, pleased with himself for bringing such a delicacy up the mountain.[2]

Watching Lightning unwrap his lunch, Hall found himself less smitten with his cold, baked potato. He spotted several slices of pizza in Hukari's food cache.

Leftover pizza on the mountain! Hall thought. *You can't get any better than that!*

~11:30 A.M.
PARKING LOT
WY'EAST DAY LODGE

Whereas the Mt. Hood Ski Patrol was responsible for patrolling the forty-one ski trails above and below the resort, the Nordic Ski Patrol teams focused on rescues in the backcountry. The organization consisted of less than a dozen men and women—a small, seemingly ragtag group of ski bums with the desire to help others. They were fully accredited by the National Ski Patrol and had performed scores of rescue missions below timberline on Mount Hood.

Kathleen Sheridan, co-director of the Nordic Ski Patrol, looked up at the peak from the parking lot. The skies were blue and clear. A complete contrast to the weather she had experienced here just two days earlier. The thirty-four-year-old had been climbing the South Side Route on Mother's Day, with a sizeable group of Mazamas. The weather had been so foul that day, visibility was lost at the top of the Magic Mile chairlift, and the club had been forced to retreat.[3]

A former EMT, Sheridan was now a student at Oregon Health & Science University. She arranged to take the rest of the day off when her organization had been called to join the search.

Sheridan entered Wy'East Day Lodge, amazed at the sheer size and scope of the SAR operation. She was used to three or four people tending to an injured cross-country skier. Here, there were so many people and so many organizations. The complexity of it all seemed staggering. She didn't envy whoever was in charge.[4]

Overhearing a radio transmission indicating Rick Harder was somewhere on the grounds of the resort, Wright took the opportunity to request Harder's presence in Base Operations.

Team 13 walked into the room. After searching their designated territory, they had hitchhiked from Highway 35 back up to the Lodge. Gerald Donahue handed Deputy Hattan a large blue mitten, stating they had discovered it at 7,300', at the base of some avalanche debris.[5] Hattan handed it to Wright just as they heard a message that Team 12 was also hitchhiking back to Base.[6] Wright wanted to further explore the area in which this mitten had been found. Donahue stated they could return to the site and intensify the efforts in that area.

Maslen knew that fine probing over a colossal slice of real estate would be extremely time-consuming. She recognized the manpower that would be required and the numerous personnel shifts that would be needed. Time was not a luxury. She could see the sense of despair in the faces of the parents, members of the media, and even SAR personnel.[7]

Deputy Williams informed reporters that roughly 100 rescue workers would be dispatched to probe the southeastern slopes of the mountain.[8] Using ten-foot aluminum probes, these searchers would poke through the snowdrifts of White River Glacier, one foot at a time. They would focus their attention on the terrain between 8,000' and 9,000'.[9]

Captain Grolbert and Lt. Stillman set about seeing to the needs of the family members of the missing climbers. Grolbert met with Lt. Hanners and decided to assign two additional personnel to the operation. Deputy Carl Witt and EM Coordinator Casey Marley were charged with aiding the families.[10]

Deputy Krebs would remain the principal interface between the rescue authorities and the families. This was an extremely difficult and emotional assignment for the man. Maslen, who worked beside him, knew when to cut Krebs' caffeine intake.[11] Still, the deputy was popping Excedrin.[12]

There were conflicting reports on the condition of the three frozen climbers. The captain learned that authorities at Emanuel were not providing any information. They may have been hampered by hospital policies. As a result, Captain Grolbert had very little information to share with families.[13]

Deputy Kennell phoned the Corvallis Mountain Rescue Unit (CMRU), 130 miles southwest of the mountain.[14] The unit, reorganized in 1975, was placed on Standby. Within minutes, however, that request was upgraded to full activation.[15]

Team 16, comprised of Nordic Ski Patrol members, exited the Lodge and donned their sunglasses. The group consisted of Kent Romney, Scott Clark, Ray Patrick, Francis Patrick, and Don Cossel.[16] They would be transported to the Hidden Lake region, west of Timberline Lodge. They were to explore a popular trail, situated between Sand Canyon and Paradise Park. If more students had fled the sanctuary of the snow cave during the whiteout, they could easily have followed the natural fall line of the mountain's topography. Such a direction would lead climbers towards Mississippi Head, Sand Canyon, or along the forested ridge east of Zigzag Canyon.

~11:45 A.M.
GAST RESIDENCE
WOODBURN

Mick Garrett had spent the morning at his grandmother's house. A call came in from the school, updating Mick on the latest news from the mountain. He was informed that the three victims at the hospital had not been identified. There were two girls and a boy. Distressed, Mick asked his dad for a ride back to campus.[17]

~11:55 A.M.
EMANUEL HOSPITAL
PORTLAND

Don parked his Porsche in a nearby parking lot and raced up a flight of stairs to the hospital. His attention went straight to a woman at the front counter, speaking on the phone. Don could tell, by listening to her side of the conversation, that it was a journalist on the other end of the line. The woman tactfully avoided the reporter's question, hung up the receiver, and greeted Penater warmly.

"Here's the deal," Don said, as calmly as he could under the circumstances. "I know you have privacy laws, but I gotta know if the two bodies you brought in from Mount Hood...was one of them an adult female?"[18] Don was unaware that a third patient had been brought to the facility. He knew his sister was the only adult female in the snow cave and believed the phrasing of his question would enable the receptionist to answer his query legally.

"I'm afraid I can't answer that question," she replied.

"Get your supervisor," Don replied, with a slightly elevated tone. The six-foot-three, former Marine leaned against the counter. He felt sorry for the receptionist but wasn't leaving until his question had been answered to his satisfaction. "Get your boss," he continued. "Get someone, cause I ain't leaving."

"But—" she continued to protest.

"Look, lady. I appreciate the situation that you're in. I don't want any names or anything. I just need to know if you have an adult female? If you don't tell me, I'm going to go down to that morgue, and I'm going to check everybody myself!"

~12:00 P.M.
BASE OPERATIONS
WY'EAST DAY LODGE

Rocky Henderson hadn't been on the mountain when the three climbers had been found. He had heard the news on the radio and drove back up to the resort.

Henderson checked-in at Base and awaited instructions. He would be added to Team 17, but the group would have to wait a while for a Huey. There were men from three SAR units waiting in a queue to hitch a ride.[19] Jeffrey Youngbluth, Dave Armstrong, Dave Bourland, John Harkness, and Mark Schneider were all PJs. Mark's twin brother—John—was a member of PMR, and no one could tell the two apart. Kent Lambert was from the Crag Rats. Dennis Alexander and Henderson represented PMR.[20] Helicopters were flying searchers to and from a relatively level section of terrain at 8,200', now known as the upper landing zone (LZ).[21]

They would have to wait their turn.

Major Jones was taking a quick break before returning to duty. He fell into conversation with a few of his coworkers. They were debating what more could be done to help in the search.

"What about dogs?" one of them inquired.[22]

Frank and John walked outside and headed down the pavement that led to the parking lot. Reporters knew who Frank was by now and immediately deluged him with questions.

"I'm scared and frightened," Frank said to the reporters. "I don't know if I want to know if Pat's in Emanuel or still up here."[23]

Although Pat was still missing, Frank had the uncontrollable urge to return home and hug his youngest son, Christopher.

John took the wheel for the somber drive home.[24]

12:56 P.M.
BASE OPERATIONS
WY'EAST DAY LODGE

Deputy Kennel made two phone calls. His first was to the 304th ARRS. Kennel asked if they would provide air transport for SAR dog teams from the Seattle area if he could procure such teams. When Kennel received confirmation that the logistics could be arranged, he telephoned King County Search and Rescue and inquired about their rescue dogs and handlers.[25]

1:00 P.M.
BASE OPERATIONS
WY'EAST DAY LODGE

Dave McClure, co-chief for PMR, walked into Base Operations.[26] His wife and Wright brought him up to speed on what had transpired during his absence. McClure had been confident that members of the missing climbing party would have crawled out of the snow cave this morning and signaled their location. The discovery of three people out in the elements, mysterious tracks that disappeared under snow drifts, and conflicting estimates on the elevation of the elusive cave were all alarming to the seasoned mountaineer.[27]

Authorities had received reports about what the terrain looked like in the immediate vicinity of where the three students had been discovered. The sites bore no physical resemblance to the details Summers had provided at his various debriefings. Tracks indicated that climbers from the OES team had descended from somewhere above 8,200'.[28] By analyzing Tuesday's weather and team movements on the mountain today, the consensus was

that the snow cave was situated somewhere a⌐
raine of White River Canyon.[29]

trip to San
Ashland,
Tempest."

~1:03 P.M.
EMANUEL HOSPITAL
PORTLAND

Sandy sat slumped in a waiting room chair. S
had asked if she could identify the patients that had
slopes of Mount Hood. This brave request had been po
Sandy heard a nurse whisper that a girl of only sixteen s⌐
be privy to such matters.[30] She contented herself with overł⌐
of conversations between reporters.

Sandy gleaned that the male victim was showing signs of in⌐
After two hours on bypass, his right ventricle began to show no⌐
contractions.[31]

~1:05 P.M.
WY'EAST DAY LODGE

Mar and Diana spotted Bishop Ladehoff and Father Malcolm Manson
The latter served as headmaster of OES. The six-foot-four man approached
the women.[32]

"How can we help?" he offered, in his British accent.[33]

"How about a Eucharist?" Mar suggested.

The priests invited everyone in the vicinity to celebrate Holy Com-
munion. When Diana received the sacrament from Fr. Manson, she felt a
sudden chill. Clearly, something was not right.[34]

~1:05 P.M.
JACKSON HOUSE
OREGON EPISCOPAL SCHOOL

Amy thought it felt strange to be home, rather than in class. After
lunch, she answered a knock at the door. It was her Aunt Tara, her cousin
Lesley, and her grandmother. They had all come in a second car while Uncle
Don was investigating what was happening in the search for Amy's mom.[35]

Amy and Lesley, both twelve, caught up on their day-to-day lives:
classes they liked, teachers they enjoyed, sports and plays they had attended. During Spring Break, Amy's mom had taken her daughter on a road

Francisco. Along their journey, they had stopped in the town of
Oregon, and attended a live performance of Shakespeare's "The

~1:10 P.M.
GAS STATION
GRESHAM

After Penater had demanded answers at Emanuel Hospital, the woman
e desk had attempted to quote privacy concerns. Don gained traction
n he threatened to head down to their morgue to personally inventory
tags. The woman walked into an adjacent room. When she emerged, she
d three words that brought the man some measure of comfort.

"No adult female," she whispered.[37]

As he listened to the sound of fuel filling the tank of his Porsche, Don
looked at Mount Hood on the horizon. It was a sunny day, and temperatures were in the mid-seventies. He couldn't believe his sister was trapped
in a cave, somewhere up on that tower of ice and snow.

It didn't feel real.

1:30 P.M.
UPPER LZ
LOWER TRIANGLE MORAINE

Rocky Henderson and his companions jumped out of the aircraft.
They nodded to the teams who were loading into the Huey for the return
trip to Base. Henderson waved to the pilot and carefully walked away from
the aircraft.

Team 17's mission was to explore a region called the White River Head-
wall. They started hiking directly toward the upper glacier near the base of
Steel Cliff. Henderson was in the lead, followed by Dennis Alexander and
Mark Schneider. They began gaining ground.[38]

Team 18 was led by Sandy Childs. His team included: Bob Caldwell,
Mike Seeley, Jeff Hartley, and Jim Boucher.[39] This team was to employ
avalanche probes and inspect the area where a smoke grenade had been
dropped hours earlier.

Searchers were hampered by increasingly warm temperatures. This presented PMR with a quandary. Volunteers had to rappel into each and every crevasse large enough to have swallowed a child. This proved dangerous and unpredictable as the heat warmed the top layers of snow. Snow bridges were likewise unstable. It was a hazardous environment for a search and rescue operation.[40] McClure and Wright were concerned that a significant accident might occur at any moment.

1:42 P.M.
WEST MORAINE
WHITE RIVER CANYON

Henderson felt strong and confident. Visibility was ideal, and winds were moderate. He heard the rotor blades of an approaching helicopter and looked up. A military Huey was making a slow pass over the team. Henderson could see Rick Harder leaning out the open door of the aircraft.[41] The Bagger was making hand signals that Rocky just couldn't understand. Confused, Henderson radioed down to Base seeking some type of interpretation.[42] Henderson thought The Bagger could be extending a friendly gesture from one volunteer to another, so he waved back.

The Huey crew had been assigned to scan the upper regions of both Palmer and White River Glaciers. They had been performing this duty when Team 17 came into view. Something caught The Bagger's attention, and he started motioning furiously.

Henderson soon realized that The Bagger wasn't sending a greeting. He was attempting to get him to turn around. The recruit spun around and saw Dennis Alexander behind him, as well as the groups' fresh tracks. There was no third man visible—only a hole in the snow.

Mark Schneider was nowhere to be seen.[43]

CHAPTER 23
MITTENS AND GLOVES

Rick Harder, who had witnessed Mark Schneider drop out of site as if someone had released a trap door, directed the helicopter to land.[1] A group of Crag Rats also descended to assist Team 17. Rocky Henderson called down to Schneider, while ten men peered down into the dark hole in the snow.

From roughly thirty feet below the surface of the moraine, Schneider responded. He hadn't broken anything, but he was pretty banged up. Unable to climb out on his own, his friends threw a line down to him. Employing ropes and pulleys, the men—significantly assisted by the mechanical advantage—retrieved their cold and injured companion.[2]

Stringfield, Radys, and O'Bannon parted ways after ten hours of searching the slopes and inspecting crevasses.[3] Team 10 had explored terrain features from 8,200' on Palmer Glacier, all the way up to Triangle Moraine.

Stringfield walked out to his car, stomping his boots to release chunks of ice and compacted snow, avoiding all requests from reporters for comments.[4]

Mar and Diana were growing more and more irritated with the media. Reporters and bystanders alike had learned that a blue mitten had been discovered on White River Glacier. Mar, upset and seeking action, turned to the nearby journalists.

"Instead of just trying to get news," she scolded, "why don't you do something useful and show a picture of that mitten on television; see if anyone recognizes it."[5]

Don Penater raced up Timberline Road, relieved that he hadn't been pulled over by the police during his journey. Approaching the parking lot, a Huey flew directly over his car, blowing snow everywhere.

"Not a good sign," he mumbled to himself.[6]

He was surprised at the sheer number of people, assembled in various knots and ranks. Where should he go to get the answers to his questions? Was there a specific individual in charge?

A passer-by announced that relatives of the missing climbers were being asked to check-in with the sheriff's department. Don noticed reporters looked like they were ready to pounce upon anyone with such a distinction, so he decided not to identify himself.

He devised a different plan altogether.

Rummaging through his car, he retrieved a pen and a pad of paper. With a renewed sense of confidence, Don began milling about the parking lot, chatting with anyone who could provide information. He blended in, he smiled, he gleaned information from SAR volunteers and deputies. With his pen and paper, Don Penater was passing as a newspaper reporter.[7]

The male patient showed further signs of improvement. As his core temperature continued to rise, his heart sustained a sinus rhythm.[8]

A priest, associated with OES, was on his way to the hospital. Hopefully, this man would recognize and identify the three students.[9]

After catching a few hours of sleep, Mike Craig was ready to lead his third team. With him on Team 19 were Chet Edwards and Bill Stevenson of

PMR.[10] They would explore the western edge of White River Glacier.

Team 20 was led by Dave McNeil, a member of Craig's previous group—Team 9. McNeil's teammates were Mark Parker and Paul Rishel, both from the Mt. Hood Nordic Ski Patrol.[11] They would be searching the gullies along the eastern edge of the glacier.

The group of men watched as Mark Schneider, one of the twins, was airlifted off the mountain.[12]

The teams continued on with their original missions. Once they reached the bottom of the Devil's Kitchen, they fanned out to explore crevasses and natural hollows in the ice.[13]

Sheriff Brooks and Captain Bradshaw entered the office spaces just as another lead came to the attention of Barry Wright.[14]

Team 16, all from the ranks of the Mount Hood Nordic Ski Patrol, had discovered an ice axe. Wright asked for more information. When the full description was read over the airwaves, hope that it belonged to the OES group were quickly dashed. It belonged to The Bagger. He had dropped the tool when The Hasty Team was descending to Silcox Hut in the blizzard.[15]

After this lead dried up, it was discovered that the blue mitten, which had been found in White River Canyon, had been positively identified as belonging to one of the missing girls. Dave McClure directed Teams 13, 19, and 20 to thoroughly investigate the area in which it had been found.[16]

A military helicopter landed at the LZ in the parking lot, and one of the pilots announced the return of Team 17. Wright, who continuously updated the map with team movements, knew Henderson and the others were up near the Devil's Kitchen. How was a *return* possible? A quick trip to the parking lot solved the mystery.

Mark Schneider had been airlifted to the LZ. As he had been a member of Henderson's group, the officer simply reported that Team 17 had returned. The rest of Schneider's colleagues were still up on the mountain, performing their assigned tasking.[17]

Walking back toward the Lodge, Wright had to pass through a tunnel of inquiries from reporters. *Why weren't the students crawling out of the snow cave on such a sunny day? Why weren't they signaling their location?* Deflecting all questions and refusing to speculate, Wright kept his thoughts to himself.

Perhaps the children weren't emerging from the cave...because they were unable to do so.[18]

~2:55 P.M.
HALLWAY
WY'EAST DAY LODGE

A member of the Forest Service approached Rick Harder, offering the use of three metal detectors, which were currently in Government Camp. Within the OES equipment cache was a metal stove, ice axes, and a handful of metal pack frames. Although unlikely, given the depth of fresh snow, metal detectors just might receive a signal. Harder relayed this information to deputies. The sheriff's department gave the thumbs up. They were willing to try anything.[19]

3:09 P.M.
MEDIA ROOM
WY'EAST DAY LODGE

Don found his way into the media room. Several deputies and members of PMR were gathered around a table at the front of the room. The audience was primarily reporters. Don, seeking any information on his missing sister, blended in with a group at the back of the room. He held his pen and paper out in front of him. To anyone in the room, he would appear to be just another reporter.[20]

McClure, looking very serious, stepped forward and introduced himself. He provided updates on team movements. Like his friend and co-chief, Barry Wright, McClure was concerned that no one had emerged from the snow cave during such ideal weather conditions. He wished Summers had insisted on taking more students with him down the mountain, but he kept that thought to himself.[21]

Cheryl Maslen, standing next to her husband, was clinging to the hope that someone inside the cave still had the presence of mind to keep their breathing holes in the ceiling open.[22]

She, too, kept that thought to herself.

A reporter asked if PMR was becoming frustrated. McClure acknowledged that they had experienced multiple disappointments. All efforts seemed fruitless. As each hour elapsed, the searchers continued to come up empty-handed. There had been voices, tracks, tools, and a mitten. Leads that led nowhere.

One journalist pointed out that there were currently three military helicopters sitting in the south parking lot. Why were they not being tasked with missions at the moment?

"Now tell me this," Don suddenly interjected. "Why can't we just go wander up there and look for them? It's not that far away."[23]

A deputy stepped forward, holding his hands up defensively.

"No, no," he said. "We have to keep control of this. Be patient and wait for the experts to do their job."

McClure turned the discussion back to strategy, providing new information. A snowcat had dropped Teams 19 and 20 off in White River Canyon, at 8,200'. These two teams were prepared to stay the night on the mountain.[24] This was the first indication that rescue workers were preparing for the possibility that the OES team could be spending another night in the snow cave. This realization was evident on the faces of the press.

The quiet that followed was interrupted by someone entering the room and handing a scrap of paper to a deputy. It was a message from Barry Wright. In White River Canyon, at 7,000', Team 13 had just come across a glove.[25]

3:15 P.M.
BASE OPERATIONS
WY'EAST DAY LODGE

It was soon revealed that the glove was not the mate to the blue mitten that had been found earlier in the day. Team 13 had placed a flag at the site of the second discovery. A search pattern, surrounding the latest glove-discovery site, was created and executed with the help of Teams 19 and 20. Snowcat 8 was redirected to the area, to lend whatever transportation assistance was needed. A Huey was assigned to provide aerial reconnaissance over the site.[26]

It was determined that the newly discovered glove belonged to Terry Swicegood. He had lost it when he took his tumble into White River Canyon.[27] The emotional roller coaster continued.

Pausing to rest and take in the view, Kathleen Sheridan heard only the teams' heavy breathing and the trickling sounds of nearby White River. She had driven down to Highway 35 and parked at White River West Sno-Park. This undeveloped pocket of the mountain was a hub of winter activities. Adrenaline junkies employing snowshoes, cross-country skis, or sleds, were a common sight here on weekends. Mercifully, it was mid-week, and only her team was in the region.

The team, on cross-country skis, had trekked up an old quarry road. The snow was deep, a welcome sight for the group who could easily see any disturbances on the ivory mounds. Everyone scanned their surroundings, looking for footprints, discarded items—anything that would indicate the passage of humans.

Standing at the forested edge of a snow bowl, Sheridan noted a low-hanging fog, lingering in the lower reaches of the canyon. *Cold and crappy*, she thought, but the cool breeze felt good on her brow. She wondered if any more of the missing OES group had departed the cave in a desperate gamble to escape. If so, could they be just around the next bend? Just behind a snow hummock in the distance? The sounds of the babbling creek continued, and the team pressed on, resuming their duties.[28]

There had been no significant developments in the case of the female patients, which medical teams had been working on for five hours. Their core temperatures had failed to rise above 68° F. Over forty perfusionists, doctors, and nurses were forced to cease life-supporting efforts on these two patients.[29] Time of death was pronounced, though their identities were not released to the public.

"There was very little chance," Dr. Barbara Lloyd, chief surgical resident, acknowledged to reporters. "They were very, very cold."[30]

"I don't think they stood too much of a chance," Nurse Woodsworth agreed. "I think we learned a lot and will be able to help others in the future."[31]

Regarding the unidentified male under their care, his core temperature upon arrival at the medical facility had been 46° F.[32] Following his time connected to the heart-lung machine, he had been warmed to 93.2° F. His heart started beating.[33]

~3:30 P.M.
JACKSON HOUSE
OREGON EPISCOPAL SCHOOL

Several of Amy's girlfriends came to her apartment to keep her and her cousin company. Aunt Tara did her best to entertain these preteens while keeping her eye on the television. Uncle Don called, periodically, with updates from the mountain. There seemed to be a constant flow of people, entering and departing the Horwell residence.

Amy's normal life had effectively been suspended. She knew the adults were monitoring her closely. *They're watching me*, she thought.

Her grandmother's attention remained focused on the news bulletins. The girls stayed fairly quiet. Occasionally, someone offered a question. It was a very somber atmosphere.[34]

Tara prompted the girls to take Lucy, Amy's dog, out for a walk. Amy knew that her mom's climbing party was experiencing difficulties, but she remained in a bubble of optimism, confident everything would work itself out in the end.[35] Amy and Leslie grabbed their tennis gear and headed out the door with the Dachshund/Scottish Terrier mix.

3:35 P.M.
PARKING LOT
WY'EAST DAY LODGE

Deputy Krebs introduced Cheryl Maslen to a dark-haired woman in her mid-forties. The woman was a psychic who had previously worked with the department. Krebs gave the newcomer a few moments before questioning her. The psychic replied that she was receiving visions of a snow cave.

Maslen raised an eyebrow, unimpressed. Information about the snow cave had been released to the public over twenty-four hours earlier. She was floored that the sheriff's department had requested the services of this woman and saw this as another sign of how desperate law enforcement felt about the situation.[36]

Coarse probing, between 8,500' and 9,000', along the west moraine, was proving fruitless.[37] An object, which had been seen flapping in the breeze, ended up being nothing but a blue streamer, dropped by a passing Huey.[38] Harder's ice axe, Swicegood's glove—every lead turned out to have a logical explanation.

Wright was feeling like the repeat victim of a desert mirage, like an oasis was just out of his reach, disappearing each time he approached.[39]

Deputy Krebs pulled McClure aside for a private conversation.[40] Working with The Bagger was proving to be a challenge. McClure felt it too. Harder was a high-energy, self-confident PJ with a lot of experience in helicopter operations. Most everyone in SAR hated being thrust into the spotlight by the press, but Harder seemed to thrive in the limelight. He was handsome and quite charming in front of a camera, but, behind the scenes, he was considered cocky, and Krebs wanted the man to be more of a team player. Harder's quote to the press about rescuing the missing children at dawn, and then throwing a hell of a party, aside; the man needed to be *managed*.[41]

"He'll only listen to you," Krebs said to McClure.[42]

"There must be something we can do," said McClure, with a shrug. There was a moment of silence between the men.

"Well," Krebs offered, with a smirk. "I could *shoot* him, ya' know?"

CHAPTER 24
SNIFFERS

Earlier in the morning, a helo had dropped a smoke grenade to mark the location of the Upper Discovery Site. Team 18 had been methodically probing the area just above the spent grenade.[1] The team had come across a glide crack running somewhat diagonally uphill. To the side of this crack was a distinctive, horizontal crevasse opening, nearly three feet wide. After watching one of their blue helmets accidentally roll into this rift, the team advanced uphill, remaining in a tight formation. With their aluminum shafts, the men had safely fine probed a 300' x 150' area.

Base Operations was in the process of pulling resources from the field. Snowcat drivers were directed to pick up four of the teams. The military helicopters would transport the other two groups, the PJs and the Crag Rats, back to the parking lot.[2] The content of these transmissions gave a clear indication that authorities were shifting personnel.

A white ambulance, a relic from the Korean War, lumbered up the final stretch of the highway and pulled into the parking lot. The Corvallis Mountain Rescue Unit (CMRU) logo was emblazoned on both sides of the vehicle. Scott Olson, his best friend, John Blaisdell, and Wayne Lederer had all been at work when they'd received activation notice for their unit.

Olson had been surprised when he got the call. Although he had watched the news coverage on Tuesday evening, he had forgotten all about the missing climbers until the call came in. Summers and a teenager had hiked out to safety so, like everyone else, Olson assumed that someone from within the cave would crawl out, signal the searchers, and that would have been the end of it.

All three men were employees with the City of Corvallis. Olson was a city engineer, Blaisdell worked as a land survey technician, and Lederer was an engineering aide. They were the first three members of CMRU to arrive on the mountain.

A tall man, wearing a blue flight suit and a helmet, had seen their signature vehicle park in the lot. He came trotting over to greet them.

"Hey, guys!" Rick Harder exclaimed. "It's so good to see you here. You're on the mission. I've got you an assignment."[3]

Olson was finding the encounter surreal—Harder seemed so energized.

5:14 P.M.
LANDING ZONE (LZ)
WY'EAST DAY LODGE

Group after group of rescue workers were returning to Base. Five times Hueys landed in the parking lot, off-loading Crag Rats, PJs, and members of PMR. Snowcats extracted additional SAR teams. Every team leader reported to McClure and Wright for proper debriefing.[4]

Volunteers were told to standby and wait for instructions. Fed, hydrated, and ready for mission tasking, patrol members were not happy with what they saw. Everyone within view seemed qualified to man avalanche probes.[5]

What are we all waiting for?

~5:20 P.M.
EMANUEL HOSPITAL
PORTLAND

The male patient had been on bypass for over six hours. The teen's heart continued to beat in sinus rhythm, yet the contractions had no force. Dr. Hill administered catecholamines in an effort to improve the force of these contractions. Improvements in skin temperature had been monitored closely, but these improvements did not extend to the youth's hands.[6] At this time, the boy was given a ten-percent chance of survival.[7]

The priest who had been dispatched to the hospital to identify the victims was unable to do so.[8]

Walking through the media room, Rocky Henderson could see anxiety on the faces of people he passed. The entire atmosphere had changed since he had last been in the Lodge.[9]

"Each parent up here is holding out for that slim ray of hope," Rich's mom told reporters. "The thing that keeps me going, the thing I cling to, is that I don't think God wants him dead."[10]

Diana and Mar walked out to their station wagon. Both women had overheard comments made by SAR workers and members of the media. Some believed the snow cave wouldn't be discovered until the summer melt. Others felt the cave would never be found. A melancholy veil seemed to be drawn over Mar. She was convinced she would never see her husband again.[11]

As Diana drove away, she realized the vehicle they were following belonged to a friend who had come to support them at the resort. They could see their friend's shoulders, heaving from tears as she drove.[12]

Four SAR dogs and their handlers, from German Sheppard Search Dogs and Columbus Search Dogs, emerged from a chopper.[13] Their arrival generated quite a commotion.

Deputies and members of the 304th ARRS had not announced that they'd been working with King County Search and Rescue in southwestern Washington to make this happen. An Air Force Reserve C-130 Hercules had been procured, and the four-engine turboprop had transported the dogs and their handlers to Portland International Airport. From there, a military helicopter flew the teams up to the mountain resort.[14]

Reporters snapped photographs as the dogs arrived. These canines were trained in wilderness search and avalanche recovery and had located skiers buried under more than six feet of snow.[15]

The sheriff's department had pulled all SAR teams off the mountain because they didn't want the scent of the volunteers interfering with the canines. Law enforcement was gambling on the dogs.

Aerial reconnaissance flights had proved useless and ground crews, working under arduous conditions, yielded no clues to the location of the missing OES team. McClure and Wright knew they'd be losing volunteers who needed to recuperate and return to their jobs. Contacting out of state rescue organizations seemed an ideal way to gain additional manpower.[16]

McClure raised the topic with Deputies Hattan and Krebs. Seattle Mountain Rescue would be activated.[17]

Jody Leach, twenty-four, walked into the office spaces looking for someone in charge. An EMT and a nursing school student, Leach was a member of CMRU. She had joined the team because her boyfriend was a member but soon found herself fascinated with the intricacies of crevasse rescue and coarse probing. She was fully qualified to perform SAR operations, but her experience working in command centers, during previous field exercises, made her an ideal candidate to help in Base Operations.

She was welcomed, led through the chaos of personnel, and introduced to Cheryl Maslen and Sue Shultz. She was shown the pads of college-ruled paper that constituted PMR's official logbook of the operation. She sat down and immediately started recording the content of incoming radio transmissions.

A reporter had managed to sneak into the office. He made his way to the women sitting around the radio table and started asking questions.

"How about, I leave an imprint of my hiking boot on your ass?" Leach offered, shooting the man a look that assured him she was quite serious.[18] The reporter made a quick getaway as the team's newest radio operator got the nod of approval from her new coworkers.

Despite the medical teams' best efforts, the male teenager was formally pronounced dead.[19]

"His heart was never able to generate enough power to come off the heart-lung pump," Dr. Long informed reporters.[20]

Deputies knew that Hillsboro Helicopters had access to a state-of-the-art, Forward-Looking Infrared (FLIR) camera. They were requesting this specialized camera for the search efforts now.

Helicopter pilot, Mike Moffitt, was contracted by a local news team and he didn't feel he could simply say, *Sorry guys, I'm outta' here.*[21] Thankfully, the sheriff's department communicated with KOIN TV. Moffitt and Hillsboro Helicopters were released to retrieve the FLIR camera.

After being turned away from identifying the three students at Emanuel Hospital, Sandy eventually returned to the school. Walking toward the dormitory, she was approached by one of the seniors. He told her there had been an identification of climbers at Emanuel.

Distraught, Sandy ran into one of the resident advisor's room to use a phone. She called Emanuel Hospital.

"Are you a member of the family?" she was asked.[22]

"No," she cried. "I'm not."

"The names of the victims have not officially been released yet," she was told.

"She's my best friend," Sandy cried. "Can you please...just tell me if it's her?" Reluctantly, the man confirmed that one of the victims was named Alison Litzenberger.

Sandy hung up the receiver. Alison—her best friend—gone.

Mike Moffitt landed his Bell 206 JetRanger at Hillsboro Helicopters, some eighty miles west of Mount Hood, and began his shut-down procedures.[23]

Moffitt stepped out of the helicopter and retrieved the infrared camera he had flown so far to obtain. He worked it onto a mounting plate under the cab of the aircraft. It slid into place, and a locking mechanism was engaged. A handful of quick-connect cords were manipulated before the procedure was considered complete.

He climbed back into the cockpit for the next leg of his journey.[24]

It had been a brief flight from Hillsboro Helicopters to the FLIR Systems headquarters in Tigard.[25] On previous assignments, Mike Moffitt had personally operated the FLIR camera, locked under the belly of his helicopter. The camera could pinpoint the hottest portions of forest fires. The Forest Service used that information to steer their firefighting resources.

The owner of Hillsboro Helicopters had contacted FLIR headquarters and requested a technical expert be prepared for pick-up in their parking lot. Curious employees watched as the JetRanger touched down on the asphalt and picked up its passenger.[26]

Huey pilots, Mullen and Jones, landed and called for their passengers to exit the aircraft. The officers had transported four dogs, their handlers, members of CMRU, and one of their own PJs to a region between 8,500' and 9,000'. They were tasked with searching the terrain around a specific crevasse that appeared to match Ralph Summer's description.[27]

After the Huey departed, Scott Olson took stock of his surroundings. Team 22 was standing in the middle of the crevasse-strewn glacier. Bill O'Brien directed everyone to rope-up into smaller teams.[28]

John Blaisdell, Wayne Lederer, and Olson were given a task—escort the dogs and their handlers through the central glacier and, above all, ensure the dogs did not fall into a crevasse.

Olson had dug several snow caves during his time but, without fail, these caves had been constructed into steep terrain. This mildly sloping glacier seemed to be an extremely illogical place to search.[29]

Gene Griswold, forty-one, was hiking toward the team. A maintenance technician for a cable television company, he was a member of CMRU. He and Hollis Ferguson had been transported up Palmer Snowfield in a snow-cat, clear up to 8,600'. Griswold had been told they needed to get up onto the peak, to take some of the stress off PMR. It was late in the day, and they hadn't been issued any avalanche probes.[30] They descended to Olson's position and joined Team 22.

7:16 P.M.
BASE OPERATIONS
WY'EAST DAY LODGE

When not volunteering with PMR, Barry Wright worked at the Bonneville Power Administration. Wayne Litzenberger was employed there as well. Wayne had called Wright directly, in the previous two days, seeking updates on the search efforts. Most everything had been shared with the public. The only extra information Barry had been able to provide was PMR never ceased operations. Even though deputies announced the cessation of ground searches—Wright and McClure's teams continued searching throughout the night. Litzenberger had been appreciative.

Learning that Wayne had lost his daughter, Alison, reinforced Wright's belief that his work with PMR would always come ahead of any other professional obligation. His immediate supervisor at BPA was not particularly supportive of his work in SAR. Wright felt, no matter what, he'd be out supporting his organization in the mountains, even if he had to take personal time off to do so.[31]

Wright could feel the weight of responsibility on his shoulders. He keenly felt the eyes of the public, staring him down. He knew—had always known—that citizens had no idea of the sheer volume of terrain that was being covered. The public demanded answers. Wright had none to offer.[32]

~7:20 P.M.
WHITE RIVER GLACIER

Team 22 was doing their best to escort the dogs and their handlers safely, but the path forward was proving difficult. Teams were roped-up and moved slowly. The handlers were not mountain climbers, and this fact was not lost on the members of CMRU.

John Harkness, a PJ, rigged a fixed line for the handlers to grasp as they worked their way across the slopes. The dogs were not used to this type of terrain as well, and the angle of ice and snow was proving too much for them. The canines repeatedly slid downhill, only to be checked by their leashes.[33] The gamble on the dogs appeared to be coming up short.

Olson was surprised to learn that the team would soon be directed to divert to Lower Triangle Moraine and, from there, catch one of the snow-cats for a ride back to Base. They were being called off the mountain, to make the slopes ready for a helicopter equipped with an infra-red camera. Apparently, their body heat would interfere with the imaging. It was perplexing. *We just got started, and now we're being extracted?*[34]

Diana and Mar walked into their home, physically drained and mentally enveloped in a numbing cloud of disbelief and denial. What would tomorrow bring?

The family had an answering machine. Diana pressed the playback button and listened to one message after another. Church members, friends, and family had left multiple offerings of love and support.

Mar, exhausted, fell asleep quickly. At some point, she experienced something...simultaneously dream and vision. An intimate conversation with her husband. "Tom," she was saying to him. "It's okay. You don't have to make it. You can let go."[35]

Manipulating the two control sticks in front of him: the cyclic—controlling movement—in his right hand; and the collective—power—in his left, Mike Moffitt was rapidly approaching the requested search sector. Barry Wright had directed Moffitt to use his FLIR camera along the western moraine of White River Glacier, between 8,000' and 8,500'. The aircraft, being an older "A" model, had been converted to a "B" model. The "A" model is 300 pounds lighter, and some pilots found the earlier model to be overly sensitive. It had hydraulic boost peddles, which newer models didn't have. This was Moffitt's first turbine, however, and he was used to how it handled.

The pilot ran fuel consumption numbers in his head. Federal requirements state that all helicopters must have twenty minutes of fuel in reserve. The JetRanger could stay aloft for three hours, but he had to shave that twenty minutes right off the top. He had fueled-up at Portland International Airport on his journey from FLIR headquarters to the mountain.

To maximize the time he could spend in the air, Moffitt would have to draw from his pilot's bag of tricks. He could idle the engine at appropriate times or, when circling, switch to a lower power setting, decreasing his fuel consumption. Pushing the threshold of the aircraft's capabilities, Moffitt arrived at 8,500', hovering only ten feet above the snow.

The operator, seated to the left of the pilot, utilized a hand-held controller while observing a 9-inch, black and white screen. He aimed the FLIR camera at the slope below. Capable of detecting temperature differentials within hundredths of a degree, the camera image appeared on the small screen.

Moffitt continued to hover, holding the aircraft as steady as possible while keeping an eye on his engine's color-coded temperature gauge. As the JetRanger was at its elevation threshold, the temperature indicator began to move from left to right. It departed the comfortable green zone and entered the yellow—cautionary—zone. Moffitt was only allowed to operate in the yellow zone for five minutes at a time.

The pilot glanced at the small TV screen near the co-pilot's seat. There, he spied distinct tracks of boot prints.

Moffitt understood that when somebody steps in the snow, compressing that section of accumulation under their boot, it will reflect temperature differently than the surrounding, uncompressed snow. The image on the screen was very distinct. *Maybe we're on to something here*, he thought excitedly.

Returning his attention to his gauges, the pilot saw the temperature indicator remained in the yellow. He was forced to break away, descend to a safer elevation, and reduce the power load before he could come around for another pass.

~8:20 P.M.
BEAUMONT SCHOOL
PORTLAND

Sitting in the stands, Frank McGinness watched the little T-ball players enjoying orange wedges and juice boxes. Looking over home plate, Frank could see Mount Hood in the distance, bathed in alpenglow. He sat in silence, knowing Pat was still up there, somewhere.

Four nights earlier, Frank had been sitting in this same spot, concerned only about the weather. It had been raining heavily, and tents had to be erected for individual portraits to be taken at home plate. There had been cheering and high-five gestures that Saturday.

Now, Frank could feel the eyes of the other parents upon him. Several of the children were even quiet, looking at him and then at their own fathers. They knew something was wrong.

Mercifully, Gary and Mary Birch came to his rescue. They offered to pick little Chris up after school the following day. Chris was well acquainted with the Birch family, and their home was a familiar environment for the child.

The McGinness' lived across the street from Rose City Cemetery in Portland. The house they rented had a second floor with a clear view of the field of tombstones. As Frank was driving Chris home, the little boy asked a troubling question.

"Is it possible my brother's dead?"[36]

"Yes," Frank replied, with a sidelong look at his son before returning his attention to the road. There was a pause.

"Well...if he's dead," Chris continued, "could we bury him in Rose City Cemetery? That way, I could keep an eye on him from the bedroom."

It was everything Frank could do, to not to lose control of the vehicle.

"Well," Frank managed to reply to his seven-year-old, "I don't know. We'll have to see."

8:28 P.M.
BASE OPERATIONS
WY'EAST DAY LODGE

Wright, exiting the office to get a breath of fresh air and to watch the sunset, was called back into the office.[37] He had a phone call from Greg Prothman of Seattle Mountain Rescue. Wright was relieved to learn that SMR would be hitting the road, immediately, and deputies could expect them to be at the Lodge between 1:00 and 2:00 a.m.[38] Wright briefed Deputy Williams on this latest development.

Descending the stairs to the media room, Williams and Wright were pelted with questions from reporters.

"Search efforts," the deputy began, "are temporarily in limbo, at least until 1:00 a.m."[39] Williams reviewed the day's events and informed the press that outside resources were being called in. The deputy was asked if these were the final SAR teams? Would the operation be called off?

"The search will continue until all persons are found," he replied.

The members of Team 22 felt like they were in a clown car. Scott Olson was in the back of an enclosed snowcat, surrounded by packs, equipment, and fellow SAR volunteers. He didn't even warrant a seat on the bench; he was just tucked on top of the supplies.

After escorting dogs and their handlers, Team 22 had been directed to begin evacuating the glacier. They had traveled west across the field of ice and then ascended, straight up the western walls of White River Canyon. After waiting some time for a snowcat, they were now slowly descending Palmer Snowfield in the dark. Over the drone of the engine, Olson held a conversation with the PJ, likewise cramped and uncomfortable in the back of the vehicle.[40]

After landing in the parking lot, Mike Moffitt looked out of the cockpit windows as the blades of his helicopter slowly spun to a stop. Everyone in the vicinity looked connected to one SAR agency or another. Members of the media were a short distance away, watching for him to exit the aircraft.

Moffitt wasn't pleased. He knew he had to inform authorities that they'd had no luck with their technical marvel.

When flying above the clouds, the infra-red camera cannot detect temperatures on the ground through cloud cover. It is capable of seeing through certain amounts of smoke, but anything with moisture—like a cloud—tended to be interpreted as a reflective surface. Data simply got bounced back, and nothing appeared on the screen.

While executing low-level passes over the glacier, the FLIR camera could detect temperature differences on the surface of the snow. The problem was, snow is a reflective surface, and any accumulation over a few inches insulates the source of that temperature variance. The camera couldn't pick up any readings. Moffitt and his technical expert had made multiple low-level passes over the designated search sector. They had found nothing.

Moffitt exited his aircraft, not angry, just very disappointed. He wished he had better news to report. He turned and suddenly found a large, foam-covered microphone in his face.

"What did you find?" a reporter asked.[41] The surprise ambush shocked Moffitt.

"No comment," he remarked.

Another snowcat pulled up to the edge of the parking lot. Nearby volunteers released the latches of the doors and, one-by-one, PJs and members of Team 22 appeared. It was, as Olson had observed, a clown car—with a seemingly impossible number of persons emerging from the cramped vehicle.

Griswold stepped out and was struck by the fact that he had never seen so many satellite dishes on top of press vehicles. A flock of media approached the team. Questions were asked, and Griswold wanted to provide information, but he knew the sheriff's department should be the one relaying such updates.[42]

Air operations had ceased at 9:43 p.m.[43] Cheryl Maslen, exhausted, made her final entry in the log for the day, "Planning a 6 AM start. Search teams high & dog teams low. Will need snowcats."[44]

Deputy Hattan took a call from Beale Air Force Base in California. He found himself speaking with an Air Force colonel. To Hattan's amazement, the colonel offered the services of a Lockheed SR-71 Blackbird, if such services were needed.

Thinking he was the victim of a prank, the deputy didn't respond. After an awkward pause, Hattan realized that the officer was sincere. The deputy had spent several years in the Air Force and knew the Blackbird was a long-range, strategic reconnaissance aircraft, capable of speeds over Mach 3. Grateful for such a generous gesture, Hattan turned down the offer, not seeing how such an aircraft could assist at this time.[45]

The pilots and crew, from the 304th ARRS, had been on enough rescues to understand that extreme caution was needed when discussing their assigned missions. The men couldn't even have a quiet conversation over cups of coffee, without members of the press shadowing them. From the squadron's perspective, any information that slipped out could rapidly be blown out of proportion. By the time news reached the next of kin, all hell could break loose. The pilots had learned to guard their knowledge as if it were classified information.

Lt. Col. Mullen was especially measured and guarded. His fellow pilot, Maj. McFadden, however, was the epitome of kinetic energy. Nicknamed "Flash," he was a man in perpetual motion.

Both men were convinced that their respective aerial reconnaissance flights had been thorough, to the point of inspecting a discarded candy wrapper, spotted from overhead. But there had been no sign of the lost climbers.

As the officers entered the restroom, their shadows followed suit, as eager for news as the pilots were to find the missing students.

McFadden understood that the journalists were just doing their job. Squadron personnel would not be talking to these reporters...even if there had been anything to report.[46]

~10:05 P.M.
TIMBERLINE LODGE

Don Penater was getting chilled, so he walked up to a side door of Timberline Lodge. It was locked. Unsure what to do next, he opted to return to Wy'East Day Lodge to find a place to sleep.

Near the entrance to the café, he grabbed a cup of coffee and sat down with a small group of men. Introductions were being made, but Don remained cautious; he only provided his first name. He learned that the men seated with him were employees of RLK & Company. Two of these men—snowcat operators—had been working high up on the mountain Monday afternoon.[47] They had been the last people to see the missing climbers as they were entering the Devil's Kitchen region. The party had then become obscured by clouds.[48]

Once his coffee was gone, Don said his goodbyes and descended the nearby stairs. He found an uncomfortable chair in which to spend the night.[49]

Action Conference, Mount Hood, 1986, Bypass Rewarming," Report No. T10-88, U.S. Army Research Institute of Environmental Medicine, Natick, MA. (February 1988): 28.

18   Hopkins, May 15, 1986.

19   Hicks, Jeff, Interview with author, I. OES Resident Advisor, January 17, 2019.

20   Dialogue comes from: Maslen, Cheryl, Interview with author, II. Wednesday, November 5, 2016.

21   Kennell, Deputy David, "Kennel's Log," CCSR. I (May 14, 1986): 76.

22   Maslen/Shultz, "1986 Rescue Log," PMR, (May 14, 1986): 27.

23   Tom Hallman, Jr. John Snell, and Rolla J. Crick, "Sunshine Lures Tourists, Spurs Rescuers to Mountain," The Oregonian, May 15, 1986.

24   Grolbert, Capt. J.T., "SAR, 86-15981," CCSR. I (May 29, 1986): 52.

25   Nalder, Eric, Jack Broom and Dave Birkland, "Mount Hood Tragedy, Three Critical, Search Continues for Missing Eight as Doctors Try to Revive Climbers," The Seattle Times, May 14, 1986.

26   Hopkins, May 15, 1986.

27   Dr. Hill, as quoted in: Wilkerson, M.D., Jim, and Murray P. Hamlet, (February 1988): 13.

28   Maslen/Shultz, (May 14, 1986): 28.

29   Maslen/Shultz, (May 14, 1986): 28.

30   Hattan, I. March 11, 2017.

31   Tom Hallman, Jr. and John Snell, "High Wind Slows Army of Searchers," The Oregonian, May 15, 1986; McGinness, Frank, OC, The McGinness Family, May 20, 2018.

32   Boatsman, Courtney, Interview with author, I. Preparations and Ascent, May 23, 2015.

33   Fitschen, Lorc.a, Interview with author, I. The OES Tragedy, January 2, 2017.

34   Dialogue exchange comes from: Whitson, John, Interview with author, I. The Climb, May 9, 2016.

35   Dialogue exchange comes from: Lane, Dee, "Classes Forgotten as Students Wait for Word of Lost Climbers," The Oregonian, May 15, 1986.

36   Douthit, Sandy, WC, Litzenberger Community Service, October 11, 2015.

37   Dialogue comes from: Lane, Dee, "Classes Forgotten as Students Wait for Word of Lost Climbers," The Oregonian, May 15, 1986.

38   Lane, Dee, "Classes Forgotten as Students Wait for Word of Lost Climbers," The Oregonian, May 15, 1986.

39   Lane, Dee, "School Calls Offers for Mount Hood Story 'Repulsive,'" The Oregonian, May 24, 1986.

40   PMR's log notes Team 10 was "in" White River Glacier, but Stringfield, interviewed in 2015, states his team never descended onto the glacier. Instead, they followed the rim that constituted the extreme eastern edge of Palmer Glacier. Stringfield, Tom, Interview with author, II. Team 10, December 19, 2015.

41   Maslen/Shultz, (May 14, 1986): 28.

42   Hopkins, May 22, 1986.

43   Hopkins, May 22, 1986.

44   Hopkins, May 22, 1986.

45   Dr. Okies, as quoted in: Wilkerson, M.D., Jim, and Murray P. Hamlet, (February 1988): 14.

46   Hopkins, May 15, 1986.

47   Dr. Orfanakis, as quoted in: Wilkerson, M.D., Jim, and Murray P. Hamlet, (February 1988): 14.

48   Dialogue comes from: Douthit, Sandra, Interview with author, I. Personal Remembrances, September 12, 2015.

Chapter 22, "Brother"

1   Dialogue comes from: Penater, Don, Interview with author, I. Personal Recollections, August 8, 2017.

2   Dialogue comes from: Hall, Ed, Interview with author, I. Hasty Team & Crag Rats, August 4, 2018.

3   Basic Group 16: "Mazamas Climb Report," Mount Hood, South Side Route, May 10, 1986. Mazamas Archives.

4   Sheridan, Kathleen, Interview with author, I. Nordic Ski Patrol, July 10, 2018.

5   This comes from an 11:35 a.m. entry in PMR's radio log. The sheriff's radio log places this around

When Ralph Summers had been interviewed Tuesday morning, he had been in an exhaustive state. Deputy Krebs was asking him, once more, to recall every detail concerning his retreat down the mountain. Hal Reese and Bruce Haynes of the Forest Service conducted this more formal request for information.[50]

Was there any other salient piece of information Summers could provide?

Newlyweds Mike Craig and Sue Shultz had been provided a little corner attic room in which to spend the night. There was a bunk bed, and the roof sloped significantly.[51] Shultz mentioned Summers and how sorry she felt for him.[52] It seemed the longer the search dragged on, the less hope there was for a favorable conclusion.[53]

The rustic interior of the room appealed to her husband, who had led three teams in the last two days. Craig sat on the lower bunk. He believed that once the public knew how often Summers was trying to get back onto the mountain, to assist in the efforts, they would forgive him for his lack of an altimeter.[54]

Downstairs, in Room 202, McClure and Maslen were exhausted.[55] With Wright remaining behind in Base Operations, McClure and Maslen tried to rest in their room. They did their best to close their eyes.

Sleep would not come easy. McClure was restless. The walls were so thin that he could hear a conversation in the adjacent room. Suddenly, the room was flooded with an obnoxiously bright light.

Maslen jumped out of bed and raced to the window. Peering through the drapes, she saw a news team below. The bright lights from the cameramen were trained directly onto the southern side of the Lodge. Maslen threw open the window and leaned out. As loudly as she could, she informed the reporters, in no uncertain terms, just how she felt about them at this moment.[56]

"The irony is," Lt. Don Vicars of the sheriff's office remarked to the press, "everyone knows they're there, someplace."[57] Vicars, in a gray flannel shirt and green down jacket, looked uneasy under the reporter's bright lights.

Privately, rescue experts had little hope for a miracle. Still, they vowed to continue the search until every climber was accounted for.[58]

Less than an hour earlier, another press release had occurred. All three teens at Emanuel Hospital had been positively identified. In addition to Alison Litzenberger, Erin O'Leary and Erik Sandvik had not survived.

Barry Wright, who had been on duty for forty-eight hours, felt the need to hear his wife's voice. Excusing himself from the office spaces, he descended the stairs and headed to the public telephones.

He phoned home. His oldest daughter was seven, while his youngest was only three. The mere thought of losing one of his own precious children was too much for the seasoned rescue veteran. When he heard his wife answer the phone, Barry Wright sobbed—uncontrollably.[59]

THURSDAY

May 15, 1986

CHAPTER 25
THE HAYSTACK

A commotion roused Barry Wright from his slumber, as fifteen volunteers from Seattle Mountain Rescue entered the room.[1] Wright greeted Greg Prothman and his men, heartened to hear that another ten volunteers were on standby.

Witnessing the arrival of these fresh volunteers, a couple of brave reporters took a few steps into the office spaces. Lt. Vicars immediately shooed them out, telling them that the search efforts would resume at dawn.[2]

Prothman asked about the weather forecast. It looked promising: easterly winds around fifteen mph, partly cloudy skies, and the freezing level would jump from 3,500' up to 10,000'.[3]

~2:10 A.M.
TIMBERLINE LODGE

Once again, Dave McClure and Cheryl Maslen were awakened by the ringing of a phone in their room. Hearing Wright's voice on the other end of the line, Maslen knew there was no emergency.

"We need you," Wright remarked.[4]

"Alright," she sighed. "We'll be there shortly."

After only a couple hours of sleep, the couple rose to face the third day of the SAR operation. Neither had brought a change of clothes or even a toothbrush. When Maslen had driven up to the Lodge, she never imagined she'd be working in the command post for multiple days. As a grad student, she was supposed to be studying this week. Her concerned thesis advisor kept tabs on her by watching the evening news. McClure's absence from academia was also keenly felt. The noted chemistry professor had already missed two lectures at Portland State University.[5]

Representatives from several agencies were assembling. Captain Grolbert, Lt. Hanners, Chief Bradshaw, and Deputy Krebs of the sheriff's department were present. Barry Wright, Cheryl Maslen, and Dave McClure of PMR were ready for the briefing. Several representatives from the 304th ARRS were in the room. Men from SMR and CMRU were in attendance.[6]

Wright provided a quick rundown on PMR personnel. Many had exhausted their bodies as well as their allotted time off from work. The new volunteers from Seattle and Corvallis had arrived just in time, fresh and anxious to contribute.[7] McClure believed they were a godsend.[8] As it stood, the sheriff's department could count on having SAR workers ready to deploy at first light.

Authorities were convinced that the snow cave was situated somewhere above 9,000', likely near the crest of the west moraine of White River Canyon. To McClure, it was highly unlikely that the three students had emerged from the shelter, *ascended* a fifty-degree slope in the face of sixty mph winds, and then ended up on the crest of the ridge where Erik had been found.[9]

In McClure's experience, exhausted climbers tended to descend and follow the most natural course possible. The best-educated guess was that the three students had departed the cave and headed south, down along the ridge. Alison and Erin had likely fallen over the ridge, sliding downhill until they came to rest in the canyon. It appeared that Erik simply collapsed atop the ridge. It was only a theory, but one that did explain many of the clues.[10]

The search efforts would consist of a systematic combing of White River Glacier, from 9,600' down to 7,500'. The first two teams would be accompanied by the search dogs.[11]

Inclement weather was causing a temporary flight restriction. The earliest a Huey could be authorized to launch was 7:00 a.m. A secondary aircraft would be available two hours later. Faced with these unforeseen flight restrictions, yet still wanting to get an early start, Hanners gave the green light to have teams transported up the mountain in snowcats, starting at

4:00 a.m.[12]

An advanced team was chosen, comprised primarily of SMR personnel. Prothman's team was instructed to meet in Base Operations at 3:15 a.m.[13]

Greg Prothman, thirty-one, consulted the nearby maps. A police officer from Renton, Washington, he was also chairman of the Mountain Rescue Council for Seattle. Paul Williams would remain in the office as SMR's base operations leader. George Sainsbury was serving as their in-town operations leader.[14]

Prothman and his Advanced Team were brought up to speed on what had happened on the mountain over the previous three days. Prothman was not surprised to learn that a climbing party from a school had gotten into trouble. He was, however, taken back when he learned that the group didn't carry an altimeter. Wright showed the men which areas of the mountain had already been searched.[15]

Prothman was the acknowledged field team leader. He was joined on the Advanced Team by Jim Cleary and Allen McGuire. These three would act as the principal climbers for the team. Bill O'Brien, of CMRU, would serve as team medic. From GSSD, Bruce Cheshire would be handling "Polly," a German shepherd, while Richard Reininger took "Rascal," a golden retriever. Everyone would wear avalanche transceivers.[16]

Prothman sat in the passenger seat of the snowcat. The remaining men and two dogs vied for space on the bench seats in the back of the rig.[17] Polly and Rascal were animated and ready for work as the snowcat began crawling up Palmer Snowfield.

Prothman hadn't climbed Mount Hood before but had skied the Magic Mile in his youth. As a police officer, well familiar with the capabilities of trained SAR dogs, he was concerned about how they would handle the terrain at higher elevations. There were crevasses and steep slopes, punctuated with occasional fields of solid ice. The climbers of the Advanced Team would need to keep a vigilant watch on the dogs and the handlers, to ensure their safety on the high-altitude terrain.[18]

Members of SMR had made an agreement within their group. Should any of them encounter non-responsive climbers, they were to say over the radio, "Send Daiber up with—" and then add a number, indicating how many had been found.[19] Prothman and Sainsbury had heard about the confusion over bodies yesterday morning and did not want a repeat performance. It was hoped that this coded message could relay necessary information but keep journalists in the dark.

4:26 A.M.
PALMER SNOWFIELD

Halfway up Palmer Snowfield, Prothman reported that winds emanated from the west and that the snowcat was traveling through a dry swirling curtain of light snow. Visibility was an impressive 100 yards, even in the dark.[20]

5:00 A.M.
TRIANGLE MORAINE

The snowcat came to a stop, roughly 500 feet below Crater Rock. The passengers began exiting the vehicle. When the last dog and handler departed the cat, the driver turned around and began his solitary descent.[21]

The Advanced Team surveyed their surroundings. They were above the clouds, and winds were still originating from the west. Visibility continued to improve. One of the men checked an altimeter. They were near 10,000'.[22]

There was an astounding amount of terrain surrounding the team. The diminutive entrance to the snow cave was hidden somewhere in this colossal haystack. Prothman felt the weight of needing *to go solve the problem*.[23]

Prothman kicked at the hard, crusted snow with one of his crampons. The wind had scoured the terrain. *This will be tough on the dogs*, he thought. Under ideal conditions, the SAR dogs he had worked with in the past had a "useful nose" for only thirty to forty-five minutes.

Scott Olson, of CMRU, was sitting in the cafeteria, drowsy from a lack of sleep. He and several of his friends had received a few hours of shut eye in a chalet room in Timberline Lodge. The telephone in the room had roused the occupants at 4:00 a.m. It was the front desk, advising them that the sheriff's department was spinning up all SAR volunteers. Olson had dressed and walked across the street to Wy'East Day Lodge, expecting to climb aboard a Huey.[24]

Gene Griswold had been grateful to have a roof over his head during the night but was growing concerned that he and his friends were not being assigned a mission. *What are we waiting for?* he wondered.[25]

Members of CMRU had already waited in the cafeteria for close to ninety minutes, unaware that the military pilots were temporarily grounded. Hungry, they helped themselves to a hearty breakfast—piping hot chili, courtesy of the Red Cross.[26]

Even at this early hour, family members of the climbers began to gather in the vicinity. Olson didn't avoid their gaze, but he didn't seek it either. It was difficult to explain to people that you simply didn't have any answers.[27]

5:32 A.M.
WEST MORAINE
WHITE RIVER CANYON

Reaching the edge of the canyon, the Advanced Team peered down the steep slopes. There appeared to be no new snow in this specific section of terrain. Intense winds had scoured spots, leaving this area resembling what it must have looked like on Monday, before the storm's arrival. Wind speeds had increased to twenty-eight mph.

Turning his attention uphill, Prothman spied a lone trail wand sticking out of the snow.[28]

5:37 A.M.
MEDIA ROOM
WY'EAST DAY LODGE

After an uncomfortable night's sleep in an armchair, Don Penater had risen early, walked outside, and watched the sunrise.[29] He decided to continue hiding his identity from reporters, allowing him to extract information from them. He bumped into Sandy James, a reporter for KOIN TV, and she seemed very likable whenever they interacted.

5:45 A.M.
PALMER GLACIER

Forty yards west of the crest of the canyon, Prothman took a series of magnetic compass bearings, relaying their findings down to Base. He estimated that the trail wand was at 10,380′. Members of his team now spotted a second trail wand, roughly 100 feet above the original marker.

The team climbed until they were near the steam vents, adjacent to Steel Cliff. Discovering two sets of boot prints, they fanned out to explore the area.[30]

5:45 A.M.
TIMBERLINE LODGE

Team 2 climbed aboard a snowcat. To reduce confusion, team numbering had started over again. Chris Madden was the leader of this new group. Tall, slender, and extremely athletic, he had once hiked the Grand Canyon—twice—in a single weekend. He was a solid rock climber and a good friend. Prothman trusted the man implicitly.[31]

With Madden were Russ Kroeker and Steve Plate of SMR, and Jim Dixon, Michael Hauty, and Harry Oakes Jr. of PMR. Accompanying these climbers were Christy Pierce of GSSD, accompanied by "Mica," and Doug Martinson of CSD with "Ranger." Both dogs were German Shepherds.[32]

Madden radioed Prothman requesting a meeting of the two teams, whenever they could rendezvous on the mountain.

6:14 A.M.
DEVIL'S KITCHEN
CRATER REGION

The Advanced Team reached the second trail wand at 10,450′. It had a red tag attached to a green stem but had no other identifying marks.[33] With the SAR dogs, team members fanned out and searched the nearby terrain.

Bill O'Brien, of CMRU, had been sent up the mountain in the first snowcat of the day. He had been told that his paramedic skills might be called upon, but that his primary role was to chaperone one of the dog handlers. O'Brien, who had that man tethered to him, had his ice axe in the ready position. Should the handler happen to fall into one of the crevasses, O'Brien could check the fall.

The handler's SAR dog repeatedly sniffed the small, fumarole vents. The stench, smelling suspiciously close to rotten eggs, was overwhelming at times.[34]

6:50 A.M.
WHITE RIVER GLACIER

Prothman directed the team to head downhill, below the second trail wand.[35] They were to inspect the entryways to the small volcanic fumaroles in the colossal bench area.

Charged with strategy, but taking the safety of all volunteers personally, Barry Wright advised Prothman to keep the dogs and handlers a safe distance from the volcanic vents.[36]

At the Advanced Team's briefing, hours ago, areas of the mountain that had already been searched had been shown to Prothman on a topographical map. Now, in the light of day, it was proving difficult to ascertain precisely where those covered areas were situated. A map is only a two-dimensional picture. Prothman was standing on a three-dimensional peak. Everything appeared different with minimal use of flagging.

Scanning the terrain below through his binoculars, he could see the whipping pennants that marked the sites where Erik, Alison, and Erin had been discovered twenty-five hours earlier.[37]

7:00 A.M.
LANDING ZONE (LZ)
WY'EAST DAY LODGE SOUTH PARKING LOT

Cheryl Maslen watched as Ralph Summers climbed aboard a military helicopter, ready for the first aerial mission of the day.[38]

Summers took a seat inside the chopper, one hand in front of his face, trying to discourage the ever-present cameramen. To nearly everyone in the area, the man appeared to be ignoring the cameras. Maslen continued watching as Summers, who had been very tolerant of the media up to this point, finally had enough. Maslen had to suppress her laughter as the consultant slowly lowered his fingers against his face...all but one. With his middle finger extended against his beard, Summers continued to wait patiently for liftoff. Maslen, chuckling in approval, turned and headed back to her post.[39]

Members of Teams 3 and 4 all hailed from the ranks of SMR. Jim Baker led Bob Ricker, Gordon Adams, and Pete Frickland on Team 3. All four volunteers were equipped with avalanche transceivers, probes, and metal detectors.[40]

Pete Bustanoby would take charge of Team 4. With him were Brian Beaman, Diane Hoff, and Ed Boulton, each brandishing avalanche probes.[41]

The teams piled into Number 8 for her third journey up the snowfield in three hours.[42]

McClure and Maslen stepped out into the cool, invigorating air. They were recognized instantly by reporters and besieged with questions. The couple had been mere faces in the crowd on Tuesday. Their features were becoming more familiar by Wednesday. Now, Thursday morning, they were recognized whenever they emerged from the office spaces.

Reporters pressed for information, but McClure could only assure everyone that they would provide data when they had something to provide.[43]

Mike Craig sat in the helo, ready to lead his fourth team of the week. Through the open door, he could see a crowd gathering to watch their departure.[44] Allen O'Bannon, Bill Stevenson, and David Allen were all heading up for their second day on the mountain. Ted Forgeron, also of PMR, had come up to help in the search. Rounding up Team 5—Dee Zduniak. She had returned to continue searching as well.

Near the helicopters, Father Malcolm Manson, the Headmaster of OES, was in the crowd. Reporters asked him for a few minutes of his time. With a camera rolling, he was asked how the families were coping with the search efforts.

"People are caring for each other," he said. "Sometimes there are people hugging each other and crying. And sometimes, people just...being quiet. It's a real tribute to the community spirit that has built up amongst these parents in the last few days."[45]

This was not Craig's first time in a rescue helicopter, but as the Huey became airborne, he marveled at the view the ride afforded him. As they flew up the mountain and the terrain of White River Glacier passed underneath, Craig could see Illumination Rock. The three-sided monolith of rock jutting out of the mountain's southwestern shoulder was sparkling majestically in the distance. *If it was any other day*, he thought, *the Rock was staged for perfect ice climbing.*[46]

If it was any other day.

CHAPTER 26
SHORT ROPE

After only nine minutes in flight, the Huey bearing Mike Craig landed on Palmer Glacier. Exiting the aircraft, he could see Team 4 up the mountain. Team 3 was moving slowly down toward Team 2. Craig's group joined in, probing assigned sections of snow with their avalanche probes.[1]

Craig listened to radio transmissions as his team worked. The terrain above 9,700' had been searched, and groups were ready to tackle the extensive south-facing slopes, directly below that position.

Lt. Vicars was fielding questions from reporters. He provided a run-down on the five teams presently probing the upper reaches of the glacier.[2]

Reporters asked about tracks the Advanced Team was following. The lieutenant stated that Prothman's men believed that the boot prints did not belong to members of the missing party. Prothman had also assured authorities that he wasn't confusing them with prints lower down on the slopes. Those belonged to previous searchers.[3]

The lieutenant also noted that two climbers, not related to the search efforts, were making a bid for the summit via the South Side Route. A solo mountaineer was also spotted on Newton Clark Glacier.[4]

Scott Olson wasn't in the best of moods. He was finally aboard a Huey, after waiting for a flight for over four hours.[5] Glancing around, he nodded at John Blaisdell and Sterling Thomas, also from CMRU.[6]

Rick Harder was motioning the trio towards a nearby sliding door. The Bagger was yelling something to the men as he opened the door, but his words were drowned out by the noise of the aircraft. Harder had his helmet on, equipped with mufflers and a radio set. A man in his element.

Olson knew they were approaching their objective and was aware of the danger of the proposed exit strategy. The plan was for the pilots to aim the nose of the aircraft straight at the steep mountain slope, around 9,700', and nudge forward ever so slowly. While the helicopter hovered, SAR volunteers were expected to climb out the side door, stand on the landing skid, and then leap to the ice and snow below. The drop might only be three or four feet, but it looked a little farther to Olson. Once individuals had hit the steep slope, they were expected to use their ice axes to brake—self-arrest—and come to a complete stop. The justification for this plan was that authorities wanted the men high up on the mountain, but there wasn't a safe place for the Huey to land.

Olson watched as the first man headed out the door without incident.[7] He moved toward the door, sat down, and carefully stretched his feet out below him. He balanced on the skid. Amid the howling winds of the rotor downwash and the roar of the engine, Olson didn't even realize The Bagger had approached him from behind.

Like a seasoned bouncer, Harder grabbed the back of Olson's pack and tossed him out the door.[8]

~8:39 A.M.
MEDIA ROOM
WY'EAST DAY LODGE

Lt. Sherwood Stillman was working with Lt. Vicars. After receiving word from coworkers upstairs, Stillman began drafting an update for the assembled reporters. The journalists wanted more information concerning the SAR dogs. How deep could the dogs detect someone buried under the snow?[9] Stillman had nothing new to provide; such information had already been disseminated.

Olson had quickly recovered from his unexpected ejection from a military Huey. He tied-in to a rope with Thomas and Blaisdell, in the shadow of Steel Cliff. Working alongside another team, they were assigned to probe the drainage area below the impressive crater wall.

Olson didn't feel the snow cave was situated in this particular area, but he was pleased not to be escorting dogs and their handlers today. Only a few feet were separating him from his colleagues, and the trio engaged in conversation as they went about their duties. So small was their assigned search sector, that their counterparts on the other search team could overhear them. Both teams began conversing together, recognizing that they'd have their sector cleared within twenty minutes.[10]

Then what?

Nearby, Pete Bustanoby spotted dark objects farther down in the same drainage.[11] He investigated the site, which turned out to be rocks.[12] The teams soon learned that this region had already been combed by teams with probes. Bustanoby noticed that the SAR volunteers, himself included, were growing increasingly frustrated.[13]

Wright and Maslen had been listening quietly as status reports came into Base. Team 3 was working their way down from about 9,700', having no hits with their metal detectors.

Another psychic was calling from Iowa, and a third was calling from Arizona. Both were offering their services, right over the telephone.[14] In the quiet room, Maslen could hear the deputy's end of the conversation. She rolled her eyes. *Psychics?* She agreed with her husband; either the probe lines would yield results, or they'd have to wait for the snow cave to melt out before it would reveal its location.[15]

Rick Harder was requesting that Greg Prothman be flown over the glacier to obtain a birds-eye view of their search sectors. Ralph Summers' presence was also requested for this flight. Wright replied that this request would be granted, but that no aircraft were available at the moment.[16]

Jody Leach was keeping track of CMRU personnel on the mountain.

Between incoming radio transmissions, she was engaged in conversation with one of the deputies. Were they still in rescue mode? Or, had they shifted to one of recovery? It was an uncomfortable topic.

"Do you think there could be people still alive in the cave?" the deputy whispered.[17]

Leach took a moment to ponder the possibilities. She had consulted PMR's log, reviewed the weather and snow conditions over the previous three days, and had a basic knowledge of the clothing and supplies Goman' team had on hand.

"Yeah," she replied. "I think there could be a couple."

9:33 A.M.
WHITE RIVER GLACIER

Prothman and Summers were scheduled to fly over the search sectors. Whenever that moment came, Prothman would pass field team leadership reigns over to Chris Madden.[18]

Directly overhead, a Huey began to hover over the sloping glacier. Wayne Lederer and Hollis Ferguson, both of CMRU, leaped out. Apparently, the last man from their unit, Gene Griswold, wasn't exiting fast enough. He was ejected out the side door before he could even prepare himself for the descent.

Flailing his arms to gain his balance in the air, Griswold landed with a *thump* in the snow. Sliding, he used his ice axe to self-arrest.[19] When he stopped, he was prone in the snow and breathing heavily. Goggles askew, he had to chuckle.

The rest of Team 6 had arrived.

10:10 A.M.
BELL UH-1 IROQUOIS HELICOPTER

Prothman and Summers strapped themselves in amid the constant vibration of the Huey. There was a slight stomach lurch as the aircraft lifted off the ice. It banked suddenly while lifting. During a moment of turbulence, The Bagger tapped his helicopter headset, a signal for the passengers to don their own. The pilot pitched the nose of the aircraft down sharply and skimmed the surface of the glacier. As the Huey made a pass over the river of ice, Harder pointed out various landmarks.[20]

Amy Horwell had been outside with her cousin. Returning to her apartment, the girls walked up the stairs and into the kitchen. Seeing the look on Aunt Tara's face, Amy knew something was wrong.

"Look," Tara began, gently. "You need to be prepared; your mom...she might not make it back."[21]

"Okay," Amy replied cautiously, not sure what to think.

Her mom was adventurous. She enjoyed activities like whitewater rafting. When they would visit family at the coast, Marion would take Amy to Cape Kiwanda, where the pair would scale to the top of the nearby sandhills. They enjoyed running and rolling down the dunes. Marion would even climb out to the headland with her daughter, despite her fear of heights.[22]

That made Amy question this whole situation. *If mom has a fear of heights, what in the world was she doing climbing a mountain?*

The Huey bearing Harder, Summers, and Prothman touched down at the foot of a steep snow slope around 7,700'. Erin and Alison had been discovered here over twenty-four hours earlier. Trail wands marked the precise location where each girl had been found, curled up in the snow. These wands had been difficult to spot from the air, so The Bagger jumped out of the helicopter to place poles, capped with brightly colored streamers, in their place.[23] This was repeated at the Upper Discovery Site.

Following this, the helicopter executed a low-level pass of the 9,200' to 9,300' levels of the glacier.

Team 6 believed there was a lack of clear communication. Blaisdell, Olson, and Thomas had finished probing the Steel Cliff drainage over an hour earlier. When they radioed down to Base, seeking another assignment, someone merely replied, *keep probing.*[24]

Olson looked around and couldn't see any other slice of real estate that could be a match for Summers' description of the cave site.

More than 300 students, faculty, family, friends, alumni, and community leaders were gathered in the chapel to note the passing of Alison Litzenberger, Erin O'Leary, and Erik Sandvik. Everyone sought solace in one another's company and in their faith.

"If you have done nothing else over the last two days," Fr. Manson said, directing his remarks to the young people in the pews. "You have shown each other, and your parents, that you love. The life you have been living is a life of love. You've got it right. You do know the way."[25]

Courtney, who had been on the climbing party for the first few hours, was in the school lobby. Reporters asked her if she would ever try to climb the mountain again; they were surprised by her answer.

"It was just one of those things that happens. I would still go up again. I'd still feel safe."[26]

Her mother agreed, saying she'd be okay sending either of her daughters up the mountain.

Jeff Hicks was having a rough day. As a resident advisor, he found so many students knocking on his door he had to prop it open. Several of the sophomores, who were scheduled to be on climbs in the weeks ahead, asked to speak to him privately. They wanted to talk about Erin, Alison, and Erik. There was a lot of *that could have been me.*[27]

The flag on campus was lowered to half-mast.[28]

At 9,700', Summers and Prothman exited the aircraft while Harder remained on board to continue aerial reconnaissance.[29]

SAR teams worked their way towards Prothman, pausing their work to discuss strategy.[30] Over the radio, they could hear that Harder was laying down smoke in a region he believed should be searched. Prothman radioed that the area in question had already been explored.[31] Moments later, The Bagger's voice came over the radio again—the area in which he was *now* flying over should be searched. Harder was referring to the Lower Hogsback.

As before, Prothman radioed that it, too, had been covered.[32]

Prothman tied Summers onto a short rope, taking the lead position. He didn't want a third man on the line. He wanted to get inside Summers' head and mine it for any information, without distractions.

He pressed the consultant for details as the two worked together, probing the snow. Summers retold his tale of navigating through the blizzard. When Summers had encountered trees, he had believed that he and Molly were below Timberline Lodge. He had actually been miles to the east. Prothman came to the realization that the consultant had no idea where he was Tuesday morning until he and Molly had come across a sign.

When pressed for details concerning the terrain surrounding the snow cave, Summers recalled the steep slope and the nearby crevasse. Prothman stopped in his tracks when he realized the consultant's description could have applied to hundreds of potential locations.[33]

10:48 A.M.
BASE OPERATIONS
WY'EAST DAY LODGE

The General Manager of Timberline Lodge offered to open the Magic Mile and Palmer chairlifts. This would help facilitate the movement of SAR workers up and down the mountain, easing the burden on the military aircraft and snowcats.[34]

Maslen didn't love this idea, as it would be nearly impossible to track the myriad of rescue workers that would be coming off the chairs.[35] Part of her job was to keep tabs on volunteers as they headed into the field, and as they safely returned from the slopes. She didn't want to lose track of anyone.

~11:00 A.M.
TRIANGLE MORAINE

Taking a short break for lunch, Bill O'Brien sat on the snow. One of the SAR dogs and its handler were having their lunches alongside him. The trio was watching a solitary figure approaching on skis, from below. It was a reporter from a major newspaper back east. Dangling from a wide neck strap, was the largest camera lens O'Brien had ever seen.

The reporter asked if he could speak with the dog handler, as readers would just love to hear about the canine alpinists. The request was granted, and an informal interview took place while O'Brien ate and observed the progress of probe lines below them.[36]

O'Brien wasn't sure how much to say. Earlier in the morning, his handler seemed nervous, but perhaps that was because they'd been on steep terrain at the time. As the morning had progressed, the areas they were inspecting had leveled out. O'Brien had supported the handler, from above, keeping him on a tight rope.[37]

11:15 A.M.
BASE OPERATIONS
WY'EAST DAY LODGE

A weather report came in from Channel 6 News. Deputy Hattan jotted down the meteorologist's weather forecast: "Cloud deck, shrouding the mountain, and fairly narrow middle high cloud cover to continue. Weather should hold through tonight. Deteriorate Friday. Continue windy. No moisture."[38]

Base asked who on the SAR teams needed to be relieved.[39]

Wright soon heard back. SMR personnel were tired, but they were going to stay on the mountain. Two of the dog handlers, however, would be escorted to the upper landing zone for extraction.[40]

Wright was harboring a dark fear that the operation would not end well. He tried to shrug the feeling that they were all, unconsciously, shifting from a rescue to a recovery operation.[41]

11:38 A.M.
WHITE RIVER GLACIER

As a police officer, Prothman employed various techniques in his attempt to glean information out of Summers. The officer kept his opinions to himself. It was his duty to locate the missing students—not to assign blame or responsibility. He befriended Summers, encouraged him, but no details emerged that assisted the men in their collective endeavor.[42]

11:47 A.M.
BASE OPERATIONS
WY'EAST DAY LODGE

Word came down from the glacier that sizeable crevasses had been encountered, large enough for men to walk inside. Another transmission, this one from Mike Craig's Team 5, indicated that these crevasses might have been explored already by members of the Crag Rats. As lunch boxes were being airlifted to the volunteers, an anxious ten minutes elapsed.

Markers were, indeed, found near the crevasses.[43] They had been searched already.

12:00 P.M.
LANDING ZONE (LZ)
WY'EAST DAY LODGE SOUTH PARKING LOT

A Huey landed, and three volunteers emerged from the aircraft. Jim Cleary, who had been working on the Advanced Team since before dawn, had come down with two dog handlers and their canines.[44] The dogs, like all the SAR teams, had been working for hours.

~12:00 P.M.
WHITE RIVER GLACIER

Zduniak stated that she thought it was essential to have Summers on the scene.[45] Pete Bustanoby reminded her that Summers was already tied-on to Prothman's rope.

Prothman, with the consultant close behind, was up near the Steel Cliff drainage. Summers repeatedly mentioned the glissade he and Schula had performed as soon as they began their journey.[46]

SAR workers had been peeling off jackets and extra layers. Morning had turned into afternoon. The sky was clear, winds were modest, and the sun was reflecting brilliantly off the ice and snow. It was a balmy 75° F.[47]

"This is the spot!" Summers suddenly exclaimed. "I recognize it!"[48]

Teams jumped into action, forming a probe line and covering the area quite thoroughly.

Nothing.

Prothman sighed. This was the second time this had happened.

12:27 P.M.
BASE OPERATIONS
WY'EAST DAY LODGE

Calls were going out to leaders of Olympic Mountain Rescue and Central Washington Mountain Rescue. If there wasn't a breakthrough soon, these teams from the north would make their way to Mount Hood by evening.[49] GSSD agreed to keep the dogs available overnight. Kevin Huntley, an advisor for Multnomah County Sheriff's Search and Rescue, Explorer Post #631, was preparing a team that would report for duty in the morning, should the search efforts extend into Friday.[50]

Maslen approached McClure and Wright. One of the news choppers was hovering too close to the teams, causing noise and interfering with communications.

Concerned, the trio discussed options.

"I'd recommend a shotgun," McClure offered, in jest.[51]

An Airforce colonel, who happened to be within earshot, overheard this conversation.

"Do you want me to close the airspace?" he offered.[52]

"Yes," Maslen replied. "Please, do."

The Colonel picked up the phone and called the Federal Aviation Administration. This resulted in an airspace closure within a fifteen-mile radius of White River Glacier. Major Charles Jones, of the 304th ARRS, was authorized to enforce this closure.[53]

12:38 P.M.
LANDING ZONE (LZ)
WY'EAST DAY LODGE SOUTH PARKING LOT

Borrowing a flight helmet from Rick Harder, McClure informed deputies that he wanted an aerial view of the search efforts.[54] There was room for him on a helicopter that was about to head up the peak.

Dodging members of the media, he walked out to the parking lot. He made his way to the military helicopter, whose rotary blades were already spinning. The side door to the aircraft slid open, and McClure climbed in. He sat on the edge, his legs dangling out the side. He wasn't strapped in and, just as he thought this might be a bad idea, the Huey lifted off the ground.[55]

CHAPTER 27
TOE THE LINE

When the SMR teams had arrived on the mountain, before sunrise, the snow had been hard-packed, requiring crampons. As the hours ticked by and the sun baked the southern slopes, the snow was turning to slush and was challenging to maneuver through. The teams had been working for hours. Greg Prothman had observed people tripping, even falling on occasion. They weren't as cognitive as they had been hours earlier.

Okay, he thought to himself. *We're going to get someone hurt here before too much longer.* Prothman gathered a group, including his senior team leaders—Chris Madden and Pete Bustanoby.

"We gotta start pulling some people off," Prothman noted.[1] This announcement was met with raised eyebrows. Some said they should remain; it would be wrong to turn back now. "Yeah, I get it," Prothman conceded. "Let's see who wants to stick around and who doesn't, but let's get some teams down to the LZ."

Prothman radioed Base, advising that fresh climbers were needed. An exit strategy for the existing teams was already being organized by one of the PJs.[2]

Bustanoby felt there was a sense of desperation in the air, and he wanted to remain on the glacier. In his mind, there were a lot of the volunteers who wouldn't retreat, even if directed to do so.[3]

Other than the pilot and co-pilot, Dave McClure was alone, his legs dangling out the left side of the aircraft. The man that deputies referred to as *Tall Gray Beard* wanted an overview of his entire search sector, starting at the upper reaches of the mountain.

Raised in Alaska, he was used to the motion of boats and small aircraft. Still, as the Huey flew up the mountain, he maintained a firm grasp while looking down from the open door.[4]

When the aircraft reached 10,000', it hovered so McClure could get a clear view of the Devil's Kitchen. The cool, crisp air smelled like spent matches, he thought. It wasn't the sulfurous geothermal fumaroles in the Kitchen that McClure wanted to view; he wanted a closer look at the base of Steel Cliff.

The Huey moved forward, beginning a slow, lengthy pass along the east rim of the volcano's crater. McClure could see steep bands of rock, capped by heavily laden cornices. Thick rime ice coated great portions of the steep walls, but it was along the base of this rampart that McClure focused his attention.[5]

~1:00 P.M.
WY'EAST DAY LODGE

Bob Freund walked into the Lodge. He was the last member of CMRU to arrive at the mountain resort. He'd had business commitments that were unbreakable.

Freund had joined a regional ski patrol when he was a student at Oregon State University. After a commission in the Navy, he was assigned to a duty station in San Diego, California. Still wanting to be involved in the mountaineering community, he volunteered with a SAR unit based out of Southern California. When his military career took him north to Seattle, Freund joined Seattle Mountain Rescue. His career eventually landed him with the Corvallis unit.

With fifty or so SAR field missions under his belt, at the age of thirty-seven, he was ready for an assignment.[6]

He spotted some of his former colleagues from SMR, who had recently returned from the upper slopes. The fatigue showed on their faces. There were about a dozen fresh climbers nearby, deliberately being held back by Maslen. They would be rotated into the field as others came down.

The extraction of Teams 1 through 6 from the field was underway. As helicopters began to arrive, the Advanced Team ensured that the searched terrain was marked clearly, with trail wands.[7]

An enticing announcement came over the airwaves. "Hot soup is available at the Red Cross."[8]

Deputy Hattan received a call from Frank Danes of Washington, stating that he was available the following morning, and he had a magnetometer in his possession.[9] The device could be used as a far more powerful metal detector than the conventional ones presently being used. Employing the device meant rescue workers could potentially search to deeper depths within the fresh snowpack, searching for ferrous metals.[10]

Only a few minutes after hanging up with Danes, Hattan received a call from Darrell Winterborn, advising him that the Mt. Hood Ski Patrol would be available in the morning.[11]

Bob Freund peered out of the chopper as the aircraft skimmed above the ivory surface of the glacier. A member of Team 7, he grasped a handheld radio. Near him, cramped together and fighting for legroom, were Dale Nelson and Jim Ruef of CMRU. Harvey Frisco and Mark Powers from PMR were part of the team as well. They would join Bill O'Brien, who had gone up with the Advanced Team early in the morning.[12] They'd all report to Prothman for assignment.

Once the Huey landed at the upper LZ, Team 7 exited the aircraft, staying low as they trotted out below the blades. As he shook Prothman's hand in greeting, Freund watched four members of SMR climb aboard the helicopter he had just exited.[13]

One helicopter was tasked with extracting thirty volunteers from the field, four climbers at a time. A smoke canister helped identify the upper landing zone.[14]

Prothman continued working with Maslen over the radio, ironing out the list of personnel remaining on the glacier. He requested more avalanche probes and water for the troops.[15]

Having been tethered closely for four-and-a-half hours, Prothman had been unable to extract any more useful information out of Summers.[16] The consultant had hiked out on Tuesday when there was almost no distinction between the sky and the snow. Summers was just as determined as his colleagues to locate the missing climbers, but he was unable to pinpoint the location of the snow cave.

Each time he would see a particularly steep stretch of terrain, near a crevasse, he'd exclaim *this is the spot!* Frantic formation of probe lines would ensue, toiling work would be performed, and yet—no results were forthcoming. This scenario played out on five occasions.

Summers' and Prothman's presence aboard a Huey was requested. The police officer disconnected Ralph from his line.[17]

Dave McClure, Deputy Hattan, Cheryl Maslen, and other operational leaders held a press conference just outside the front entrance to the building.[18] Some of these people had received less than six hours of sleep in the last sixty-five, and it showed.

McClure could only imagine how teenagers had battled the elements. He was doing his best to appear calm and determined as he gauged the faces of those assembled. There was an oppressive air of sadness. He kept going over statistics in his head. *What time had Goman's party started climbing? How long had they been out in the elements before entering the snow cave? What clothing and equipment did they have in their possession? How long had they been in the cave?* He knew the answers to all these questions and understood the odds his teams were up against. McClure felt the pressure. He knew that the missing party might not be discovered until the snow cave melted out.[19]

Like her husband, Maslen felt they were now on a recovery mission, rather than a rescue operation. She kept these feelings to herself, not wanting the media to blow such a statement out of proportion.[20]

Pete Bustanoby, of SMR, maintained a positive outlook in front of the families. Like McClure and Maslen, however, he privately believed the tide had turned. They had surely entered recovery mode.[21]

3:15 P.M.
BELL UH-1 IROQUOIS HELICOPTER
OVER WHITE RIVER GLACIER

Back on a helicopter, Summers thought he recognized something in the region of the glacier due west of Steel Cliff. The consultant asked the pilot to land so that they could inspect the site on foot. The location just seemed to feel right.[22]

At 8,140' on the glacier, Summers tied-in, yet again, to Prothman's line. Summers produced his compass. Recalling the reading he had taken near the entrance to the cave on Tuesday morning, he continued his efforts to identify the site.

Bill O'Brien was leading a probe line just a hundred yards farther uphill. This team had only been exploring a newly assigned section of the glacier for a few minutes when The Bagger called O'Brien down to his position.

Harder informed O'Brien that Summers believed they were in the right area.[23]

~3:25 P.M.
MCGINNESS RESIDENCE
PORTLAND

Having no air-conditioning, Frank McGinness had all his fans running at full speed and all doors in the home flung wide open. His phone rang.

Frank had a good friend, who was very well connected politically. That friend had used his clout to make some phone calls, resulting in a call from Oregon Senator, Mark O. Hatfield, to an officer of the 304th ARRS. A colonel was now calling Frank at his residence.

When asked how he could be of service, Frank let the officer know, they could find Patrick and the other missing kids and get them down off that mountain.

"We're doing the best we can up there," the colonel responded.[24]

"Well," Frank replied, dissatisfied. "I just want to make sure that it is the best. I may have been just a staff sergeant, but I know what kind of bull can come down from the top." Frank then lit into the colonel, venting to the hilt.

3:30 P.M.
WHITE RIVER GLACIER

Summers stated that he had a very hot feeling about the terrain just east of their position.[25] Rick Harder directed twenty-eight volunteers to march uphill for a bit, before lining up, facing east.[26]

Bob Freund dutifully lined up with his colleagues and heard The Bagger call out that they'd be using the fine probe technique. This surprised Freund. He was sure they'd be directed to begin coarse probing.[27]

Scott Olson, only a few feet away from Summers and Harder, was confused too. *Fine probing? We don't need to probe every twelve inches.* Olson stood there, holding a ten-foot long EMT conduit, which he was using as an avalanche probe. He thought about saying something, but he held his tongue and did as he was told.[28]

Coarse probing has searchers line up, separated an arm's length apart. The formation would probe outside their left foot, take a step, then probe outside their right foot. It's used when leadership wants to cover a lot of ground, quickly, yet it does have its drawbacks. The principal disadvantage is that fewer probe holes are made in the snow.

Fine probing, however, is employed when leaders are confident that what they're looking for is in the immediate vicinity.

"Ready!" a PJ called out to the group.

Freund saw that they'd be working their way east, towards the pole capped with a brightly colored streamer. This marked the spot where Erik Sandvik had been found the previous morning.[29]

"Probe left!" the PJ ordered.[30]

Freund sank his avalanche probe into the snow—to his left—and could tell that snow deposits were beginning to harden. Although the aluminum shaft had penetrated fully, there was definite resistance to the movement.

"Probe center!" came the next command.

Freund knew that fine probing is very thorough, but it is extremely time-consuming for the time and energy that is expended.

"Probe right!" the PJ ordered.

Are we wasting time? Freund thought to himself. If they were looking for a lone person, that was known to have fallen in a general vicinity, then yes, this was the technique to employ. Since they were looking for a snow cave containing eight people, roughly fifteen feet away from a large equipment cache, Freund would have opted for the coarse probe technique. Scott Olson and several other members of CMRU agreed, grumbling under their breath.[31]

"Advance!" the PJ called out.

Freund, along with his colleagues, took a step forward and the probing process was repeated. Shoulder-to-shoulder, team members plunged their probes into the snowpack; slowly and methodically, they advanced in unison.

Pete Bustanoby was somewhat irritated as The Bagger had insisted on taking charge of the twenty-three-man probe line, even though it had already been created by members of CMRU.[32]

The mammoth team went high, sweeping as far as they could to the east. When they reached the corniced ridge, they looked at one another and shrugged their shoulders.

Nothing.

~3:40 P.M.
LANDING ZONE (LZ)
WY'EAST DAY LODGE SOUTH PARKING LOT

Having hiked out to safety two days earlier with Summers, Molly Schula was observing the search efforts through a pair of binoculars.

Don Penater recognized her from the news broadcasts and made his way to her side.

"Do you have your fingers crossed under those sleeves?" he asked.[33] Looking up at the glacier, Don saw a helicopter landing at the upper LZ. He introduced himself as Marion Horwell's brother, not as a reporter as he had allowed others to believe.

Don knew Molly was just a teen, and he didn't have any harsh feelings towards her. He just wanted information concerning his sister. He asked Molly why she and Summers hadn't returned the shovel to the occupants of the cave. Molly teared up, looked down at the pavement, and walked away.[34]

Reporters from *The Oregonian* approached Penater. The man who had been passing himself off as a journalist had, somehow, been identified. With the full understanding that he was Marion Horwell's brother, a reporter asked what Don's thoughts were considering the condition of the missing climbers.

"They're probably dead," he sighed, "but you gotta try. What do you think I'm still here for?"[35]

Nearby, Father Roy Coulter brushed his gray hair with his hand, the sunshine highlighting his widow's peak. As dean of the Cathedral of St. John at OES, Coulter knew the families well and was doing his best to provide them with some measure of comfort during their mountain vigil. By wearing his white clerical collar, Coulter became a lightning rod for journalists.

"They've been very stalwart," he said to a reporter, who had asked of the condition of the worried parents. "It's one of those situations when, in every hour that passes, there is less hope for survival."[36]

4:00 P.M.
WHITE RIVER GLACIER

The previous search sector had taken an hour to inspect. The probe line dropped about 300 feet in elevation and lined up again.[37] Master Sergeant Charlie Ek would be placed ahead of the crew, scouting for hidden crevasses with his probe. Ek tied-in to another PJ, Airman Gary Dugan, who would serve as his anchorman should he accidentally fall into one of these gaping maws.[38]

Roughly 150 feet behind Ek and Dugan came the wave of volunteers. Rick Harder and Technical Sergeant Joel Kasprzak—a paramedic with the Portland Fire Bureau—were following the probe line, carrying shovels in the event that anything was discovered.[39]

"How do we know how deep these people are buried," someone from the group asked, "and what is it going to feel like?"[40]

Bob Freund explained to a newer volunteer that it was never good to presume that one's probe was sinking straight down. They're made of lightweight aluminum. As they descend through the snow, they can bend and veer off at an angle. When you've been probing hard snow for hours, then suddenly encounter some light resistance—a buried person—you can instinctively *push* through. It was a harsh reality, but a very real possibility that volunteers needed to accept.[41]

Lt. Col. Mullen had become the on-scene commander, as far as the squadron personnel were concerned. Maj. McFadden was serving as the on-site duty officer in the LZ, overseeing communication and coordination. A couple approached.

"First of all," the man began, "we want to just tell you how much we really appreciate what you're doing."[42]

Mullen paused several seconds before replying.

"Oh," he said. "Thank you very much."

"You've done everything you could possibly do," the gentleman continued. "We just want to tell you how much we, absolutely, appreciate your efforts but, we're pretty much resigned to the fact that our child is gone. If you haven't found them by now, there's no way you're going to find her now. We're going to go home. We wanted to tell you, again, how much we really appreciate your efforts."

McFadden watched as the couple disappeared into the rows of cars in the parking lot. These were parents who had taken the time to express their gratitude while facing an agonizing truth—the hope of finding their daughter diminished with every passing hour.[43]

Prothman recognized that it was time for him, personally, to leave the search efforts. He needed to arrange transportation down the mountain, be debriefed by authorities, and drive over three hours to his home in Renton. He had only had an hour or two of sleep during the previous two days, and he had to report to work in the morning.

He unclipped Summers from his line. Except for an occasional helicopter flight over the glacier, the two men had been roped together for more than five hours. As Prothman coiled his rope, he said his goodbyes to Pete Bustanoby, the newly designated field team leader.[44]

Maslen continued manning the radio while her husband walked to a small, private room on the first floor of the Lodge. Deputies Hattan and Krebs, Barry Wright, and Greg Prothman were in attendance.

What is our status now? What are our plans for this evening? If the cave is not found today, what is our plan for tomorrow? These were just some of the questions being batted about.

Prothman believed the teams should stop using the SAR dogs as well as the metal detectors. Too much new snow had fallen. The OES party was too deep to be detected by these methods.[45]

Krebs asked about the status of the probe lines. For two days, authorities were used to seeing three to four-man teams of workers searching specific, targeted areas. Today, there was a virtual phalanx of personnel, combing the slopes with aluminum probes. Teams had started converging.

McClure complimented the efforts of Prothman and his team, recognizing that they had processed more real-time information than authorities could decipher at Base.

Hattan asked McClure for his overall assessment of the day's operation.

"We've done the best we can," McClure sighed, "and yet, we're not getting anywhere."[46]

The plan for the remainder of the day was to continue swapping out exhausted volunteers with fresh personnel.[47] The wind was picking up, and clouds were rolling in. Starting at 6:00 p.m., searchers would be picked off the glacier.[48] The consensus within the room was that probe lines were the best possible strategy for the task.

And, if the cave is not found today?

PMR didn't have the authority to call off an operation. That was a legal decision they were not empowered to make. Such responsibility fell to Sheriff Bill Brooks. Plans were made to continue searching on Friday. If there were no findings by some point tomorrow, volunteers might be pulled from the field. Then, only the spring thaw would reveal the snow cave's location.

CHAPTER 28
DAIBER

Word had spread that foul weather was on the horizon. The increased winds and poor conditions appeared to be returning. As a result of the weather forecast, search efforts for the day were scheduled to cease at 6:00 p.m.

Paul Williams had been growing apprehensive about retrieving his SMR personnel from the glacier. He heard from someone that search operations might cease soon, so he approached a deputy with his concerns.[1] The officer assured him that all SAR workers would be safely extracted before sunset.

Still concerned, Williams came trotting down the road that divided the two buildings. He asked some helicopter pilots about retrieving his personnel.[2] The pilots advised him that members of the probe line wanted to finish the search sector they were presently exploring before coming down.[3]

Deputy Kennel and Deputy Serafin peered down from their seats in a Huey. Observing the ground forces below them, they were not disappointed. The remnants of the original teams had joined together and were advancing as one colossal force. There were twenty-seven people working in unison.[4]

Over the airwaves came an announcement. The first wave of volunteers would be picked up by snowcat at 5:40 p.m. It looked as if the missing climbers would be spending another night in their snow cave.

The long probe line was advancing from west to east, toward the ridge which dropped down into White River Canyon.[5] Charlie Ek and Airman Dugan, who were scouting ahead of the main party, began descending the thirty-five-degree slope. The company, staying in line, followed roughly fifty feet behind.[6]

Mike Craig kept his eye on Ralph Summers. Though the consultant had believed he'd recognized terrain features several times during the day, something about his body language was different this time. *He's close*, Craig thought. *He's close, and he can't hide it.*[7]

About fifty feet down the embankment, around 8,200', Ek encountered a narrow crevasse. Dugan had him on belay as Ek hopped over the glide crack and explored the area in front of him with his ten-foot probe. The aluminum shaft sank. Suddenly, there it was—a soft resistance.

"Get me the shovel!" Ek demanded.[8] Someone handed over the shovel, and the PJ began digging furiously. Four feet down, he could see a green backpack and a yellow tarp.[9]

The equipment cache!

Watching the discovery unfold, Summers quickly pointed to a spot ten feet south of the cache. Ek, Ed Bolton, and Scott Olson turned and began probing the new area as the consultant continued pointing.[10]

Olson was suddenly aware that the news helicopters were producing an obnoxious amount of noise. Looking at the snow in front of him, he saw a glove and presumed it to be one of the victims. Four feet of fresh snow had fallen during the storm, yet this glove was lying on the surface of the pack. Olson took another step forward and sank his probe into the snow. He felt the give and realized he had discovered a void—*there it is.*[11]

Since the PJs were not roped in with the main probe team, they were given the task of digging. Ek and Kasprzak began tossing shovelful after shovelful of snow over their shoulders.

On the ridge, Bob Freund and Bill O'Brien were observing the excavation. Freund realized the search portion of the operation had just concluded, and they had immediately shifted into rescue mode. Nobody had discussed what the on-site rescue operation would look like.

Freund and O'Brien instructed anyone with a shovel to descend to the cave and offer their assistance.

"What we really need to do," O'Brien remarked, "as soon as we get some heart monitors up here, is get patches on all these people."[12]

Olson started ascending back up to Freund's position. He was a city engineer and knew he could contribute to the rigging system that would be needed to transport the victims. The word *patients* never entered his mind. Surely, there would be no survivors.[13]

~5:25 P.M.
LANDING ZONE (LZ)
WY'EAST DAY LODGE SOUTH PARKING LOT

The Bagger's voice came across Maj. McFadden's Air Force radio, requesting a switch to a previously agreed upon second frequency. A private channel, between the two men, was opened.

"Okay," Harder began. "We found something."[14]

"Okay..." McFadden replied quietly. "What do you need?"

"I'll call you back. We may need some things, and we may need 'em fast."

McFadden slowly approached one of his flight engineers.

"I want you to go over—don't make a big deal out of it—but, strip all the stuff out of 6-2."[15] He instructed the engineer to remove any unnecessary supplies and equipment from the helicopter bearing the tail number 82462. This would lighten the overall weight of the bird. The enlisted man got to work without questioning the order.

McFadden walked over to two pilots.

"When you get a chance," McFadden said, "kindly go over and check out your helicopter. Basically, do a pre-flight, but make it very casual looking."[16] The major's expression and tone delivered the message that this was no mere request—something was up.

Next, McFadden walked up beside one of the deputies.

Maintaining his low-key demeanor, he leaned in close enough so only the deputy could hear his words.

"Look, they've found something on the mountain, and this place is going to go crazy in about ten minutes."[17]

"What do you want me to do," said the deputy.

"Just keep everybody back."

Code 1244   283

5:28 P.M.
BASE OPERATIONS
WY'EAST DAY LODGE

SMR Base Operations Leader, Paul Williams, radioed his teams, telling them to prepare for departure. Pete Bustanoby's voice came back over the airwaves.

"Have you consulted with Daiber?"[18]

Williams was shocked by this response. The phrase was incredibly close to the code SMR had prearranged, to note the discovery of deceased personnel. It was not, however, followed by a number.

Williams walked into the adjacent room to report this communique. A deputy had just received a similar, coded message from the PJs.[19]

5:38 P.M.
WEST MORAINE
WHITE RIVER GLACIER

After digging down more than four feet, Charlie Ek exposed a portion of the void. Dropping down onto his belly, he stuck his head down into the hole.[20]

The odor was unmistakable. They had found the cave.[21] Ek, Kasprzak, and The Bagger all heard a faint moan from inside the shelter.[22]

"Hey!" Kasprzak yelled out to the volunteers in the probe line. "Somebody's talking to me!"[23]

~5:38 P.M.
BASE OPERATIONS
WY'EAST DAY LODGE

Static and crackling dominated the airwaves, but Jody Leach distinctly heard one word. *Digging*. Then...silence.

"Have you got them?" Leach inquired over the radio.[24] No reply. More and more rescue workers congregated around the radio. "What's going on?" she pressed.

"We have patients!" came Rick Harder's voice over the airwaves.[25]

Overjoyed by the transmission, McClure and Maslen grabbed their jackets and radios, determined to get out into the parking lot to render whatever assistance they could. Wright offered to man the radio.[26] Shultz took over the PMR log. As each new piece of information came in, the adrenalin affected her normally precise penmanship.

Radio transmissions between the mountain, Base Operations, and the medics in the parking lot were coming in rapid fire. SAR workers on the glacier were already requesting rescue sleds and specific medical supplies.[27] Triage carts, warm clothing, and blankets were being loaded aboard the first helicopter. Boxes containing intubation equipment and intravenous lidocaine were also rushed outside.[28]

~5:40 P.M.
WEST MORAINE
WHITE RIVER GLACIER

Bob Freund was watching from the top of the ridge when he heard Kasprzak yell out, indicating that someone inside the cave was making noise. Patients would need to be evacuated quickly, yet safely. There were enough qualified personnel on the ridge to affect an evacuation, but not enough equipment.

Freund looked at the thin crevasse that was situated between him and the discovery site. He could see that each victim would have to be pulled straight uphill on a rescue sled, crossing the potentially dangerous obstacle along the way.

He also knew that many of his colleagues had been working since before dawn. Rescue workers were physically and mentally drained. Freund wondered how they could ensure that none of the volunteers were involved in an accident themselves, while the patient evacuation was underway.

"Let's gather the probes," he said to Scott Olson.[29]

Believing that the final stages of the operation might occur after sunset, Freund asked his friends to jam their probes into the snow, forming crossed "X" patterns, all along the uphill side of the glide crack. Hopefully, this would prevent anyone from wandering too close to the crevasse.[30]

~5:44 P.M.
TIMBERLINE LODGE

The news had reached the resort. A man came running from Timberline Lodge down to the parking lot. He gave the thumbs-up sign and was grinning from ear-to-ear. A parent of one of the missing students saw this man's face and dropped to his knees.[31]

Don Penater felt relief too, but in his heart, he remained a realist. He knew how long the team had been in the snow cave. He knew he'd soon have the answers he was seeking, and he began pacing.[32]

Ek and Kasprzak pulled out an ice axe and a backpack from the cave. A bit farther in, they came upon the yellow raincoat. Removing this, Kasprzak was overjoyed by what he saw.

"We got people! We got people!" he hollered.[33]

Those at Base wanted to know the location of the cave. One of the on-site SAR workers responded. The shelter was directly underneath a spent smoke grenade, which had been dropped from a Huey to mark the Upper Discovery Site.[34] A streamer, attached to a pole, stood just yards away, whipping quietly in the breeze. It marked the spot where Erik Sandvik had been found, thirty-five hours earlier.[35]

Freund and Olson discussed the need to rig a pulley system. As the weight of a single person on a sled was not heavy, and the slope was only around thirty-five-degrees, they opted to perform a 1:1 raising. By employing a single pulley block, the sled would rise a foot in elevation for every foot the team pulled on the line.

Freund looked for a suitable site to rig the necessary system. He wanted it to terminate as close to the entrance of the cave as possible, but the glide crack crossed directly in their path. Finding a small snow bridge that spanned a section of the crack, he sank his ice axe directly above the bridge's position.

The snow cave was roughly fifty feet down the slope from the far side of the ice bridge. Using one of the 150-foot dynamic climbing-ropes for the pulley system, the workers on the ridge would have around 100 feet of spare line at their disposal.[36]

Rigging a single pulley, Freund passed the bitter end of one of the climbing ropes through a small pulley block.[37]

His quick thinking paid immediate dividends, as the first helicopter bearing the supplies landed about two hundred yards to the southwest.[38]

CMRU was ready to get to work again.

6:00 P.M.
GOMAN-YATES RESIDENCE
PORTLAND

As Mar and Diana were about to leave for the midweek Eucharist and potluck at St. John's in Milwaukie, their telephone rang.[39] A friend was on the other end of the line, and she didn't bother with pleasantries.

"Turn on the TV!" she cried. "They found them!"[40]

There was only one small television in the house, upstairs in the sewing room. The pair ran up the stairs.

~6:02 P.M.
OREGON EPISCOPAL SCHOOL
PORTLAND

When Amy Horwell was only seven, she and her mother had gone to the grocery store.

"Amy," Marion said quietly. "Look over there."[41] By the main doors to the store, a woman had a cardboard box with a little dachshund-Scottish terrier mix. "Free," the sign read. Unable to resist her daughter's smile and pleading eyes, the family acquired a new member that day.

Now, five years later, Amy was taking Lucy for a walk on campus.[42] A group of upperclassmen approached her, excitedly.

"They've found the snow cave!" the older kids announced. "They're okay," they assured her.[43]

~6:02 P.M.
HIGHWAY 26

Heading away from the mountain, a Ford Taurus was just passing the town of Government Camp when the news came over the radio. The snow cave had been found. Greg Prothman nearly turned his vehicle around. After all, he was only seven miles away from the resort.

Would there be any survivors?

As Prothman passed the towns of Rhododendron and Mt. Hood Village, he began to examine the day's events. He'd been working with Ralph Summers for hours. He wondered what else he could have said or done to get inside the consultant's head. Prothman was facing a three-and-a-half-hour drive home to Renton, alone with his thoughts. [44]

Enough snow had been removed to expose the tunnel and the front of the cave.[45] Charlie Ek saw two teenagers lying in the entranceway, one on top of the other.[46] A male and a female; neither were wearing a hat, and they were barely conscious.[47]

The Bagger directed Ek to crawl farther into the cave, while Harder began working on the boy. He placed a thermometer inside his patient's mouth. The boy's jaw was clenched, and he was shivering, causing the device to break.[48]

Ek was making every effort not to disturb the first two patients as he cautiously crawled into the cave. The PJ, trying to steady himself, reached up to touch the roof of the snow cave. There were no visible air holes in the ceiling.[49] With Bagger and another PJ tending to the first two patients, Ek's job was to check for signs of life amid the remaining six climbers. In a 4'x6' cavity, armed only with a stethoscope, he set to work.[50]

Dick Sandvik called Frank, to personally invite him to Erik's memorial service on the weekend. Frank was monitoring CNN News as he spoke to his friend.

"Have you heard any update on the search effort," Dick asked.[51]

"Dick!" Frank exclaimed. "You're not going to believe this, but they have just found the snow cave." CNN was announcing at that very moment. "They say there are survivors."

"Oh, great!" Dick shot back. "Oh, God...oh, *shit*."

The range of emotions these two fathers shared over the phone was overwhelming. Euphoria was tempered with caution. Hope was put in check by the knowledge that Dick had already lost his son. Pat had spent another night and a full day on the mountain. Could he be alive?

"Do you know any more?" Dick asked after a substantial pause in the conversation.

"No. Turn it on."

"What channel?"

"CNN. Go turn your TV on!"

As other SAR workers continued to dig, exposing more and more of the shelter to the light of day, Pete Bustanoby was making his way inside to be of assistance.[52] Looking down at the girl that a PJ was assessing, he was somewhat shocked. Removing his glove, Bustanoby gently touched her pale face. He felt the heat from his fingers draining into her freezing flesh. The girl moaned softly, slightly opening her eyes.[53]

The seasoned SAR worker was filled with an overwhelming desire to get off the peak. Everything within him told him to descend and get back down amid civilization. Though survivors had been found, he was still wracked with grief, unable to suppress the next, inevitable question.

How many had perished?[54]

CHAPTER 29
THE RELAY

When Mick Garrett had ventured out to the main campus, teachers and fellow students offered him kind words and hugs. He had very little interaction with many of these people, before Monday's field trip.[1] Around campus, the campaign posters for Erin's run for student body president had been quietly taken down.[2]

The dorm lounge was a space for campus residents to socialize or study, like a family room for those who lived away from home. It held a ping pong table, a television, and comfy furniture. Mick had spent most of the day in the lounge, escaping to familiar surroundings.

As he was eating a slice of pizza, there was a news flash. Rescue workers had discovered the snow cave. Mick felt elated and relieved.

With her arms piled high with blankets from the historic inn, Maslen counted eight stretchers lined up in a row on the pavement. Extra oxygen bottles, medication, and the blankets were being staged. It didn't look as though there were enough supplies for the eight patients that would need to be assessed and stabilized for transport. She could see a couple of ambulances in the lot but knew they wouldn't be used. All of the hypothermic climbers would need to be airlifted to regional hospitals. After adding the blankets to the mounting supplies, Maslen followed the lead of other volunteers, tucking intravenous solution bags inside her jacket to keep them as close to body temperature as possible.[3]

Even though they were busy tending to their duties, the first responders stole quick hugs from one another, relieved that progress was being made. Soon, they'd be able to provide the medical services that had brought them to the mountain.[4]

The first flight had already departed, bearing triage equipment, warm clothing, an electrocardiogram with grid strips, and extra batteries.[5] Now, Sergeant John Harkness and Airman Dave Armstrong began loading the specific medical supplies and equipment that The Bagger had requested over the radio.[6] Intravenous lidocaine, the first of the akja sleds, and additional life packs were among the items being loaded onto the second flight.[7]

Initially, Harkness and Armstrong were in charge of the triage area in the landing zone.[8] The sheriff's department was pleased with their ongoing services but wanted medical responsibility transferred to civilians. Deputy Hattan turned official responsibility for the triage area over to Lane Wintermute of the Hoodland Fire District, and Phil Moyer of Alpine Ambulances. These men would determine which incoming patients would be sent to which medical facility.[9]

As Maslen heard more requests for supplies over her radio handset, she scribbled a list in a notebook, trying not to drop the I.V. bags tucked inside her coat.

"Cheryl!" came a familiar voice. Maslen turned to see Deputy Krebs. "You're with me," he stated firmly.[10]

~6:06 P.M.
SNOW CAVE
WHITE RIVER GLACIER

Bill O'Brien descended from the ridge crest to the exposed cave site. He caught a glimpse of the first two patients. A boy was lying partially atop a girl.[11] He reminded Harder that he was a paramedic with the city of Albany and could be of assistance. The Bagger instructed him to back away from the cave. His crew had all of the medical needs covered.[12] O'Brien backed off and started back up the slope.[13]

Harder placed an oxygen mask over the lower portion of his patient's face. Another PJ did the same for the girl. Fifteen liters of oxygen per minute began flowing.[14] The medics were unable to get a carotid pulse on either victim, yet both teens were in and out of consciousness.

Patients #1 and #2 were carefully extracted from their positions and laid out—supine—on a level platform of snow, just outside the cave. Medics could now work on them while other SAR workers continued digging.[15]

As he was ascending the slope, O'Brien stopped, turned around, and returned to the cave, ignoring The Bagger's prior request to back away.[16] He spied two Lifepaks (EKGs) arriving on the scene and, as he ran cardiac arrest calls on a regular basis—with this specific type of Lifepak—he felt the urge to contribute to the cause.

The male patient was becoming more vocal. He was nearly shouting, unintelligibly, in brief moments of agitation. His gaze was roving, side-to-side, with no purposeful eye contact.[17] The girl's eyes were open, but moving slowly.[18]

O'Brien was shocked to see that both patients were not properly insulated. He ordered hats and more blankets.[19] As these items were being procured, he passed his own Therm-a-Rest sleeping pad to one of the PJs.[20]

The EKG machines were situated on the sides of the first two patients. Harder continued working on the boy while another PJ tended to the girl.

O'Brien recognized the device. Manufactured by Physio-Control, it was called the Lifepak 5. It had two batteries and a wire, that split into three wires, with snaps on each end. Round, sticky foam patches—two inches in diameter—with conductive gel centers, were attached to these snaps. These three "leads" were to be attached to the patients. O'Brien watched the progress, mentally checking off the required steps as they were performed.[21] If everything went smoothly, the procedure would only take a minute, and it would translate the heart's electrical activity into small line tracings on a paper printout.

O'Brien saw some hesitancy on the part of the PJ tending to the girl. It seemed that he was confused as to where to place the leads. *Attach the red lead to the lower left side of her chest*, O'Brien thought to himself. *Attach the white lead under or above her clavicle . . . Let's go, let's go.* Seeing that the PJ appeared puzzled by the color of the third wire, O'Brien told him where it should be placed.[22] Once completed, the PJ flipped the switch.[23]

The machine didn't respond.

O'Brien couldn't believe it. The batteries were dead. A runner had to be sent up to the LZ, to obtain extras.[24] Hopefully, the second set would be charged.

Gene Griswold reached the cave's entrance and noticed it was very near to a steep slope. If any of the paramedics stepped too far back from the cave, they would be in jeopardy of falling off. He believed the medics were so focused on their work that a misstep was a very real possibility. He took up a position between the patients and the lip of the drop-off. Griswold

Ric Conrad

was now serving as a safety watch for Harder, O'Brien, and the PJs.[25]

O'Brien was handed the replacement batteries. Being familiar with the equipment, he quickly swapped them out and tried the test again.[26] It worked; paper, depicting wave-like patterns, began spitting out of the device.

The Bagger, monitoring the boy's test results, grabbed the radio.

"Patient #1 is male, young," his voice sounded over the airwaves. "When I put a thermometer in his mouth, he bites it off. EKG is as follows: very slow, pulse rate about forty."[27] A normal pulse for a teenager is seventy-five to eighty beats per minute. Harder requested that authorities relay these details to a doctor at Emanuel Hospital. The Bagger said his patients were conscious, alert, and in sinus rhythm.[28]

O'Brien was taken aback by the transmission. He reached over and examined the boy's EKG test results for himself. He saw a green, illuminated waveform of the heart's electrical activity. O'Brien knew he was looking at a wide, complex atrial fibrillation. He saw these patterns all the time when confronted with elderly patients suffering from heart failure. The only difference in this boy's specific rhythms was that each wave was wider—due to extreme hypothermia.[29]

O'Brien looked at both patients. At the moment, they were both unconscious. He was baffled as to why The Bagger had completely blown the level of consciousness, as well as misinterpreted the EKG rhythms.[30]

To help alleviate, though not eliminate, the possibility of arrhythmia, Harder had one of his PJs try to start an intravenous line to pump lidocaine into Patient #1. O'Brien leaned over and informed Harder that lidocaine doesn't work in cases of extreme hypothermia. I.V.'s were unlikely to be established.

The PJs quickly discovered that the veins in the teen's limbs had collapsed because of the extreme cold.[31] Lidocaine, through an I.V., wouldn't work.

The Bagger grabbed the radio, requesting authorization to use lidocaine intramuscularly.[32]

"Stand by," Jody Leach replied.[33]

The Bagger's request to administer lidocaine into the muscle was denied by a doctor.[34]

Harder radioed Base again, seeking to consult with a different doctor. This request was submitted. O'Brien knew lidocaine was only given by an intravenous route, in a conscious patient. Patient's #1 and #2 were unconscious at the moment. Lidocaine was never given intramuscularly, and he stated as much to The Bagger.[35] He pushed for Harder to forgo the I.V. attempts, and the radio calls seeking authorization to use the drug. *Let's get moving.*[36]

Within minutes, a second physician was patched-in to Jody Leach. Harder, again, asked for permission to inject lidocaine directly into the muscle of his patients.[37]

"The doctor wants to know," Leach's voice came over the airwaves, "why lidocaine?"[38]

Harder requested the input of a third doctor.[39]

Mike Craig descended from the ridge, down to the cave, and what he saw stopped him in his tracks. O'Brien and The Bagger were busy, each attending a teenager. Behind the first two patients, workers had removed the roof of the snow cave. Inside the now exposed interior, were the remaining members of the OES climbing party. Two adults were sitting upright, with their legs stretched out and their eyes open. Father Tom had his back to the mountain while Marion sat across from him. Four teens were stacked like cordwood atop Tom and Marion's legs. It looked as though the adults were trying to prop the children up, to get them out of the snowmelt that their collective body heat had created. It was a profoundly moving scene.[40]

Griswold, only a few feet away, was equally moved. He saw snow where he didn't want to see it, partially obscuring brightly colored parkas within the cave. He had two children, only a few years older than the kids in the cave. Griswold understood that he was experiencing a moment of identity transference. *Those are someone's children...they could easily have been mine.* Trying not to let these emotions betray his professional demeanor, he looked away.[41]

Craig could see the partially exposed equipment cache nearby, filled with backpacks and items that could have been used as insulating warmth and protection from the snow and water inside the cave. He considered the storm, the high winds, and how frightened the students must have been. He couldn't help but wonder what the members of the party had been through.

They did the best they could, he thought.[42]

Bob Freund sent some of the crew down towards the LZ at Lower Tri-angle Moraine, to intercept an inbound Huey. He was pleased to see, even from this distance, that akja sleds had been brought up to the glacier and would be at the ridge crest shortly.

When the rescue sleds arrived, he noticed the lack of handles on these models. There were chains at the apex, however, and Freund was quick to seize hold of one of these, linking it to the end of the climbing rope with the use of a carabiner. The pulley system was now complete.

The team slowly paid out the line and watched as the sled descended the natural fall-line of the thirty-five-degree slope. The anchor had been placed perfectly, and the akja, upon reaching the glide crack, slid smoothly over the narrow snow bridge that spanned the gap. As the men continued to pay out the line, the sled continued its journey down to the cave.[43]

The EKG reading indicated that Patient #2 had a pulse rate of only thirty beats per minute. The Bagger reported that their female patient was suffering from atrial fibrillation, an irregular beating of the heart muscle.[44]

Harder, O'Brien, and the PJs were at the limit of medical assistance they could provide at the site. The Bagger wanted Life Flight to standby for the evacuation of the first two patients.[45]

During his career, Harder had witnessed five of his patients go into cardiac arrest, right as he and his colleagues commenced moving them from the field.[46]

The first akja sled reached the cave and was unclipped from the rope.

Freund's team, fifty feet higher uphill, gathered up the line and sent down a second sled. When this akja was delivered to the cave site, it was unclipped from the rope and set aside in the snow. Because the terrain was not flat, there was no room for more sleds at the cave; a relay system would need to be created.[47]

"I've made a command decision," Harder radioed Base, not waiting for the response from the third doctor he had requested.[48] "We are going to evacuate now."[49]

"How many are you sending?" came the reply.

"We'll have more than two."[50]

The Bagger radioed Maj. McFadden on the private frequency.

"I've got one ready for transport," Harder remarked.[51]

"No problem," McFadden replied. "I'll have a bird up for you in a few minutes." He gave the signal for one of the military helicopters to take off. As the noise diminished, he turned to address the inquisitive crowd.

"Look," he said. "We have a survivor."[52] The officer's experience hadn't prepared him for the reaction this announcement created. He thought it resembled the dropping of raw meat into a pool of piranha. The deputies did an admirable job holding the media back.

The extraction of the patients occurred with extreme caution. Patient #1 was carefully lifted and placed into the aluminum akja sled. SAR volunteers strapped him in; everyone performed these tasks as delicately as possible.

As the sled was towed gently up the snow slope, The Bagger stayed with his patient, carefully monitoring his oxygen flow.[53] The akja had runners built into the bottom. This enabled the craft to track nicely and prevented the sled from shifting sideways.[54]

Freund observed this progress from the pulley block. Once the akja reached his position, he unclipped it from a carabiner, and seven men took charge of the patient. An empty sled was lowered down to the cave, and the relay continued.

The seven volunteers transported the teen 150-yards west, and slightly downhill, to the awaiting Huey.

Doctors at Emanuel radioed Leach, wanting to know how many climbers had been found alive. She relayed that question up to Harder.[55] He didn't reply. He was too busy orchestrating the transport of patients down to the triage center. Each patient would be accompanied by a Life Flight nurse and at least one PJ.[56] The Bagger and Technical Sergeant Joel

Kasprzak climbed aboard the first chopper.[57]

6:41 P.M.
LANDING ZONE (LZ)
WY'EAST DAY LODGE SOUTH PARKING LOT

Recognizing that there was plenty of manpower on the scene, Pete Bustanoby had yielded to the voices in his head, the ones telling him to descend. He had returned to the parking lot with Ed Boulton; both were exhausted.[58]

Walking across the parking lot, they informed a deputy that the position of field leader had been turned over to Bill O'Brien of CMRU.[59] The men found themselves surrounded by reporters.

When asked about the reaction of SAR workers when the cave was found, Bustanoby sighed.

"I got tears in my eyes," he replied. "There was a lot of back-slapping. It turned out so much better than we thought it would. It was fantastic. Kids were alive—it was a miracle."[60]

A cameraman from KGW News pulled Don Penater aside, asking him what he thought of the unfolding operation.

"The only thing that worries me," Don remarked, "is the definition of the word *alive*. They termed the others not dead on arrival, the three. With this hypothermia, I don't know. Forty-five-degree body temperature—not real alive, but we'll just have to see."[61]

~6:47 P.M.
WEST MORAINE
WHITE RIVER GLACIER

Freund looked down towards the snow cave. Another patient was being strapped in an akja. The sled was then rigged for hauling. A Ratchet hitch was employed so that, in the event any rescue worker tripped, the ratchet would catch the line and prevent the sled from sliding back down the hill.

A dozen people grabbed hold of the slack line. As Freund called out the order, "Haul!" the volunteers held fast to the rope and began walking parallel with the glide crack, activating the pulley system. Freund was so focused on the task that he didn't notice a news helicopter filming the operation.[62]

~6:48 P.M.
SNOW CAVE
WHITE RIVER GLACIER

Workers were instructed to gently remove the remaining six patients, strap oxygen masks on them, and evacuate them to the LZ.[63] Charlie Ek, who had been tasked with evaluating those in the cave, had not detected heartbeats with his stethoscope.

Mike Craig was emotionally spent. He quietly observed the ongoing evacuation procedures. The only two defibrillators had departed with Harder and Kasprzak, in case the first two patients encountered any trouble.[64] *Six patients to go.* Craig didn't want to witness what he was seeing—those on the bottom layer of the pile were being cut out of their clothing with paramedic scissors.[65] They had frozen to the floor and to one another.

6:57 P.M.
LANDING ZONE (LZ)
WY'EAST DAY LODGE SOUTH PARKING LOT

Bystanders were watching as the military helicopter bearing Patient #1, accompanied by Rick Harder, landed in the roped-off section of the parking lot.[66]

Deputy Hattan was on the team that raced forward to remove the teen from the Huey. The deputy looked down into the boy's open eyes. The look on the teen's face was not fear. Hattan could see that the youth knew he was finally safe.[67]

The team carefully transported their patient into a Life Flight helicopter.[68] All air vents on the aircraft were opened, to keep the inside temperature consistent.[69] The nurse had been told not to warm the bodies of the incoming climbers—an attempt to avoid further injury.[70]

The aircraft lifted off from the staging area, heading to Providence Hospital in Portland.[71]

Deputy Hattan, filled with emotion, flashed a bright smile and a triumphant thumbs-up to nearby reporters.[72]

~7:05 P.M.
INTERSTATE 5
WOODBURN

Although he had devoted Tuesday and Wednesday afternoon to the search efforts, Rocky Henderson was now over eighty miles away, driving

298   Ric Conrad

south along Interstate 5. Over his car radio, he heard the announcement that the cave had been discovered. Patients were being airlifted to regional hospitals. Overjoyed, and grinning from ear-to-ear, Henderson celebrated by slamming the dashboard, repeatedly, with his free hand.

Finding survivors was a miracle.[73]

7:30 P.M.
PROVIDENCE MEDICAL CENTER
PORTLAND

As the Life Flight touched down on the helipad, ten medical personnel raced toward the aircraft. Dr. Leo Marx, a cardiovascular expert, supervised as Patient #1 was transported to a waiting gurney.[74]

The teen was taken to an operating room where nearly a dozen physicians, nurses, and specialists were awaiting his arrival. Doctors removed his ski cap and oxygen mask, before transferring him from the gurney to the operating table.[75] Their patient appeared to be struggling, incoherent, and was not responding to verbal stimuli. His face was red, and his cheeks were puffy. Some portions of his limbs were red, while others were pale. He was breathing on his own, and his pulse rate was in the 50s.[76]

The professionals tending to him were wary of restraining him, as such restrictions might trigger more stress. Someone took his bladder temperature—71.6° Fahrenheit. An anesthesiologist began administering oxygen but had yet to intubate the patient.[77]

Doctors were confronted with vascular access concerns. No peripheral veins were available. Groin punctures had to be performed after a Doppler ultrasound was employed to find the vein and artery.

Without warning, the patient developed ventricular fibrillation.[78]

CHAPTER 30
SIGNING OFF

7:35 P.M.
LANDING ZONE (LZ)
WY'EAST DAY LODGE SOUTH PARKING LOT

Barry Wright had rarely left Base Operations in sixty-two hours. The only four hours of sleep he had received had been on a cot, fifteen feet from his desk. Having served as one of the key strategists for three days, never abandoning his post, Barry felt the need to make a hands-on contribution. In the parking lot, Deputy Krebs directed him to join one of the teams waiting at the LZ.

Jody Leach walked outside as well. Even though sunset was an hour away, this was the first daylight she had experienced all day. Being cooped up in Base, manning one of the radio sets for hours, she was ready to see the evacuation procedures underway in the parking lot.[1]

A Huey bearing Patients #3 and #4, a girl and boy respectively, landed nearby. Wright and other workers raced forward. The kids were covered with more blankets, and the team transported them to a Life Flight helicopter. Looking down at the boy's face, Barry's heart began to ache. The teen was gone.[2]

The man who had signed the Search and Rescue log as *Barry Wright—NEVER OUT—PMR*, mentally checked out. The haunting image of the boy's face, framed in sandy curls, burned into his memory.

~7:45 P.M.
MCGINNESS RESIDENCE
PORTLAND

Frank, anxiously watching the news and waiting for any information regarding Pat, heard a helicopter flying over his house. Racing out into his front yard, he saw a Life Flight helicopter, most likely heading to nearby Emanuel Hospital.

His heart jumped. *Is my son aboard one of those aircraft?*

He ran back inside and phoned the school.

"Listen," he pleaded to the woman on the other end of the line. "What's going on?"[3] He was desperately seeking any information about Patrick.

"Well," the woman replied cautiously, "our center here is going to disseminate all of the information." That was the only fact that she could offer at this time.

Hanging up the phone, Frank decided to head straight to the school.

7:48 P.M.
EMANUEL HOSPITAL
PORTLAND

The helicopter bearing Patient #2 landed at Emanuel. She was bundled neatly under several blankets. The patient's face was swollen, her arms were folded across her chest, and her legs were stiff. Delirious and unable to communicate, she seemed to stare at the trauma team members who were transferring her to a gurney.[4] Breaths were shallow, at a rate of only twelve per minute.[5]

She was whisked away to a room that had been preheated to 80° F. Her body temperature was 73.4° F.[6] The teen was gently placed on a heated blanket, and an anesthesiologist began administering 105.8° F humidified oxygen. Even after these measures had been taken, the patient's temperature dropped another degree within minutes.[7]

7:49 P.M.
LANDING ZONE (LZ)
WY'EAST DAY LODGE SOUTH PARKING LOT

Chief Bradshaw and Captain Grolbert asked Deputy Krebs how they could be of assistance. The captain was directed to join one of the six-person stretcher teams.[8] The men were soon unloading Patient #5, a boy, from a Huey.

Patient #6, who followed, was easily identifiable. An adult male with a beard. Fr. Goman. *Tom.*

Ground volunteers expected to load these two patients into a civilian aircraft, but none was present. Not wanting to wait around for an in-bound Life Flight helicopter, the patients were re-loaded, back onto the military chopper. It was unclear which hospital, if any, could accommodate such a large helicopter; this concern would have to be resolved—and soon.

The medical team working with Patient #1 had acted quickly. To facilitate the boy's rapid resuscitation, they elected to perform a sternotomy and immediately instituted cardiopulmonary bypass. Paddles were put on shortly after. The teen had responded, and an organized rhythm was restored.

Doctors worked amid a sea of tubes, needles, and various pumps. For just a moment, these medical professionals parted like the Red Sea to permit a photographer to lean in and snap a photo of the patient. The photograph would be used for identification.[9]

Don Penater had grabbed all his gear and was headed to his car. He had just heard Deputy Williams' grim statement to the press. Williams had reported that all eight patients had been removed from the snow cave. Patient #1 was a responsive male who was flown to Providence. Patient #2 was a responsive female who was flown to Emanuel. Patients #3 and #4 were not breathing and were en route to OHSU. Williams conceded that the condition of the remaining four patients was unknown, but that some were breathing.[10]

A Huey landed, and Patient #7 was offloaded. She was gently carried to an awaiting civilian aircraft.[11]

Don shouted questions over the noise. No one in the parking lot seemed to understand the precise identification or destinations of individual patients. Don tossed his belongings into his car. He figured that some of the victims would be flown to Emanuel, so he began his descent of Timberline Road, heading towards Highway 26.

Let's see what this Porsche can do.[12]

The final patient was transferred from military to civilian aircraft. Patient #8 was a grown woman. The dean of students for the upper school—Marion Horwell—began her flight to St. Vincent Medical Center in Portland.[13]

As the last patient departed the mountain on a helicopter, Deputy

Hattan's eyes filled with tears.

"I got a miracle going," he said to nearby reporters. "We never completely lost hope but...it wasn't looking real promising. But this is what makes it all worthwhile."[14] The emotion carried in his voice.

Volunteers from the Red Cross approached relatives of the climbers. Families were asked if they would congregate in the cafeteria so that authorities could give them the most recent information.

Cheryl Maslen had the sense that someone was walking too close to her, and it caused her to flinch. As she turned around, there was no one there. She was alone. Then, it happened again. When it happened a third time, Cheryl realized she was beginning to hallucinate.[15] She was emotionally spent. She decided she should write something in the official log before she completely lost it.

A reporter approached her as she scribbled an entry concerning the OES climbers: "All 8 confirmed down."[16]

"What's next?" he inquired.[17]

Cheryl pondered the question for a moment. She could feel her emotional dam beginning to crumble. Staring at the parking lot, littered with equipment, she knew the answer to the question.

"I'm going to sit down and cry."

~8:00 P.M.
ST. JOHN THE EVANGELIST EPISCOPAL CHURCH
MILWAUKIE

Roughly forty people attended the service, including Diana and Mar. They knew the snow cave had been discovered but assumed it would take some time for the patients to be removed from the shelter. Mar had informed authorities that she and Diana would be at church, only two miles from home, where they could be reached if there were any developments.[18]

They were surrounded by friends when the long-awaited call arrived. Tom was being flown to Good Samaritan Hospital. While Mar was on the phone, Diana could hear a helicopter in the distance.[19]

~8:05 P.M.
EMANUEL HOSPITAL
PORTLAND

Patient #2 had been connected to a heart-lung machine for the rewarming process. In her first two minutes on bypass, with flows up to three liters per minute, her heart rate had increased. Now, doctors closely monitored the EKG readouts.[20]

On the west side of the Willamette River, high up on Marquam Hill, Patients #3 and #4 arrived at the OHSU helipad. Patient #3, a girl, had a temperature of 42.8°F and no detectable heartbeat.[21]

Patient #4's temperature registered at 53.6°F.[22] One of the cardiac surgeons described the youth as "ice cold and quite stiff."[23] The boy was rushed into surgery; his mouth was clenched too tight for an airway tube.

On the east side of the Willamette River, Patient #7 arrived at Emanuel with no discernable heartbeat. Her core body temperature was 44° F.[24]

Relatives and friends of Marion Horwell congregated in the living room of her apartment. Most everyone was glued to the television screen, waiting for a phone call. *Was Marion alive? Which medical facility had she been taken to?* The family waited for the answers to these crucial questions.

When she learned the snow cave had been discovered, Amy was under the belief that her mother was okay and would be home shortly. Armed with this knowledge, she asked Aunt Tara if she could go outside. Tara allowed this, with the sole provision that Amy venture no farther than the nearby playground as the sun was low in the sky.

Amy ignored this parameter, walking down to Fanno Creek at the edge of the school's boundary. Rolling up her jeans, she waded into the water. She'd always loved playing in the stream. As she waded in deeper, the icy water came up higher on her legs. It felt good on this warm, Spring evening.

A woman's shouts caught her attention. Amy looked up from the creek to see her aunt in the distance, running towards her.

"Amy!" Tara shouted. "We have to get to the hospital!"[25]

Amy rushed up the bank of the creek and unrolled the first of her pant legs. Continued pleading from her aunt caused the girl to forgo unrolling the second, and off she shot—running towards Tara. She headed uphill, along a short stretch of road that led to the main parking lot. She noticed a group of students turning to look her way. Amy felt self-conscious.[26]

Scott Olson was on the first wave of evacuation flights down to the parking lot. As he stepped out of the aircraft, he scanned the area, littered with equipment and rescue gear. Cloisters of people were working on the chaos. Olson saw Sheriff Bill Brooks heading straight towards him.

"Would you be willing to go on *The Today Show* first thing tomorrow morning?" the sheriff asked.[27]

Olson didn't even pause to consider the offer.

"No way," he replied, shaking his head as he began walking towards the Lodge. Olson failed to notice a patch of black ice and he slipped. He sprawled out onto the pavement. Exhausted and somewhat embarrassed, he rose to his feet and limped into the building.[28]

Doctors suddenly recoiled as their patient woke up on the operating table. Dr. Long watched as the teen slowly uncrossed her arms and began moving. Although startling, the movements were a welcome sight to doctors, as it told them the patient's upper torso was not dealing with neurological injuries.[29]

Eight blocks west of Good Samaritan Hospital, the Air Force helicopter bearing Patient #5 and Patient #6 landed between two baseball fields in Wallace Park. The hospital didn't have a helipad, so the patients were being delivered here, to be transferred to the hospital by an ambulance. CPR had been administered to both patients during the flight.[30]

The sun was setting as the final patient landed at a hospital.[31] Marion's body temperature was a mere 34° F.[32]

Patient #2 had been on bypass for thirty minutes. Her EKG readings showed sinus tachycardia, an elevated rate of impulses. She was given six units of red blood cells and fresh frozen plasma.[33]

The girl's hands moved, back and forth, and Dr. Long noted that she had had ulnar neuropraxia in both. She was unable to extend her fingers completely.[34]

Fr. Richard Toll and his wife had driven Mar and Diana from the church to the hospital. The group soon learned more about Tom and the youth who had been delivered to the same facility.

No heartbeat had been detected on either patient when they were up in the snow cave, during the helicopter flight, on the ambulance ride, or upon their arrival at the hospital. There was only the quivering of heart muscles, no true contractions—fine ventricular fibrillation. The two patients were rushed into operating room 7260, where they were connected to heart-lung machines. Tom's core temperature was 66° F. The boy registered at 41°F.[35]

"We're trying to save him," doctors informed Mar and Diana. "We're trying to slowly rewarm him."[36]

"Whatever you can do," Mar begged. "Just save him. Please."

Bill O'Brien, who had tended patients as a paramedic up at the snow cave, jumped out of a helicopter as it landed in the parking lot. Walking away from the aircraft, he caught sight of Rick Harder, surrounded by hungry reporters.[37]

Nearby, Cheryl Maslen was checking-in the last wave of her volunteers. She'd arrived on the mountain believing she'd only be needed in Base Operations for a few hours on Tuesday morning. When the last SAR worker was checked in, Cheryl made her final entry in the PMR log— "Signing off."[38]

Dr. Asaph informed reporters that the temperature of Patient #1 had been raised, on average, 1.8° F every five minutes.[39] The doctor added that the boy's forearm showed signs of muscle necrosis, yet none of the blistering associated with frostbite.[40]

In seventy-five minutes, the medical team had managed to raise the teen's core temperature from 71.6° to a normal 98.6° F.[41]

Doctors had tried everything they could for Patients #3 and #4. The boy's chest had been opened, and blood clots were discovered in his heart. Such clots prevent the use of the heart-lung machine.[42]

The girl had arrived even colder than her companion. The medical teams had to make the same difficult decision. At this point, the two youths were legally pronounced dead.[43]

Dr. Lowe noted that the cause of death for both patients was *profound hypothermia*. Speaking on behalf of the medical specialists who had attended the teens, Lowe added, "We were sorry we couldn't have done better, but we gave it our best shot."[44]

Patient #2 was taken off the heart-lung machine. Her heartrate had only been thirty beats per minute upon arrival, but she had improved dramatically. Dr. Clark Chipman noted that his patient had been sedated and transferred to the ICU.[45]

"We are very optimistic," he stated to reporters.[46]

Elsewhere in the hospital, the medical specialists who were working with Patient #7 had not been successful. The girl was pronounced dead.[47]

9:00 P.M.
PARKING LOT
WY'EAST DAY LODGE

Lt. Gene Hanners was overseeing the demobilization process of the rescue organizations.[48] All SAR teams were off the mountain slopes by 8:44 p.m.[49] Many of CMRU's personnel had volunteered to stay overnight; they'd head up to the snow cave in the morning to retrieve equipment and personal belongings of the OES team. SMR's car caravan had already departed as they had a three-hour drive ahead of them. Most of the parents had left, and one by one, the number of vehicles in the lot diminished.

Several memorable vehicles and aircraft had also departed. The military's fuel truck and the Red Cross truck were both on the road already. The Life Flight helicopters and one of the military helicopters had all left with patients. The news choppers and vans were departing for Portland, making their way to various hospitals. One of the civilian helicopters, however, remained. Mike Moffitt had received authorization from his employer to the use their Bell 206 JetRanger in the morning, to assist CMRU.

With all patients evacuated, the pilots of the remaining four military aircraft began start-up procedures. Pulling up slowly, they lifted off the pavement of the lower LZ for the last time. Once airborne, the four came together, flying in formation as the crimson twilight faded in the west.[50]

Near the entrance to Wy'East Day Lodge, Dave McClure, Cheryl Maslen, Pete Bustanoby, Rick Harder, and Ralph Summers fielded questions from the remaining press.[51] In the bright lights from television cameras, limited information was given.[52] Lt. Vicars remained in Base, coordinating communications with the Red Cross and the local hospitals.

Frank had been seeking information on campus. He knew his son had been evacuated from the mountain, but to which medical facility remained a mystery to him. He managed to learn that the Red Cross had been working with each hospital, and they were beginning to untangle the identification and locations of each patient.

The Red Cross would have the answers he was seeking. When Frank called the volunteer organization, however, all he received was an answering service.

Confused and on edge, he walked out to one of the courtyards where he bumped into the school's headmaster, Fr. Malcolm Manson. The headmaster told Frank that he had just learned that Susan McClave had passed away at OHSU.

Frank asked him if he knew anything about his son. Manson said he had no knowledge of Patrick and recommended that Frank check with the Red Cross, right off the Fremont Bridge, on the far side of the river.[53]

Don Penater took the Lloyd Center exit off Highway 84, illuminated by an amber streetlight. Executing a right turn onto Union, he slowed down and stopped at a red light.[54] Suddenly, there were women tapping on his window and calling out to him. Startling him from his thoughts about his sister, Don quickly recognized what was happening. He was a middle-aged man, driving a Porsche and stopped along Union Avenue. The sun had set, and he was in a sketchy part of town. Don waved the prostitutes away and hit the gas when the light turned green.

Unbelievably, the entire scene played out again when he got caught at another stoplight.

"Screw this!" he spat when the scene played out a third time.[55] He raced forward and ran through six red lights on his journey. He turned down a side street, nearly running headlong into a police car.

Don stuck his head out the window and yelled, "Where the hell is Emanuel Hospital?"[56]

Jeff Hicks was walking through the hall towards the dorm lounge. Without even realizing it, he was fast becoming an essential resource for relaying medical updates on Father Tom and the other members of his team. There was a payphone on campus and a phone in the office. Jeff had one in his apartment as well. These phones stayed busy as information continued pouring in. Parents were calling from various hospitals around the greater Portland area. Whenever Jeff would receive an update, he'd break the news to those maintaining their vigil in Marion's apartment. Then, he'd head to the dorm lounge to update the students.

The advisor could see Mick and other kids congregated around the TV. They'd been watching news updates for the last three hours, since the announcement that the snow cave had been discovered. The kids all looked at Jeff when he entered the room.

He broke the news that Susan had been pronounced dead at OHSU Hospital.[57]

CHAPTER 31
ULTIMATE
KNOWLEDGE

Mick was reeling from the shock. Susan had died. She was one of those girls that everyone liked. Popular, partly because she was a natural leader, but mostly because she was nice and outgoing with everyone she encountered on campus.

On TV, the news anchor reported that a male patient appeared to be doing well at Providence. A female teenager, over at Emanuel, was faring even better. Finally, some good news.

The resident advisor entered the room again. This time Jeff informed everyone that Pat McGinness had died at OHSU.

Mick had just finished pouring the contents of a plastic bottle of Sprite into a large cup. Perhaps he was numb, or maybe in shock, but he was still standing in the same place, grasping the empty bottle, when Jeff came back a few moments later. Another call had come in. Tasha Amy had died at Emanuel. As grief and anger overtook Mick, he crushed the plastic bottle in his hand and then pounded his fist on the ping pong table.[1]

Sharon Ritter, the second-in-command of the Portland office, recognized Frank McGinness, as he walked towards her.

"Frank," she said, looking quite puzzled. "What are you doing here?"[2]

The Red Cross had received a donation of some upscale furniture only a month earlier. Ritter had approached Frank at the time, seeking a quote on furniture refinishing. He obliged her and soon won the bid.

While Frank had been working on the project, Ritter had stopped by his workshop. Pat had been in the shop that day, working on his high school science project entitled, "Light Effect on Wood Finish Furniture." Ritter ended up having a long conversation with the teen, concerning different wood species, stains, and various amounts of light exposures.

"Pat..." It was all that Frank could say, in response to Sharon's question.

"Oh, My God . . . No!" Sharon responded, remembering that Pat attended OES. She picked up the phone and began making calls on his behalf, doing what she could to reunite father and son.

Frank stayed in front of the reception desk, mentally adrift in a sea of fear and denial. His friend, Dick, had already lost his boy. He knew that the parents of Alison and Erin had been dealt their heaviest blow yesterday, and tonight, the parents of Susan were confronted with a parent's worst fear.

This can't be happening.

"Mr. McGinness," a volunteer behind the counter repeated, waking Frank from his somber thoughts. "You have a call from OHSU."[3] She handed Frank the telephone receiver. A man identified himself as a doctor.

"I regret to inform you," the doctor continued, "that your son has passed away."

"Are you sure?" Frank inquired, knowing there were troubles identifying the teens.

"Yes," the doctor replied. "There are two representatives here from OES. They have brought pictures, and they have said it is, undeniably, your son."

Frank slid down into a chair, devastated.[4]

10:00 P.M.
ST. VINCENT MEDICAL CENTER
PORTLAND

Amy and her family had been escorted to a private room, where they had been waiting for word about Marion's condition.[5] Don had yet to find his family.

Amy and her cousin, escorted by Aunt Tara, wandered off to the ladies' room. As they were washing their hands, the girls started playing around with the automatic faucets, making a game out of the running water.[6] A nurse stuck her head into the room and said a doctor was waiting to speak with everyone.

The girls dried their hands and returned to the private room. Amy hopped up onto the lap of one of her family members.

A man in green scrubs sat down in a chair, facing the girl.

"I'm very sorry," he said plainly, "but, your mother didn't survive."[7]

For days, the twelve-year-old had been living in a self-created bubble of optimism, refusing to even contemplate that her mom wouldn't come home. Amy's bubble collapsed around her.

Don Penater burst through the door and entered the waiting room, finally finding his family after a desperate search. Lesley ran into her dad's arms, telling him that Aunt Marion had died.

Don's mind was racing. *Hypothermia? Suffocation? She must have died up in the cave*, he reasoned. Not necessarily a religious man, the Vietnam veteran understood the pronouncement of death was merely a legal formality. Marion could have been gone hours earlier. *Dead was dead*. A priest approached the grieving man.

"Get away from me," Don whispered.[8]

~10:15 P.M.
304th AIR RESCUE AND RECOVERY SQUADRON
PORTLAND INTERNATIONAL AIRPORT

The squadron was welcoming their new commander, the legendary Jim Sehorn. The officer was a former member of the 469th Tactical Fighter Squadron, flying combat missions over Southeast Asia during the Vietnam War. He'd spent five years in the Hanoi Hilton after being shot down.

As luck would have it, today was his first day on the job as the squadron's commander. Half his unit had been up on the mountain, and their contributions to the operation were being extolled on the evening news. Lives had been saved.

Upon their return to base, a couple of cases of beer had magically appeared.

"Well," Sehorn said to his men while they were celebrating. "I guess I got to see what it is you guys do."[9]

There was cause for celebration. The cave had been found, and they had saved people that would have died if not for the dedicated work of rescuers.

Maj. McFadden, indulging in a beer, was impressed by the innate goodness of humanity. *People are willing to invest their time and energy—to go and save strangers who managed to put themselves in a shitty spot.*[10]

Not everyone had survived. There were folks who did not get to celebrate.

~10:20 P.M.
RODNEY HOUSE
OREGON EPISCOPAL SCHOOL

In the dorm lounge, the students heard that Father Tom and Rich Haeder had both been taken to Good Samaritan Hospital and had a decent prognosis. Rich was a good friend of Mick's while Tom was Mick's academic advisor, mentor, and role-model, all rolled into one.

Because Mick hadn't attended OES his freshmen year, he had been required to take freshman biology class as a sophomore. He ended up sitting next to Rich, and the two hit it off right away, despite being in different grades. This year, they sat at the same table in physics.

In these classes, they'd become bosom buddies, often whispering and joking with each other. Mick really enjoyed that short time before the day's lesson started, when the two would discuss their lives outside of school. They never spent time together off campus, being in different grades and having different circles of friends and interests.[11]

That didn't seem to make much sense now.

When Jeff Hicks received a call from Don at the hospital, informing him that Marion had died, the revelation came as quite a blow. He became friends with Don, Marion, and the rest of her family, several years back when he'd lived in Pacific City. Marion had slight traces of an English accent, merely a remnant of her years living in England. She was a strong person.

Now, thinking of his friend, Jeff felt a wave of guilt wash over him. He had helped talk Marion into the climb. Having been on several successful trips with Father Tom before, he had no reservations about recommending the mountain to Marion.

"It's a long walk," he had told her. "It's going to be fine."[12] He urged her to participate as it would help build her credibility with the students on campus.[13]

Jeff walked into the dorm lounge again, informing the kids that Marion Horwell was recently pronounced dead at St. Vincent Hospital.

Mick couldn't believe what was happening.[14]

Frank McGinness stood in a long, sterile hallway of the hospital.

"Your son is in that room," the coroner said, nodding towards a door.[15]

Frank steeled himself for what lay ahead as he followed the man. He had prepared himself to be entering a mortuary, so he was surprised to see that the hospital had set up a special room for the sole purpose of the formal identification. There were two gurneys visible. Frank saw a teenage girl's lengthy hair, emerging from underneath a white sheet. The coroner explained that it was Susan McClave.[16] On the other gurney—Patrick. Because some of his blonde hair was peeking out from underneath the sheet, Frank knew it was his boy, even before the material was pulled back.

Lt. Vicars completed his final call to the Red Cross in Portland. Through a coordinated effort with each hospital, the Red Cross had positively identified all eight patients.

Vicars compiled his notes, reviewed his findings with superiors, and prepared the next press release. Although authorities knew that some of the patients had not survived, they didn't have confirmation that families had been informed. The public would have to wait for further details.

The identities of each patient, as well as their current location, was released at 10:30 p.m. In this press release, SAR volunteers learned: Giles Thompson had been flown to Providence Medical Center; Tasha Amy and Brinton Clark had been admitted to Emanuel Hospital; Susan McClave and Pat McGinness had been taken to OHSU; Father Tom Goman and Rich Haeder had been transported to Good Samaritan Hospital; and Marion Horwell had been flown to St. Vincent Medical Center. Brinton and Giles were described as responsive. Their six companions were listed as unresponsive.

No further details were included.[17]

Deputy Mike Hattan was exhausted. With the exception of an occasional cat nap, he had been up for days. Although he had not attended the final news conference, Hattan would not be free of television cameras. His superiors had sent him home with specific instructions: get some sleep, don a clean uniform, and report to Portland's Channel 2 News studio at four o'clock in the morning. There, the deputy was to meet up with Dr. Ben Bachulis of Emanuel Hospital. The duo would be interviewed on ABC's *Good Morning America*.[18]

Mar and Diana were surrounded by Diana's sons, members of Tom's family, Fr. Toll, and Bishop Ladehoff.

A pair of surgeons entered the room. They approached Mar and spoke softly.

"We'd like you to come downstairs now," said one of the doctors.[19] Mar asked if Father Toll and Bishop Ladehoff could accompany her and Diana. The surgeons agreed to the request.

The Doctors led the group down a staircase and ushered everyone into an anteroom. They were all asked to put on scrubs. Once the group was adequately covered, they were handed masks and led towards a nearby operating room. As they drew closer, a doctor suddenly emerged from the room, cursing and ripping off his own mask. He cast it onto the floor before noticing that he wasn't alone. Embarrassed, he excused himself and exited the area.

"This is not good," Diana whispered.[20]

As the group entered the operating room, they could see Tom, lying on a table, surrounded by medical staff, EKG machines, and various monitors. Overhead, operating lights and surgical booms vied for space in the cramped quarters. It was a claustrophobic environment, sterile and nearly devoid of color. Tom's head and lips were swollen, but the women recognized him. Mar was frightened, instinctively reaching out for Father Toll's arm.

One of the priests administered Last Rites.

Sandy just heard that Pat died, and she was unable to process the devastating blow. Feeling isolated, she looked around the room. Two school counselors shared office spaces, but there was a divider down the center.

What am I going to do now?

Her close friend Erik was gone. Her best friend Alison was gone. And now, the boy she loved was gone. Forever. Crippling numbness set in as her world crumbled.

Wanting to confide in someone, she thought of her childhood friend, Kim, now a sophomore at Beaverton High School. Even though it was late in the evening, Sandy reached for the phone. She caught herself dialing her most familiar number. It was Alison's number.[21] It was so natural.

She hung up the phone, and dialed Kim.

"What am I going to do now?" Sandy sobbed.[22]

After a late meal, Scott Olson was washing his hands in the restroom. Looking up at the mirror, he saw his reflection and had to shake his head. He had completely forgotten to apply sunscreen all day, and his whole face and neck were severely sunburned.[23]

Departing the restroom, Olson returned to his friends from Corvallis Mountain Rescue Unit: Bob Freund, Jody Leach, and Bill O'Brien. The group was having drinks in the Ram's Head Bar.[24] Located on the second-floor circular mezzanine, overlooking the Head House and its towering stone chimney. Tonight, on the Sheriff's tab, the bar would remain open to accommodate SAR volunteers.[25]

All eyes would turn to the television behind the bar, when updates on the patients were announced. Freund and his friends were used to rescuing adult climbers. These were kids. *This was different.*[26]

Freund was just about to say something when another breaking update was announced. Rich Haeder had been pronounced dead at 10:53 p.m., at Good Samaritan Hospital. The room became quiet as sorrow and disappointment sunk in. Freund shook his head in disbelief. *How could this happen?*

The atmosphere in the establishment had been a bit surreal. Jon Tullis heard a ruckus up in the bar from his position at the front desk in the lobby below. Rick Harder and his entourage had made their way across the mezzanine. The Bagger entered the bar with shouts of celebration, the sounds you hear after a triumphant sporting victory.[27]

Scott Olson turned his head towards the commotion, in time to see Harder leap up onto a table. Olson couldn't believe what he was seeing and glanced uncomfortably at nearby reporters. The Bagger had everyone's attention as he gave a speech and did a little dance.[28]

Who's the loud guy? Jody Leach thought to herself.[29]

Tullis recognized the reality of the situation. With the vast amount of experience SAR volunteers had under their belts, most rescue leaders had nearly given up hope on finding anyone alive. The Bagger was celebrating the fact that survivors *had* been found. Two children would be permitted to grow to adulthood.[30] With this knowledge, coupled with adrenaline, Harder was celebrating life. He was doing his best to block out the grim news.

Leach could agree with the concept of celebration but disapproved of the volume level. She had no issue with the toasting and the chatting and had undoubtedly taken the Sheriff up on his generosity. Already passing the boundary between tipsy and well-oiled, she had slid down the banister of the Lodge, when she had journeyed to the pay phone on the ground floor. She wanted to call her mom and personally let her know there were survivors.[31]

Ed Hall was more than aware that his friend tended to rub some people the wrong way; Harder pushed people's buttons, he could be domineering, and he continually referred to himself in the third person. "Come, talk to The Bagger," he would say.[32] He was supremely confident. But if you were lost, Bagger was the man you wanted to come for you.

Once they had settled into a table, Harder's volume decreased dramatically. Soon, Hall could see something was wrong with his friend.

"Hey, what's wrong?" Ed asked.[33]

"That smoke grenade that was thrown out of the helo yesterday," The Bagger quietly remarked. "It landed on top of the snow cave."[34]

Alongside Barry Wright, Sue Shultz, and Dave McClure, Maslen had been incredibly focused on their mission.

Now, with the operation concluded, McClure and Maslen had one final fear. If their rescue pager went off again, within the next seventy-two hours, PMR would not be able to place resources in the field. The entire unit was spent. If any mountaineer dared to climb Mount Hood and ran into trouble, PMR would be unable to respond.[35]

McClure switched off his pager.[36]

Cheryl climbed into her Volvo, which had been parked in the lot since Tuesday morning. She headed down Timberline Road and encountered a hitchhiker. Not one to pick up such travelers, she hoped that having someone else in the car would help her stay awake. Unfortunately, the hitchhiker only needed a ride to Government Camp.

McClure and Wright were in PMR's Suburban. Once they hit a dark stretch of Highway 26, Dave fell asleep at the wheel, and he woke up with the rig in a ditch. He managed to extricate the truck and complete their journey home.[37] Barry slept through the entire affair.

Mick was sitting on the floor of the dorm lounge, still watching the late-night news reports on television. Brinton and Giles appeared to be doing well.

Rich had been pronounced dead at 10:53 p.m., and Father Tom passed away at 11:05 p.m.[38]

The OES climbing party had started with twenty souls: seven had turned back prior to the storm's arrival; two had hiked out to safety; two had survived the snow cave; nine had lost their lives.

The losses were staggering. It was too much. A mental fog descended over Mick.[39]

After Last Rites, Tom's family left the room. As they removed their hospital scrubs, Mar suggested moving everyone into the hospital chapel. There, she delivered the news that the rewarming attempt had failed.[40]

At some point, reporters found Mar. Again, she somehow found the strength to share the news.

"I want the world to know how wonderful Tom was," she stated. "He gave of himself. I know, on the mountain, he would have been the one to put himself at the greatest risk to protect the lives of his students. He treated students as people. He taught them something about integrity, and they recognized it."[41]

When asked about waiting days to determine her husband's fate, Mar added, "The strain of not knowing was much worse than the ultimate knowledge of death."[42]

Though Giles remained in critical condition, doctors were optimistic.[43]

"Given 100 people who have made it this far," Dr. Duane Bletz told reporters, "eighty would survive."[44] Bletz, a cardiac surgeon, noted that Giles' core temperature had been restored, the heart-lung machine had been disconnected, and the patient was moving his arms and head. Even his blood pressure remained steady. When reporters heard these facts from the doctor, someone asked why this student fared better than his companions.

"He had pretty good equipment on, "Bletz replied, "He had a good pair of rubber pants, a good pair of wool pants; a real husky fellow. With a little luck, he'll be out of here in eight to ten days with a little frostbite."[45]

Brinton was taken off a respirator, and her parents were able to see her.[46] Dr. William Long informed reporters that his patient was awake and doing well, given the circumstances. Brinton's pulse was strong, her blood pressure had leveled out, and her neurological functions had improved. Her parents, both physicians, were well aware of the difficult road ahead.[47]

Frank found a couch in the hospital. He sat down, trying to absorb everything that had taken place over the last few days. Fathers should not outlive their sons. None of this made sense.

"I have some simple questions for you," the coroner remarked. "We can do it later. Since you're here though, it would only take five minutes of your time. It would only be yes or no questions, and I thought I'd save you the grief of having to come back."[48]

Frank was mentally elsewhere.

He was back in Philadelphia, on a hot day in August. He was with five-year-old Patrick, looking for their seats aboard a Boeing 707, non-stop flight to San Francisco. Pat was fascinated with the jet's four engines and the colorfully dressed flight attendants. Father and son found their seats near the rear of the aircraft.

While fastening their seatbelts, Frank noticed something strange about the other passengers. Of the nearly 180 aboard, over half of them were garbed in various religious attire. There were Catholic nuns, smiling at his boy. There were Jewish men, with yarmulke caps. There were Muslim men, Protestant ministers, and scores of Catholic priests. There were far too many religious leaders aboard this single flight for it to be a coincidence.

The weeklong, International Eucharist Congress, an interfaith ecumenical gathering of scholars and church leaders from around the globe, had recently concluded.[49] These leaders were now making their way to San Francisco, for connecting international flights that would take them home.

A collective sigh of relief went up throughout the cabin when the air-conditioning kicked in. It was August, and Philadelphia was hot, muggy, and hadn't encountered a decent breeze in weeks.

The plane took off around 6:15 p.m. and rapidly made its way up to the cloud ceiling that was hanging over the City of Brotherly Love. Frank sighed heavily. He had been looking forward to the flight. Since the jetliner was heading west, passengers would enjoy a lengthy sunset. Time would seem to stand still, if only for a while. Young Pat alternated his gaze between the strange assembly of people and the view out the small window.

As the jetliner climbed above the clouds, no one appeared to be talking on the plane. Frank found the silence unnerving. Perhaps the sea of religious leaders aboard were all talked out? *Was there nothing left to say?*

"Hey, Dad," Pat called out while elbowing his father. "Are we in Heaven yet?"[50]

There was a dramatic pause as Frank began to blush profusely. Then, slowly, beginning in the rows nearby, a ripple effect of suppressed laughter could be heard. Row after row joined in. It couldn't be contained, and the cabin occupants enjoyed the moment of levity and child-like faith. People wanted to know the identity of the darling little boy, and flight attendants were soon congregating around Frank's son.

With parental blessing, Pat walked up and down the aisle, more than happy to shake hands and engage in conversation with the passengers. He chuckled. He asked questions. His curiosity stayed with him for the rest of his short life.

CHAPTER 32
AUTUMN

BRINTON CLARK

Brinton spent weeks recovering from her injuries.[1] After graduating from OES in 1988, she went on to study at Stanford.[2]

After earning a degree in human biology, she served for two years in Ghana with the Peace Corps. When her work in Africa was complete, she attended medical school. She graduated in 2001 from the University of California, San Francisco.[3]

She declines interview requests, but acquiesced on one occasion, when *The Oregonian* ran an article on the tenth anniversary of the ill-fated climb.

"I was only fifteen," she said. "I needed to work on getting better. It's not productive to look back. I don't do a lot of second-guessing. I survived, and many wonderful things happened to me. I lived. *Why* is not a question that has plagued me."[4]

She is presently a doctor at Providence Medical Center in Portland, Oregon.

GILES THOMPSON

Doctors were forced to amputate both of Giles' legs, one below the knee, the other, above.[5] Neither surgery nor his experience on the mountain kept Giles out of the alpine environment for long.

"He was amazing," Courtney Boatsman remarked. "After the tragedy, he came out of the gate running. Once he got his prosthetics, there was nothing that was going to stop him."[6]

Following graduation from OES in 1988, Giles attended Colorado College, to have easy access to mountains.[7] He returned to a favorite pastime of his youth—skiing.[8]

He earned a degree in drama and moved to Seattle.[9] He became a master artisan for companies such as the ACT Theater and the Teatro ZinZanni Company.[10] His expertise with special effects have been highly praised.

As a father, he now has a better understanding of what an ordeal the parents of the missing students had to undergo during those difficult times on Mount Hood.[11] He never discussed his experiences with Molly or Brinton but says he is much more comfortable with the topic these days.[12]

"Erin and Susan, Erik and Patrick, and Richard and Tasha," Giles said in a rare interview, "They all had such special qualities. They all paid a terrible price. In my heart, they are all with me. Not daily. I don't live for them. But they are there. The reality is that they are with me, and I with them."[13]

RALPH SUMMERS

Summers went to work for a hospital in Portland, counseling mental health patients. Using his phenomenal level of energy to counsel juvenile delinquents, he also earned an advanced degree in sociology.

"I call it productive avoidance," he told a reporter in the years that followed. "I found a way to spend my energy beneficially to handle the stress. Some people drink. Some become reclusive. Fortunately, I've found something productive, something to occupy my time while I continue to heal."[14]

MOLLY SCHULA

Molly graduated from OES, one month after the tragedy. She attended the University of Oregon in Eugene.[15] An English major, she graduated with a bachelor's degree and married one of the attorneys that represented Oregon Episcopal School during a lawsuit.[16]

COURTNEY BOATSMAN

Courtney graduated from OES in 1988. She graduated from Lewis and Clark College with a degree in molecular biology. She married and had a child. Courtney never returned to the mountain for an ascent, though she still harbors the desire to do so. She became the Director of Client Services at MolecularMD, a corporation in Portland that provides diagnostic services and products for specific cancer therapies.

"The Oregon Episcopal School's Basecamp program was very well thought out," she remarks, "and the people who were involved in it were at the highest level of excellence and expertise in their fields."[17] She remains a staunch supporter of her Alma mater and educational programs that introduce youth to the outdoors.

LORCA FITSCHEN

Lorca became the first recipient of the annual Susan E. McClave scholarship. Each year, this is awarded to the OES senior who best exemplifies a "giving spirit toward others."[18] With this scholarship in hand, Lorca went on to become a Germaine Thompson Scholar at Mills College in Oakland, California. After graduating with a Bachelor of Arts in French Studies, she went on to earn a Master of Arts degree in International Studies at the University of Washington.

Lorca moved to Bozeman, Montana, where she's raising a family and lives as a leadership and resilience educator. She is a consultant and TEDx speaker on the subjects of resilience design, compassion, recovery from tragedy, and joy. She is also on the faculty of the Human Leadership Development Program at Montana State University.[19]

She hasn't returned to Mount Hood to make a fourth bid for the summit but states the desire to do so remains.[20]

JOHN WHITSON

John was elected student body president, his senior year at OES.[21] After graduating in 1988, he moved to San Francisco. Returning to Oregon, he founded Holy Mountain, an independent record company. Through signing emerging psychedelic and hard rock bands, John contributes to Portland's reputation for musical diversity.

There are those who consider him a critic of OES and of Fr. Goman in particular, but John merely opposes blind followers. He cannot understand why his fellow students didn't turn back, as he did, before the party ascended into the Devil's Kitchen. Regarding the school, he states, "The darkness for me, was their inability to acknowledge that they were at fault."[22]

MICK GARRETT

Mick attended college at the University of Washington and earned a Bachelor of Science degree from their College of Engineering. He has worked as a search engine marketing analyst, consulting for Microsoft, Amazon, Getty Images, and Recreational Equipment, Inc. (REI).[23]

Mick is a singer, songwriter, and producer for novelty indie rock band *Monkeyshorts*. At the 13th annual Independent Music Awards, the band was nominated in the category of Cover Songs for their bluegrass version of *Nine Inch Nails'* "Closer."

Describing himself as being fairly reserved by nature, Mick shied away from reporters and writers for decades. He never climbed Mount Hood again, though he remains an avid hiker.

SANDY DOUTHIT

The emotional turmoil from losing Pat and Alison caused Sandy to feel isolated on campus. She moved back to California, halfway through her junior year.

She felt rudderless and unsure of how she should proceed in life. Eventually, she earned a bachelor's degree in sociology from the University of Alaska. A marriage, in 2002, resulted in the happiness she was seeking, including a son and daughter. Sandy received the full support and blessing of the Litzenberger family when her daughter's middle name was announced—Alison.

Acknowledging the Basecamp program had its problems, Sandy believes that OES instilled in her a sense of duty and the need to give back to one's community. Over the years she has served as a candy striper at Emanuel Hospital, a volunteer rape crisis counselor in Alaska, an educational tutor at the Boys & Girls Clubs of America, a Girl Scout leader, an AWANA leader, and co-leader of the East Valley CHADD Community Group.[24]

AMY HORWELL

Amy stayed with her uncle and aunt in Pacific City for a month after she lost her mom. She already had her annual summer plane ticket to visit her father in England, but in 1986, it became a one-way journey. Acknowledging that she was "a devastated, traumatized twelve-year-old girl," Amy moved to England feeling lost, alone, and uprooted from the life she knew.[25]

She graduated with a bachelor's degree in Psychology in 1995 and earned a master's degree in Criminology a year later. In 2002, she completed a Ph.D. in social work, focusing her attention on sexually abused children. She subsequently trained in Counselling Psychology and Integrative Psychotherapy, earning her Psychology doctorate. Amy now works as a psychologist for the UK's National Health Service (NHS) and as a psychotherapist in private practice.[26]

Amy and her husband have a daughter and a son. The growing family has settled in Southend-on-Sea, a seaside resort town in Essex.

She has thought a lot about the tragedy. One thought makes a reappearance time and time again—her mother's decision not to turn back the day of the fateful climb. The knowledge that Marion could have turned back with Sharon and Hilary, with Courtney and Lorca, with Mick and John, or even with Dee Zduniak, is something Amy has struggled with for decades.[27]

DON PENATER

Don continued living in Pacific City, selling real estate. He became a commercial fisherman in the early years of the Twenty-First Century, utilizing his Dory boat and a new trawler.

In 2007, he lost his wife Tara, due to another traumatic and tragic incident. Don moved to Carmel, California to be closer to family. The veteran is proud of his niece, Amy Horwell, who found a challenging and rewarding career helping others.[28]

MAR GOMAN

"What happened ripped my life open," Mar notes. "As painful as it was, there was new growth for me."[29] She feels like she has led two different lives, one before Tom's death and one after—both good and rewarding, yet both including pain as well as joy.[30]

Following Tom's death, Mar and Diana went their separate ways. Mar has been in a civil union with her partner, Virginia Lindley, for over thirty years and they have a home in Ridgefield, Washington.

Mar continues to work as a mixed-media artist and likes working with cast-offs from a consumer society. She has been significantly influenced by naïve art, outsider art, and tribal art. She is best-known for *Pharmacy of the Soul*, a series of boxes and antique cabinets she fills with small sculptures, altered bottles, scrolls, and found objects.[31] Her work is featured at galleries around the Pacific Northwest.

FRANK MCGINNESS

Frank remembers the kindness of friends and strangers in the wake of the tragedy. "I had potato salad for a week-and-a-half," he smiled, "three different varieties."[32] His journey has not been an easy one.

Just a few months before the tragedy, Frank had a wife, two children, and a thriving business. By September 1986, he was divorced, filed for bankruptcy, and had lost Patrick. His youngest son, Christopher, went to live with his mother, 3,000 miles away.[33]

One of Frank's great pleasures in life has been watching his son, Chris, grow into a productive and respected adult. Chris is a meteorologist, who graduated from Penn State University on a track scholarship. He is married and is a traffic reporter in the Portland area. He and his wife had a son in 2017. Frank's grandson is his pride and joy. He is named—Patrick.[34]

BOB FREUND

Bob remained with Corvallis Mountain Rescue Unit for several years, serving as their president on multiple occasions. During that time, he logged an additional thirty field missions, primarily around Mount Jefferson and Central Oregon. He is now considered an emeritus member of the organization.

"I no longer go out in the field," he remarks. "Occasionally, when they have missions in the Santiam Pass area, I'll go run radio relay for them."[35] Bob was a radio engineer for the Oregon Department of Transportation (ODOT), overseeing their statewide microwave system.

He contributed his time and talents to the Santiam Pass Ski Patrol as well, working to promote ski and backcountry safety around the Hoodoo Ski Area. He has been recognized as an "Outstanding Alpine Patroller" several times, by the National Ski Patrol.

ED HALL

Ed continued volunteering his services with PMR. He's made over 100 ascents of the mountain and became an Honorary Member of the Crag Rats. His idyllic cabin near the mountain narrowly survived the '96 Flood. He and his wife decided to sell and take their daughters to live in the outskirts of Boring, Oregon.

He took early retirement after twenty-seven years with the Portland Fire Bureau. He went to work for United States Senator, Jeff Merkley. For over seven years, Ed covered the state, focusing on labor-oriented issues. He also served as the Senator's Clackamas County field representative, which kept him connected to the mountain.[36]

RICK HARDER

Master Sergeant Richard A. Harder helped to rescue over 300 people during his twenty-three-year career as a PJ attached to the 304th ARRS. The Bagger served the City of Roses for twenty years as a rescue paramedic for the Portland Fire Bureau.

He gave various presentations to youth groups around the state, teaching them the essentials to surviving in the wild.

"This is going to happen again," he said after the tragedy, "because people don't know how to handle themselves up there, and they aren't teaching their kids. I've got a son, and I want to prevent this. If parents want their kids to learn survival, they should let them spend a night in the back yard."[37]

The Bagger died, at the age of forty-four, from a heart attack.

"He was always the first to volunteer and always ready," said Lt. Col. Dave Ellis of the 304th. "When it came to winter skills, underwater rescues, and everything in between, he set the standard."[38]

ROCKY HENDERSON

The raw recruit has always considered his first rescue call—the '86 Tragedy—his *Baptism by Fire*.[39] During the 1990s, he served for four years as PMR's president. He later served a two-year term as president of the national Mountain Rescue Association (MRA), and later served as their fundraising chairman. Henderson has also served as PMR's Rescue Systems and Equipment Committee Chairman, putting his considerable technical skills to work evaluating new equipment and methodology for incorporation into their rope rescue systems.[40] He continues to be an active mountain rescue team leader.

"Rocky has been the public face of the organization for so long," notes Tom Stringfield, "that, even though we now have an official public information officer, some of the local reporters just have Rocky on speed dial."[41]

MARK KELSEY

The man who had climbed Hood around twenty-five times by May 1986, has now tread her summit slopes 460 times. Most of these ascents occurred between 1992 and 2002 when Mark ran the mountaineering division of the Northwest School of Survival. This was a permitted company, allowed to guide on the peak for commercial purposes.

Kelsey went on to teach avalanche and winter survival training courses in Oregon, Washington, Wyoming, New Hampshire, and upstate New York. He additionally taught flat-plains survival techniques in the Dakotas.

Time has not diminished his penchant for exploration. Whether it's kayaking, skiing, climbing, or spending time with his daughter, life remains an adventure. His left forearm bears a tattoo: *45°22'25"N 121°41'45"W*—the coordinates of the summit of Mount Hood.[42]

HAL LILLYWHITE

Hal became president of H.F. Lillywhite, LLC, which offered consulting and seminars on the topic of making good decisions. He has written books, both novels, and non-fiction, as well as several articles concerning search and rescue operations.

"Boy, did that mountain give me an education," Hal states, regarding the tragedy.[43]

Alongside Rocky Henderson and Tom Stringfield, Hal continues to volunteer his time and talents to PMR.

BILL O'BRIEN

In the aftermath of the tragedy, Bill felt the need to distance himself from mountain rescue. "I was just so damaged," he remarked in 2017, "from seeing things that I had never seen before in my rescues."[44] This, coming from a man who once tended to kids who died in a car crash; the children bearing an uncanny resemblance to his own preschool and elementary school-aged children. "I had seen horrible things, but nothing like this."

Alongside Jeromy Adolf, Bill sent letters to all thirty-six county sheriffs in Oregon. In these letters, they stated that individual members of CMRU desired a statewide mountain rescue organization be created—the Oregon Mountain Rescue Council (OMRC). This group provided closer coordination between regional mountain SAR units and became a centralized body for the state's ongoing efforts in mountain safety education.[45] Bill served as this new organization's chairman for a year, only stepping down when he was confident the unit was self-sustaining. It was his hope—which came to fruition—that the organization would fold in nicely within the nationally recognized Mountain Rescue Association.

Bill is no longer in CMRU. He retired as a paramedic in 2011, after serving the community of Albany for twenty-eight years.

GREG PROTHMAN

"It was one of the more difficult ones," Greg recalls of the tragedy. "I've done a lot of search and rescue work. A lot of rescues. Picked up a lot of bodies in the mountains, but that was one where I felt there *must* have been something else I could have done."[46]

In the late summer of 1986, Greg departed the Renton Police Department to become the Assistant Manager for the city of Des Moines, Washington. He went on to serve as the Manager for nine years. He joined Wadron & Company, a local executive recruitment firm, but soon left to form his own business.[47] The Prothman Company, founded in 2001, is an Issaquah-based consulting firm specializing in regional and national executive recruitment staffing.

The Seattle native remains a member of Seattle Mountain Rescue. He served as their chairman from 1986 through 1990 and again from 2002 through 2004.[48] He is also a volunteer EMT/firefighter for the city of Snoqualmie, and he enjoyed a thirty-year relationship with the Crystal Mountain Ski Patrol. In 2016, Prothman joined the Summit Guard Ski Patrol to work alongside his son. Since the elder Prothman is new to the Summit Guard crew, his fellow patrol members have affectionately dubbed him—*the rookie.*

TOM STRINGFIELD

When Tom returned to his office at Hoffman Construction Company, the day after his participation in the SAR effort, he went to see his boss to explain why he had been AWOL the previous day. Instead of the mild rebuke he expected, Cecil Drinkward offered thanks. Tom learned that his boss was the OES Board Chairman.

An avid outdoorsman, but not a climber, Drinkward said he wanted to learn exactly what the school was asking students to do during these climbing trips. He asked Tom to take him to the summit of the mountain so he could experience it for himself. Within two weeks, they made the journey together.[49]

Tom continued to manage construction projects, most notably the Oregon Convention Center in downtown Portland. He retired from his civil engineering and construction management careers in 1992 and three years later, married his girlfriend at Timberline Lodge. They had been dating for eighteen years.

"You can't rush into some things," he notes, with a knowing smile.[50]

Tom remains the longest-serving member of PMR. He served on their rescue crews, on their board, and as their organization's president on two different occasions. He also served on the initial board of the Oregon Mountain Rescue Council. Around 2009, he removed himself from PMR's active rescue squads. "I'm seventy," he recently remarked. "I can't keep up with the twenty-five-year-olds." Tom entered into an advisory role.

One of his most recent contributions to the organization came in 2014, after a climber entered an uncontrolled slide into a volcanic fumarole in the crater region on Mount Hood. Knowing that a climber had perished in such a vent in 1934, Tom headed up a project that developed the documented protocol for handling such unique situations. This led to PMR procuring the necessary funds to purchase a RAE Systems MultiRAE, 4-channel, handheld gas analyzer. As of 2015, the unit can use its new hazardous gas detector in future fumarole operations.[51]

MIKE CRAIG

Mike never formally resigned from PMR. He drifted away after this mission, physically and socially. He and his wife continue to work as chiropractors in Vancouver, Washington.

Around 1998, Mike inherited the family farm in Ridgefield. Descended from farmers, he enjoys the simpler, holistic life these days: building furniture and raising hogs, geese, and goats.[52] He sold the tractor years ago, deeming horse or ox-power a far more attractive alternative.

SUE SHULTZ

Only a few weeks after the bodies had been recovered from the snow cave, Sue asked her husband, Mike Craig, if he could take her up to the site. Nursing a hip injury, Sue was forced to hike backward, gaining 2,200 feet in elevation from Timberline Lodge. Mike showed her where the snow cave had been, and together they burned incense and began to feel some of the pressure in their lives lifting. It was an emotional pilgrimage for both.[53]

The 1986 Mount Hood Tragedy was Sue's first and last mission with PMR. Along with her husband, she drifted away from the organization. She felt the whole event was so overwhelming; she simply had to walk away.[54]

These days, Sue is busy working at her chiropractic clinic, tending to her organic garden, and working tirelessly to increase the public's awareness and acceptance of Asian medicine and acupuncture.[55]

CHERYL MASLEN

Cheryl completed her doctoral thesis, "The cloning and characterization of DNA probes which detect restriction fragment length polymorphisms on human chromosomes 11q and 16q." She graduated with her doctorate from Oregon Health Sciences University in May 1987.[56] She went on to a post-doctoral fellowship at Shriner's Hospital for Children in Portland. After four years at Shriner's, she joined the faculty of OHSU.[57]

She has spent the last thirty years working in molecular biology. Her work takes advantage of the fact that scientists know the sequence of the human genome. She sequences individual genomes from people with different types of heart defects to determine how they differ genetically from people who do not have such defects. This provides her, and her colleagues, with insight into the causes of cardiovascular malformations and how they might be better treated.

Cheryl periodically reflects upon the SAR efforts during the tragedy. "Mount Hood hasn't changed in the past thirty years," Maslen notes. "It still has the potential to be a very dangerous place and should be treated with respect. It is not a walk to the top, as I so often hear people say. It is a technical climb, even on the south side. No one should die up there due to ignorance of the true nature of this beautiful place."[58]

ED KREBS

Deputy Krebs spent the following thirteen years with the Clackamas County Sheriff's Department. In his decades of service, he worked in SAR, narcotics, patrol, and the motor units, in three counties: Lincoln, Clackamas, and Polk. He retired in 1999, enjoying time with his children and grandchildren, his pride and joy.

In addition to mountain climbing and skydiving, Ed loved riding motorcycles and having coffee with his Vietnam War buddies from the *USS Bugara*.[59] Ed Krebs passed away in October 2017.

MIKE HATTAN

"I have never been through anything that drained me more, physically and emotionally," Hattan recalls. "It was an extremely emotional period."[60] He resigned from the Clackamas County Sheriff's Office two years after the tragedy and went into private business. Mike was only out of uniform a couple of months when he was recruited into the sheriff's reserve division, serving as a training officer. He retired as a reserve captain.

He began working for Clackamas County in traffic engineering and focused on emergency incident response. For twenty years, he was on call twenty-four hours a day, 365 days a year. He finally retired in 2016.

"Search and rescue was really personal for me," he grins. "That was my baby."[61] Mike joined the Clackamas County Sheriff's Posse in 2005, continuing SAR work, but this time, with a view from the saddle.

He continues to update his skills and learn new technologies by attending the annual Pacific Northwest Search and Rescue Conference, and through his position on the Mounted SAR Council.

DAVE MCCLURE

The quiet and reserved "Tall Grey Beard" continued serving as the department chair for Portland State University's chemistry department. He spent a year on sabbatical at Oxford, focused on low-temperature thermodynamics. Although he officially retired from PSU in 2002, as Emeritus Professor of Chemistry, he continued to serve as chair of the department until 2005. He joined the Physics Department, as an Adjunct Professor of Physics and taught graduate courses. Dave has also served as House Manager for the PSU Opera program.

As for his recommendations to today's climbers, mounting an attempt on Mount Hood, he always refers back to the '86 Tragedy. "Do *not* underestimate how hard the climb is, especially, the effect of elevation on your energy reserves. What starts as a beautiful day on Hood, can change very abruptly when the fog and weather roll in, and it often happens at the lower elevations before you are aware of it. Once that occurs, and you are unable to see the Lodge, you are in trouble; you had better know what you're doing. Whiteout conditions are very common, and if the weather does not clear before dark, you will find yourself in the same situation that led to the OES Tragedy."[62]

BARRY WRIGHT

After seventeen years volunteering in mountain SAR operations, Barry retired from PMR.[63] His thirty-second ascent of Mount Hood, in 2004, was the last time he walked her summit slopes.

After forty-one-years of federal service, he retired from the Bonneville Power Administration. Since then, he's climbed Mount St. Helens and Volcán de Agua in Guatemala. Regarding the slow decline of his ascents, he notes, "You kind of recognize your mortality. You're not going to live forever."[64]

"Of all the organizations I have ever belonged to," he beams with pride, "Portland Mountain Rescue is still the best. I can't praise them enough for their dedication to maintaining the freedom of the hills that we love to climb."[65]

BIBLIOGRAPHY

RECORDED INTERVIEWS

Boatsman (Fuller), Courtney, Interview with author, I. *Preparations and Ascent*, May 23, 2015.

Craig, Mike and Sue Shultz, Interview with author, I. *Tuesday through Thursday*, June 10, 2018.

Douthit (Radtke), Sandra, Interview with author, I. *Personal Remembrances*, September 12, 2015.

Ek, Charlie, Interview with author, I. *The OES Tragedy*, May 6, 2017.

Fitschen (Smetana), Lorca, Interview with author, I. *The OES Tragedy*, January 2, 2017.

Freund, Robert, Interview with author, I. *Patient Evacuations*, June 18, 2017.

Garrett, Mick, Interview with author, I. *Wy'East Day Lodge to Palmer*, September 14, 2015.

—Interview with author, II. *Palmer Down to Timberline*, September 14, 2015.

Goman, Mar, and Diana Yates, Interview with author, I. *The Vigil*, March 12, 2016.

—Interview with author, II. *Looking Back*, March 12, 2016.

Griswold, Gene, Interview with author, I. *Personal Recollections*, November 13, 2018.

Hall, Ed, Interview with author, I. *Hasty Team & Crag Rats*, August 4, 2018.

Hattan, Mike, Interview with author, I. *Personal Remembrances*, March 11, 2017.

Henderson, Rocky, Interview with author, I. *The Raw Recruit*, March 9, 2015.

—Interview with author, II. *Rescuers Rescuing Rescuers*, March 9, 2015.

Hicks, Jeff, Interview with author, I. *OES Resident Advisor*, January 17, 2019.

Horwell, Amy, Interview with author, I. *Personal Remembrances*, April 9, 2017.

Janeck, Jerry, Interview with author, I. *The OES Tragedy*, June 10, 2017.

Kelsey, Mark, Interview with author, I. *Team 1 and Team 8*, November 3, 2018.

Krank, Ky, Interview with author, I. *Team 6*, June 29, 2018.

Leach (Sergienkl), Jody, Interview with author, I. *Base Operations*, November 18, 2018.

Lillywhite, Hal, Interview with author, I. *A Memorable Lesson*, January 16, 2016.

McClure, Dave, and Cheryl Maslen, Interview with author, I. *Tuesday*, October 8, 2016.

—Interview with author, II. *Wednesday*, November 5, 2016.

—Interview with author, III. *Thursday*, January 14, 2017.

—Interview with author, IV. *Thursday, Part II*, January 14, 2017.

McFadden, Ken, Interview with author, I. *Helo 3*, May 25, 2019.

—Interview with author, II. *Helo 3*, May 25, 2019.

McGinness, Frank, Interview with author, I. *Sunday through Wednesday*, August 2, 2015.

—Interview with author, II. *Wednesday through Sunday*, August 2, 2015.

—Interview with author, III. *Patrick McGinness*, October 10, 2015.

—Interview with author, IV. *Are We in Heaven Yet*, May 20, 2018.

—Interview with author, V. *Black Hole*, March 24, 2019.

Moffitt, Mike, Interview with author, I. *Hillsboro Helicopters*, August 3, 2018.

O'Brien, Bill, Interview with author, I. *Personal Recollections*, July 30, 2017.

—Interview with author, II. *Personal Recollections*, July 30, 2017.

Olson, Scott, Interview with author, I. *Team 22 & 6A*, October 21, 2018.

Penater, Don, Interview with author, I. *Personal Recollections*, August 8, 2017.

Prothman, Greg, Interview with author, I. *Field Team Leader*, April 2, 2017.

Sheridan, Kathleen, Interview with author, I. *Nordic Ski Patrol*, July 10, 2018.

Stringfield, Tom, Interview with author, I. *Wednesday's Rescue Efforts*, December 9, 2015.

—Interview with author, II. *Team 10*, December 19, 2015.

Whitson, John, Interview with author, I. *The Climb*, May 9, 2016.

Wright, Barry, Interview with author, I. *The Early Efforts*, April 13, 2015.

—Interview with author, II. *The Latter Efforts*, April 13, 2015.

—Interview with author, III. *Thursday*, November 6, 2018.

ORAL COMMUNICATIONS (OC)

Boatsman, Courtney, Oral Communication with author, *Giles Thompson*, May 23, 2015.

Douthit, Sandra, Oral Communication with author, *Erik Sandvik*, September 12, 2015.

Fitschen, Lorca, Oral Communication with author, *Background*, July 27, 2015.

Garrett, Mick, Oral Communication with author, *Fr. Thomas Goman*, September 14, 2015.

—Oral Communication with author, *Giles Thompson*, September 14, 2015.

—Oral Communication with author, *Climbing Team Configurations*, November 30, 2015.

Hattan, Mike, Oral Communication with author, *The Media*, March 11, 2017.

Henderson, Rocky, Oral Communication with author, *Team 17*, January 11, 2016.

—Oral Communication with author, *Lack of an Altimeter*, September 10, 2016.

Krank, Ky, Oral Communication with author, *Pre-Interview Conversation*, June 28, 2018.

Maslen, Cheryl, Oral Communication with author, *Wednesday*, September 10, 2016.

McGinness, Frank, Oral Communication with author, *Constricting Snow Cave Entrance*, October 10, 2015.

—Oral Communication with author, *The McGinness Family*, May 20, 2018.

—Oral Communication with author, *The Viewing*, October 12, 2018.

O'Regan, Judy, Oral Communication with author, *Personal Recollections*, December 3, 2018.

Wright, Barry, Oral Communication with author, *Cries for Help*, April 13, 2015.

—Oral Communication with author, *Wednesday*, January 11, 2016.

—Oral Communication with author, *The Possibilities*, September 10, 2016.

WRITTEN COMMUNICATIONS (WC)

Boatsman, Courtney, Correspondence with author, *The Sprays' Room*, November 16, 2015.

Brett, Bill, Correspondence with author, *Number 8*, April 8, 2015.

Conrad, Ric, *Interview Notes with Mike Craig and Sue Shultz*, June 10, 2018.

Fitschen (Smetana), Lorca, Correspondence with author, *Updated Autumn Section*, March 13, 2019.

Garrett, Mick, Correspondence with author, *Timberline Lodge Accommodations*, September 28, 2015.

—Correspondence with author, *Palmer Glacier Turnaround*, September 28, 2015.

—Correspondence with author, *Manuscript Corrections*, November 6, 2015.

—Correspondence with author, *The Hallway Meeting*, November 15, 2015.

—Correspondence with author, *Meeting with Authorities*, November 17, 2015.

—Correspondence with author, *Haeder, Sr. and Schula*, November 17, 2015.

—Correspondence with author, *The Sprays' Room*, November 17, 2015.

—Correspondence with author, *John Whitson*, November 21, 2015.

—Correspondence with author, *OES Dorm Layout*, April 29, 2017.

—Correspondence with author, *Silcox Hut*, October 8, 2018.

Goman, Mar, Correspondence with author, *Corrections to Autumn Section*, February 14, 2016.

    —Correspondence with author, *Summary of Tom Goman's Climbing Experience*, February 14, 2016.

    —Correspondence with author, *Corrections to Tom Goman's Background*, February 14, 2016.

Hall, Ed, Correspondence with author, *Silcox Hut*, October 8, 2018.

Henderson, Rocky, Correspondence with author, *Silcox Hut*, October 8, 2018.

Horwell, Amy, Correspondence with author, *Amendments/Additions–Sunday Night*, April 14, 2017.

    —Correspondence with author, *Amendments/Additions–Monday-Thursday*, April 15, 2017.

    —Correspondence with author, *Marion Horwell*, April 15, 2017.

    —Correspondence with author, *Amendments*, April 27, 2017.

Kelsey, Mark, Correspondence with author, *Climbing Clothes*, November 5, 2018.

Krank, Ky, Correspondence with author, *The Six Questions*, July 11, 2018.

    —Correspondence with author, *Corrections to Chapter 17*, August 26, 2018.

Lillywhite, Hal, Correspondence with author, *Silcox Hut*, October 8, 2018.

Maslen, Cheryl, Correspondence with author, *Autumn Section*, November 8, 2016.

McClure, Dave, Correspondence with author, *Autumn Section*, November 10, 2016.

McGinness, Frank, Correspondence with author, *Tuesday Morning's Call*, June 11, 2018.

O'Brien, Bill, Correspondence with author, *Patient Evacuation*, July 29, 2017.

    —Correspondence with author, *The SAR Dogs*, December 12, 2018.

    —Correspondence with author, *The Bagger*, December 17, 2018.

    —Correspondence with author, *Manuscript Corrections*, December 29, 2018.

    —Correspondence with author, *The SAR Dogs II*, December 30, 2018.

    —Correspondence with author, *Manuscript Corrections II*, January 10, 2019.

    —Correspondence with author, *Snow Cave Memories*, January 12, 2019.

Olson, Scott, Correspondence with author, *Additions to Recorded Interview*, October 31, 2018.

    —Correspondence with author, *Manuscript Corrections*, November 8, 2018.

Prothman, Greg, Correspondence with author, *Corrections to Autumn Section*, April 5, 2017.

    —Correspondence with author, *Manuscript Corrections*, April 13, 2017.

Radtke, Sandy, Correspondence with author, *Polypropylene Underwear*, August 25, 2015.

    —Correspondence with author, *Manuscript Corrections*, October 8, 2015.

    —Correspondence with author, *Litzenberger Community Service*, October 11, 2015.

    —Correspondence with author, *Relationship with Pat McGinness*, October 15, 2015.

    —Correspondence with author, *The Note*, March 30, 2019.

    —Correspondence with author, *Dialing Alison*, April 8, 2019.

Stringfield, Tom, Correspondence with author, I. *Rocky Henderson*, December 17, 2015.

    —Correspondence with author, *Cecil Drinkward*, September 27, 2018.

Tullis, Jon, Correspondence with author, *Personal Recollections*, July 9, 2017.

Wright, Barry, Correspondence with author, *Avalanche on Leuthold Couloir*, June 12, 2015.

    —Correspondence with author, *Wayne Litzenberger & the BPA*, July 23, 2018.

Yates, Diana, Correspondence with author, *Manuscript Corrections and Additions*, June 28, 2016.

    —Correspondence with author, *FurDur Tom*, June 3, 2018.

    —Correspondence with author, *St. John the Evangelist*, December 10, 2018.

ADDITIONAL SOURCES IN ALPHABETICAL ORDER

AMERICAN ALPINE JOURNAL (AAJ)
Golden, Colorado

McArthur, Lewis L., "Thomas Gordon Goman," (In Memorium) *American Alpine Journal*, XXIX, No. 61 (December 1987): 354-355.

CLACKAMAS COUNTY SHERIFF'S REPORT (CCSR)

Brooks, Sheriff Bill, "Clackamas County Sheriff's Department Report: Mount Hood Search and Rescue, May 12–15, 1986," *CCSR*. II. (May 18, 1986): 252-262.

Freund, Robert, "Mission Record #86-02," Corvallis Mountain Rescue, *CCSR*, II. (May 19, 1986): 202-204.

Goman, Fr. Thomas, "Climbing and Backcountry Travel Register," U.S. Forest Service, *CCSR*, I. (May 12, 1986): 18-19.

Grolbert, Capt. J.T., "Search and Rescue, 86-15981," *CCSR*. I. (May 29, 1986): 51-53.

Hanners, Lt. Gene W., "Search and Rescue (Supplemental) - Agencies Involved," *CCSR*. I (May 25, 1986): 43-44.

—"Search and Rescue (Supplemental) - Agencies Involved," *CCSR*. I (May 25, 1986): 45-48.

—"Supervisor's Daily Report," *CCSR*. I (May 12, 1986): 55.

Hattan, Deputy Mike, "Hattan's Log," *CCSR*. I (May 12, 1986): 74-75.

Kennell, Deputy David, "Oregon SAR Mission Data Sheet, Case #86-15981," *CCSR*. I (May 12, 1986): 1-2.

—"Chuck Reynolds," *CCSR*. I (May 12, 1986): 68.

—"Kennel's Log," *CCSR*. I (May 12, 1986): 69-73; 75-78.

—"Preliminarily Response - Special Report," *CCSR*. I (May 16, 1986): 20-26.

Krebs, Deputy Ed, "Missing Person Reports: 86-15993 (Amy); 86-15992 (Clark); 86-15991 (Goman); 86-15990 (Haeder); 86-15989 (Horwell); 86-15988 (Litzenberger); 86-15987 (McClave); 86-15986 (McGinness); 86-15985 (O'Leary); 86-15984 (Sandvik); 86-15983 (Thompson); 86-15982 (Schula); 86-15981 (Summers)," *CCSR*. I (May 12, 1986), 7-17.

Reininger, Richard, "Correspondence with Lt. Stillman," German Shepherd Search Dogs, *CCSR*. II (May 27, 1986), 233.

Romney, Kent, "OES School - Mt. Hood Search and Rescue (Critique)," Mt. Hood Nordic Ski Patrol, *CCSR*. II (June 7, 1986), 199-201.

Shultz, Susan, "Portland Base Notes," *CCSR*. I (May 13-15, 1986): 101-148.

Stillman, Lt. Sherwood, "S.A.R. - Mt. Hood," *CCSR*. I (May 22, 1986): 49-50.

—"Press Release Update - Six Teams around Crater Rock," *CCSR*. I (May 15, 1986): 58.

Summers, Ralph, "This is How I Understood My Role in Working With the Oregon Episcopal School," *CCSR*. II (May 18, 1986), 217-220.

—"Notes dictated by Ralph Summers, Regarding the Mount Hood Climb by OES Students on May 12, 1986," *CCSR*. II (May 18, 1986), 221-232.

Vicars, Lt. Don, "Press Release Update - Dog Teams and Probers," *CCSR*. I (May 15, 1986): 58.

—"Press Release Update - (Hospital) Locations of Hikers," *CCSR*. I (May 15, 1986): 59.

—"Press Release Update - Thursday's SAR Strategy," *CCSR*. I (May 15, 1986): 60.

Williams, Deputy Russ, "Press Release Update - Snow Cave Discovery & First Hour," *CCSR*. I (May 15, 1986): 61.

Unknown, "Debriefing Molly Schula (Unknown deputy's notes)," *CCSR*. I (May 13, 1986): 96.
—"Sign-in Sheets," *CCSR*. I (May 13-15, 1986): 86-95.
—"Base Operations - Duty Assignments," *CCSR*. I (May 14, 1986): 42.
—"Timberline Lodge Room Assignments," *CCSR*. II (May 14, 1986): 240.
—"Team Organization Forms," *CCSR*. I (May 13-15, 1986): 149-186.
—"List of Climbers," *CCSR*. I (May 16, 1986): 27-29.
—"Rescue Log," *CCSR*. I (May 16, 1986): 30-32.
—"Meeting with Ralph Summers," *CCSR*. I (May 30, 1986): 33.
—"Notes," *CCSR*. I (May 30, 1986): 35.
—"Rescue Workers - Timberline Lodge Room Locations," *CCSR*. I (May 30, 1986): 41.

GARRETT COLLECTION
Seattle, Washington

Goman, FrDr. Tom, Correspondence with Mick Garrett, *ACT Acceptance Letter*, Circa June 1985.
—Memorandum: *Readers for the Advanced Climbing Team Essays - 1985-86*, Circa Spring 1985.
—Memorandum: *Parents of Students Selected for the Advanced Mountaineering Team* (Permission to Climb), Circa June 1985.
Unknown, "Remembrance Gathering: Marion Penater Horwell, 1944–1986 (Bulletin),"
Episcopal Parish of St. John the Baptist, Oregon Episcopal School, (May 20, 1986): 1-7.
—Memorial Service: "Richard Leyden Haeder, Jr. (Bulletin)", Church of Jesus Christ of Latter Day Saints, (May 20, 1986): 1-4.

KGW NEWS
Portland, Oregon

Dooris, Pat, "Trapped on Mt. Hood: Remembering the 1986 Tragedy," KGW.COM, May 12, 2015.

LINCOLN MEMORIAL PARK AND FUNERAL HOME
Portland, Oregon

Obituary, "In Memory of Edwin Wayne Krebs (1947–2017)," Lincoln Memorial Park and Funeral Home, Portland, OR, Circa October 2017.

MAGAZINE ARTICLES

Lillywhite, Harold F., "Field Report: School Accident on Mount Hood," *Advanced Rescue Technology*, VII: 2 (April-May, 2004): 62-65.
Plummer, William, "Step by Step, A Routine Hike up Mount Hood Turns Into a Nightmare That Kills Nine," *People* magazine, XXV: 22, (June 2, 1986): 50-52.
Roskelley, John, "The Mt. Hood Tragedy - Did it Have to Happen?" *Backpacker* magazine, XIV: 5, (September 1986): 50–53.

Toutonghi, Pauls, "The House of Mourning," *Outside* magazine, (November 2018): 62-73.

MAZAMA ANNUAL
Portland, Oregon

Bangs, Cameron and Don Batten, "High School Climbing Tragedy," *Mazama Annual*, LXVIII: 13 (December 1986): 24-26.

Bryan, Bill, "304th ARRS–Helping Rescue," *Mazama Annual*, LXIII: 13 (December 1981): 42-43.

Collins, J.R. and Phillips, Kenneth, "Fumaroles on Mount Hood," *Mazama Annual*, XVII: 12, (December 1935): 19.

MAZAMAS ARCHIVES
Portland, Oregon

MANUSCRIPTS, MAZAMAS COLLECTION/BASIC GROUP - 16

Basic Group 16: "Mazamas Climb Report," Mount Hood, South Side Route, May 10, 1986. The Mazamas Collection.

MOFFITT COLLECTION
Hillsboro, Oregon

Moffitt, Mike, "Aircraft Pilot's Logbook," Bell 206 JetRanger helicopter, (May 14–15, 1986): 1.

MCGINNESS COLLECTION
Portland, Oregon

McGinness, Pat, "Photographs, 1986 OES Climb," McGinness Collection, (May 12, 1986).

Penater, Don, "Memo regarding Interview with Molly Schula, McGinness Collection, (June 19, 1986): 1-6.

Zduniak, Dee, "Statement of Dee Zduniak," Interview with Elden Rosenthal, McGinness Collection, (August 2, 1986): 1-4.

NEWSPAPER ARTICLES

Lodi News-Sentinel, The

Unknown, "Three Die, Eight Are Lost on Survival Hike," *Lodi News-Sentinel*, May 15, 1986.
—"Snow Cave Discovered," *Lodi News-Sentinel*, May 16, 1986.

Oregon Journal

Unknown, "Big Lift for Skiers," *Oregon Journal*, October 29, 1939.

Buker, Paul, "Guelph Uses Tenacious Defense to Whip 'Invincible' Hull 3-1," *The Oregonian*, May 13, 1986.

Danks, Holly, "Survivor of Climb on Mount Hood Loses Both Legs," *The Oregonian*, May 19, 1986.

—"Climbers' Love of Life Celebrated," *The Oregonian*, May 20, 1986.

Danks, Holly, and Tom Hallman, Jr., "Parents View Report with Sense of Relief," *The Oregonian*, July 25, 1986.

Erickson, Steve, "Rescuers Ecstatic at Finding Climbers," *The Oregonian*, May 16, 1986.

—"Father Eulogizes Son Lost to Mount Hood," *The Oregonian*, May 21, 1986.

Hallman, Jr., Tom, "Winds Halt Rescue of 11 Trapped on Mount Hood," *The Oregonian*, May 14, 1986.

—"Mount Hood's Deadly Deceit," *The Oregonian*, May 12, 1996.

—Tom Hallman, Jr. John Snell, and Rolla J. Crick, "Sunshine Lures Tourists, Spurs Rescuers to Mountain," *The Oregonian*, May 15, 1986.

—Tom Hallman, Jr. and John Snell, "High Wind Slows Army of Searchers," *The Oregonian*, May 15, 1986.

—Tom Hallman, Jr. and John Snell, "Anxious Parents Can Only Wait and Hope," *The Oregonian*, May 15, 1986.

—Tom Hallman, Jr. and John Snell, "Nightmare on Mount Hood," *The Oregonian*, May 18, 1986.

—Tom Hallman, Jr. and John Snell, "The Week on Mount Hood," *The Oregonian*, May 18, 1986.

—Tom Hallman, Jr., Sura Rubenstein, and Holly Danks, "Doctors Fight to Save Two Climbers; 6 Die After Rescue From Snow Cave," *The Oregonian*, May 16, 1986.

—Tom Hallman, Jr., Sura Rubenstein, and Holly Danks, "Timberline Celebration Premature," *The Oregonian*, May 16, 1986.

Hopkins, Oz, "Medical Team Battles in Vain for Lives of Three Young Climbers," *The Oregonian*, May 15, 1986.

—"Climbing Tragedy Offers Medical Insights," *The Oregonian*, May 22, 1986.

Lane, Dee, "Classes Forgotten as Students Wait for Word of Lost Climbers," *The Oregonian*, May 15, 1986.

—"School Family Mourns Victims of Mountain," *The Oregonian*, May 16, 1986.

—"Shared Faith Provides Hope, Refuge," *The Oregonian*, May 16, 1986.

—"School Calls Offers for Mount Hood Story 'Repulsive,'" *The Oregonian*, May 24, 1986.

—Lane, Dee and Kathie Durbin, "Basecamp Project Supported by Students, Parents; Other Schools Wary," *The Oregonian*, May 16, 1986.

—"From Tragedy Rises Triumph of Pair's Survival," *The Oregonian*, May 17, 1986.

—"Headmaster Leads OES Back From Grief," *The Oregonian*, September 16, 1986.

Lesage, Pete, "'Rookie Line' Helps Hawks Put Away Guelph 6-4," *The Oregonian*, May 12, 1986.

O'Neill, Patrick, "Pair Describe Ordeal During Ill-fated Mount Hood Climb," *The Oregonian*, March 23, 1990.

—"Mother Tells of Anger Over Son's Death," *The Oregonian*, March 29, 1990.

—"Surviving Students, Guide Testify on Doomed Mount Hood Climb," *The Oregonian*, April 3, 1990.

—Rubenstein, Sura and John Painter, Jr., "Weather on Mount Hood Went From Bad to Worse," *The Oregonian*, May 16, 1986.

Snell, John, "Thompson Learning to Walk Again," *The Oregonian*, August 24, 1986.

—"Hood Disaster Survivor Clark Leaves Hospital," *The Oregonian*, May 29, 1986.

—"Rescuers Fear Another Tragedy," *The Oregonian*, May 10, 1987.

Unknown, "Weather Report," (forecast) *The Oregonian*, May 11, 1986.

—"Weather Report," (forecast) *The Oregonian*, May 12, 1986.

—"Weather Report," (forecast) *The Oregonian*, May 13, 1986.

—"Weather Report," (forecast) *The Oregonian*, May 14, 1986.

—"Weather Report," (forecast) *The Oregonian*, May 15, 1986.

—"Nightmare on Mount Hood," *The Oregonian*, May 15, 1986.

—"Workers at Five Hospitals Labor to Save Climbers," *The Oregonian*, May 16, 1986.

—"Funerals, Memorial Services Set For Five Victims of Climbing Tragedy," *The Oregonian*, May 17, 1986.

—"Services Planned for Students, Educators Lost to Mountain," *The Oregonian*, May 18, 1986.

Philadelphia Inquirer, The

Dubin, Murray, "8 Climbers Found in Cave On Mt. Hood; 2 Are Alive," *The Philadelphia Inquirer*, May 16, 1986.

Unknown, "Today in Philadelphia History: 41st International Eucharist Congress Begins," *The Philadelphia Inquirer*, August 1, 2013.

Sacramento Bee, The

Akre, Brian S., "Mount Hood Climbers Cling to Life," *The Sacramento Bee*, May 16, 1986.

Unknown, "Mount Hood Snowstorm Kills 3," *The Sacramento Bee*, May 15, 1986.

—"Mt. Hood Survivors Fight for Their Lives," *The Sacramento Bee*, May 17, 1986.

Seattle Times, The

King, Marsha, "A Student Who Turned Back Reflects on Mount Hood Climb," *The Seattle Times*, May 16, 1986.

Nalder, Eric, Jack Broom and Dave Birkland, "Mount Hood Tragedy, Three Critical, Search Continues for Missing Eight as Doctors Try to Revive Climbers," *The Seattle Times*, May 14, 1986.

Seven, Richard, "Lingering Regrets," *The Seattle Times (Pacific)*, May 8, 1988.

Unknown, "Bodies of Three Climbers Found on Mount Hood, *The Seattle Times*, May 14, 1986.

—"Climbing Experts Raise Questions About Hood Climb," *The Seattle Times*, May 22, 1986.

—"Richard Harder, Air Force Specialist (Obituary)," *The Seattle Times*, November 23, 1996.

Willamette Week

Clark, Taylor, "The Survivor," (Giles Thompson) *Willamette Week*, November 10, 2004.

OREGON PUBLIC BROADCASTING
Portland, Oregon

Baer, April, "Mt. Hood Climbing Has Seen Many Changes in 25 Years Since OES Tragedy," Oregon Public Broadcasting news article, May 10, 2011.

PORTLAND MOUNTAIN RESCUE (PMR)
Portland, Oregon

Basecamp Inquiry Committee (BIC), "Synopsis of Our Findings Regarding the O.E.S. Basecamp Program and the Mt. Hood Accident," (July 22, 1986):1-2.

—"Review of the O.E.S. Basecamp Program," (July 22, 1986):1-11.

—"Analysis of the O.E.S. Mt. Hood Accident - May 1986," (July 22, 1986):1-27.

—"Appendix A: List of Resources Used by O.E.S. Inquiry Committee," (July 22, 1986):1.

—"Appendix B: Mt. Hood Weather May 9-13, 1986," by Charles M. Feris, Meteorologist, Bonneville Power Administration (July 22, 1986):1-2.

Brooks, Bill, "Transcript of Search and Rescue Meeting," Portland Mountain Rescue, (June 4, 1986): 1-80.

Goman, Fr. Thomas, "Sophomore Climb - 1986," memorandum to Sam Dibbins, (April 26, 1986): 1-2.

Maslen/Shultz, "1986 Oregon Episcopal School Tragedy Rescue Log," Portland Mountain Rescue, (May 13-15, 1986): 1-54.

McClure, Dr. David W., "The OES Climbing Tragedy on Mt. Hood," Portland Mountain Rescue (August, 1986): 1-8.

Schula, Molly, Untitled Statement, Portland Mountain Rescue, (May 1986): 1-21.

Stringfield, Tom, "Mountain Rescue Critique," Portland Mountain Rescue, (June 4, 1986): 1-6.

Summers, Ralph, "Statement of Ralph Summers," Statement provided to Basecamp Inquiry Committee. (June 9, 1986), 1-10.

Wright, Barry, "PMR Rescue Callout," Portland Mountain Rescue, (May 13, 1986): 1.

Unknown, "Portland Mountain Rescue Membership List," Portland Mountain Rescue, (November 12, 1985): 1-2.

—"Portland Mountain Rescue Membership List," Portland Mountain Rescue, (October 10, 1986): 1-7.

RADTKE COLLECTION
Chandler, Arizona

Birch, Kim, written correspondence with Sandra Douthit, "The Phone Rings," (March 18, 1987): 1.

Goman, Fr. Thomas, "Sophomore Climb - 1986," memorandum to Sam Dibbins, (April 26, 1986): 1.

McGinness, Patrick, "My Special Object," notes, (October 21, 1984): 1.

Radtke, Sandra, "20th Reunion", remembrance notes (Pat McGinness), (May 12, 2006): 1-4.

OES Coordinating Council, Correspondence with Oregon Episcopal Community, OES Peoplecare, (June 20, 1986): pp. 1–5.

Sandvik, Erik, written correspondence with Sandra Douthit, (February 8, 1985): 1-2.

Unknown, "Mass of Christian Burial: Erin Kathleen "Carmel" O'Leary (Bulletin)", Saint Elizabeth Catholic Church, (May 17, 1986): 1-2.

—"Memorial Service: Alison Kae Litzenberger (Bulletin)", St. Michael and All Angels Episcopal Church, (May 17, 1986): 1-12.

—"Memorial Service: Patrick Francis McGuiness (Bulletin)", St. Michael and All Angels Episcopal Church, (May 19, 1986): 1-7.

SEATTLE MOUNTAIN RESCUE (SMR)
Seattle, Washington

Bustanoby, Pete, "Mount Hood Rescue - Synopsis," Mountain Rescue Council, (Circa June 1986): 9-11.

Sainsbury, George, "Mission Report," Mountain Rescue Council, (November 1986): 1-5.

—"In-Town Operations Leader Report," Mountain Rescue Council, (Circa June 1986): 5-7.

Williams, Paul, "Base Operations Leader Report," Mountain Rescue Council, (Circa June 1986): 7-8.

Unknown, "Mt. Hood, Search - Rescue - Recovery," Mountain Rescue Council newsletter, (November 1986): 1-14.

SIGNPOST FOR NORTHWEST TRAILS

Miller, Jim "The Oregon Episcopal School Climb," *Signpost for Northwest Trails.* XXV (May, 1990).

SOCIAL MEDIA

cascadiahealthcare.com/practitioners/susan-k-shultz-d-c-eam.

Oregon Episcopal School. [Susan E. McClave Award]. (2017) Retrieved from ‹https://www.oes.edu/page.cfm?p=849›

Oregon Mountain Rescue Council. [Formation and Purpose]. (2017) Retrieved from ‹http://corvallis-mountainrescue.org/omrc/›

"Sunrise and Sunset Times, May 12–15, 1986." (2017) Retrieved from ‹https://www.sunrisesunset.com›

Thompson, G. [Giles]. (2019). Retrieved from ‹https://www.facebook.com/giles.thompson.507›

Unknown (July 31, 2014). Retrieved from ‹http://shiversofdelight.blogspot.com/2014/07/mar-goman-pharmacy-of-soul.html›

—(August 7, 2014). *304th Rescue Squadron.* Factsheets: 920th Rescue Wing, retrieved from ‹http://920rqw.afrc.af.mil/›

—(March 16, 2019). *www.amyhorwell.com.*

UNITED STATES ARMY
Medical Research & Development

Wilkerson, M.D., Jim, and Murray P. Hamlet, D.V.M., "Medical After Action Conference, Mount Hood, 1986, Bypass Rewarming," Report No. T10-88, U.S. Army Research Institute of Environmental Medicine, Natick, MA. (February 1988): 1-174.

Danes, Z. Frank, "Testimony Pertaining to the Character and Qualifications of Reverend Dr. Thomas Gordon Goman," Written Correspondence to OES Basecamp Inquiry Committee, (July 19, 1986): 1-6.

—"Memorial Service: Rev. Dr. Thomas Gordon Goman (Bulletin)," St. John's Episcopal Church, (May 19, 1986): 1-4.

Endnotes

Chapter 1, "Mother's Day"

1   McGinness, Frank, OC, The McGinness Family, May 20, 2018.

2   Douthit, Sandra, Interview with author, I. Personal Remembrances, September 12, 2015.

3   Dialogue exchanges between McGinness and his sons come from: McGinness, Frank, Interview with author, I. Sunday through Wednesday, August 2, 2015.

4   Lane, Dee, "Shared Faith Provides Hope, Refuge," The Oregonian, May 16, 1986.

5   Erickson, Steve, "Father Eulogizes Son Lost to Mount Hood," The Oregonian, May 21, 1986.

6   Lane, May 16, 1986.

7   Dialogue exchange comes from: Douthit, I, September 12, 2015.

8   Tom Hallman, Jr. and John Snell, "Nightmare on Mount Hood," The Oregonian, May 18, 1986.

9   Unknown, "Weather Report," (forecast) The Oregonian, May 11, 1986.

10   Basecamp Inquiry Committee (BIC), "Synopsis of Our Findings Regarding the O.E.S. Basecamp Program and the Mt. Hood Accident," (July 22, 1986):5; Hallman, Jr. & Snell, May 18, 1986; Yates, Diana, WC, Manuscript Corrections and Additions, June 28, 2016.

11   Lane, May 16, 1986.

12   Douthit, I, September 12, 2015.

13   All Sandvik jokes listed come from: Sandvik, Erik, WC with Sandra Douthit, (February 8, 1985): 1.

14   Douthit, I, September 12, 2015.

15   Lane, May 16, 1986; Douthit, Sandra, OC, Erik Sandvik, September 12, 2015.

16   Unknown, "Funerals, Memorial Services Set for Five Victims of Climbing Tragedy," The Oregonian, May 17, 1986.

17   Douthit, OC, September 12, 2015.

18   Dialogue exchange comes from: McGinness, I. August 2, 2015.

19   Dialogue exchange comes from: McGinness, I. August 2, 2015.

20   Age determined by: Krebs, Ed, "Missing Person Report 86-15990 (Richard Haeder. Jr.)," CCSR. I (May 12, 1986), 8.

21   Plummer, William, "Step by Step, A Routine Hike up Mount Hood Turns Into a Nightmare That Kills Nine," People magazine, XXV: 22, (June 2, 1986); Summers providing the list comes from: Unknown, "Meeting with Ralph Summers," CCSR. I (May 30, 1986): 33; Hallman, Jr. & Snell, May 18, 1986.

22   Hallman, Jr. & Snell, May 18, 1986.

23   BIC, (July 22, 1986): 5; O'Neill, Patrick, "Mother Tells of Anger Over Son's Death," The Oregonian, March 29, 1990.

24   McArthur, Lewis L., "Thomas Gordon Goman," (In Memorium) AAJ, XXIX, No. 61 (December 1987): 355.

25   Yates, Diana, and Mar Goman, Interview with author, I. The Vigil, March 12, 2016.

26   Yates, Diana, WC, FurDur Tom, June 3, 2018.

27   Goman, Mar, WC, Corrections to Tom Goman's Background, February 14, 2016.

28   Danes, Z. Frank, "Testimony Pertaining to the Character and Qualifications of Reverend Dr. Thomas Gordon Goman," WC to OES BIC, (July 19, 1986): 4.

29   Yates, I. March 12, 2016.

30   Dialogue comes from: Goman, I. March 12, 2016.

31   Mar Goman believes Tom arrived at the school between 8:00 p.m.–9:00 p.m.

32   Unknown, "Services Planned for Students, Educators Lost to Mountain," The Oregonian, May 18, 1986.

33   Douthit, I, September 12, 2015; Garrett, Mick, Interview with author, I. Wy'East Day Lodge to Palmer, September 14, 2015.

34   Horwell, Amy, WC, Amendments/Additions–Sunday, April 14, 2017.

35   Horwell, Amy, Interview with author, I. Personal Remembrances, April 9, 2017; Horwell, WC, April 14, 2017.

36   Dialogue comes from: McGinness, I, August 2, 2015.

37   Boatsman, Courtney, Interview with author, I. Preparations and Ascent, May 23, 2015.

38   King, Marsha, "A Student Who Turned Back Reflects on Mount Hood Climb," The Seattle Times, May 16, 1986.

39   Boatsman, I. May 23, 2015.

40   Garrett, Mick, WC, OES Dorm Layout, April 29, 2017.

41   Unknown, "Services Planned for Students, Educators Lost to Mountain," The Oregonian, May 18, 1986; Hallman, Jr. & Snell, May 18, 1986.

42   In 2015, Douthit, Boatsman, and Garrett all agreed on this point.

43   Douthit, I, September 12, 2015.

44   Unknown, "Meeting with Ralph Summers," CCSR. I (May 30, 1986): 33.

45   Fitschen and Boatsman agree that ACT members were checking the students' backpacks and equipment prior to boarding the bus. Fitschen adds, however, that ACT members were assisting—that Fr. Goman and others were helping as well. Fitschen, Lorca, Interview with author, I. The OES Tragedy, January 2, 2017; Boatsman, I, May 23, 2015.

46   Hallman, Jr. & Snell, May 18, 1986.

47   Dialogue exchange comes from, Hallman, Jr. & Snell, May 18, 1986.

48   Other sources claim Amy was fifteen. The sheriff department's missing person's report lists her date of birth as January 5, 1970. Krebs, Deputy Ed, "Missing Person Report 86-15993 (Tasha Amy)," CCSR. I (May 12, 1986), 5.

49   Boatsman, I, May 23, 2015.

50   Unknown, "Services Planned for Students, Educators Lost to Mountain," The Oregonian, May 18, 1986.

51   Danks, Holly, "Climbers' Love of Life Celebrated," The Oregonian, May 20, 1986.

52   Douthit, I, September 12, 2015.

53   Boatsman, I, May 23, 2015.

54   O'Neill, Patrick, "Surviving Students, Guide Testify on Doomed Mount Hood Climb," The Oregonian, April 3, 1990.

55   Dialogue comes from: Whitson, John, Interview with author, I. The Climb, May 9, 2016.

56   Whitson, I. May 9, 2016.

57   Garrett, I, September 14, 2015.

58   Douthit, I, September 12, 2015.

59   Snell, John, "Thompson Learning to Walk Again," The Oregonian, August 24, 1986.

60   Boatsman, Courtney, OC, Giles Thompson, May 23, 2015.

61   Hallman, Jr., Tom, "Mount Hood's Deadly Deceit," The Oregonian, May 12, 1996.

62   BIC, (July 22, 1986): 3.

63   Douthit, I, September 12, 2015. Neither Boatsman, Fitschen, Garrett, or Whitson could recall—precisely—whether the Sprays rode up to the mountain on the bus, or took a private automobile. Hilary Spray declined an interview for this project.

64   Whitson felt that Litzenberger was the smartest student in their class.

65   Lane, May 16, 1986.

66   Douthit, I, September 12, 2015.

Chapter 2, "Father Tom's Posse"

1   Boatsman, Courtney, Interview with author, I. Preparations and Ascent, May 23, 2015.

2   Dialogue comes from: Whitson, I. May 9, 2016.

3   Danes, Z. Frank, "Testimony Pertaining to the Character and Qualifications of Reverend Dr. Thomas Gordon Goman," WC to OES BIC, (July 19, 1986): 3.

4   Goman, Mar, WC, Corrections to Tom Goman's Background, February 14, 2016; McArthur, Lewis

L., "Thomas Gordon Goman," (In Memorium) AAJ, XXIX, No. 61 (December 1987): 355.

5   Goman, Mar, WC, Summary of Tom Goman's Climbing Experience, February 14, 2016.

6   McGinness, Frank, Interview with author, I. Sunday through Wednesday, August 2, 2015.

7   Unknown, "List of Climbers," CCSR. I (May 16, 1986): 27.

8   Tom Hallman, Jr. and John Snell, "Nightmare on Mount Hood," The Oregonian, May 18, 1986.

9   Dialogue exchange comes from: Hallman, Jr. & Snell, May 18, 1986.

10   Unknown, "Funerals, Memorial Services Set For Five Victims of Climbing Tragedy," The Oregonian, May 17, 1986.

11   Fitschen, Lorca, Interview with author, I. The OES Tragedy, January 2, 2017.

12   Garrett, I. September 14, 2015.

13   Douthit, I. September 12, 2015.

14   Fitschen, I. January 2, 2017.

15   Dialogue comes from: Fitschen, I, January 2, 2017.

16   Fitschen, I, January 2, 2017.

17   Garrett, I, September 14, 2015.

18   McGinness, Frank, OC, The McGinness Family, May 20, 2018.

19   Lane, Dee and Kathie Durbin, "Basecamp Project Supported by Students, Parents; Other Schools Wary," The Oregonian, May 16, 1986.

20   Lane, Dee, "Classes Forgotten as Students Wait for Word of Lost Climbers," The Oregonian, May 15, 1986.

21   Lane & Durbin, May 16, 1986.

22   Lane & Durbin, May 16, 1986.

23   Unknown, "Mt. Hood, Search—Rescue—Recovery," Mountain Rescue Council newsletter, (November 1986): 8.

24   Garrett, I. September 14, 2015.

25   Goman, Fr. Thomas, "Sophomore Climb—1986," memorandum to Sam Dibbins, Radtke Collection, (April 26, 1986): 1.

26   Garrett, I. September 14, 2015.

27   Goman, FrDr. Tom, Memorandum: Readers for the Advanced Climbing Team Essays—1985-86, Circa Spring 1985; Goman, FrDr. Tom, Memorandum: Parents of Students Selected for the Advanced Mountaineering Team (Permission to Climb), Circa June 1985.

28   Goman, FrDr. Tom, Correspondence with Mick Garrett, ACT Acceptance Letter, Circa June 1985.

29   Garrett, Mick, OC, Climbing Team Configurations, November 30, 2015.

30   Fitschen, Lorca, OC, Background, July 27, 2015.

31   Garrett, Mick, WC, Manuscript Corrections, November 6, 2015.

32   Garrett, I., September 14, 2015.

33   Whitson, I, May 9, 2016.

34   Danks, Holly, and Tom Hallman, Jr., "Parents View Report with Sense of Relief," The Oregonian, July 25, 1986.

35   Zduniak, Dee, "Statement of Dee Zduniak," Interview with Elden Rosenthal, McGinness Collection, (August 2, 1986): 1.

36   Tullis, Jon, WC, Personal Recollections, July 9, 2017.

37   Zduniak, (August 2, 1986): 1.

38   Tullis, WC, July 9, 2017.

39   Dialogue exchange comes from: O'Regan, Judy, OC, Personal Recollections, December 3, 2018.

Chapter 3, "A Weather Eye"

1   BIC, "Analysis of the O.E.S. Mt. Hood Accident—May 1986," (July 22, 1986): 5.

2   Schula, Molly, Untitled Statement, PMR, (May 1986): 1.

3   Yates, Diana, and Mar Goman, Interview with author, I. The Vigil, March 12, 2016.

4   Yates & Goman, I. March 12, 2016.

5	Boatsman, Courtney, Interview with author, I. Preparations and Ascent, May 23, 2015.

6	Whitson, John, Interview with author, I. The Climb, May 9, 2016.

7	Garrett, Mick, Interview with author, I. Wy'East Day Lodge to Palmer, September 14, 2015.

8	Radtke, Sandy, Correspondence with author, The Note, March 30, 2019.

9	All information in this section concerning the relationship between Pat McGinness and Dandy Douthit comes from: Douthit, Sandra, Interview with author, I. Personal Remembrances, September 12, 2015.

10	McGinness, Frank, Interview with author, I. Sunday through Wednesday, August 2, 2015.

11	Whitson, I. May 9, 2016.

12	Tom Hallman, Jr. and John Snell, "Nightmare on Mount Hood," The Oregonian, May 18, 1986.

13	Dr. Long, as quoted in: Wilkerson, M.D., Jim, and Murray P. Hamlet, D.V.M., "Medical After Action Conference, Mount Hood, 1986, Bypass Rewarming," Report No. T10-88, U.S. Army Research Institute of Environmental Medicine, Natick, MA. (February 1988): 147.

14	Krebs, Ed, "Missing Person Report 86-15981 (Ralph Summers)," CCSR. I (May 12, 1986), 17. Some reports list Summers as thirty-one, but he was born on October 31, 1955. Unknown, "List of Climbers," CCSR. I (May 16, 1986): 27.

15	Unknown, "Climbing Experts Raise Questions About Hood Climb," The Seattle Times, May 22, 1986.

16	Summers, Ralph, "Statement of Ralph Summers," Statement provided to BIC. (June 9, 1986), 2.

17	Summers, Ralph, "This is How I Understood My Role in Working With the OES," CCSR. II (May 18, 1986), 218.

18	Summers, Ralph, "Notes dictated by Ralph Summers, Regarding the Mount Hood Climb by OES Students on May 12, 1986," CCSR. II (May 18, 1986), 221.

19	Garrett, I. September 14, 2015.

20	Whitson, I. May 9, 2016.

21	Boatsman, I. May 23, 2015.

22	Rubenstein, Sura and John Painter, Jr., "Weather on Mount Hood Went From Bad to Worse," The Oregonian, May 16, 1986.

23	Schula, (May 1986): 1.

24	Schula, (May 1986): 1.

25	Fitschen, Lorca, Interview with author, I. The OES Tragedy, January 2, 2017.

26	Schula, (May 1986): 1.

27	Garrett, I. September 14, 2015.

28	Schula, (May 1986): 1.

29	Summers, (June 9, 1986), 2.

30	McGinness, Pat, "Photographs, 1986 OES Climb," McGinness Collection, (May 12, 1986).

31	Goman, Fr. Thomas, "Climbing and Backcountry Travel Register," U.S. Forest Service, CCSR, (May 12, 1986): 18-19.

32	In her typed statement, Schula indicated that Fr. Goman had already had this form filled out. Garrett and Summers recall the priest filling it out on the scene.

33	Dialogue exchange comes from: Garrett, I. September 14, 2015.

Chapter 4, "That Nagging Feeling"

1	Summers, Ralph, "Statement of Ralph Summers," Statement provided to BIC. (June 9, 1986), 2.

2	BIC, "Analysis of the O.E.S. Mt. Hood Accident—May 1986," (July 22, 1986): 11; Kennell, David, "Preliminarily Response—Special Report," CCSR. I (May 16, 1986): 26.

3	Schula, Molly, Untitled Statement, PMR, (May 1986): 1.

4	BIC, (July 22, 1986): 11.

5	Garrett, Mick, Interview with author, I. Wy'East Day Lodge to Palmer, September 14, 2015; Summers, (June 9, 1986), 3.

6	Schula, (May 1986): 1.

7   Unknown, "Friendly Hike is Deadly for Group," Lodi News-Sentinel, May 19, 1986.

8   Hayakawa, Alan R., "Hood's Lure for Climbers Takes Toll Over Years," The Oregonian, May 15, 1986.

9   Hayakawa, May 15, 1986.

10   Boatsman, Courtney, Interview with author, I. Preparations and Ascent, May 23, 2015.

11   Whitson, John, Interview with author, I. The Climb, May 9, 2016. Contrary to what Whitson and Boatsman reported, Schula notes in her written statement that she was not able to see the stars, but could see the Lodge.

12   Garrett, Mick, Interview with author, I. Wy'East Day Lodge to Palmer, September 14, 2015.

13   Schula, (May 1986): 1-2.

14   BIC, (July 22, 1986): 11–12.

15   Schula, (May 1986): 2.

16   Schula, (May 1986): 2.

17   Summers, Ralph, Untitled supplemental page concerning Richard Haeder, Jr., Marion Horwell, Patrick McGinness, Giles Thompson, Susan McClave, and Fr. Tom Goman, WC, (June 12, 1986): 1. Though Summers notes that McGinness and Thompson were near the front, Schula added that Haeder, Jr. was there as well.

18   Douthit, Sandra, "20th Reunion", remembrance notes (Pat McGinness), (May 12, 2006): 1.

19   Dialogue comes from: Douthit, (May 12, 2006): 1.

20   Schula, (May 1986): 2.

21   Summers, (June 9, 1986), 3.

22   Plummer, William, "Step by Step, A Routine Hike up Mount Hood Turns Into a Nightmare That Kills Nine," People magazine, XXV: 22, (June 2, 1986).

23   BIC., (July 22, 1986): 12.

24   Zduniak, Dee, "Statement of Dee Zduniak," Interview with Elden Rosenthal, McGinness Collection (August 2, 1986): 1-2.

25   Garrett, I. September 14, 2015.

26   Summers, Ralph, "Notes dictated by Ralph Summers, Regarding the Mount Hood Climb by OES Students on May 12, 1986," CCSR. II (May 18, 1986), 221.

27   BIC, (July 22, 1986): 11.

28   Summers, (May 18, 1986), 221.

29   Boatsman, I. May 23, 2015.

30   Summers, (May 18, 1986), 221.

31   Unknown, "Big Lift for Skiers," Oregon Journal, October 29, 1939.

32   McArthur, Lewis L., "Silcox Hut: Then and Now," Mazama Annual, LXXIII: 14, (December 1991): 53; MS2004.008, "Silcox Hut," Restoration and Adaptive Use. The Mazamas Collection.

33   Schula, (May 1986): 2.

34   Garrett, I. September 14, 2015.

35   Summers, (May 18, 1986), 221.

36   Summers, (June 9, 1986), 3.

37   Garrett, Mick, WC, Silcox Hut, October 8, 2018.

38   Schula, (May 1986): 2.

39   Dialogue comes from: Garrett, I. September 14, 2015.

40   Summers, Ralph, Untitled supplemental page concerning Richard Haeder, Jr., Marion Horwell, Patrick McGinness, Giles Thompson, Susan McClave, and Fr. Tom Goman, WC, (June 12, 1986): 1.

41   Schula, (May 1986): 3.

42   Dialogue comes from: Garrett, I. September 14, 2015.

43   Schula, (May 1986): 3.

44   Garrett, I. September 14, 2015.

45   "Sunrise and Sunset Times, May 12–15, 1986." (2017) Retrieved from ‹https://www.sunrisesunset.com›

46   Zduniak, (August 2, 1986): 2.

47   Summers, Ralph, Untitled supplemental page concerning Richard Haeder, Jr., Marion Horwell, Patrick McGinness, Giles Thompson, Susan McClave, and Fr. Tom Goman, WC, (June 12, 1986): 1.

48   Zduniak, (August 2, 1986): 2.

49   Zduniak, (August 2, 1986): 2.

50   Dooris, Pat, "Trapped on Mt. Hood: Remembering the 1986 Tragedy," KGW.COM, May 12, 2015.

51   BIC, (July 22, 1986): 12.

52   Boatsman, I. May 23, 2015.

53   Boatsman, I. May 23, 2015.

54   King, Marsha, "A Student Who Turned Back Reflects on Mount Hood Climb," The Seattle Times, May 16, 1986.

55   Boatsman, I. May 23, 2015.

56   Fitschen, Lorca, Interview with author, I. The OES Tragedy, January 2, 2017.

57   Dialogue exchange comes from: Boatsman, I. May 23, 2015.

58   Schula, (May 1986): 3.

59   Dialogue exchange comes from: Fitschen, I. January 2, 2017.

60   Dialogue comes from: Schula, (May 1986): 3.

61   Garrett, I. September 14, 2015.

62   Schula, (May 1986): 3.

63   Dialogue comes from: Boatsman, I. May 23, 2015.

64   Schula, (May 1986): 3.

65   Boatsman, I. May 23, 2015.

66   King, May 16, 1986.

67   Garrett, I. September 14, 2015.

68   Garrett, I. September 14, 2015.

69   Boatsman, I. May 23, 2015.

70   The precise time for this break, at a position just below the top shack of Palmer chairlift, is open for debate. The BIC believed it to be around 8:00 a.m. Summers' statement, dated June 9, 1986, agrees with this time. Zduniak's statement lists this milestone as 9:30 a.m. Schula's statement does not list a time, nor does Summers' May 18, 1986 statement to authorities.

71   McGinness, Pat, "Photographs, 1986 OES Climb," McGinness Collection, (May 12, 1986).

72   Garrett, Mick, OC, Giles Thompson, September 14, 2015.

73   Hallman, Jr., Tom, "Mount Hood's Deadly Deceit," The Oregonian, May 12, 1996.

74   Hallman, Jr., May 12, 1996.

75   Garrett, Mick, Interview with author, II. Palmer Down to Timberline, September 14, 2015.

76   Garrett, I. September 14, 2015.

77   Garrett, Mick, WC, Palmer Glacier Turnaround, September 28, 2015.

78   Whitson, I. May 9, 2016.

79   Dialogue comes from: Whitson I. May 9, 2016.

80   Horwell's condition and dialogue come from: Whitson, I. May 9, 2016; Bella, Rick, "Student Says Teacher Goaded Climbers up Mount Hood," The Oregonian, March 16, 1990.

81   Whitson, I. May 9, 2016.

82   Garrett, II. September 14, 2015.

83   Schula's 1986 statement and Garett's 2015 interviews both state Susan McClave was feeling quite strong and motivated at this point.

84   Dialogue comes from: Garrett, II. September 14, 2015.

85   Garrett, WC, September 28, 2015.

86   Garrett, WC, September 28, 2015.

87   Schula, (May 1986): 4.

88   Farewell dialogue between students and faculty comes from: Garrett, II. September 14, 2015.

89   Lane, Dee, "Classes Forgotten as Students Wait for Word of Lost Climbers," The Oregonian, May

15, 1986.

90   McGinness, Frank, Interview with author, I. Sunday through Wednesday, August 2, 2015.

91   Summers, (May 18, 1986), 222; BIC, (July 22, 1986): 13.

92   Summers, (May 18, 1986), 222.

93   Schula, (May 1986): 4.

94   Schula, (May 1986): 4.

95   Schula, (May 1986): 4-5.

96   Schula, (May 1986): 5.

97   Schula, (May 1986): 5.

98   McGinness, Pat, "Photographs, 1986 OES Climb," McGinness Collection, (May 12, 1986).

99   Summers, (May 18, 1986), 222.

100   Zduniak, (August 2, 1986): 2-3.

101   Dialogue exchange comes from: Schula, (May 1986): 5.

102   Schula, (May 1986): 5.

103   Zduniak, (August 2, 1986): 3.

104   Summers, Ralph, "Statement of Ralph Summers," Statement provided to BIC. (June 9, 1986), 4.

105   Schula, (May 1986): 5.

106   BIC, (July 22, 1986): 13.

107   Zduniak, (August 2, 1986): 3.

108   Unknown, "Climbing Experts Raise Questions About Hood Climb," The Seattle Times, May 22, 1986.

Chapter 5, "The Devil's Kitchen"

1   Zduniak, Dee, "Statement of Dee Zduniak," Interview with Elden Rosenthal, McGinness Collection, (August 2, 1986): 3.

2   According to Garrett, he and Whitson sat down over some beers years later and had a frank and open conversation about the 1986 OES climb. Men now, rather than the teenagers they were years earlier, they were able to ease one another's concerns and provided one another with some measure of comfort; the decision for Whitson to turn back was not met by Garrett with anger, but rather, with genuine relief.

3   Dialogue comes from: Garrett, Mick, Interview with author, II. Palmer Down to Timberline, September 14, 2015.

4   Garrett, Mick, WC, The Sprays' Room, November 17, 2015.

5   Boatsman, Courtney, WC, The Sprays' Room, November 16, 2015.

6   Fitschen, Lorca, Interview with author, I. The OES Tragedy, January 2, 2017.

7   Garrett, Mick, WC, Timberline Lodge Accommodations, September 28, 2015; Garrett, Mick, WC, Manuscript Corrections, November 6, 2015.

8   Zduniak, (August 2, 1986): 3.

9   Summers, Ralph, "Notes dictated by Ralph Summers, Regarding the Mount Hood Climb by OES Students on May 12, 1986," CCSR. II (May 18, 1986), 223.

10   Schula, Molly, Untitled Statement, PMR, (May 1986): 6.

11   Hallman, Jr., Tom, "Mount Hood's Deadly Deceit," The Oregonian, May 12, 1996.

12   Schula, (May 1986): 6.

13   Schula, (May 1986): 6.

14   Schula, (May 1986): 6.

15   Schula, (May 1986): 6.

16   Collins, J.R. and Phillips, Kenneth, "Fumaroles on Mount Hood," Mazama Annual, XVII: 12, (December 1935): 19.

17   Schula, (May 1986): 7.

18   Summers, (May 18, 1986), 223.

19   Schula, (May 1986): 7.

20   Summers, (May 18, 1986), 223.

21   Summers later stated, "It is my understanding that I was hired more as a consultant to the group. It was made very clear to me by Father Tom Goman that they did not want me to jump in and take over as the leader on the days they were climbing. Thus, if I had a job description, I would consider myself as a consultant." Summers, Ralph, "This is How I Understood My Role in Working With the OES," CCSR. II (May 18, 1986), 220.

22   Schula, (May 1986): 7.

23   Schula, (May 1986): 7.

24   Summers, (May 18, 1986), 223.

25   Schula, (May 1986): 7-8.

26   Dialogue comes from: Schula, (May 1986): 8.

27   McClure, Dr. David W., "The OES Climbing Tragedy on Mt. Hood," PMR, (August 1986): 1.

28   Dialogue exchange comes from: Schula, (May 1986): 8.

29   Schula, (May 1986): 8.

30   O'Leary appears to have been the only student carrying a wristwatch. Schula, (May 1986): 8.

31   Summers, (May 18, 1986), 223.

32   Summers, (May 18, 1986), 223.

33   Schula, (May 1986): 8.

34   Dialogue comes from: Schula, (May 1986): 8.

35   Summers, Ralph, "Statement of Ralph Summers," Statement provided to BIC. (June 9, 1986), 5.

36   Summers, (May 18, 1986), 223.

37   One source places the highest point reached as 11,135 feet, but this is inaccurate. Such an elevation figure would have meant the team passed through the Pearly Gates, which did not take place.

38   Dialogue exchange comes from: McGinness, Frank, Interview with author, I. Sunday through Wednesday, August 2, 2015.

39   Hallman, Jr. & Snell's article, "The Week on Mount Hood," which appeared in The Oregonian on May 18, 1986, lists 3:45 p.m. as the turnaround time. That milestone is listed as "by four o'clock in the afternoon" in McClure's report to PMR. In John Roskelley's article for Backpacker magazine, the turn-around time is listed as 5:00 p.m. These time differences may be attributed to the fact that the call for retreat came around 3:15 p.m., yet the team spent an hour tending to McGinness, who was suffering from hypothermia, prior to continuing with the descent.

40   Summers, (May 18, 1986), 223.

41   Schula, (May 1986): 9.

42   BIC, "Analysis of the O.E.S. Mt. Hood Accident—May 1986," (July 22, 1986): 14.

43   Dialogue comes from: Schula, (May 1986): 9.

44   Schula, (May 1986): 9.

45   McClure, (August, 1986): 1.

46   Summers, (May 18, 1986), 224.

47   Schula, (May 1986): 9.

48   Schula, (May 1986): 10.

49   Dialogue comes from: Schula, (May 1986): 10.

50   Summers, (May 18, 1986), 224.

51   Summers, (May 18, 1986), 224.

52   Dialogue comes from: Schula, (May 1986): 10.

53   Summers, (May 18, 1986), 224.

54   Schula, (May 1986): 10.

55   Schula, (May 1986): 10.

56   Summers, (May 18, 1986), 224.

57   Schula, (May 1986): 10.

58   Summers, (May 18, 1986), 224.

59   Summers, (May 18, 1986), 224.

60   Schula, (May 1986): 10.

61   Summers, (May 18, 1986), 224.

62   Schula, (May 1986): 10; Summers, (May 18, 1986), 224.

63   Dialogue comes from: Schula, (May 1986): 10.

Chapter 6, "Alabaster Skies"

1   Summers, Ralph, "Notes dictated by Ralph Summers, Regarding the Mount Hood Climb by OES Students on May 12, 1986," CCSR. II (May 18, 1986), 225.

2   Schula, Molly, Untitled Statement, PMR, (May 1986): 10.

3   Summers, (May 18, 1986), 225.

4   Summers, (May 18, 1986), 225.

5   Schula, (May 1986): 11.

6   Schula, (May 1986): 10.

7   Summers, (May 18, 1986), 225.

8   Summers, (May 18, 1986), 225.

9   Tom Hallman, Jr. and John Snell, "The Week on Mount Hood," The Oregonian, May 18, 1986.

10   Tom Hallman, Jr. and John Snell, "High Wind Slows Army of Searchers," The Oregonian, May 15, 1986.

11   Tom Hallman, Jr. and John Snell, "Nightmare on Mount Hood," The Oregonian, May 18, 1986.

12   Schula, (May 1986): 11.

13   Schula, (May 1986): 11.

14   Schula, (May 1986): 11.

15   Summers, (May 18, 1986), 225.

16   Schula, (May 1986): 11.

17   Summers, (May 18, 1986), 225.

18   Dialogue comes from: Summers, (May 18, 1986), 226.

19   Summers, (May 18, 1986), 226.

20   Summers, (May 18, 1986), 226.

21   Dialogue comes from: Schula, (May 1986): 11.

22   Schula, (May 1986): 11.

23   Dialogue comes from: Schula, (May 1986): 11.

24   Unknown Deputy, "Debriefing Molly Schula (Unknown deputy's notes)," CCSR. I (May 13, 1986): 96.

25   Dialogue comes from: Summers, (May 18, 1986), 227.

26   Summers, (May 18, 1986), 227.

27   Summers, (May 18, 1986), 227.

28   O'Neill, Patrick, "Pair Describe Ordeal During Ill-fated Mount Hood Climb," The Oregonian, March 23, 1990.

29   Unknown Deputy, (May 13, 1986): 96.

30   Unknown Deputy, (May 13, 1986): 96.

31   Dialogue comes from: Summers, (May 18, 1986), 227.

32   Unknown Deputy, (May 13, 1986): 96.

33   Schula, (May 1986): 12.

34   Summers, (May 18, 1986), 227.

35   Garrett, Mick, WC, Manuscript Corrections, November 6, 2015.

36   King, Marsha, "A Student Who Turned Back Reflects on Mount Hood Climb," The Seattle Times, May 16, 1986.

37   Garrett, Mick, WC, The Sprays' Room, November 17, 2015.

38   Dialogue comes from: Garrett, Mick, Interview with author, II. Palmer Down to Timberline, September 14, 2015.

39   Since their founding, the team had been called the Winter Hawks. In May 2009, they re-branded

themselves the Winterhawks.

40   Lesage, Pete, "'Rookie Line' Helps Hawks Put Away Guelph 6-4," The Oregonian, May 12, 1986; Horwell, Amy, WC, Amendments/Additions–Monday, April 15, 2017.

41   Buker, Paul, "Guelph Uses Tenacious Defense to Whip 'Invincible' Hull 3-1," The Oregonian, May 13, 1986.

42   Hicks, Jeff, Interview with author, I. OES Resident Advisor, January 17, 2019.

43   Horwell, Amy, Interview with author, I. Personal Remembrances, April 9, 2017.

44   Schula, (May 1986): 12.

45   Schula, (May 1986): 12.

46   Summers, (May 18, 1986), 227.

47   Summers, (May 18, 1986), 227.

48   Hallman, Jr., Tom, "Mount Hood's Deadly Deceit," The Oregonian, May 12, 1996.

49   Unknown Deputy, (May 13, 1986): 96; Schula, (May 1986): 13.

50   Summers, (May 18, 1986), 228.

51   Summers, (May 18, 1986), 228.

52   Summers, (May 18, 1986), 228.

53   Summers, (May 18, 1986), 228.

54   Summers, (May 18, 1986), 228.

55   Bangs, Cameron and Don Batten, "High School Climbing Tragedy," Mazama Annual, LXVIII: 13 (December 1986): 25.

56   Dialogue exchange comes from two sources: Schula, (May 1986): 13; Summers, (May 18, 1986), 228.

57   Summers, (May 18, 1986), 228.

Chapter 7, "Puzzle Box"

1   Summers, Ralph, "Notes dictated by Ralph Summers, Regarding the Mount Hood Climb by OES Students on May 12, 1986," CCSR. II (May 18, 1986), 229.

2   Summers, (May 18, 1986), 229.

3   Schula, Molly, Untitled Statement, PMR, (May 1986): 14.

4   Dialogue between O'Leary and Sandvik comes from: Schula, (May 1986): 13-14.

5   Schula, (May 1986): 14.

6   Schula, (May 1986): 14.

7   O'Leary assisting comes from: Schula, (May 1986): 14. Litzenberger assisting comes from: Summers, (May 18, 1986), 229.

8   Dialogue comes from: Schula, (May 1986): 14.

9   Schula (May 1986): 14.

10   Dialogue exchange comes from: McGinness, Frank, Interview with author, I. Sunday through Wednesday, August 2, 2015.

11   Dialogue between Buck and McGinness comes from: McGinness, I. August 2, 2015.

12   Summers, (May 18, 1986), 229.

13   "Sunrise and Sunset Times, May 12–15, 1986." (2017) Retrieved from ‹https://www.sunrisesunset.com›

14   Garrett, Mick, Interview with author, II. Palmer Down to Timberline, September 14, 2015.

15   Dialogue comes from: Fitschen, Lorca, Interview with author, I. The OES Tragedy, January 2, 2017.

16   Whitson, John, Interview with author, I. The Climb, May 9, 2016.

17   Dialogue comes from: Fitschen, I. January 2, 2017.

18   Garrett, I. September 14, 2015.

19   Bangs, Cameron and Don Batten, "High School Climbing Tragedy," Mazama Annual, LXVIII: 13 (December 1986): 25.

20   Summers, (May 18, 1986), 229.

21   Dialogue comes from: Summers, (May 18, 1986), 229.

22   Schula, (May 1986): 14.

23   Summers, (May 18, 1986), 229.

24   Dialogue comes from: Summers, (May 18, 1986), 229.

25   Summers, (May 18, 1986), 229.

26   Garrett, Mick, OC, Fr. Thomas Goman, September 14, 2015.

27   Boatsman, Courtney, Interview with author, I. Preparations and Ascent, May 23, 2015.

28   Dialogue exchange between Summers and Goman comes from: Summers, (May 18, 1986), 230.

29   Dialogue between Summers and McGinness Comes from: Summers, (May 18, 1986), 230.

30   Hallman, Jr., Tom, "Mount Hood's Deadly Deceit," The Oregonian, May 12, 1996.

31   Plummer, William, "Step by Step, A Routine Hike up Mount Hood Turns into a Nightmare That Kills Nine," People magazine, XXV: 22, (June 2, 1986).

32   O'Neill, Patrick, "Surviving Students, Guide Testify on Doomed Mount Hood Climb," The Oregonian, April 3, 1990.

33   Summers, (May 18, 1986), 230.

34   Reynolds, Charles, "Transcript of SAR Meeting," PMR, (June 4, 1986): 4-5.

35   Hanners, Lt. Gene W., "Supervisor's Daily Report," CCSR. I (May 12, 1986): 55.

36   Hanners, (June 4, 1986): 3-5.

37   Hanners, Lt. Gene W., "SAR (Supplemental)—Agencies Involved," CCSR. I (May 25, 1986): 45.

38   Schula, (May 1986): 14.

39   Summers, (May 18, 1986), 230.

40   Schula, (May 1986): 15.

41   Penater, Don, "Memo regarding Interview with Molly Schula," McGinness Collection, (June 19, 1986): 1-6.

42   Schula (May 1986), 15.

43   Schula, (May 1986): 15.

44   Schula, (May 1986): 15.

45   Dialogue comes from: Schula, (May 1986): 15.

46   Schula, (May 1986): 15.

47   Dialogue comes from: Penater, Don, Interview with author, I. Personal Recollections, August 8, 2017.

48   Dialogue comes from: Schula, (May 1986): 15.

49   Schula, (May 1986): 15.

50   Tom Hallman, Jr. and John Snell, "Nightmare on Mount Hood," The Oregonian, May 18, 1986.

51   Dialogue comes from: Goman, Mar, Interview with author, I. The Vigil, March 12, 2016.

52   Goman and Yates, I. March 12, 2016.

53   Tullis, Jon, WC, Personal Recollections, July 9, 2017.

Chapter 8, "Grapevine"

1   Hanners, Gene, "Transcript of SAR Meeting," PMR, (June 4, 1986): 6.

2   Hanners, Lt. Gene W., "SAR (Supplemental)—Agencies Involved," CCSR. I (May 25, 1986): 45

3   Kennel, David, "Chuck Reynolds," CCSR. I (May 12, 1986): 68.

4   Dialogue comes from: Tullis, Jon, WC, Personal Recollections, July 9, 2017.

5   Garrett, Mick, Interview with author, II. Palmer Down to Timberline, September 14, 2015.

6   Dialogue comes from: McGinness, Frank, Interview with author, I. Sunday through Wednesday, August 2, 2015.

7   Dialogue comes from: Douthit, Sandra, Interview with author, I. Personal Remembrances, September 12, 2015.

8   Dialogue comes from: Douthit, I. September 12, 2015.

9   Fitschen, Lorca, Interview with author, I. The OES Tragedy, January 2, 2017.

10   Whitson, John, Interview with author, I. The Climb, May 9, 2016.

11   Garrett, II. September 14, 2015.

12   Tullis, Jon, WC, Personal Recollections, July 9, 2017.

13   Tullis, WC, Personal Recollections, July 9, 2017.

14   Tullis' call to the CCSO was placed at 10:15 p.m. Kennel, David, "Chuck Reynolds," CCSR. I (May 12, 1986): 68.

15   One source states both deputies were dispatched. Another source says Kennel was sent Monday night and Krebs arrived early Tuesday morning. Krebs passed away in 2017 and Kennel declined to be interviewed for this book.

16   Hanners, (June 4, 1986): 6.

17   Obituary, "In Memory of Edwin Wayne Krebs (1947–2017)," Lincoln Memorial Park and Funeral Home, Portland, OR, October 2017.

18   Goman, Fr. Thomas, "Climbing and Backcountry Travel Register," U.S. Forest Service, CCSR, (May 12, 1986): 18-19.

19   Summers was most likely not standing beside Goman when this document was filled out, as evidenced by two factors. First, Goman misspelled Summers' name on the register. Secondly, the spaces next to items labeled Skis and Wands, were left blank even though Summers carried both.

20   Kennell, David, "Preliminarily Response—Special Report," CCSR. I (May 16, 1986): 20.

21   Buker, Paul, "Guelph Uses Tenacious Defense to Whip 'Invincible' Hull 3-1," The Oregonian, May 13, 1986.

22   Dialogue comes from: Horwell, Amy, Interview with author, I. Personal Remembrances, April 9, 2017.

23   Hicks, Jeff, Interview with author, I. OES Resident Advisor, January 17, 2019.

24   Tullis, WC, July 9, 2017.

25   Hanners, (May 25, 1986): 45.

26   Tullis, WC, July 9, 2017.

27   Hallman, Jr. Tom, "Winds Halt rescue of 11 Trapped on Mount Hood," The Oregonian, May 14, 1986.

28   Schula, Molly, Untitled Statement, PMR, (May 1986): 15.

29   Tom Hallman, Jr. and John Snell, "Nightmare on Mount Hood," The Oregonian, May 18, 1986.

30   Hallman, May 14, 1986.

31   O'Neill, Patrick, "Surviving Students, Guide Testify on Doomed Mount Hood Climb," The Oregonian, April 3, 1990.

32   Hallman, Jr., Tom, "Mount Hood's Deadly Deceit," The Oregonian, May 12, 1996; Garrett, II. September 14, 2015.

Chapter 9, "The Call Out"

1   McClure, Dave, "Transcript of SAR Meeting," PMR, (June 4, 1986): 9.

2   Maslen, Cheryl, Interview with author, I. Tuesday, October 8, 2016.

3   Wright, Barry, WC, Avalanche on Leuthold Couloir, June 12, 2015.

4   Wright, Barry, Interview with author, I. The Early Efforts, April 13, 2015.

5   McClure, (June 4, 1986): 9.

6   Wright, I. April 13, 2015.

7   Kennell, Deputy David, "Kennel's Log," CCSR. I (May 12, 1986): 69.

8   Wright, Barry, "PMR Rescue Callout," PMR, (May 13, 1986): 1.

9   McClure, (June 4, 1986): 9.

10   Wright, (May 13, 1986): 1.

11   Wright, I. April 13, 2015.

12   Craig, Mike, Interview with author, I. Tuesday through Thursday, June 10, 2018.

13   Conrad, Ric, Interview Notes with Mike Craig and Sue Shultz, June 10, 2018.

14   Shultz, Sue, Interview with author, I. Tuesday through Thursday, June 10, 2018.

15   Shultz, I. June 10, 2018.

16   Kennell, (May 12, 1986): 69.

17   Boatsman, Courtney, Interview with author, I. Preparations and Ascent, May 23, 2015.

18   Henderson, Rocky, Interview with author, I. The Raw Recruit, March 9, 2015.

19   Kennell, David, "Preliminarily Response—Special Report," CCSR. I (May 16, 1986): 21; Kennell, (May 12, 1986): 69.

20   Kennell, (May 12, 1986): 69.

21   Dialogue comes from: Lillywhite, Harold F., "Field Report: School Accident on Mount Hood," Advanced Rescue Technology, VII: 2 (April-May, 2004): 62.

22   Lillywhite, Hal, Interview with author, I. A Memorable Lesson, January 16, 2016.

23   Unknown, "Richard Harder, Air Force Specialist (Obit)," The Seattle Times, November 23, 1996.

24   Ek, Charlie, Interview with author, I. The OES Tragedy, May 6, 2017.

25   Harder, Rick, "Transcript of SAR Meeting," PMR, (June 4, 1986): 8.

26   Hall, Ed, Interview with author, I. Hasty Team & Crag Rats, August 4, 2018.

27   Dialogue comes from: Schula, Molly, Untitled Statement, PMR, (May 1986): 15.

28   Dialogue comes from: Schula, (May 1986): 16.

29   Rubenstein, Sura and John Painter, Jr., "Weather on Mount Hood Went From Bad to Worse," The Oregonian, May 16, 1986; Schula, (May 1986): 16.

30   Summers, Ralph, "Notes dictated by Ralph Summers, Regarding the Mount Hood Climb by OES Students on May 12, 1986," CCSR. II (May 18, 1986), 231. According to Dr. Bangs, the shovel merely slid away sometime during the night. Cameron Bangs and Don Batten, "High School Climbing Tragedy," Mazama Annual, LXVIII: 13 (December 1986): 25. Schula also stated that the shovel slid away. Schula, (May 1986): 16.

31   Maslen, I. October 8, 2016.

32   McClure, (June 4, 1986): 9.

33   McClure, (June 4, 1986): 9

34   Schula, (May 1986): 16.

35   Schula, (May 1986): 16.

36   Harder, (June 4, 1986): 8.

37   Diana Yates recalled. "It had to be us. We knew they [Boatsman, Garrett, Whitson, and Fitschen] were sleeping upstairs." Mar Goman added, "I don't remember [Harder] waking us up. I think it was probably us, because nobody else was there. Goman, Mar, I. March 12, 2016.

38   Harder, (June 4, 1986): 8.

39   Hall, I. August 4, 2018.

40   Kelsey, Mark, Interview with author, I. Team 1 and Team 8, November 3, 2018.

41   Hall, I. August 4, 2018.

42   Hallman, Jr., Tom, "Mount Hood's Deadly Deceit," The Oregonian, May 12, 1996.

43   Garrett, Mick, WC, Meeting with Authorities, November 17, 2015.

44   Garrett, Mick, WC, The Hallway Meeting, November 15, 2015. Tom Stringfield notes, "Today, PMR volunteers wear identical red team parkas, with logos and a big white RESCUE label on the sleeve. We began having red team parkas made in 2000. At the time of the OES mission, PMR members provided their own parkas, in whatever colors they chose."

45   Boatsman, I. May 23, 2015.

46   Garrett, I. September 14, 2015.

47   Garrett, Mick, WC, Haeder, Sr. and Schula, November 17, 2015; Garrett, I. September 14, 2015.

48   Hanners, Lt. Gene W., "SAR (Supplemental)—Agencies Involved," CCSR. I (May 25, 1986): 45.

49   Harder, (June 4, 1986): 8-9.

50   McClure, Dr. David W., "The OES Climbing Tragedy on Mt. Hood," PMR, (August 1986): 2.

51   Henderson, I. March 9, 2015.

52   Unknown, "Weather Report," (forecast) The Oregonian, May 13, 1986.

53   Unknown, "Notes," CCSR. I (May 30, 1986): 35.

54   Henderson, March 9, 2015.

Chapter 10, "Tall Grey Beard"

1   McClure, Dave, Interview with author, I. Tuesday, October 8, 2016.

2   McClure, Dr. David W., "The OES Climbing Tragedy on Mt. Hood," PMR, (August 1986): 2.

3   Wright, Barry, Interview with author, I. The Early Efforts, April 13, 2015.

4   Hanners, Lt. Gene W., "SAR (Supplemental)—Agencies Involved," CCSR. I (May 25, 1986): 45.

5   McClure, Dave, "Transcript of SAR Meeting," PMR, (June 4, 1986): 15.

6   Stillman, Lt. Sherwood, "S.A.R.—Mt. Hood," CCSR. I (May 22, 1986): 49.

7   Shultz, Susan, Interview with author, I. Tuesday through Thursday, June 10, 2018.

8   Janeck, Jerry, Interview with author, I. The OES Tragedy, June 10, 2017.

9   Janeck, I. June 10, 2017.

10   Lillywhite, Hal, Interview with author, I. A Memorable Lesson, January 16, 2016.

11   Schula, Molly, Untitled Statement, PMR, (May 1986): 16.

12   Dialogue exchange comes from: Schula, (May 1986): 16.

13   Henderson, Rocky, Interview with author, I. The Raw Recruit, March 9, 2015.

14   Henderson, I. March 9, 2015 and Hattan, Mike, Interview with author, I. Personal Remembrances, March 11, 2017.

15   Wright, I. April 13, 2015.

16   Unknown, "Notes," CCSR. I (May 30, 1986): 35.

17   Wright, I. April 13, 2015.

18   Unknown, "Climbing Experts Raise Questions About Hood Climb," The Seattle Times, May 22, 1986.

19   McClure, (August 1986): 2.

20   Wright, I. April 13, 2015.

21   Baer, April, "Mt. Hood Climbing Has Seen Many Changes in 25 Years Since OES Tragedy," OPB news article, May 10, 2011.

22   McClure, (August 1986): 2-3.

23   "Sunrise and Sunset Times, May 12–15, 1986." (2017) Retrieved from ‹https://www.sunrisesunset.com›

24   History of the squadron comes from: Unknown, (August 7, 2014). 304th Rescue Squadron. Factsheets: 920th Rescue Wing, retrieved from ‹http://920rqw.afrc.af.mil/›.

25   Bryan, Bill, "304th ARRS–Helping Rescue," Mazama Annual, LXIII: 13 (December 1981): 42.

26   Jones, Maj. Charles, "Transcript of SAR Meeting," PMR, (June 4, 1986): 12.

27   Tom Hallman, Jr. John Snell, and Rolla J. Crick, "Sunshine Lures Tourists, Spurs Rescuers to Mountain," The Oregonian, May 15, 1986.

28   Stobell, Fred, "Transcript of SAR Meeting," PMR, (June 4, 1986): 28-29.

29   Youngbluth, Jeff, "Transcript of SAR Meeting," PMR, (June 4, 1986): 26.

30   Unknown, "Team Organization Forms," CCSR. I (May 13, 1986): 149; Unknown, "PMR Membership List," PMR, (November 12, 1985): 1-2.

31   Unidentified, "Transcript of SAR Meeting," PMR, (June 4, 1986): 23.

32   McClure, (June 4, 1986): 15.

33   Ed Hall believed The Hasty Team alone was in the first snowcat. Hall, Ed, Interview with author, I. Hasty Team & Crag Rats, August 4, 2018.

34   Unknown, "Team Organization Forms," CCSR. I (May 13, 1986): 153; Unknown, "PMR Membership List," PMR, (November 12, 1985): 1-2.

35   Glenn, Steve, "Transcript of SAR Meeting," PMR, (June 4, 1986): 17.

36   Kennell, David, "Preliminarily Response—Special Report," CCSR. I (May 16, 1986): 21.

37   Dooris, Pat, "Trapped on Mt. Hood: Remembering the 1986 Tragedy," KGW.COM, May 12, 2015.

38   Bill Brett notes that this same snowcat was also referred to as "Ole Blue," due to an earlier, blue paint job.

39   Brett, Bill, WC, Number 8, April 8, 2015.

40   Shultz, I. June 10, 2018.

41   Shultz, Sue, "1986 Rescue Log," PMR, (May 13, 1986): 1.

42   Schultz, (May 13, 1986): 1.

43   Janeck, I. June 10, 2017.

44   Wilkerson, M.D., Jim, and Murray P. Hamlet, D.V.M., "Medical After Action Conference, Mount Hood, 1986, Bypass Rewarming," Report No. T10-88, U.S. Army Research Institute of Environmental Medicine, Natick, MA. (February 1988): 1.

45   Kelsey, Mark, WC, Climbing Clothes, November 5, 2018.

46   McClure, I. October 8, 2016.

47   Glenn, (June 4, 1986): 17.

Chapter 11, "The Hasty Teams"

1   Dialogue exchange comes from two sources: McGinness, Frank, WC, Tuesday Morning's Call, June 11, 2018 and McGinness, Frank, Interview with author, I. Sunday through Wednesday, August 2, 2015.

2   Dialogue and overall scene where party members shift to upright positions comes from: Schula, Molly, Untitled Statement, PMR, (May 1986): 16.

3   Maslen/Shultz, "1986 Rescue Log," PMR, (May 13, 1986): 1.

4   Barry Wright stated that, in the days ahead, PMR ended up using more of the ski patrol's communication devices than their own.

5   Shultz, Sue, Interview with author, I. Tuesday through Thursday, June 10, 2018.

6   Conrad, Ric, Interview Notes with Mike Craig and Sue Shultz, June 10, 2018.

7   Dialogue comes from: Maslen, Cheryl, Interview with author, I. Tuesday, October 8, 2016.

8   Maslen, I. October 8, 2016.

9   McClure, Dave, Interview with author, I. Tuesday, October 8, 2016.

10   Maslen/Shultz, (May 13, 1986): 1.

11   Hall, Ed, Interview with author, I. Hasty Team & Crag Rats, August 4, 2018.

12   Attempts to establish this communication link proved fruitless and as a result, Harder's request became forgotten in the ensuing operation.

13   Janeck, Jerry, Interview with author, I. The OES Tragedy, June 10, 2017.

14   Stringfield, Tom, "Mountain Rescue Critique," PMR, (June 4, 1986): 2.

15   Janeck, I. June 10, 2017.

16   Janeck, I. June 10, 2017.

17   Dialogue comes from Janeck, I. June 10, 2017.

18   Maslen/Shultz, (May 13, 1986): 1.

19   Horwell, Amy, Interview with author, I. Personal Remembrances, April 9, 2017.

20   Jones, Charles, "Transcript of SAR Meeting," PMR, (June 4, 1986): 29.

21   Hoffmann, Dick, "Transcript of SAR Meeting," PMR, (June 4, 1986): 14.

22   Glenn, Steve, "Transcript of SAR Meeting," PMR, (June 4, 1986): 17.

23   Glenn, (June 4, 1986): 17.

24   Dialogue comes from: Maslen/Shultz, (May 13, 1986): 2.

25   Dialogue exchange comes from: Douthit, Sandra, Interview with author, I. Personal Remembrances, September 12, 2015.

26   Schula, (May 1986): 16.

27   Schula, (May 1986): 17.

28   Swicegood, Terry, "Transcript of SAR Meeting," PMR, (June 4, 1986): 21.

29   Unknown, "Team Organization Forms," CCSR. I (May 13, 1986): 155.

30   McClure, I. October 8, 2016.

31   Swicegood, (June 4, 1986): 21.

32   McClure, I. October 8, 2016.

33   Conrad, Ric, Interview Notes with Mike Craig and Sue Shultz, June 10, 2018.

34   Unknown, "Team Organization Forms," CCSR. I (May 13, 1986): 157; Unknown, "PMR Membership List," PMR, (November 12, 1985): 1-2.

35 Swicegood, (June 4, 1986): 21.

36 Conrad, Ric, Interview Notes with Mike Craig and Sue Shultz, June 10, 2018.

37 Craig, I., June 10, 2018.

38 Craig, I. June 10, 2018.

39 Brett, Bill, WC, Number 8, April 8, 2015.

40 Maslen/Shultz, (May 13, 1986): 2.

41 Conrad, Ric, Interview Notes with Mike Craig and Sue Shultz, June 10, 2018.

42 Summers, Ralph, "Notes dictated by Ralph Summers, Regarding the Mount Hood Climb by OES Students on May 12, 1986," CCSR. II (May 18, 1986), 231.

43 Dialogue comes from: Hallman, Jr., Tom, "Mount Hood's Deadly Deceit," The Oregonian, May 12, 1996.

44 Summers, (May 18, 1986), 231.

45 O'Neill, Patrick, "Surviving Students, Guide Testify on Doomed Mount Hood Climb," The Oregonian, April 3, 1990.

46 Dialogue exchange comes from: Schula, (May 1986): 17.

47 Summers, (May 18, 1986), 231.

48 Summers, (May 18, 1986), 231.

49 Summers, (May 18, 1986), 231.

50 Dialogue exchanges regarding Summers' request for a partner comes from: Schula, (May 1986): 17, unless otherwise specified.

51 Summers, (May 18, 1986), 232.

52 Dialogue comes from: Summers, (May 18, 1986), 232.

53 Dooris, Pat, "Trapped on Mt. Hood: Remembering the 1986 Tragedy," KGW.COM, May 12, 2015.

54 Schula, (May 1986): 19.

55 Dialogue exchange comes from Jim Miller, "The OES Climb," Signpost for Northwest Trails. XXV (May, 1990).

56 Dialogue comes from: Schula, (May 1986): 17.

57 Dialogue exchange comes from: Schula, (May 1986): 18.

58 Dialogue comes from: Hallman, Jr., Tom, "Winds Halt Rescue of 11 Trapped on Mount Hood," The Oregonian, May 14, 1986.

Chapter 12, "Desperate Gamble"

1 McClure, Dave, "Transcript of SAR Meeting," PMR, (June 4, 1986): 19.

2 Maslen/Shultz, "1986 Rescue Log," PMR, (May 13, 1986): 2; Glenn, Steve, "Transcript of SAR Meeting," PMR, (June 4, 1986): 17.

3 Summers stated he believed his departure time from the cave was "about 8:00 a.m.," Summers, Ralph, "Transcript of SAR Meeting," PMR, (June 4, 1986): 21.

4 Dialogue comes from: Schula, Molly, Untitled Statement, PMR, (May 1986): 18.

5 Dialogue comes from: Schula, (May 1986): 18.

6 Harder, Rick, "Transcript of SAR Meeting," PMR, (June 4, 1986): 18–19.

7 Rick Harder, as quoted in: Wilkerson, M.D., Jim, and Murray P. Hamlet, D.V.M., "Medical After Action Conference, Mount Hood, 1986, Bypass Rewarming," Report No. T10-88, U.S. Army Research Institute of Environmental Medicine, Natick, MA. (February 1988): 110.

8 Hall, Ed, Interview with author, I. Hasty Team & Crag Rats, August 4, 2018.

9 Kelsey, Mark, Interview with author, I. Team 1 and Team 8, November 3, 2018.

10 Harder, (June 4, 1986): 16.

11 Dialogue comes from: Henderson, Rocky, Interview with author, I. The Raw Recruit, March 9, 2015.

12 Swicegood, Terry, "Transcript of SAR Meeting," PMR, (June 4, 1986): 21-22.

13 Dialogue comes from: Maslen, Cheryl, Interview with author, I. Tuesday, October 8, 2016.

14 Maslen/Shultz, (May 13, 1986): 2.

15 Kelsey, I. November 3, 2018.

16 Henderson, I. March 9, 2015.

17 Youngbluth, Jeffrey, "Transcript of SAR Meeting," PMR, (June 4, 1986): 26.

18 Dialogue comes from: Hall, I. August 4, 2018.

19 Harder, (June 4, 1986): 17.

20 Dialogue exchange comes from: Hall, I. August 4, 2018.

21 Schula, (May 1986): 19.

22 Dialogue exchange comes from: Schula, (May 1986): 18-20, unless otherwise specified.

23 Dialogue exchange comes from: Summers, Ralph, "Notes dictated by Ralph Summers, Regarding the Mount Hood Climb by OES Students on May 12, 1986," CCSR. II (May 18, 1986), 232.

24 Schula, (May 1986): 19.

25 Nalder, Eric, Jack Broom and Dave Birkland, "Mount Hood Tragedy, Three Critical, Search Continues for Missing Eight as Doctors Try to Revive Climbers," The Seattle Times, May 14, 1986.

26 In Schula's written statement to authorities, she additionally mentioned seeing a "mirage," but did not list what it was she felt she saw. Schula, (May 1986): 19.

27 Jones, Charles, "Transcript of SAR Meeting," PMR, (June 4, 1986): 29.

28 Jones, (June 4, 1986): 12-13.

29 Jones, (June 4, 1986): 30.

30 Glenn, (June 4, 1986): 17.

31 Petrie, Craig, "Transcript of SAR Meeting," PMR, (June 4, 1986): 12.

32 Maslen/Shultz, (May 13, 1986): 4.

33 Glenn, (June 4, 1986): 18.

34 McClure, Dr. David W., "The OES Climbing Tragedy on Mt. Hood," PMR, (August 1986): 3.

35 Unidentified, "Transcript of SAR Meeting," PMR, (June 4, 1986): 18.

36 Janeck, Jerry, Interview with author, I. The OES Tragedy, June 10, 2017.

37 Hallman, Jr., Tom, "Mount Hood's Deadly Deceit," The Oregonian, May 12, 1996.

38 McGinness, Frank, OC, Constricting Snow Cave Entrance, October 10, 2015.

39 McGinness, OC, October 10, 2015.

40 Wilkerson & Hamlet. (February 1988): 18.

41 Whitson, John, Interview with author, I. The Climb, May 9, 2016; McGinness, OC, October 10, 2015.

42 Hallman, Jr., Tom, "Mount Hood's Deadly Deceit," The Oregonian, May 12, 1996.

43 Dialogue exchanges, as well as the journey through the canyon, come from: Schula, (May 1986): 20.

44 Unknown, "Debriefing Molly Schula (Unknown deputy's notes)," CCSR. I (May 13, 1986): 96.

45 Dialogue exchange comes from: Schula, (May 1986): 20.

46 Schula, (May 1986): 20-21.

47 Harder, (June 4, 1986): 17; Hall, I. August 4, 2018.

48 Maslen, I. October 8, 2016.

49 Dialogue exchange comes from: Schula, (May 1986): 21.

50 Dialogue exchange comes from Jim Miller, "The OES Climb," Signpost for Northwest Trails. XXV (May, 1990).

51 Perceived identity of the ski lift comes from: Schula, (May 1986): 21. According to Tom Hallman's newspaper article, Summers recognized the chairlift as belonging to Mt. Hood Meadows. According to Schula's written statement, however, Summers believed it to be one just below Timberline Lodge. Hallman, Jr., Tom, "Winds Halt Rescue of 11 Trapped on Mount Hood," The Oregonian, May 14, 1986.

52 Dialogue comes from: Schula, (May 1986): 21.

53 Dialogue comes from: Schula, (May 1986): 21.

54 Henderson, Rocky, WC, Summers and Schula, February 23, 2016.

55 Dialogue comes from: Schula, (May 1986): 21.

56 Hall, I. August 4, 2018.

57 Dialogue comes from: Kelsey, I. November 3, 2018.

58   Dialogue comes from: Hall, I. August 4, 2018.

59   Dialogue comes from: Kelsey, I. November 3, 2018.

60   Kelsey, I. November 3, 2018.

61   Hall, I. August 4, 2018.

62   Schula, (May 1986): 21.

63   Maslen/Shultz, (May 13, 1986): 4.

64   Janeck, Jerry, "Transcript of SAR Meeting," PMR, (June 4, 1986): 20.

65   Janeck, I. June 10, 2017. Interviewed in 2018, Ed Hall said the winds were so loud, it is unclear whether Harder had a clear communication line with Glenn. On the other hand, Hall had been on previous SAR missions where Harder had turned down helicopter flights off the mountain when Hall would have preferred to catch a ride. Hall, I. August 4, 2018.

66   Hall, I. August 4, 2018.

67   Kelsey, I. November 3, 2018.

Chapter 13, "Ant Colony"

1   Dialogue exchange comes from: McGinness, Frank, Interview with author, I. Sunday through Wednesday, August 2, 2015.

2   Krebs, Ed, "Transcript of SAR Meeting," PMR, (June 4, 1986): 24.

3   With the exception of occasional misquotes, McClure felt that the media performed a valuable service during the ordeal. McClure, Dr. David W., "The OES Climbing Tragedy on Mt. Hood," PMR, (August, 1986): 7.

4   All dialogue in the interior of the Head House comes from: McGinness, I. August 2, 2015.

5   Dialogue comes from: Yates, Diana, and Mar Goman, Interview with author, I. The Vigil, March 12, 2016.

6   Goman, I. March 12, 2016.

7   Whitson, John, Interview with author, I. The Climb, May 9, 2016.

8   Garrett, Mick, Interview with author, II. Palmer Down to Timberline, September 14, 2015.

9   Dialogue exchange between Krebs and reporters comes from: Dooris, Pat, "Trapped on Mt. Hood: Remembering the 1986 Tragedy," KGW.COM, May 12, 2015.

10   Dialogue exchange comes from: McGinness, Frank, Interview with author, V. Black Hole, March 24, 2019.

11   Dialogue comes from: McGinness, Frank, Interview with author, V. Black Hole, March 24, 2019.

12   Maslen/Shultz, "1986 Rescue Log," PMR, (May 13, 1986): 5; Glenn, Steve, "Transcript of SAR Meeting," PMR, (June 4, 1986): 18.

13   Maslen/Shultz, (May 13, 1986): 6.

14   Dooris, May 12, 2015.

15   Dialogue exchange comes from: McGinness, I. August 2, 2015.

16   McGinness, I. August 2, 2015.

17   Maslen/Shultz, (May 13, 1986): 6.

18   Maslen/Shultz, (May 13, 1986): 6.

19   Shultz, Sue, Interview with author, I. Tuesday through Thursday, June 10, 2018.

20   Summers, Ralph, "Transcript of SAR Meeting," PMR, (June 4, 1986): 37.

21   Dialogue comes from: Conrad, Ric, Interview Notes with Mike Craig and Sue Shultz, June 10, 2018.

22   Dooris, May 12, 2015.

23   Tom Hallman, Jr. and John Snell, "High Wind Slows Army of Searchers," The Oregonian, May 15, 1986.

24   Youngbluth, Jeff, "Transcript of SAR Meeting," PMR, (June 4, 1986): 38.

25   Youngbluth, (June 4, 1986): 38.

26   Maslen/Shultz, (May 13, 1986): 6; Youngbluth, (June 4, 1986): 38.

27   Wright, Barry, Interview with author, I. The Early Efforts, April 13, 2015; McClure's report to PMR states that Summers estimated the snow cave's position as being between 8,000' and 9,000'.

28   Youngbluth, (June 4, 1986): 26. The elevation figure in PMR's log is 7,600'. Interviewed in 2015, Henderson stated this was inaccurate; 7,200' was the elevation figure that was transmitted over the airwaves. Youngbluth, quoted only weeks after the tragedy, is in agreement.

29   Summers, (June 4, 1986): 37.

30   Lt. Gene Hanners reported that neither Summers nor Schula could precisely pinpoint the location of the snow cave on a map.

31   Wright, I. April 13, 2015.

32   Maslen, I. October 8, 2016; Maslen, Cheryl, "Transcript of SAR Meeting," PMR, (June 4, 1986): 38.

33   Maslen/Shultz, (May 13, 1986): 5.

34   Henderson, Rocky, Interview with author, I. The Raw Recruit, March 9, 2015.

35   Bearing of 43° comes from two sources: Swicegood, (June 4, 1986): 22; Maslen, (May 13, 1986): 7.

36   Maslen/Shultz, (May 13, 1986): 5-7.

37   Garrett, Mick, Interview with author, II. Palmer Down to Timberline, September 14, 2015.

38   Whitson, I. May 9, 2016.

39   Fitschen, Lorca, Interview with author, I. The OES Tragedy, January 2, 2017.

40   Boatsman, Courtney, Interview with author, I. Preparations and Ascent, May 23, 2015.

41   Boatsman, I. May 23, 2015.

42   Dooris, May 12, 2015.

43   Garrett, II. September 14, 2015.

44   Hallman, Jr., Tom, "Mount Hood's Deadly Deceit," The Oregonian, May 12, 1996.

45   Miller, Jim, "The OES Climb," Signpost for Northwest Trails. XXV (May, 1990); Hallman, Jr., Tom, "Mount Hood's Deadly Deceit," The Oregonian, May 12, 1996.

Chapter 14, "Rescuers Rescuing Rescuers"

1   Hicks, Jeff, Interview with author, I. OES Resident Advisor, January 17, 2019.

2   Maslen/Shultz, "1986 Rescue Log," PMR, (May 13, 1986): 7.

3   Maslen/Shultz, (May 13, 1986): 7.

4   Janeck, Jerry, "Transcript of SAR Meeting," PMR, (June 4, 1986): 20.

5   McGinness, Frank, Interview with author, I. Sunday through Wednesday, August 2, 2015.

6   Dialogue comes from: Radtke, Sandra, "20th Reunion", remembrance notes (Pat McGinness), (May 12, 2006): 1-2.

7   Radtke, (May 12, 2006): 1-2.

8   Swicegood, Terry, "Transcript of SAR Meeting," PMR, (June 4, 1986): 22.

9   Lillywhite, Harold F., "Field Report: School Accident on Mount Hood," Advanced Rescue Technology, VII: 2 (April-May, 2004): 63.

10   Lillywhite, Hal, Interview with author, I. A Memorable Lesson, January 16, 2016.

11   Lillywhite, I. January 16, 2016.

12   Craig, Mike, "Transcript of SAR Meeting," PMR, (June 4, 1986): 23.

13   Bangs, Cameron and Don Batten, "High School Climbing Tragedy," Mazama Annual, LXVIII: 13 (December 1986): 25.

14   Henderson, Rocky, Interview with author, I. The Raw Recruit, March 9, 2015.

15   Conrad, Ric, Interview Notes with Mike Craig and Sue Shultz, June 10, 2018.

16   Swicegood, Terry, "Transcript of SAR Meeting," PMR, (June 4, 1986): 22.

17   Jones, Charles, "Transcript of SAR Meeting," PMR, (June 4, 1986): 30.

18   Maslen/Shultz, (May 13, 1986): 7-8.

19   Maslen/Shultz, (May 13, 1986): 8.

20   Janeck, Jerry, Interview with author, I. The OES Tragedy, June 10, 2017.

21   Hattan, Mike, OC, The Media, March 11, 2017.

22   Maslen/Shultz, (May 13, 1986): 8.

23   Maslen/Shultz, (May 13, 1986): 8.

24   Henderson, I. March 9, 2015.

25   The description of Swicegood's fall comes from five sources: Lillywhite, I, January 16, 2016; Henderson, I, March 9, 2015; Swicegood, (June 4, 1986): 22; and Lillywhite, (April-May, 2004): 63; Maslen/Shultz, (May 13, 1986): 8.

26   Kennell, David, "Preliminarily Response—Special Report," CCSR. I (May 16, 1986): 22.

27   Tom Hallman, Jr. John Snell, and Rolla J. Crick, "Sunshine Lures Tourists, Spurs Rescuers to Mountain," The Oregonian, May 15, 1986.

28   Hallman, Jr., Tom, "Winds Halt Rescue of 11 Trapped on Mount Hood," The Oregonian, May 14, 1986.

29   Dialogue exchange comes from: McGinness, Frank, Interview with author, I. Sunday through Wednesday, August 2, 2015.

30   Maslen/Shultz, (May 13, 1986): 8.

31   Lillywhite, I. January 16, 2016.

32   Henderson, I. March 9, 2015.

33   Lillywhite, I. January 16, 2016.

34   Craig, Mike, Interview with author, I. Tuesday through Thursday, June 10, 2018.

35   Craig, I., June 10, 2018.

36   Henderson, I. March 9, 2015.

37   McGinness, I. August 2, 2015.

38   Maslen/Shultz, (May 13, 1986): 8.

39   Hall, Ed, Correspondence with author, Silcox Hut, October 8, 2018; Henderson, Rocky, WC, Silcox Hut, October 8, 2018.

40   Kelsey, Mark, Interview with author, I. Team 1 and Team 8, November 3, 2018.

41   Hall, Ed, Interview with author, I. Hasty Team & Crag Rats, August 4, 2018.

42   Rick Harder, as quoted in: Wilkerson, M.D., Jim, and Murray P. Hamlet, D.V.M., "Medical After Action Conference, Mount Hood, 1986, Bypass Rewarming," Report No. T10-88, U.S. Army Research Institute of Environmental Medicine, Natick, MA. (February 1988): 110-111.

43   Lillywhite, (April-May, 2004): 63.

44   Swicegood, (June 4, 1986): 22-23.

45   Dialogue comes from: Janeck, I. June 10, 2017.

46   Janeck, I. June 10, 2017.

47   McClure, Dr. David W., "The OES Climbing Tragedy on Mt. Hood," PMR, (August, 1986): 2.

48   Summers, (May 18, 1986), 226.

49   Janeck, I. June 10, 2017.

50   Maslen/Shultz, (May 13, 1986): 7.

51   Unknown, "Team Organization Forms," CCSR. I (May 13, 1986): 158.

52   Hall, Ed, Interview with author, I. Hasty Team & Crag Rats, August 4, 2018.

53   Dooris, May 12, 2015.

54   Maslen/Shultz, (May 13, 1986): 8.

55   Janeck, I. June 10, 2017.

56   Maslen/Shultz, (May 13, 1986): 9.

57   Petrie, Craig, "Transcript of SAR Meeting," PMR, (June 4, 1986): 12.

58   McClure, Dave, and Cheryl Maslen, Interview with author, I. Tuesday, October 8, 2016.

Chapter 15, "The Three Amigos"

1   Maslen/Shultz, "1986 Rescue Log," PMR, (May 13, 1986): 10.

2   Maslen/Shultz, (May 13, 1986): 10.

3   Henderson, Rocky, Interview with author, I. The Raw Recruit, March 9, 2015.

4   Maslen/Shultz, (May 13, 1986): 10.

5   Maslen/Shultz, (May 13, 1986): 10.

6   Youngbluth, Jeff, "Transcript of SAR Meeting," PMR, (June 4, 1986): 27.

7   Larson, Terry, "Transcript of SAR Meeting," PMR, (June 4, 1986): 23.

8   Maslen/Shultz, (May 13, 1986): 11.

9   Conrad, Ric, Interview Notes with Mike Craig and Sue Shultz, June 10, 2018.

10   Craig, Mike, Interview with author, I. Tuesday through Thursday, June 10, 2018.

11   Conrad, Ric, Interview Notes with Mike Craig and Sue Shultz, June 10, 2018.

12   Maslen/Shultz, (May 13, 1986): 10; Kennell, Deputy David, "Kennel's Log," CCSR. I (May 12, 1986): 72.

13   Maslen/Shultz, (May 13, 1986): 11.

14   Maslen, Cheryl, Interview with author, I. Tuesday, October 8, 2016.

15   Youngbluth, (June 4, 1986): 27; Henderson, I. March 9, 2015.

16   Henderson, I. March 9, 2015.

17   Henderson, Rocky, OC, Lack of an Altimeter, September 10, 2016.

18   Maslen/Shultz, (May 13, 1986): 11.

19   Youngbluth, (June 4, 1986): 27.

20   Youngbluth, (June 4, 1986): 27.

21   Dialogue comes from Tom Hallman, Jr. John Snell, and Rolla J. Crick, "Sunshine Lures Tourists, Spurs Rescuers to Mountain," The Oregonian, May 15, 1986.

22   Maslen/Shultz, (May 13, 1986): 12.

23   Maslen/Shultz, (May 13, 1986): 12.

24   Maslen/Shultz, (May 13, 1986): 12.

25   Jones, Charles, "Transcript of SAR Meeting," PMR, (June 4, 1986): 30.

26   Rick Harder, as quoted in: Wilkerson, M.D., Jim, and Murray P. Hamlet, D.V.M., "Medical After Action Conference, Mount Hood, 1986, Bypass Rewarming," Report No. T10-88, U.S. Army Research Institute of Environmental Medicine, Natick, MA. (February 1988): 110-111.

27   Dialogue comes from: Hopkins, Oz, "Climbing Tragedy Offers Medical Insights," The Oregonian, May 22, 1986.

28   Harder, (February 1988): 110-111.

29   Maslen/Shultz, (May 13, 1986): 12.

30   Zduniak, Dee, "Statement of Dee Zduniak," Interview with Elden Rosenthal, McGinness Collection, (August 2, 1986): 4.

31   Unidentified, "Transcript of SAR Meeting," PMR, (June 4, 1986): 28.

32   Maslen/Shultz, (May 13, 1986): 12.

33   Maslen/Shultz, (May 13, 1986): 12.

34   Hanners, Lt. Gene W., "SAR (Supplemental)—Agencies Involved," CCSR. I (May 25, 1986): 46.

35   Krebs, Ed, "Transcript of SAR Meeting," PMR, (June 4, 1986): 38.

36   McClure, Dr. David W., "The OES Climbing Tragedy on Mt. Hood," PMR, (August 1986): 3.

37   Henderson, I. March 9, 2015.

38   Jones, (June 4, 1986): 30 and 36.

39   Jones, (June 4, 1986): 30-31.

Chapter 16, "Voices in the Dark"

1   Maslen, Cheryl, Interview with author, I. Tuesday, October 8, 2016; Tom Hallman, Jr. John Snell, and Rolla J. Crick, "Sunshine Lures Tourists, Spurs Rescuers to Mountain," The Oregonian, May 15, 1986; Hanners, Lt. Gene W., "SAR (Supplemental)—Agencies Involved," CCSR. I (May 25, 1986): 46.

2   Tom Hallman, Jr. John Snell, and Rolla J. Crick, "Sunshine Lures Tourists, Spurs Rescuers to Mountain," The Oregonian, May 15, 1986; Hanners, (May 25, 1986): 46.

3   Maslen/Shultz, (May 13, 1986): 13.

4   Maslen/Shultz, (May 13, 1986): 13.

5   Krebs, Ed, "Transcript of SAR Meeting," PMR, (June 4, 1986): 25.

6   Petrie, Craig, "Transcript of SAR Meeting," PMR, (June 4, 1986): 31.

7   Tullis, Jon, WC, Personal Recollections, July 9, 2017.

8   O'Regan, Judy, OC, Personal Recollections, December 3, 2018.

9   Dialogue comes from: Krank, Ky, Interview with author, I. Team 6, June 29, 2018.

10   Unidentified, "Transcript of SAR Meeting," PMR, (June 4, 1986): 28; Maslen/Shultz (May 13, 1986): 13.

11   Hattan, Mike, Interview with author, I. Personal Remembrances, March 11, 2017.

12   Hanners, (May 25, 1986): 46.

13   Maslen, I, October 8, 2016.

14   Hanners, (May 25, 1986): 46.

15   Krank, I, June 29, 2018.

16   Krank, Ky, "Transcript of SAR Meeting," PMR, (June 4, 1986): 32.

17   Unknown, "Team Organization Forms," CCSR. I (May 13, 1986): 161; Unknown, "PMR Membership List," PMR, (November 12, 1985): 1-2.

18   Tom Hallman, Jr. and John Snell, "Nightmare on Mount Hood," The Oregonian, May 18, 1986.

19   Krank, I, June 29, 2018.

20   Henderson, Rocky, Interview with author, I. The Raw Recruit, March 9, 2015.

21   McClure, Dave, "Transcript of SAR Meeting," PMR, (June 4, 1986): 39.

22   Dialogue comes from: McGinness, Frank, Interview with author, I. Sunday through Wednesday, August 2, 2015.

23   Maslen/Shultz, (May 13, 1986): 14.

24   Krank, (June 4, 1986): 32.

25   Krank, I, June 29, 2018.

26   Krank, I, June 29, 2018.

27   Kennell, David, "Preliminarily Response—Special Report," CCSR. I (May 16, 1986): 23.

28   Tom Hallman, Jr. and John Snell, "The Week on Mount Hood," The Oregonian, May 18, 1986; Hallman, Jr., Tom, "Winds Halt Rescue of 11 Trapped on Mount Hood," The Oregonian, May 14, 1986.

29   Stillman, Lt. Sherwood, "S.A.R.—Mt. Hood," CCSR. I (May 22, 1986): 49.

30   Grolbert, Capt. J.T., "SAR, 86-15981," CCSR. I (May 29, 1986): 51.

31   "Sunrise and Sunset Times, May 12–15, 1986." (2017) Retrieved from ‹https://www.sunrisesunset.com›.

32   Maslen, I, October 8, 2016.

33   Hattan, Deputy Mike, "Hattan's Log," CCSR. I (May 12, 1986): 74; Hanners, (May 25, 1986): 46.

34   Krank, (June 4, 1986): 32.

35   Dialogue comes from: Krank, I, June 29, 2018.

36   Krank, I, June 29, 2018.

37   Krank, (June 4, 1986): 32.

38   Tom Hallman, Jr. and John Snell, "Nightmare on Mount Hood," The Oregonian, May 18, 1986.

39   Krank, I, June 29, 2018.

40   Unknown, "PMR Membership List," PMR, (November 12, 1985): 1-2.

41   Unknown, "Team Organization Forms," CCSR. I (May 13, 1986): 167; Unknown, "PMR Membership List," PMR, (October 10, 1986): 1-7.

42   Dialogue comes from: Penater, Don, Interview with author, I. Personal Recollections, August 8, 2017.

43   McGinness, I, August 2, 2015.

44   Dialogue comes from: McGinness, I, August 2, 2015.

45   Krank, I, June 29, 2018.

46   Dialogue comes from: Tom Hallman, Jr. and John Snell, "Nightmare on Mount Hood," The Oregonian, May 18, 1986.

47   Dialogue comes from: Hattan, I, March 11, 2017.

48   Tom Hallman, Jr. John Snell, and Rolla J. Crick, "Sunshine Lures Tourists, Spurs Rescuers to Mountain," The Oregonian, May 15, 1986.

49   Dialogue comes from: Tom Hallman, Jr. John Snell, and Rolla J. Crick, "Sunshine Lures Tourists, Spurs Rescuers to Mountain," The Oregonian, May 15, 1986; Tom Hallman, Jr. and John Snell, "Night-

mare on Mount Hood," The Oregonian, May 18, 1986.

50   Dialogue comes from: Hallman, Jr., Tom, "Winds Halt Rescue of 11 Trapped on Mount Hood," The Oregonian, May 14, 1986.

51   Krebs, (June 4, 1986): 35.

52   Krank, (June 4, 1986): 32.

53   Unknown, "Rescue Log," CCSR. I (May 16, 1986): 32.

54   Krank, I, June 29, 2018.

55   Dialogue exchange comes from: Krank, I, June 29, 2018.

56   McClure, David, "The OES Climbing Tragedy on Mt. Hood," (August, 1986): 3; Wright, Barry, OC, Cries for Help, April 13, 2015.

57   Krank, (June 4, 1986): 32.

58   Hattan, I. March 11, 2017.

59   Maslen, I. October 8, 2016.

60   Unknown, "Rescue Workers—Timberline Lodge Room Locations," CCSR. I (May 30, 1986): 41.

61   Lillywhite, Hal, Interview with author, I. A Memorable Lesson, January 16, 2016.

62   Maslen/Shultz, (May 13, 1986): 15.

Chapter 17, "Fireflies"

1   Dialogue exchange comes from: McGinness, Frank, Interview with author, I. Sunday through Wednesday, August 2, 2015.

2   Unknown, "Timberline Lodge Room Assignments," CCSR. II (May 14, 1986): 240.

3   Goman, Mar, WC, Corrections to Tom Goman's Background, February 14, 2016.

4   Yates, Diana, and Mar Goman, Interview with author, I. The Vigil, March 12, 2016.

5   Unknown, "Team Organization Forms," CCSR. I (May 15, 1986): 168.

6   Maslen/Shultz, "1986 Rescue Log," PMR, (May 14, 1986): 16.

7   Unknown, "Team Organization Forms," CCSR. I (May 14, 1986): 171.

8   Craig, Mike, Interview with author, I. Tuesday through Thursday, June 10, 2018.

9   Maslen/Shultz, (May 14, 1986): 15.

10   Maslen/Shultz, (May 14, 1986): 15.

11   Hattan, Mike, Interview with author, I. Personal Remembrances, March 11, 2017.

12   Stringfield, Tom, Interview with author, I. Wednesday's Rescue Efforts, December 9, 2015.

13   Krank, Ky, Interview with author, I. Team 6, June 29, 2018.

14   Lt. Hanner's report states that the snowcat "turned over," but Barry Wright and Cheryl Maslen dispute this claim. They stated that only the front end of the cat fell forward.

15   Hattan, I. March 11, 2017.

16   Maslen/Shultz, (May 14, 1986): 17; McClure, Dave, "The OES Climbing Tragedy on Mt. Hood," (August, 1986): 3.

17   Time stamp comes from: Maslen/Shultz, (May 14, 1986): 17.

18   McDaniels, Larry, "Transcript of SAR Meeting," PMR, (June 4, 1986): 39.

19   Maslen/Shultz, (May 14, 1986): 17.

20   Maslen, Cheryl, Interview with author, II. Wednesday, November 5, 2016.

21   Maslen/Shultz, (May 14, 1986): 17.

22   Maslen/Shultz, (May 14, 1986): 17.

23   Kelsey, Mark, Interview with author, I. Team 1 and Team 8, November 3, 2018.

24   Timing of flare lighting comes from PMR rescue logs.

25   Maslen/Shultz, (May 14, 1986): 18; Kelsey, I. November 3, 2018.

26   Maslen/Shultz, (May 14, 1986): 18.

27   Krank, Ky, WC, Corrections to Chapter 17, August 26, 2018.

28   Krank, Ky, WC, The Six Questions, July 11, 2018.

29   Maslen, II. November 5, 2016.

30   Stringfield, Tom, "Mountain Rescue Critique," PMR, (June 4, 1986): 1; Krebs, Ed, "Transcript of

SAR Meeting," PMR, (June 4, 1986): 10-11.

31   Maslen, II. November 5, 2016.

32   Stringfield, (June 4, 1986): 1; Arens, John, "Transcript of SAR Meeting," PMR, (June 4, 1986): 11.

33   Hattan, Deputy Mike, "Hattan's Log," CCSR. I (May 12, 1986): 74.

34   McDaniels, Larry, "Transcript of SAR Meeting," PMR, (June 4, 1986): 39.

35   Maslen/Shultz, (May 14, 1986): 19.

36   Maslen/Shultz, (May 14, 1986): 19.

37   Krank, WC, Corrections to Chapter 17, August 26, 2018.

38   Dialogue comes from: Krank, Ky, OC, Pre-Interview Conversation, June 28, 2018.

39   McDaniels, (June 4, 1986): 39.

40   Maslen/Shultz, (May 14, 1986): 19.

41   Maslen/Shultz, (May 14, 1986): 19.

42   Kelsey, Mark, Interview with author, I. Team 1 and Team 8, November 3, 2018.

43   Janeck, Jerry, Interview with author, I. The OES Tragedy, June 10, 2017.

44   Kelsey, I. November 3, 2018.

45   Unknown, "Weather Report," (forecast) The Oregonian, May 14, 1986.

46   Hattan, I. March 11, 2017.

47   Maslen/Shultz, (May 14, 1986): 19.

48   Unknown, "Base Operations—Duty Assignments," CCSR. I (May 14, 1986): 42.

49   Unknown, "Rescue Log," CCSR. I (May 16, 1986): 32.

50   Kennell, David, "Preliminarily Response—Special Report," CCSR. I (May 16, 1986): 23.

Chapter 18, "The Fog of War"

1   Snell, John, "Rescuers Fear Another Tragedy," The Oregonian, May 10, 1987.

2   Unknown, "Team Organization Forms," CCSR. I (May 14, 1986): 172.

3   Stringfield, Tom, Interview with author, I. Wednesday's Rescue Efforts, December 9, 2015.

4   Maslen/Shultz, "1986 Rescue Log," PMR, (May 14, 1986): 20.

5   Stringfield, I. December 9, 2015.

6   Hanners, Lt. Gene W., "Search and Rescue (Supplemental)—Agencies Involved," CCSR. I (May 25, 1986): 46-47.

7   Wright, Barry, "Transcript of SAR Meeting," PMR, (June 4, 1986): 40.

8   Wright, Barry, OC, Wednesday, January 11, 2016.

9   Maslen/Shultz, (May 14, 1986): 20.

10   Harder, Rick, "Transcript of SAR Meeting," PMR, (June 4, 1986): 43.

11   McGinness, Frank, Interview with author, I. Sunday through Wednesday, August 2, 2015.

12   Dialogue comes from: McGinness, Frank, I. August 2, 2015.

13   Wright, Barry, Interview with author, I. The Early Efforts, April 13, 2015.

14   Maslen, Cheryl, Interview with author, I. Tuesday, October 8, 2016.

15   Moffitt, Mike, "Aircraft Pilot's Logbook," Bell 206 JetRanger helicopter, (May 14, 1986): 1.

16   Moffitt, Mike, Interview with author, I. Hillsboro Helicopters, August 3, 2018.

17   Stringfield, I. December 9, 2015; Maslen/Shultz, (May 14, 1986): 21.

18   Dialogue exchange comes from: Hall, Ed, Interview with author, I. Hasty Team & Crag Rats, August 4, 2018.

19   Krank, Ky, Interview with author, I. Team 6, June 29, 2018.

20   McClure, Dave, and Cheryl Maslen, Interview with author, II. Wednesday, November 5, 2016.

21   The number of family members listed comes from Nalder, Eric, Jack Broom and Dave Birkland, "Mount Hood Tragedy, Three Critical, Search Continues for Missing Eight as Doctors Try to Revive Climbers," The Seattle Times, May 14, 1986.

22   Dialogue from family members during the departure of this aircraft comes from: Tom Hallman, Jr. and John Snell, "High Wind Slows Army of Searchers," The Oregonian, May 15, 1986.

23   McGinness, I. August 2, 2015.

24   Tom Hallman, Jr. John Snell, and Rolla J. Crick, "Sunshine Lures Tourists, Spurs Rescuers to Mountain," The Oregonian, May 15, 1986.

25   The inclusion of Harder, Youngbluth, and Nesbit comes from: Harder, Rick, "Transcript of SAR Meeting," PMR, (June 4, 1986): 43. The inclusion of Ek comes from: Ek, Charlie, Interview with author, I. The OES Tragedy, May 6, 2017.

26   Dialogue comes from: Tom Hallman, Jr. and John Snell, "High Wind Slows Army of Searchers," The Oregonian, May 15, 1986.

27   Tom Hallman, Jr. John Snell, and Rolla J. Crick, "Sunshine Lures Tourists, Spurs Rescuers to Mountain," The Oregonian, May 15, 1986.

28   Maslen, II. November 5, 2016.

29   Maslen/Shultz, (May 14, 1986): 21.

30   Tom Hallman, Jr. John Snell, and Rolla J. Crick, "Sunshine Lures Tourists, Spurs Rescuers to Mountain," The Oregonian, May 15, 1986.

31   Tom Hallman, Jr. and John Snell, "Nightmare on Mount Hood," The Oregonian, May 18, 1986.

32   McGinness, I. August 2, 2015.

33   "Sunrise and Sunset Times, May 14, 1986." (2017) Retrieved from ‹https://www.sunrisesunset.com›.

34   Kelsey, Mark, Interview with author, I. Team 1 and Team 8, November 3, 2018.

35   Harbour, Carl, "Transcript of SAR Meeting," PMR, (June 4, 1986): 42.

36   Janeck, Jerry, Interview with author, I. The OES Tragedy, June 10, 2017.

37   Rich, David, "Transcript of SAR Meeting," PMR, (June 4, 1986): 51.

38   Maslen, II. November 5, 2016.

39   Summers, Ralph, "Transcript of SAR Meeting," PMR, (June 4, 1986): 53-54.

40   Ek, Charlie, Interview with author, I. The OES Tragedy, May 6, 2017.

41   Maslen/Shultz, (May 14, 1986): 22.

42   Maslen, II. November 5, 2016.

43   Tom Hallman, Jr. and John Snell, "High Wind Slows Army of Searchers," The Oregonian, May 15, 1986; Hanners, Lt. Gene W., "SAR (Supplemental)—Agencies Involved," CCSR. I (May 25, 1986): 46; Krebs, Ed, "Transcript of SAR Meeting," PMR, (June 4, 1986): 44. Charlie Ek theorizes that the sentence Harder uttered was, "We have a visual on two possible survivors" and that the word possible might have been garbled when overheard by authorities. Ek, Charlie, Interview with author, I. The OES Tragedy, May 6, 2017.

44   Maslen, Cheryl, Interview with author, II. Wednesday, November 5, 2016. The Conrad Collection.

45   Harder, Rick, "Transcript of SAR Meeting," PMR, (June 4, 1986): 43.

46   Krebs, (June 4, 1986): 45.

47   Maslen/Shultz, (May 14, 1986): 21.

48   Conrad, Ric, Interview Notes with Mike Craig and Sue Shultz, June 10, 2018.

49   McGinness, I. August 2, 2015.

50   Tom Hallman, Jr. and John Snell, "Nightmare on Mount Hood," The Oregonian, May 18, 1986.

51   Summers, Ralph, "Transcript of SAR Meeting," PMR, (June 4, 1986): 53.

52   Youngbluth, Jeffrey, "Transcript of SAR Meeting," PMR, (June 4, 1986): 49.

53   Krebs, (June 4, 1986): 61.

54   Youngbluth, (June 4, 1986): 49.

55   Dialogue comes from: Tom Hallman, Jr. and John Snell, "Nightmare on Mount Hood," The Oregonian, May 18, 1986.

56   Dialogue comes from: Unknown, "Three Die, Eight Are Lost on Survival Hike," Lodi News-Sentinel, May 15, 1986.

57   Youngbluth, (June 4, 1986): 49.

58   Dr. Okies, as quoted in: Wilkerson, M.D., Jim, and Murray P. Hamlet, D.V.M., "Medical After Action Conference, Mount Hood, 1986, Bypass Rewarming," Report No. T10-88, U.S. Army Research Institute of Environmental Medicine, Natick, MA. (February 1988): 28.

59   Maslen/Shultz, (May 14, 1986): 22.

60   Harder, (June 4, 1986): 43-44.

61   Janeck, I. June 10, 2017.

62   Harder, (June 4, 1986): 43; Rick Harder, as quoted in: Wilkerson, M.D., Jim, and Murray P. Hamlet (February 1988): 111.

63   Kelsey, I. November 3, 2018.

64   Janeck, I. June 10, 2017.

Chapter 19, "Vital Signs"

1   Stringfield, Tom, Interview with author, I. Wednesday's Rescue Efforts, December 9, 2015.

2   Maslen/Shultz, "1986 Rescue Log," PMR, (May 14, 1986): 22.

3   Kennell, Deputy David, "Kennel's Log," CCSR. I (May 14, 1986): 75.

4   Kelsey, Mark, Interview with author, I. Team 1 and Team 8, November 3, 2018.

5   Rich, David, "Transcript of SAR," PMR, (June 4, 1986): 51; Janeck, Jerry, Interview with author, I. The OES Tragedy, June 10, 2017.

6   Kelsey, I. November 3, 2018.

7   Krebs, Ed, "Transcript of SAR Meeting," PMR, (June 4, 1986): 46.

8   Summer, David, "Transcript of SAR Meeting," PMR, (June 4, 1986): 47.

9   Maslen, Cheryl, Interview with author, II. Wednesday, November 5, 2016.

10   Tom Hallman, Jr. John Snell, and Rolla J. Crick, "Sunshine Lures Tourists, Spurs Rescuers to Mountain," The Oregonian, May 15, 1986.

11   Dialogue comes from: Tom Hallman, Jr. John Snell, and Rolla J. Crick, "Sunshine Lures Tourists, Spurs Rescuers to Mountain," The Oregonian, May 15, 1986.

12   Yates, Diana, and Mar Goman, Interview with author, I. The Vigil, March 12, 2016.

13   McGinness, Frank, Interview with author, I. Sunday through Wednesday, August 2, 2015.

14   Maslen/Shultz, (May 14, 1986): 23.

15   McGinness, I. August 2, 2015.

16   Dialogue comes from: Tom Hallman, Jr. John Snell, and Rolla J. Crick, "Sunshine Lures Tourists, Spurs Rescuers to Mountain," The Oregonian, May 15, 1986.

17   Dialogue exchange comes from: McGinness, I. August 2, 2015.

18   McGinness, I. August 2, 2015.

19   Maslen/Shultz, (May 14, 1986): 23.

20   Unknown, "Base Operations—Duty Assignments," CCSR. I (May 14, 1986): 42.

21   Tom Hallman, Jr. and John Snell, "Nightmare on Mount Hood," The Oregonian, May 18, 1986.

22   Grolbert, Capt. J.T., "SAR, 86-15981," CCSR. I (May 29, 1986): 51.

23   Hanners, Lt. Gene W., "SAR (Supplemental)—Agencies Involved," CCSR. I (May 25, 1986): 46.

24   Schneider, John, "Transcript of SAR Meeting," PMR, (June 4, 1986): 50-51.

25   Harder, Rick, "Transcript of SAR Meeting," PMR, (June 4, 1986): 49.

26   Harder, (June 4, 1986): 49.

27   Youngbluth, Jeffrey, "Transcript of SAR Meeting," PMR, (June 4, 1986): 51.

28   Radys estimated that they arrived at 6:15 a.m. yet the radio log entry for their arrival is listed as 6:33 a.m.

29   Stringfield, Tom, Interview with author, II. Team 10, December 19, 2015.

30   Radys, Al, "Transcript of SAR Meeting," PMR, (June 4, 1986): 47.

31   Maslen/Shultz, (May 14, 1986): 23.

32   Maslen/Shultz, (May 14, 1986): 23.

33   Stringfield, II. December 19, 2015; Wright, Barry, Interview with author, III. Thursday, November 6, 2018.

34   Krebs, (June 4, 1986): 61; Craig, Mike, Interview with author, I. Tuesday through Thursday, June 10, 2018.

35   Dialogue exchange comes from: Craig, I. June 10, 2018.

36   Lillywhite, Hal, Interview with author, I. A Memorable Lesson, January 16, 2016.

37   Lillywhite, I. January 16, 2016.

38   Maslen/Shultz, (May 14, 1986): 24.

39   Kennell, Deputy David, "Kennel's Log," CCSR. I (May 14, 1986): 75.

40   PMR periodically flew a law enforcement officer from southern Arizona up to the City of Roses, to teach a course on tracking missing personnel. Stringfield, and most of his colleagues, had taken this course. Stringfield, I. December 9, 2015.

41   Maslen/Shultz, (May 14, 1986): 24.

42   Stringfield, I. December 9, 2015.

43   Maslen/Shultz, (May 14, 1986): 24.

44   Kennell, Deputy David, "Kennel's Log," CCSR. I (May 14, 1986): 75.

45   Maslen/Shultz, (May 14, 1986): 25.

46   Dialogue exchange comes from: Kelsey, I. November 3, 2018.

47   Janeck, I. June 10, 2017.

48   Schneider, (June 4, 1986): 51.

49   Janeck, I. June 10, 2017.

Chapter 20, "Code 1244"

1   McGinness, Frank, OC, Initial Introductions, May 2, 2015.

2   Tullis, Jon, WC, Personal Recollections, July 9, 2017.

3   Maslen, Cheryl, Interview with author, I. Tuesday, October 8, 2016.

4   Hanners, Lt. Gene W., "SAR (Supplemental)—Agencies Involved," CCSR. I (May 25, 1986): 46.

5   Maslen/Shultz, "1986 Rescue Log," PMR, (May 14, 1986): 25.

6   Unknown, "Team Organization Forms," CCSR. I (May 15, 1986): 173.

7   Unknown, "Team Organization Forms," CCSR. I (May 15, 1986): 174.

8   Unidentified, "Transcript of SAR Meeting," PMR, (June 4, 1986): 42.

9   Janeck, Jerry, Interview with author, I. The OES Tragedy, June 10, 2017.

10   Shultz, Sue, Interview with author, I. Tuesday through Thursday, June 10, 2018.

11   Conrad, Ric, Interview Notes with Mike Craig and Sue Shultz, June 10, 2018.

12   Shultz, I. June 10, 2018.

13   Kelsey, Mark, Interview with author, I. Team 1 and Team 8, November 3, 2018.

14   Hanners, Lt. (May 25, 1986): 46.

15   Hanners, Lt. (May 25, 1986): 46.

16   Dialogue comes from the following source unless otherwise specified: McGinness, Frank, Interview with author, II. Wednesday through Sunday, August 2, 2015.

17   Hicks, Jeff, Interview with author, I. OES Resident Advisor, January 17, 2019.

18   Dialogue comes from: McGinness, II. August 2, 2015.

19   Dialogue comes from: McGinness, II. August 2, 2015.

20   Dialogue comes from: McGinness, II. August 2, 2015.

21   Hanners, Lt. (May 25, 1986): 46.

22   Hicks, I. January 17, 2019.

23   McGinness, I. August 2, 2015.

24   Wright, Barry, OC, The Possibilities, September 10, 2016.

25   Unknown, "Team Organization Forms," CCSR. I (May 14, 1986): 175.

26   Unknown, "Bodies of Three Climbers Found on Mount Hood, The Seattle Times, May 14, 1986.

27   Tom Hallman, Jr. and John Snell, "Anxious Parents Can Only Wait and Hope," The Oregonian, May 15, 1986.

28   Hallman, Jr., Tom, "Mount Hood's Deadly Deceit," The Oregonian, May 12, 1996.

29   Dialogue comes from: Yates, Diana, WC, Manuscript Corrections and Additions, June 28, 2016.

30   Dialogue comes from: Yates, Diana, and Mar Goman, Interview with author, I. The Vigil, March 12, 2016.

31   Goman, I. March 12, 2016.

32 Hanners, (May 25, 1986): 46.

33 Maslen/Shultz, (May 14, 1986): 26.

34 Maslen, I. October 8, 2016.

35 Maslen/Shultz, (May 14, 1986): 26; Unknown, "PMR Membership List," PMR, (November 12, 1985): 1.

36 Kennell, Deputy David, "Kennel's Log," CCSR. I (May 14, 1986): 75.

37 Dialogue comes from: Hicks, I. January 17, 2019.

38 Dialogue exchange comes from Hanners, Lt. (May 25, 1986): 47.

39 Krebs, Ed, "Transcript of SAR Meeting," PMR, (June 4, 1986): 45.

40 Kennell, (May 14, 1986): 75; Wright, Barry, OC, The Possibilities, September 10, 2016.

41 Wright, OC, September 10, 2016.

42 Wright is not the only one who failed to see this entry in the sheriff's log. Lt. Hanners and Deputy Krebs were not privy to this information as well.

43 Harder, Rick, "Transcript of SAR," PMR, (June 4, 1986): 45.

44 Krebs, (June 4, 1986): 46.

45 Hanners, Lt. (May 25, 1986): 47.

46 Hanners, Lt. (May 25, 1986): 47.

47 Hanners, Lt. (May 25, 1986): 47.

48 Hattan, Mike, Interview with author, I. Personal Remembrances, March 11, 2017.

49 Dialogue between Hattan and Harder comes from: Hattan, I. March 11, 2017.

50 Harder, (June 4, 1986): 43.

51 Hattan, I. March 11, 2017.

52 Hanners, Lt. (May 25, 1986): 47.

53 Hanners, Lt. (May 25, 1986): 47.

54 Kennell, (May 14, 1986): 75.

55 Dialogue comes from: Hattan, I. March 11, 2017.

Chapter 21, "Command and Control"

1 Hattan, Mike, Interview with author, I. Personal Remembrances, March 11, 2017.

2 Wright, Barry, OC, The Possibilities, September 10, 2016.

3 Stringfield, Tom, "Mountain Rescue Critique," PMR, (June 4, 1986): 5.

4 Wright, Barry, Interview with author, II. The Latter Efforts, April 13, 2015. In 2015, Wright, Stringfield, and Henderson—interviewed separately—all agreed upon this point.

5 Harder, Rick, "Transcript of SAR Meeting," PMR, (June 4, 1986): 49.

6 Wright, OC, September 10, 2016.

7 Dialogue comes from: Hattan, I. March 11, 2017.

8 Hattan, I. March 11, 2017.

9 Dialogue exchange comes from Dooris, Pat, "Trapped on Mt. Hood: Remembering the 1986 Tragedy," KGW.COM, May 12, 2015.

10 Dialogue comes from: Penater, Don, Interview with author, I. Personal Recollections, August 8, 2017.

11 Hopkins, Oz, "Medical Team Battles in Vain for Lives of Three Young Climbers," The Oregonian, May 15, 1986.

12 Dialogue comes from: Nalder, Eric, Jack Broom and Dave Birkland, "Mount Hood Tragedy, Three Critical, Search Continues for Missing Eight as Doctors Try to Revive Climbers," The Seattle Times, May 14, 1986.

13 Hopkins, May 15, 1986.

14 Wright, II. April 13, 2015.

15 Unknown, "Team Organization Forms," CCSR. I (May 14, 1986): 177.

16 Hopkins, May 15, 1986.

17 Dr. Okies, as quoted in: Wilkerson, M.D., Jim, and Murray P. Hamlet, D.V.M., "Medical After

1:30 p.m. Unknown, "Rescue Log," CCSR. I (May 16, 1986): 31.

6   Maslen/Shultz, "1986 Rescue Log," PMR, (May 14, 1986): 29; Wright, Barry, OC, Wednesday, January 11, 2016.

7   Maslen, Cheryl, OC, Wednesday, September 10, 2016; McClure, Dr. Dave W., "The OES Climbing Tragedy on Mt. Hood," PMR, (August, 1986): 4.

8   Another source states it was forty-five rescue workers. Nalder, Eric, Jack Broom and Dave Birkland, "Mount Hood Tragedy, Three Critical, Search Continues for Missing Eight as Doctors Try to Revive Climbers," The Seattle Times, May 14, 1986.

9   Tom Hallman, Jr. and John Snell, "Anxious Parents Can Only Wait and Hope," The Oregonian, May 15, 1986.

10   Grolbert, Capt. J.T., "Search and Rescue, 86-15981," CCSR. I (May 29, 1986): 52.

11   Maslen, Cheryl, Interview with author, I. Tuesday, October 8, 2016.

12   McClure, Dave, Interview with author, I. Tuesday, October 8, 2016.

13   Grolbert, Capt. J.T., (May 29, 1986): 52.

14   Kennell, David, "Preliminarily Response—Special Report," CCSR. I (May 16, 1986): 23.

15   Freund, Robert, Interview with author, I. Patient Evacuations, June 18, 2017.

16   Unknown, "Team Organization Forms," CCSR. I (May 14, 1986): 178; Krebs, Ed, "Transcript of SAR Meeting," PMR, (June 4, 1986): 62

17   Garrett, Mick, Interview with author, II. Palmer Down to Timberline, September 14, 2015.

18   Dialogue exchange comes from: Penater, I. August 8, 2017.

19   Henderson, Rocky, OC, Team 17, January 11, 2016.

20   Unknown, "Team Organization Forms," CCSR. I (May 13, 1986): 179.

21   Henderson, Rocky, Interview with author, I. The Raw Recruit, March 9, 2015.

22   Dialogue comes from: Jones, Charlie, "Transcript of SAR Meeting," PMR, (June 4, 1986): 68.

23   Dialogue comes from: Tom Hallman, Jr. and John Snell, "High Wind Slows Army of Searchers," The Oregonian, May 15, 1986.

24   McGinness, Frank, Interview with author, II. Wednesday through Sunday, August 2, 2015.

25   Kennell, (May 16, 1986): 23.

26   McClure, Dave, "Transcript of SAR Meeting," PMR, (June 4, 1986): 39.

27   McClure, Dave, II. November 5, 2016.

28   Hanners, Lt. Gene W., "SAR (Supplemental)—Agencies Involved," CCSR. I (May 25, 1986): 48; Henderson, Rocky, OC, Team 17, January 11, 2016.

29   McClure, (August, 1986): 4.

30   Douthit, Sandra, Interview with author, I. Personal Remembrances, September 12, 2015.

31   Dr. Hill, as quoted in: Wilkerson, M.D., Jim, and Murray P. Hamlet, D.V.M., "Medical After Action Conference, Mount Hood, 1986, Bypass Rewarming," Report No. T10-88, U.S. Army Research Institute of Environmental Medicine, Natick, MA. (February 1988): 13.

32   Height and title come from: Lane, Dee, "Headmaster Leads OES Back From Grief," The Oregonian, September 16, 1986.

33   Dialogue exchange comes from: Goman, Mar, and Diana Yates, Interview with author, I. The Vigil, March 12, 2016.

34   Yates, I. March 12, 2016.

35   Horwell, Amy, WC, Amendments/Additions–Tuesday, April 15, 2017.

36   Horwell, Amy, Interview with author, I. Personal Remembrances, April 9, 2017.

37   Dialogue comes from: Penater, I. August 8, 2017.

38   Henderson, I. March 9, 2015.

39   Unknown, "Team Organization Forms," CCSR. I (May 14, 1986): 181.

40   McClure, (August, 1986): 4.

41   Henderson, I. March 9, 2015.

42   Maslen/Shultz, (May 14, 1986): 31.

43   Henderson, I. March 9, 2015.

Chapter 23, "Mittens and Gloves"

1   PMR's log notes, "2:00 (p.m.). 3 rescue people in crevasse in White River Canyon. Bagger has equiptment [sic] and P.J.s on the ground—all people OK. Rescue in progress. Team 17." Maslen/Shultz, "1986 Oregon Episcopal School Tragedy Rescue Log," PMR, (May 14, 1986): 31. In interviewing members of PMR in 2015 and 2016, it is apparent that this reference to three climbers in a crevasse is, in reality, only Mark Schneider.

2   Henderson, Rocky, Interview with author, I. The Raw Recruit, March 9, 2015.

3   Maslen/Shultz, "1986 Rescue Log," PMR, (May 14, 1986): 31.

4   Stringfield, Tom, Interview with author, I. Wednesday's Rescue Efforts, December 9, 2015.

5   Dialogue comes from: Goman, Mar, Interview with author, I. The Vigil, March 12, 2016.

6   Dialogue comes from: Penater, Don, Interview with author, I. Personal Recollections, August 8, 2017.

7   Penater, I. August 8, 2017.

8   Dr. Hill, as quoted in: Wilkerson, M.D., Jim, and Murray P. Hamlet, D.V.M., "Medical After Action Conference, Mount Hood, 1986, Bypass Rewarming," Report No. T10-88, U.S. Army Research Institute of Environmental Medicine, Natick, MA. (February 1988): 13.

9   Kennell, Deputy David, "Kennel's Log," CCSR. I (May 14, 1986): 77.

10   Unknown, "Team Organization Forms," CCSR. I (May 14, 1986): 182.

11   Unknown, "Team Organization Forms," CCSR. I (May 14, 1986): 183.

12   Unknown, "Team Organization Forms," CCSR. I (May 14, 1986): 179.

13   Henderson, I. March 9, 2015.

14   Kennell, (May 14, 1986): 77.

15   Maslen/Shultz, (May 14, 1986): 32.

16   Maslen/Shultz, (May 14, 1986): 32.

17   Maslen/Shultz, (May 14, 1986): 32; Henderson, Rocky, OC, Team 17, January 11, 2016.

18   Wright, Barry, OC, Wednesday, January 11, 2016.

19   Krebs, Ed, "Transcript of SAR Meeting," PMR, (June 4, 1986): 63; Harder, Rick, "Transcript of SAR Meeting," PMR, (June 4, 1986): 63.

20   Penater, I. August 8, 2017.

21   McClure, II. November 5, 2016.

22   Maslen, II. November 5, 2016.

23   Dialogue comes from: Penater, I. August 8, 2017.

24   Maslen/Shultz, (May 14, 1986): 32.

25   Maslen/Shultz, (May 14, 1986): 33; Wright, Barry, OC, Wednesday, January 11, 2016.

26   Maslen/Shultz, (May 14, 1986): 33.

27   Maslen/Shultz, (May 14, 1986): 35.

28   Sheridan, Kathleen, Interview with author, I. Nordic Ski Patrol, July 10, 2018.

29   Unknown, "Mount Hood Snowstorm Kills 3," The Sacramento Bee, May 15, 1986.

30   Dialogue comes from: Hopkins, Oz, "Medical Team Battles in Vain for Lives of Three Young Climbers," The Oregonian, May 15, 1986.

31   Dialogue comes from: Hopkins, May 15, 1986.

32   Dr. Hill, as quoted in: Wilkerson, M.D., Jim, and Murray P. Hamlet, (February 1988): 13.

33   Unknown, "Three Die, Eight Are Lost on Survival Hike," Lodi News-Sentinel, May 15, 1986.

34   Horwell, Amy, WC, Amendments/Additions–Tuesday, April 15, 2017.

35   Horwell, Amy, Interview with author, I. Personal Remembrances, April 9, 2017.

36   McClure, II. November 5, 2016.

37   McClure, (August, 1986): 4.

38   Maslen/Shultz, (May 14, 1986): 34.

39   Wright, Barry, OC, The Possibilities, September 10, 2016.

40   Though the Sheriff's log states that Krebs departed Base at 4:02 p.m., to catch some sleep, PMR leadership states that the deputy had not yet departed.

41   Maslen, I. October 8, 2016.

42   Dialogue exchange comes from: McClure, I. October 8, 2016.

Chapter 24, "Sniffers"

1   Maslen/Shultz, "1986 Rescue Log," PMR, (May 14, 1986): 35.

2   Maslen/Shultz, (May 14, 1986): 34-35.

3   Dialogue comes from: Olson, Scott, Interview with author, I. Team 22 & 5B, October 21, 2018.

4   Maslen/Shultz, (May 14, 1986): 35.

5   Unidentified member of the Nordic Patrol, "Transcript of SAR Meeting," PMR, (June 4, 1986): 68.

6   Dr. Hill, as quoted in: Wilkerson, M.D., Jim, and Murray P. Hamlet, D.V.M., "Medical After Action Conference, Mount Hood, 1986, Bypass Rewarming," Report No. T10-88, U.S. Army Research Institute of Environmental Medicine, Natick, MA. (February 1988): 13 and 125.

7   Kennell, Deputy David, "Kennel's Log," CCSR. I (May 14, 1986): 78.

8   Grolbert, Capt. J.T., "SAR, 86-15981," CCSR. I (May 29, 1986): 52.

9   Baer, April, "Mt. Hood Climbing Has Seen Many Changes in 25 Years Since OES Tragedy," OPB news article, May 10, 2011.

10   Dialogue comes from: Tom Hallman, Jr. and John Snell, "3 Climbers Die; Fate of 8 Unknown," The Oregonian, May 15, 1986.

11   Goman, Mar, Interview with author, I. The Vigil, March 12, 2016.

12   Yates, Diana, Interview with author, I. The Vigil, March 12, 2016.

13   Unknown, "Rescue Log," CCSR. I (May 16, 1986): 31.

14   Tom Hallman, Jr. John Snell, and Rolla J. Crick, "Sunshine Lures Tourists, Spurs Rescuers to Mountain," The Oregonian, May 15, 1986.

15   Reininger, Richard, "Correspondence with Lt. Stillman," German Shepherd Search Dogs, CCSR. II (May 27, 1986), 233.

16   McClure, Dave, "The OES Climbing Tragedy on Mt. Hood," (August, 1986): 4.

17   Williams, Paul, "Transcript of SAR Meeting," PMR, (June 4, 1986): 11.

18   Dialogue comes from: Leach, Jody, Interview with author, I. Base Operations, November 18, 2018.

19   Tom Hallman, Jr. and John Snell, "3 Climbers Die; Fate of 8 Unknown," The Oregonian, May 15, 1986.

20   Dialogue comes from: Hopkins, Oz, "Medical Team Battles in Vain for Lives of Three Young Climbers," The Oregonian, May 15, 1986.

21   Moffitt, Mike, Interview with author, I. Hillsboro Helicopters, August 3, 2018.

22   Dialogue exchange comes from: Douthit, Sandra, Interview with author, I. Personal Remembrances, September 12, 2015.

23   Moffitt, Mike, "Aircraft Pilot's Logbook," Bell 206 JetRanger helicopter, (May 14, 1986): 1.

24   Moffitt, I. August 3, 2018.

25   Moffitt, (May 14, 1986): 1.

26   Moffitt, I. August 3, 2018.

27   Jones, Charlie, "Transcript of SAR Meeting," PMR, (June 4, 1986): 68.

28   Maslen/Shultz, (May 14, 1986): 36.

29   Olson, I. October 21, 2018.

30   Griswold, Gene, Interview with author, I. Personal Recollections, November 13, 2018.

31   Wright, Barry, WC, Wayne Litzenberger & the BPA, July 23, 2018.

32   Wright, Barry, OC, Wednesday, January 11, 2016.

33   Harkness, John, "Transcript of SAR Meeting," PMR, (June 4, 1986): 69.

34   Olson, I. October 21, 2018.

35   Goman, I. March 12, 2016.

36   Dialogue exchange comes from: McGinness, Frank, Interview with author, II. Wednesday through Sunday, August 2, 2015.

37   "Sunrise and Sunset Times, May 14, 1986." (2017) Retrieved from ‹https://www.sunrisesunset.com›

38   Wright, Barry, OC, Wednesday, January 11, 2016.

39   Dialogue at press briefing comes from: Williams, Deputy Russ, "Press Release Update—Search in Limbo," CCSR. I (May 14, 1986): 60.

40   Olson, I. October 21, 2018.

41   Dialogue exchange comes from: Moffitt, I. August 3, 2018.

42   Griswold, I. November 13, 2018.

43   Unknown, "Rescue Log," CCSR. I (May 16, 1986): 31.

44   Maslen/Shultz, (May 14, 1986): 37.

45   Hattan, Mike, Interview with author, I. Personal Remembrances, March 11, 2017.

46   McFadden, Ken, Interview with author, I. Helo 3, May 25, 2019.

47   Dee Zduniak recalls interacting with these two repairmen. Zduniak, Dee, "Statement of Dee Zduniak," Interview with Elden Rosenthal, McGinness Collection, (August 2, 1986): 3.

48   Unknown, "Climbing Experts Raise Questions About Hood Climb," The Seattle Times, May 22, 1986.

49   Penater, Don, Interview with author, I. Personal Recollections, August 8, 2017.

50   Haynes, Bruce, "Transcript of SAR Meeting," PMR, (June 4, 1986): 37.

51   Shultz, Sue, Interview with author, I. Tuesday through Thursday, June 10, 2018.

52   Conrad, Ric, Interview Notes with Mike Craig and Sue Shultz, June 10, 2018.

53   Craig, Mike, Interview with author, I. Tuesday through Thursday, June 10, 2018.

54   Conrad, June 10, 2018.

55   Unknown, "Timberline Lodge Room Assignments," CCSR. II (May 14, 1986): 240.

56   Maslen, Cheryl, Interview with author, II. Wednesday, November 5, 2016.

57   Dialogue comes from: Tom Hallman, Jr. and John Snell, "Nightmare on Mount Hood," The Oregonian, May 18, 1986.

58   Hallman, Jr. & Snell, May 18, 1986.

59   Wright, Barry, Interview with author, II. The Latter Efforts, April 13, 2015.

Chapter 25, "The Haystack"

1   Wright, Barry, Interview with author, II. The Latter Efforts, April 13, 2015.

2   Vicars, Lt. Don, "Press Release Update—Thursday's SAR Strategy," CCSR. I (May 15, 1986): 60.

3   Unknown, "Weather Report," (forecast) The Oregonian, May 15, 1986.

4   Dialogue comes from Maslen, Cheryl, Interview with author, II. Wednesday, November 5, 2016.

5   Maslen, II. November 5, 2016.

6   Wright, Barry, OC, The Possibilities, September 10, 2016.

7   Sainsbury, George, "Mission Report," Mountain Rescue Council, (Circa June 1986): 1; Hanners, Lt. Gene W., "SAR (Supplemental)—Agencies Involved," CCSR. I (May 25, 1986): 48.

8   McClure, Dave, Interview with author, III. Thursday, January 14, 2017.

9   McClure, Dr. David W., "The OES Climbing Tragedy on Mt. Hood," PMR, (August, 1986): 5.

10   McClure, (August, 1986): 5.

11   Grolbert, Capt. J.T., "SAR, 86-15981," CCSR. I (May 29, 1986): 52.

12   Hanners, (May 25, 1986): 48.

13   Maslen/Shultz, "1986 Rescue Log," PMR, (May 15, 1986): 69-70.

14   Prothman, Greg, Interview with author, I. Field Team Leader, April 2, 2017.

15   Wright, OC, September 10, 2016.

16   Unknown, "Team Organization Forms," CCSR. I (May 15, 1986): 150.

17   Williams, Paul, "Base Operations Leader Report," Mountain Rescue Council, (Circa June 1986): 7.

18   Prothman, I, April 2, 2017.

19   Williams, (Circa June 1986): 7.

20   Maslen/Shultz, (May 15, 1986): 38.

21   Maslen/Shultz, (May 15, 1986): 38.

22   Maslen/Shultz, (May 15, 1986): 38.

23 Prothman, I, April 2, 2017.

24 Olson, Scott, Interview with author, I. Team 22 & 6A, October 21, 2018.

25 Griswold, Gene, Interview with author, I. Personal Recollections, November 13, 2018.

26 Olson, Scott, WC, Additions to Recorded Interview, October 31, 2018.

27 Olson, I, October 21, 2018.

28 Maslen/Shultz, (May 15, 1986): 38.

29 "Sunrise and Sunset Times, May 12–15, 1986." (2017) Retrieved from ‹https://www.sunrisesunset.com›

30 Maslen/Shultz, (May 15, 1986): 39.

31 Prothman, I, April 2, 2017.

32 Unknown, "Team Organization Forms," CCSR. I (May 15, 1986): 152.

33 Maslen/Shultz, (May 15, 1986): 39.

34 O'Brien, Bill, WC, The SAR Dogs, December 12, 2018.

35 Maslen/Shultz, (May 15, 1986): 39-40.

36 Maslen/Shultz, (May 15, 1986): 40.

37 Prothman, I, April 2, 2017.

38 Unknown, "Rescue Log," CCSR. I (May 16, 1986): 30.

39 Maslen, II, November 5, 2016; McClure, Dave, and Cheryl Maslen, III, January 14, 2017.

40 Unknown, "Team Organization Forms," CCSR. I (May 15, 1986): 154.

41 Unknown, "Team Organization Forms," CCSR. I (May 15, 1986): 156.

42 Maslen/Shultz, (May 15, 1986): 40.

43 McClure and Maslen, III, January 14, 2017.

44 Conrad, Ric, Interview Notes with Mike Craig and Sue Shultz, June 10, 2018.

45 Dialogue comes from: Dooris, Pat, "Trapped on Mt. Hood: Remembering the 1986 Tragedy," KGW.COM, May 12, 2015.

46 Craig, Mike, Interview with author, I. Tuesday through Thursday, June 10, 2018.

Chapter 26, "Short Rope"

1 Maslen/Shultz, "1986 Rescue Log," PMR, (May 15, 1986): 41.

2 Vicars, Lt. Don, "Press Release Update—Dog Teams and Probers," CCSR. I (May 15, 1986): 58.

3 Maslen/Shultz, (May 15, 1986): 42.

4 Maslen/Shultz, (May 15, 1986): 40.

5 Olson, Scott, WC, Additions to Recorded Interview, October 31, 2018.

6 Unknown, "Team Organization Forms," CCSR. I (May 15, 1986): 163.

7 Olson, WC, October 31, 2018.

8 Olson, Scott, Interview with author, I. Team 22 & 6A, October 21, 2018.

9 Stillman, Lt. Sherwood, "Press Release Update—Six Teams around Crater Rock," CCSR. I (May 15, 1986): 58.

10 Olson, I, October 21, 2018.

11 Maslen/Shultz, (May 15, 1986): 42.

12 Bustanoby, Pete, "Mount Hood Rescue—Synopsis," Mountain Rescue Council, (Circa June 1986): 9.

13 Bustanoby, Pete, "Transcript of SAR Meeting," PMR, (June 4, 1986): 71.

14 Maslen/Shultz, (May 15, 1986): 42.

15 Maslen, Cheryl, Interview with author, III. Thursday, January 14, 2017.

16 Maslen/Shultz, (May 15, 1986): 43.

17 Dialogue exchange comes from: Leach, Jody (Sergienkl), Interview with author, I. Base Operations, November 18, 2018.

18 Maslen/Shultz, (May 15, 1986): 43.

19 Griswold, Gene, Interview with author, I. Personal Recollections, November 13, 2018.

20 The Bagger had initially boarded this Huey in the parking lot. It had taken off at 10:00 a.m. Maslen/

Shultz, (May 15, 1986): 43. Thirty years later. Prothman remembered the details of this flight, but can't recall whether he and Summers were flown down the mountain to meet with Harder, or if Harder flew up to pick them up. Summers stated to authorities that he had only taken one flight on Thursday. The Bagger, most likely, flew up to retrieve Prothman and Summers.

21   Dialogue exchange comes from: Horwell, Amy, Interview with author, I. Personal Remembrances, April 9, 2017.

22   Horwell, Amy, WC, Marion Horwell, April 15, 2017.

23   Maslen/Shultz, (May 15, 1986): 43.

24   Olson, I, October 21, 2018.

25   Dialogue comes from: Lane, Dee, "School Family Mourns Victims of Mountain," The Oregonian, May 16, 1986.

26   Dialogue comes from: King, Marsha, "A Student Who Turned Back Reflects on Mount Hood Climb," The Seattle Times, May 16, 1986.

27   Hicks, Jeff, Interview with author, I. OES Resident Advisor, January 17, 2019.

28   Unknown, "Mt. Hood Survivors Fight for Their Lives," The Sacramento Bee, May 17, 1986.

29   Maslen/Shultz, (May 15, 1986): 43.

30   Maslen/Shultz, (May 15, 1986): 43.

31   Maslen/Shultz, (May 15, 1986): 43.

32   Maslen/Shultz, (May 15, 1986): 44.

33   Prothman, Greg, Interview with author, I. Field Team Leader, April 2, 2017.

34   Maslen/Shultz, (May 15, 1986): 44.

35   Maslen, III, January 14, 2017.

36   O'Brien, Bill, WC, The SAR Dogs, December 12, 2018.

37   O'Brien, Bill, WC, The SAR Dogs II, December 30, 2018.

38   Hattan, Deputy Mike, "Hattan's Log," CCSR. I (May 15, 1986): 82.

39   Maslen/Shultz, (May 15, 1986): 44.

40   Maslen/Shultz, (May 15, 1986): 44.

41   Wright, Barry, Interview with author, III. Thursday, November 6, 2018.

42   Prothman, I, April 2, 2017.

43   Maslen/Shultz, (May 15, 1986): 45.

44   Maslen/Shultz, (May 15, 1986): 45.

45   Bustanoby, (Circa June 1986): 9.

46   Bustanoby, (June 4, 1986): 71.

47   Maslen/Shultz, (May 15, 1986): 48.

48   Dialogue comes from: Prothman, I, April 2, 2017.

49   Sainsbury, George, "Transcript of SAR Meeting," PMR, (June 4, 1986): 14.

50   Hattan, Deputy Mike, "Hattan's Log," CCSR. I (May 15, 1986): 82.

51   Dialogue comes from: McClure, Dave, Interview with author, I. Tuesday, October 8, 2016. McClure and Maslen originally believed this conversation took place on Tuesday, but it was, in fact, on Thursday.

52   Dialogue exchange comes from: Maslen, I, October 8, 2016.

53   Maslen/Shultz, (May 15, 1986): 46.

54   Maslen/Shultz, (May 15, 1986): 46.

55   McClure, Dave, III, January 14, 2017.

Chapter 27, "Toe the Line"
1   Dialogue comes from: Prothman, Greg, Interview with author, I. Field Team Leader, April 2, 2017.

2   Maslen/Shultz, "1986 Rescue Log," PMR, (May 15, 1986): 46.

3   Bustanoby, Pete, "Transcript of SAR Meeting," PMR, (June 4, 1986): 71.

4   McClure, Dave, and Cheryl Maslen, Interview with author, III. Thursday, January 14, 2017.

5   Harder, Rick, "Transcript of SAR Meeting," PMR, (June 4, 1986): 72.

6   Freund, Robert, Interview with author, I. Patient Evacuations, June 18, 2017.

7 Maslen/Shultz, (May 15, 1986): 47.

8 Maslen/Shultz, (May 15, 1986): 47.

9 Hattan, Deputy Mike, "Hattan's Log," CCSR. I (May 15, 1986): 83.

10 Frank Danes was a physics professor at the University of Puget Sound. He was a close family friend of the Gomans and had been on many climbs with Father Tom. Danes had been invited to accompany the OES Team on May 12, 1986, but was unable to attend due to other commitments.

11 Hattan, (May 15, 1986): 83.

12 Unknown, "Team Organization Forms," CCSR. I (May 15, 1986): 166.

13 Freund, I, June 18, 2017.

14 Maslen/Shultz, (May 15, 1986): 47-8.

15 Maslen/Shultz, (May 15, 1986): 48.

16 Prothman, Greg, Interview with author, I. Field Team Leader, April 2, 2017.

17 Prothman, I, April 2, 2017.

18 Maslen/Shultz, (May 15, 1986): 48.

19 McClure, Dr. David W., "The OES Climbing Tragedy on Mt. Hood," PMR, (August, 1986): 5.

20 Maslen, Cheryl, Interview with author, III. Thursday, January 14, 2017.

21 Seven, Richard, "Lingering Regrets," The Seattle Times (Pacific), May 8, 1988.

22 Tom Hallman, Jr., Sura Rubenstein, and Holly Danks, "Timberline Celebration Premature," The Oregonian, May 16, 1986.

23 O'Brien, Bill, WC, The Bagger, December 17, 2018.

24 Dialogue comes from: McGinness, Frank, Interview with author, II. Wednesday through Sunday, August 2, 2015.

25 Prothman, I, April 2, 2017.

26 Olson, Scott, Interview with author, I. Team 22 & 6A, October 21, 2018.

27 Freund, I, June 18, 2017.

28 Olson, I, October 21, 2018.

29 Maslen/Shultz, (May 15, 1986): 49.

30 Dialogue comes from: Freund, I, June 18, 2017.

31 Olson, I, October 21, 2018.

32 Bustanoby, Pete, "Mount Hood Rescue—Synopsis," Mountain Rescue Council, (Circa June 1986): 10.

33 Dialogue comes from: Hallman, Rubenstein, and Danks, May 16, 1986.

34 Penater, Don, Interview with author, I. Personal Recollections, August 8, 2017.

35 Dialogue comes from: Hallman, Rubenstein, and Danks, May 16, 1986.

36 Dialogue comes from: Akre, Brian S., "Mount Hood Climbers Cling to Life," The Sacramento Bee, May 16, 1986.

37 Bustanoby, Pete, "Transcript of SAR Meeting," PMR, (June 4, 1986): 72; Maslen/Shultz, (May 15, 1986): 49.

38 Ek, Charlie, Interview with author, I. The OES Tragedy, May 6, 2017.

39 Tom Hallman, Jr. and John Snell, "Nightmare on Mount Hood," The Oregonian, May 18, 1986.

40 Dialogue comes from: Freund, I, June 18, 2017.

41 Freund, I, June 18, 2017.

42 Dialogue exchange comes from: McFadden, Ken, Interview with author, I. Helo 3, May 25, 2019.

43 McFadden, I. May 25, 2019. McFadden later learned that these two individuals were the parents of Brinton Clark.

44 Prothman, I, April 2, 2017; Bustanoby, Pete, "Mount Hood Rescue—Synopsis," Mountain Rescue Council, (Circa June 1986): 9.

45 Prothman, I, April 2, 2017.

46 Dialogue comes from: McClure, David, Interview with author, IV. Thursday, Part II, January 14, 2017.

47 Bustanoby, (Circa June 1986): 9.

48   Maslen/Shultz, (May 15, 1986): 49.

Chapter 28, "Daiber"

1   Williams, Paul, "Base Operations Leader Report," Mountain Rescue Council, (Circa June 1986): 8.

2   Williams, (Circa June 1986): 8.

3   Bustanoby, Pete, "Mount Hood Rescue—Synopsis," Mountain Rescue Council, (Circa June 1986): 10.

4   Figure of 27 comes from: Maslen/Shultz, "1986 Rescue Log," PMR, (May 15, 1986): 50.

5   Rick Harder, as quoted in: Wilkerson, M.D., Jim, and Murray P. Hamlet, D.V.M., "Medical After Action Conference, Mount Hood, 1986, Bypass Rewarming," Report No. T10-88, U.S. Army Research Institute of Environmental Medicine, Natick, MA. (February 1988): 111.

6   Freund, Robert, Interview with author, I. Patient Evacuations, June 18, 2017.

7   Craig, Mike, Interview with author, I. Tuesday through Thursday, June 10, 2018.

8   Dialogue comes from: Ek, Charlie, Interview with author, I. The OES Tragedy, May 6, 2017.

9   Bustanoby, Pete, "Transcript of SAR Meeting," PMR, (June 4, 1986): 72.

10   Olson, Scott, Interview with author, I. Team 22 & 6A, October 21, 2018.

11   Olson, I. Team 22 & 6A, October 21, 2018; Olson, Scott, WC, Additions to Recorded Interview, October 31, 2018.

12   Dialogue comes from: Freund, I, June 18, 2017.

13   Olson, I, October 21, 2018.

14   Dialogue exchange between Harder and McFadden comes from: McFadden, Ken, Interview with author, I. Helo 3, May 25, 2019.

15   Dialogue comes from: McFadden, I. May 25, 2019.

16   Dialogue comes from: McFadden, I. May 25, 2019.

17   Dialogue exchange between McFadden and the deputy comes from: McFadden, I. May 25, 2019.

18   Dialogue comes from: Williams, Paul, "Base Operations Leader Report," Mountain Rescue Council, (Circa June 1986): 8.

19   Williams, (Circa June 1986): 8.

20   Bustanoby, Pete, "Transcript of SAR Meeting," PMR, (June 4, 1986): 72.

21   Bustanoby, (Circa June 1986): 10.

22   Erickson, Steve, "Rescuers Ecstatic at Finding Climbers," The Oregonian, May 16, 1986; Ek, Charlie, Interview with author, I. The OES Tragedy, May 6, 2017; Harder, Rick, as quoted in: Wilkerson, M.D., (February 1988): 26.

23   Dialogue comes from: Plummer, William, "Step by Step, A Routine Hike up Mount Hood Turns Into a Nightmare That Kills Nine," People magazine, XXV: 22, (June 2, 1986).

24   Dialogue comes from: Leach, Jody (Sergienkl), Interview with author, I. Base Operations, November 18, 2018.

25   Dialogue comes from: Seven, Richard, "Lingering Regrets," The Seattle Times (Pacific), May 8, 1988.

26   McClure, Dave, and Cheryl Maslen, Interview with author, III. Thursday, January 14, 2017.

27   McClure and Maslen, III, January 14, 2017.

28   Maslen/Shultz, (May 15, 1986): 51.

29   Dialogue comes from: Freund, I, June 18, 2017.

30   Freund, I, June 18, 2017.

31   Tom Hallman, Jr., Sura Rubenstein, and Holly Danks, "Timberline Celebration Premature," The Oregonian, May 16, 1986.

32   Dialogue comes from: Penater, Don, Interview with author, I. Personal Recollections, August 8, 2017.

33   Dialogue comes from: Tom Hallman, Jr. and John Snell, "Nightmare on Mount Hood," The Oregonian, May 18, 1986.

34   Maslen/Shultz, (May 15, 1986): 52; Wright, Barry, Interview with author, III. Thursday, November

6, 2018.

35   Bustanoby, (June 4, 1986): 72.

36   Freund, I, June 18, 2017.

37   Freund, I, June 18, 2017.

38   Rick Harder, as quoted in: Wilkerson, M.D., (February 1988): 111.

39   Yates, Diana, WC, Manuscript Corrections and Additions, June 28, 2016; Yates, Diana, WC, St. John the Evangelist, December 10, 2018.

40   Dialogue comes from: Yates, Diana, and Mar Goman, Interview with author, I. The Vigil, March 12, 2016.

41   Dialogue comes from: Horwell, Amy, Interview with author, I. Personal Remembrances, April 9, 2017.

42   Interviewed in 2017, Horwell couldn't recall whether she was walking her dog at this point or just coming from a tennis match. Horwell, Amy, WC, Amendments, April 27, 2017.

43   Dialogue comes from: Horwell, WC, April 27, 2017.

44   Prothman, Greg, Interview with author, I. Field Team Leader, April 2, 2017.

45   Rick Harder, as quoted in: Wilkerson, M.D., (February 1988): 112.

46   O'Brien, Bill, "Transcript of SAR Meeting," PMR, (June 4, 1986): 74; Maslen/Shultz, (May 15, 1986): 52.

47   O'Brien, (June 4, 1986): 74; Maslen/Shultz, (May 15, 1986): 52.

48   Erickson, Steve, "Rescuers Ecstatic at Finding Climbers," The Oregonian, May 16, 1986.

49   Molly Schula had stated that breathing holes were present on Monday night. Schula, Molly, Untitled Statement, PMR, (May 1986): 16.

50   Ek, I, May 6, 2017.

51   Dialogue exchange comes from: McGinness, Frank, Interview with author, II. Wednesday through Sunday, August 2, 2015.

52   Danks, Holly, "Survivor of Climb on Mount Hood Loses Both Legs," The Oregonian, May 19, 1986.

53   Seven, Richard, "Lingering Regrets," The Seattle Times (Pacific), May 8, 1988; Erickson, Steve, "Rescuers Ecstatic at Finding Climbers," The Oregonian, May 16, 1986.

54   Seven, May 8, 1988.

Chapter 29, "The Relay"

1   Garrett, Mick, Interview with author, II. Palmer Down to Timberline, September 14, 2015.

2   Tom Hallman, Jr. and John Snell, "Nightmare on Mount Hood," The Oregonian, May 18, 1986.

3   Maslen, Cheryl, Interview with author, III. Thursday, January 14, 2017.

4   Tom Hallman, Jr., Sura Rubenstein, and Holly Danks, "Timberline Celebration Premature," The Oregonian, May 16, 1986.

5   O'Brien, Bill, WC, Manuscript Corrections, December 29, 2018.

6   Hallman and John Snell, May 18, 1986.

7   Maslen/Shultz, "1986 Rescue Log," PMR, (May 15, 1986): 51.

8   Bustanoby, Pete, "Transcript of SAR Meeting," PMR, (June 4, 1986): 73.

9   Hattan, Mike, Interview with author, I. Personal Remembrances, March 11, 2017; Bustanoby, (June 4, 1986): 73.

10   Dialogue comes from: Maslen, III, January 14, 2017.

11   O'Brien, Bill, WC, Snow Cave Memories, January 12, 2019.

12   O'Brien, Bill, WC, The Bagger, December 17, 2018.

13   O'Brien, WC, January 12, 2019.

14   Rick Harder, as quoted in: Wilkerson, M.D., Jim, and Murray P. Hamlet, D.V.M., "Medical After Action Conference, Mount Hood, 1986, Bypass Rewarming," Report No. T10-88, U.S. Army Research Institute of Environmental Medicine, Natick, MA. (February 1988): 112.

15   O'Brien, WC, January 12, 2019.

16   O'Brien, WC, January 12, 2019.

17   O'Brien, WC, January 12, 2019.

18   O'Brien, Bill, Interview with author, II. Personal Recollections, July 30, 2017.

19   O'Brien, WC, December 29, 2018.

20   O'Brien, Bill, Correspondence with author, Manuscript Corrections II, January 10, 2019.

21   O'Brien, WC, December 29, 2018.

22   O'Brien, WC, December 29, 2018; O'Brien, WC, January 10, 2019.

23   O'Brien states that the third wire on a Lifepak 5 could be black or green. Its lead would mirror the white lead on the patient's upper left chest. These gave three angles in which to sense electrical impulses through the heart, and a fourth, averaged test as well. "That third lead, with its two-color options, was what caused the confusion, but was very basic and should not have thrown a medic." O'Brien, WC, December 29, 2018.

24   O'Brien, WC, January 10, 2019.

25   Griswold, Gene, Interview with author, I. Personal Recollections, November 13, 2018.

26   O'Brien, Bill, "Transcript of SAR Meeting," PMR, (June 4, 1986): 74.

27   Dialogue comes from: Hallman and Snell, May 18, 1986; Rick Harder, as quoted in: Wilkerson, M.D., (February 1988): 112.

28   O'Brien, WC, December 17, 2018.

29   O'Brien, WC, January 10, 2019.

30   O'Brien, WC, December 29, 2018.

31   Rick Harder, as quoted in: Wilkerson, M.D., (February 1988): 112.

32   O'Brien, WC, December 17, 2018.

33   Dialogue comes from: O'Brien, WC, December 17, 2018.

34   O'Brien, WC, December 17, 2018.

35   O'Brien, WC, December 29, 2018.

36   O'Brien, WC, January 12, 2019.

37   Rick Harder, as quoted in: Wilkerson, M.D., (February 1988): 112.

38   Dialogue comes from: O'Brien, WC, December 17, 2018.

39   O'Brien, WC, December 17, 2018. At a 1988 medical conference, Harder stated, "Eventually, we called Emanuel Hospital and asked the flight nurse to get permission to give lidocaine, but we were unable to receive the radio reply." Rick Harder, as quoted in: Wilkerson, M.D., (February 1988): 112.

40   Craig, Mike, Interview with author, I. Tuesday through Thursday, June 10, 2018.

41   Griswold, Gene, Interview with author, I. Personal Recollections, November 13, 2018.

42   Craig, I, June 10, 2018.

43   Freund, Robert, Interview with author, I. Patient Evacuations, June 18, 2017.

44   Maslen/Shultz, (May 15, 1986): 51.

45   Maslen/Shultz, (May 15, 1986): 51.

46   Harder, Rick, "Transcript of SAR Meeting," PMR, (June 4, 1986): 77.

47   Freund, I, June 18, 2017.

48   O'Brien, WC, January 12, 2019. Harder recalled that it was a flight nurse at Emanuel Hospital that he asked permission. Rick Harder, as quoted in: Wilkerson, M.D., (February 1988): 112.

49   Dialogue comes from: O'Brien, WC, January 10, 2019.

50   The specific time that Thompson's sled began moving comes from Rick Harder, as quoted in: Wilkerson, M.D., (February 1988): 112.

51   Dialogue between Harder and McFadden comes from: McFadden, Ken, Interview with author, I. Helo 3, May 25, 2019.

52   Dialogue comes from: McFadden, I. May 25, 2019.

53   Harder, Rick, as quoted in: Wilkerson, M.D., (February 1988): 26.

54   Freund, I, June 18, 2017.

55   O'Brien, WC, January 12, 2019.

56   Maslen/Shultz, (May 15, 1986): 52.

57   Ek, Charlie, Interview with author, I. The OES Tragedy, May 6, 2017.

58   Bustanoby, Pete, "Mount Hood Rescue—Synopsis," Mountain Rescue Council, (Circa June 1986): 11.

59   Bustanoby, (Circa June 1986): 11.

60   Dialogue comes from: Erickson, Steve, "Rescuers Ecstatic at Finding Climbers," The Oregonian, May 16, 1986.

61   Dialogue comes from: Dooris, Pat, "Trapped on Mt. Hood: Remembering the 1986 Tragedy," KGW. COM, May 12, 2015.

62   Freund, I, June 18, 2017; Freund, Robert, "Mission Record #86-02," CMRU, CCSR, II. (May 19, 1986): 204; Bustanoby, (Circa June 1986): 11.

63   Harder recalls that the last patient departed the snow cave at 7:09 p.m. Rick Harder, as quoted in: Wilkerson, M.D., (February 1988): 112.

64   Ek, I, May 6, 2017.

65   Craig, I, June 10, 2018.

66   Harder recalls this time milestone as 7:07 p.m. rather than 6:57 p.m. Rick Harder, as quoted in: Wilkerson, M.D., (February 1988): 112.

67   Hattan, Mike, Interview with author, I. Personal Remembrances, March 11, 2017.

68   Unknown, "Snow Cave Discovered," Lodi News-Sentinel, May 16, 1986.

69   Harder, Rick, as quoted in: Wilkerson, M.D., (February 1988): 27.

70   Unknown, "Workers at Five Hospitals Labor to Save Climbers," The Oregonian, May 16, 1986.

71   Tom Hallman, Jr. and John Snell, "The Week on Mount Hood," The Oregonian, May 18, 1986; Tom Hallman, Jr., Sura Rubenstein, and Holly Danks, "Doctors Fight to Save Two Climbers; 6 Die After Rescue From Snow Cave," The Oregonian, May 16, 1986.

72   Dooris, May 12, 2015.

73   Henderson, Rocky, Interview with author, II. Rescuers Rescuing Rescuers, March 9, 2015.

74   Unknown, "Snow Cave Discovered," Lodi News-Sentinel, May 16, 1986.

75   Unknown, "Workers at Five Hospitals Labor to Save Climbers," The Oregonian, May 16, 1986.

76   Dubin, Murray, "8 Climbers Found in Cave On Mt. Hood; 2 Are Alive," The Philadelphia Inquirer, May 16, 1986.

77   Dr. Asaph, as quoted in: Wilkerson, M.D., (February 1988): 136.

78   Dr. Asaph, as quoted in: Wilkerson, M.D., (February 1988): 143.

Chapter 30, "Signing Off"

1   Leach, Jody (Sergienkl), Interview with author, I. Base Operations, November 18, 2018.

2   Wright, Barry, Interview with author, II. The Latter Efforts, April 13, 2015.

3   Dialogue exchange comes from: McGinness, Frank, Interview with author, II. Wednesday through Sunday, August 2, 2015.

4   Unknown, "Snow Cave Discovered," Lodi News-Sentinel, May 16, 1986.

5   Dr. Long, as quoted in: Wilkerson, M.D., Jim, and Murray P. Hamlet, D.V.M., "Medical After Action Conference, Mount Hood, 1986, Bypass Rewarming," Report No. T10-88, U.S. Army Research Institute of Environmental Medicine, Natick, MA. (February 1988): 79-80.

6   Other sources say 71.6° or 73° F, but the author is going with the temperature stated by her physician, Dr. Long. Wilkerson, M.D., (February 1988): 79-80.

7   Dr. Long, as quoted in: Wilkerson, M.D., (February 1988): 80.

8   Grolbert, Capt. J.T., "Search and Rescue, 86-15981," CCSR. I (May 29, 1986): 53.

9   Dubin, Murray, "8 Climbers Found in Cave On Mt. Hood; 2 Are Alive," The Philadelphia Inquirer, May 16, 1986.

10   Williams, Russ, "Press Release Update—Snow Cave Discovery & First Hour," CCSR. I (May 15, 1986): 61.

11   Rick Harder, as quoted in: Wilkerson, M.D., (February 1988): 112.

12   Penater, Don, Interview with author, I. Personal Recollections, August 8, 2017.

13   Rick Harder, as quoted in: Wilkerson, M.D., (February 1988): 112.

14   Dialogue comes from: Tom Hallman, Jr., Sura Rubenstein, and Holly Danks, "Timberline Celebration Premature," The Oregonian, May 16, 1986.

15   Maslen, Cheryl, Interview with author, I. Tuesday, October 8, 2016.

16   Maslen/Shultz, "1986 Rescue Log," PMR, (May 15, 1986): 53.

17   Dialogue exchange comes from: Maslen, I, October 8, 2016.

18   Yates, Diana, WC, St. John the Evangelist, December 10, 2018.

19   Yates, Diana, Interview with author, I. The Vigil, March 12, 2016.

20   Dr. Long, as quoted in: Wilkerson, M.D., (February 1988): 80.

21   Unknown, "Workers at Five Hospitals Labor to Save Climbers," The Oregonian, May 16, 1986.

22   Tom Hallman, Jr., Sura Rubenstein, and Holly Danks, "Doctors Fight to Save Two Climbers; 6 Die After Rescue From Snow Cave," The Oregonian, May 16, 1986.

23   Dialogue comes from: Tom Hallman, Jr. and John Snell, "Nightmare on Mount Hood," The Oregonian, May 18, 1986.

24   Unknown, "Workers at Five Hospitals Labor to Save Climbers," The Oregonian, May 16, 1986.

25   Dialogue comes from: Horwell, Amy, WC, Amendments, April 27, 2017.

26   Horwell, WC, April 27, 2017.

27   Dialogue exchange comes from: Olson, Scott, Interview with author, I. Team 22 & 6A, October 21, 2018; Olson, Scott, WC, Additions to Recorded Interview, October 31, 2018.

28   Olson, Scott, WC, Manuscript Corrections, November 8, 2018.

29   Dr. Long, as quoted in: Wilkerson, M.D., (February 1988): 145.

30   Rick Harder was later quoted as saying CPR was performed on Haeder, Jr. only. Harder, Rick, as quoted in: Wilkerson, M.D., (February 1988): 27.

31   "Sunrise and Sunset Times, May 12–15, 1986." (2017) Retrieved from ‹https://www.sunrisesunset.com›

32   Hallman and John Snell, May 18, 1986.

33   Dr. Long, as quoted in: Wilkerson, M.D., (February 1988): 80.

34   Dr. Long, as quoted in: Wilkerson, M.D., (February 1988): 146.

35   Hallman and John Snell, May 18, 1986.

36   Dialogue exchange comes from: Goman, Mar, Interview with author, I. The Vigil, March 12, 2016.

37   O'Brien, Bill, Interview with author, II. Personal Recollections, July 30, 2017.

38   Maslen/Shultz, (May 15, 1986): 52.

39   Dr. Asaph, as quoted in: Wilkerson, M.D., (February 1988): 139.

40   Dr. Asaph, as quoted in: Wilkerson, M.D., (February 1988): 139.

41   Dubin, May 16, 1986.

42   Hopkins, Oz, "Climbing Tragedy Offers Medical Insights," The Oregonian, May 22, 1986.

43   Pat McGinness' death certificate lists his time of death as 8:40 p.m.

44   Dialogue comes from: Unknown, "Workers at Five Hospitals Labor to Save Climbers," The Oregonian, May 16, 1986.

45   Tom Hallman, Jr., Sura Rubenstein, and Holly Danks, "Doctors Fight to Save Two Climbers; 6 Die After Rescue From Snow Cave," The Oregonian, May 16, 1986.

46   Dialogue comes from: Unknown, "Workers at Five Hospitals Labor to Save Climbers," The Oregonian, May 16, 1986.

47   Hallman, Rubenstein, and Danks, May 16, 1986.

48   Grolbert, Capt. J.T., "SAR, 86-15981," CCSR. I (May 29, 1986): 53.

49   Kennell, David, "Preliminarily Response—Special Report," CCSR. I (May 16, 1986): 25.

50   McFadden, Ken, Interview with author, I. Helo 3, May 25, 2019.

51   Stillman, Lt. Sherwood, "S.A.R.—Mt. Hood," CCSR. I (May 22, 1986): 49.

52   Bustanoby, Pete, "Mount Hood Rescue—Synopsis," Mountain Rescue Council, (Circa June 1986): 11; McClure, Dave, and Cheryl Maslen, Interview with author, III. Thursday, January 14, 2017.

53   McGinness, Frank, Interview with author, II. Wednesday through Sunday, August 2, 2015.

54   Union Avenue was renamed Martin Luther King Jr. Blvd in 1990.

55   Dialogue comes from: Penater, Don, Interview with author, I. Personal Recollections, August 8, 2017.

56   Dialogue comes from: Penater, I, August 8, 2017.

57   Garrett, Mick, Interview with author, II. Palmer Down to Timberline, September 14, 2015. In 2019, Jeff Hicks could not recall breaking the news to the kids in this manner, but acknowledged that these were Garrett's memories.

Chapter 31, "Ultimate Knowledge"

1   Garrett, Mick, Interview with author, II. Palmer Down to Timberline, September 14, 2015.

2   Dialogue exchange comes from: McGinness, Frank, Interview with author, II. Wednesday through Sunday, August 2, 2015.

3   Dialogue comes from: McGinness, II, August 2, 2015.

4   All dialogue concerning McGinness' time at The Red Cross comes from: McGinness, II, August 2, 2015.

5   Horwell, Amy, WC, Amendments/Additions–Thursday, April 15, 2017.

6   Horwell, Amy, WC, Amendments, April 27, 2017.

7   Dialogue comes from: Horwell, Amy, Interview with author, I. Personal Remembrances, April 9, 2017.

8   Dialogue comes from: Penater, Don, Interview with author, I. Personal Recollections, August 8, 2017.

9   Dialogue comes from: McFadden, Ken, Interview with author, I. Helo 3, May 25, 2019.

10   McFadden, I. May 25, 2019.

11   Garrett, II, September 14, 2015.

12   Dialogue comes from: Hicks, Jeff, Interview with author, I. OES Resident Advisor, January 17, 2019.

13   Hicks, I, January 17, 2019.

14   Garrett, II, September 14, 2015.

15   Dialogue between McGinness and the coroner comes from: McGinness, II, August 2, 2015.

16   McGinness, Frank, OC, The Viewing, October 12, 2018.

17   Vicars, Lt. Don, "Press Release Update—(Hospital) Locations of Hikers," CCSR. I (May 15, 1986): 59.

18   Hattan, Mike, Interview with author, I. Personal Remembrances, March 11, 2017.

19   Dialogue comes from: Yates, Diana, and Mar Goman, Interview with author, I. The Vigil, March 12, 2016.

20   Dialogue comes from: Yates, I, March 12, 2016.

21   Radtke, Sandy, WC, Dialing Alison, April 8, 2019.

22   Dialogue comes from: Birch, Kim, WC with Sandra Douthit, "The Phone Rings," (March 18, 1987): I.

23   Olson, Scott, WC, Additions to Recorded Interview, October 31, 2018.

24   O'Brien, Bill, Interview with author, II. Personal Recollections, July 30, 2017.

25   Leach, Jody (Sergienkl), Interview with author, I. Base Operations, November 18, 2018.

26   Freund, Robert, Interview with author, I. Patient Evacuations, June 18, 2017.

27   Tullis, Jon, WC, Personal Recollections, July 9, 2017; Tullis, Jon, WC, Manuscript Corrections, July 26, 2017.

28   Olson, Scott, Interview with author, I. Team 22 & 6A, October 21, 2018.

29   Leach, I, November 18, 2018.

30   Tullis, WC, July 9, 2017.

31   Leach, I, November 18, 2018.

32   Dialogue comes from: Hall, Ed, Interview with author, I. Hasty Team & Crag Rats, August 4, 2018.

33   Dialogue comes from: Hall, I, August 4, 2018.

34   Dialogue comes from: Hall, I, August 4, 2018.

35   Maslen, Cheryl, Interview with author, I. Tuesday, October 8, 2016.

36   McClure, David, Interview with author, I. Tuesday, October 8, 2016.

37   McClure, David, Interview with author, III. Thursday, January 14, 2017. In 2018, Wright was unable to recall how he got home. Cheryl Maslen, however, stated Wright drove rode home with her husband in the Suburban.

38   Freund, Robert, Interview with author, I. Patient Evacuations, June 18, 2017.

39   Garrett, II, September 14, 2015.

40   Yates and Goman, I, March 12, 2016.

41   Dialogue comes from: Tom Hallman, Jr., Sura Rubenstein, and Holly Danks, "Doctors Fight to Save Two Climbers; 6 Die After Rescue From Snow Cave," The Oregonian, May 16, 1986.

42   Dialogue comes from: Hallman, Rubenstein, and Danks, May 16, 1986.

43   Akre, Brian S., "Mt. Hood Survivors Fight for Their Lives," The Sacramento Bee, May 17, 1986.

44   Dialogue comes from: Hallman, Rubenstein, and Danks, May 16, 1986.

45   Dialogue comes from: Hallman, Rubenstein, and Danks, May 16, 1986; Unknown, "Workers at Five Hospitals Labor to Save Climbers," The Oregonian, May 16, 1986.

46   Akre, May 17, 1986.

47   Lane, Dee, "From Tragedy Rises Triumph of Pair's Survival," The Oregonian, May 17, 1986.

48   Dialogue comes from: McGinness, II, August 2, 2015.

49   Unknown, "Today in Philadelphia History: 41st International Eucharist Congress Begins," The Philadelphia Inquirer, August 1, 2013.

50   Dialogue comes from: McGinness, Frank, Interview with author, IV. Are We in Heaven Yet, May 20, 2018.

Chapter 32, "Autumn"

1   Snell, John, "Hood Disaster Survivor Clark Leaves Hospital," The Oregonian, May 29, 1986.

2   Hallman, Jr., Tom, "Mount Hood's Deadly Deceit," The Oregonian, May 12, 1996.

3   Clark, Taylor, "The Survivor," (Giles Thompson) Willamette Week, November 10, 2004.

4   Dialogue comes from: Hallman, Jr., May 12, 1996.

5   Clark, November 10, 2004.

6   Dialogue comes from: Boatsman, Courtney, Interview with author, I. Preparations and Ascent, May 23, 2015.

7   Garrett, Mick, OC, Giles Thompson, September 14, 2015.

8   Hallman, Jr., May 12, 1996.

9   Hallman, Jr., May 12, 1996.

10   Thompson, Facebook, n.d., circa 2019.

11   Hallman, Jr., May 12, 1996.

12   Clark, November 10, 2004.

13   Dialogue comes from: Hallman, Jr., May 12, 1996.

14   Dialogue comes from: Seven, Richard, "Lingering Regrets," The Seattle Times (Pacific), May 8, 1988.

15   O'Neill, Patrick, "Surviving Students, Guide Testify on Doomed Mount Hood Climb," The Oregonian, April 3, 1990.

16   Hallman, Jr., May 12, 1996.

17   Dialogue comes from: Boatsman, I, May 23, 2015.

18   Oregon Episcopal School. [Susan E. McClave Award]. (2017) Retrieved from ‹https://www.oes.edu/page.cfm?p=849›; Fitschen, Lorca, Interview with author, I. The OES Tragedy, January 2, 2017.

19   Fitschen (Smetana), Lorca, Correspondence with author, Updated Autumn Section, March 13, 2019.

20   Fitschen, I, January 2, 2017.

21   Garrett, Mick, WC, John Whitson, November 21, 2015.

22   Dialogue comes from: Whitson, John, Interview with author, I. The Climb, May 9, 2016.

23   Garrett, Mick, Interview with author, II. Palmer Down to Timberline, September 14, 2015.

24   Radtke, Sandy, WC, Manuscript corrections, October 8, 2015.

25   Horwell, Amy, Interview with author, I. Personal Remembrances, April 9, 2017.

26   www.amyhorwell.com.

27   Horwell, I, April 9, 2017.

28   Penater, Don, Interview with author, I. Personal Recollections, August 8, 2017.

29   Dialogue comes from: Hallman, Jr., May 12, 1996.

30   Goman, Mar, WC, Corrections to Autumn Section, February 14, 2016.

31   Unknown, "Mar Goman: Pharmacy of the Soul," Shivers of Delight, July 31, 2014.

32   Dialogue comes from: McGinness, Frank, Interview with author, II. Wednesday through Sunday, August 2, 2015.

33   Hallman, Jr., May 12, 1996.

34   McGinness, Frank, OC, The McGinness Family, May 20, 2018.

35   Dialogue comes from; Freund, Robert, Interview with author, I. Patient Evacuations, June 18, 2017.

36   Hall, Ed, Interview with author, I. Hasty Team & Crag Rats, August 4, 2018.

37   Seven, Richard, "Lingering Regrets," The Seattle Times (Pacific), May 8, 1988.

38   Unknown, "Richard Harder, Air Force Specialist (Obituary)," The Seattle Times, November 23, 1996.

39   Henderson, Rocky, Interview with author, II. Rescuers Rescuing Rescuers, March 9, 2015.

40   Stringfield, Tom, WC, I. Rocky Henderson, December 17, 2015.

41   Dialogue comes from: Stringfield, Tom, Interview with author, I. Wednesday's Rescue Efforts, December 9, 2015.

42   Kelsey, Mark, Interview with author, I. Team 1 and Team 8, November 3, 2018.

43   Dialogue comes from: Lillywhite, Hal, Interview with author, I. A Memorable Lesson, January 16, 2016.

44   Dialogue Comes from: O'Brien, Bill, Interview with author, II. Personal Recollections, July 30, 2017.

45   Oregon Mountain Rescue Council. [Formation and Purpose]. (2017) Retrieved from ‹http://corvallismountainrescue.org/omrc/›.

46   Dialogue comes from: Prothman, Greg, Interview with author, I. Field Team Leader, April 2, 2017.

47   Prothman, Greg, WC, Manuscript Corrections, April 13, 2017.

48   Prothman, Greg, WC, Corrections to Autumn Section, April 5, 2017.

49   Stringfield, Tom, WC, Cecil Drinkward, September 27, 2018.

50   Dialogue comes from: Stringfield, I, December 9, 2015.

51   Stringfield, I, December 9, 2015.

52   Conrad, Ric, WC, Interview Notes with Mike Craig and Sue Shultz, June 10, 2018.

53   Shultz, Sue, Interview with author, I. Tuesday through Thursday, June 10, 2018.

54   Conrad, WC, June 10, 2018.

55   cascadiahealthcare.com/practitioners/susan-k-shultz-d-c-eam.

56   Maslen, Cheryl, Interview with author, IV. Thursday, Part II, January 14, 2017.

57   Maslen, IV, January 14, 2017.

58   Dialogue comes from: Maslen, Cheryl, WC, Autumn Section, November 8, 2016.

59   Obituary, "In Memory of Edwin Wayne Krebs (1947–2017)," Lincoln Memorial Park and Funeral Home, Portland, OR, Circa October 2017.

60   Dialogue comes from: Hattan, Mike, Interview with author, I. Personal Remembrances, March 11, 2017.

61   Dialogue comes from: Hattan, I, March 11, 2017.

62   Dialogue comes from: McClure, Dave, WC, Autumn Section, November 10, 2016.

63   Wright, Barry, Interview with author, II. The Latter Efforts, April 13, 2015.

64   Dialogue comes from: Wright, II, April 13, 2015.

65   Wright, Barry, WC, I. Avalanche on Leuthold Couloir, June 12, 2015.

Ric Conrad